# THE POLITICS OF MELODRAMA

# THE POLITICS OF MELODRAMA

THE CULTURAL AND POLITICAL LIVES OF
IHSAN ABDEL KOUDDOUS
AND
GAMAL ABDEL NASSER

Jonathan Smolin

STANFORD UNIVERSITY PRESS
Stanford, California

Stanford University Press
Stanford, California

© 2025 by Jonathan Smolin. All rights reserved.

No part of this book may be reproduced or transmitted in any form or by any means, electronic or mechanical, including photocopying and recording, or in any information storage or retrieval system, without the prior written permission of Stanford University Press.

Printed in the United States of America on acid-free, archival-quality paper.

Library of Congress Cataloging-in-Publication Data
Names: Smolin, Jonathan, author.
Title: The politics of melodrama : the cultural and political lives of Ihsan Abdel Kouddous and Gamal Abdel Nasser / Jonathan Smolin.
Description: Stanford, California : Stanford University Press, 2025. | Includes bibliographical references and index.
Identifiers: LCCN 2024009291 (print) | LCCN 2024009292 (ebook) | ISBN 9781503640238 (cloth) | ISBN 9781503641273 (paperback) | ISBN 9781503641280 (ebook)
Subjects: LCSH: 'Abd al-Qaddūs, Ihsān—Influence. | 'Abd al-Qaddūs, Ihsān—Political and social views. | Nasser, Gamal Abdel, 1918-1970—Friends and associates. | Arabic fiction—Political aspects—Egypt—History—20th century. | Authors, Egyptian—20th century—Political and social views. | Egypt—History—Revolution, 1952—Influence. | Egypt—Politics and government—1952-1970.
Classification: LCC PJ7804.Q3 Z887 2024 (print) | LCC PJ7804.Q3 (ebook) | DDC 892.7/36—dc23/eng/20240311
LC record available at https://lccn.loc.gov/2024009291
LC ebook record available at https://lccn.loc.gov/2024009292

Cover design: Jason Anscomb
Cover images: Ihsan Abdel Kouddous (1943), photo courtesy of the Abdel Kouddous family. Illustrations from *Rose El Youssef* magazine, 1953-59.
Typeset by Newgen in Cardea OTCE 10/14.5

*For Noah*

# CONTENTS

| | | |
|---|---|---|
| | LIST OF ILLUSTRATIONS | ix |
| | ACKNOWLEDGMENTS | xi |
| | NOTE ON TRANSLITERATION AND TRANSLATION | xv |
| INTRODUCTION | Analyzing Ihsan Abdel Kouddous | 1 |
| ONE | Casting Calls | 27 |
| TWO | The Erased Revolutionary | 72 |
| THREE | The Psychology of the Revolution | 116 |
| FOUR | The Time of Resistance | 165 |
| FIVE | The Greatest Splendor of Victories | 206 |
| SIX | The Time of Defeats | 251 |
| CONCLUSION | The Time of Denial | 299 |
| | NOTES | 309 |
| | BIBLIOGRAPHY | 339 |
| | INDEX | 351 |

ILLUSTRATIONS

FIGURE 1.  Naguib Mahfouz congratulating Ihsan Abdel Kouddous for winning the Egyptian state prize for best film in 1957.   31

FIGURE 2.  Fatima Youssef and Mohamed El-Tabii, editor in chief of *Rose El Youssef*, smiling on their way to prison in 1934.   33

FIGURE 3.  Cover of *Rose El Youssef*, 2 December 1936.   35

FIGURE 4.  Ihsan Abdel Kouddous, December 1943.   39

FIGURE 5.  Cover of *Rose El Youssef*, 31 December 1951.   68

FIGURE 6.  Ihsan Abdel Kouddous, early 1950s, perhaps speaking on behalf of the Free Officers.   85

FIGURE 7.  Installment of *I'm Free* with Amina and Abbas. *Rose El Youssef*, 3 August 1953.   110

FIGURE 8.  "The Secret Gang That Rules Egypt." *Rose El Youssef*, 22 March 1954.   121

FIGURE 9.  Cover of *Rose El Youssef*, 26 July 1954.   125

FIGURE 10.  Installment of *Where's My Life? Rose El Youssef*, 23 November 1953.   130

FIGURE 11.  Ihsan Abdel Kouddous beside the 1955 Fathi Mahmoud statue of him in chains.   137

## LIST OF ILLUSTRATIONS

FIGURE 12. Ihsan Abdel Kouddous at home with director Salah Abou Seif and the stars of the 1957 film adaptation of *The Empty Pillow*. — 146

FIGURE 13. Final installment of *The Barred Road*. *Rose El Youssef*, 11 April 1955. — 158

FIGURE 14. Ihsan Abdel Kouddous with Ahmed Mazhar. — 161

FIGURE 15. First installment of *I Do Not Sleep*. *Rose El Youssef*, 3 October 1955. — 169

FIGURE 16. Ihsan Abdel Kouddous at his desk at *Rose El Youssef*, mid-1950s. — 171

FIGURE 17. The only known photograph of Ihsan Abdel Kouddous with Gamal Abdel Nasser, taken with Syrian leaders in Damascus in early 1958. Originally published in *Rose El Youssef*, 16 January 1989. — 210

FIGURE 18. First installment of the Third Girl from *Girls in Summer*. *Sabah al-Khayr*, 25 September 1958. — 217

FIGURE 19. Poster for the 1960 film adaptation of the Third Girl from *Girls in Summer*. — 226

FIGURE 20. Installment of *The Sun Never Sets* with Layla and her piano teacher. *Rose El Youssef*, 24 August 1959. — 234

FIGURE 21. Hanan al-Shaykh, taken in Beirut by Ihsan Abdel Kouddous, 1963. — 253

FIGURE 22. Ihsan Abdel Kouddous with admirers, early 1960s. — 259

FIGURE 23. Installment of the First Eye with Hashim and Amina from *A Nose and Three Eyes*. *Rose El Youssef*, 28 October 1963. — 265

FIGURE 24. Installment of the Second Eye with Uncle Abdou and Nagwa from *A Nose and Three Eyes*. *Rose El Youssef*, 30 March 1964. — 277

FIGURE 25. Ihsan Abdel Kouddous beside Gamal Kamel's 1965 painting "The Son Humanity." — 293

ACKNOWLEDGMENTS

Years ago, when I was learning Arabic at the University of Chicago, I first encountered the short stories of Ihsan Abdel Kouddous. I was mesmerized—they were page-turners, full of scandal and romantic desire, driving me forward to each climactic conclusion. My Arabic professor at the time, Farouk Mustafa, told our class that Ihsan was one of the most important Arabic writers of the twentieth century but that critics had completely ignored him because they considered his fiction to be lowbrow melodrama. Someone needs to write a book about Ihsan, Farouk told our class. He cryptically added that Ihsan's work, with its unparalleled scope and popularity, is a unique lens through which to understand the Egypt of Gamal Abdel Nasser.

After focusing my research on Morocco for years, I decided in 2017 that I would write my next book on Egypt. Remembering Farouk's comment to our class so many years earlier, I thought that surely someone must have written that book on Ihsan by now. I looked everywhere, and to my surprise, Ihsan was still being ignored. How was this possible? I started rereading Ihsan's fiction, and I was mesmerized once again. I spoke at length about Ihsan with the legendary writer Ahmed Khaled Tawfik, who enthusiastically encouraged me to take on the project. Alaa Al Aswany, perhaps the most important living Egyptian novelist, did the same. Once I started reading old issues of *Rose El Youssef* magazine, which Ihsan edited and where he not only serialized his fiction but also published political editorials, I discovered an entirely new and unexpected aspect to my project. In addition to being the trailblazing writer of romantic melodrama, Ihsan was a searing voice of dissent calling for revolution well before the 23 July 1952 coup d'état as well as a stunning opponent of Nasser as he entrenched dictatorship in Egypt. How did Ihsan play such different roles? As I collected more and more issues of *Rose El Youssef* and began reading his fiction not as published books but as weekly installments embedded in the political context of each issue, I discovered that there were not, in fact, two Ihsans. Lining up the installments of his serialized fiction with the political editorials—together with contemporaneous events in Ihsan's life—showed that he was indeed being political, at least through metaphor and allegory, when he wrote fiction. Perhaps this was what Farouk meant when he said that Ihsan's fiction is a unique lens through which to understand Nasser's Egypt. It is my hope that this book does justice to the project that Farouk suggested all those years ago as well as to his memory. Thank you, Farouk.

I would not have been able to collect the thousands of magazines necessary to complete this project without the help of Mohamed Shoair and Mohammad Rabie. Both served as crucial early interlocutors for this project and also introduced me to Mohamed Sadek, whose Arabic magazine and newspaper collection rivals that of any library in the world. Sadek was able to find an incredible array of primary material for this project, not only magazines that Ihsan edited but also hundreds of articles published about him in the Egyptian press over the years. I am extremely grateful for Sadek's persistent help as well as his warm hospitality. Thanks to generous funding from Dartmouth's Scholarly Innovation and Advancement Award, the Jane and Raphael Bernstein Professorship in Asian Studies, and the Leslie Center for Humanities, I was able to collect most of the material for this project with the help of Sadek in Cairo, Michael Hopper at Harvard Library, and Marlis J. Saleh at the University of Chicago Library.

Once I met the Abdel Kouddous family, I was able to fill in crucial gaps. I am extremely grateful for their warmth, hospitality, and generosity during the research, writing, and editing stages. Their enthusiasm to preserve Ihsan's memory is truly inspiring. I am grateful for their patience and kindness with my many requests, from photographing pages of magazines and newspapers to locating copies of interviews and television programs. It has been an honor and privilege to have their unwavering help and support for this project.

I could not have completed this book without Hanan al-Shaykh. I am extremely fortunate that she has been so open, kind, and enthusiastic in discussing her time with Ihsan. Hanan helped me piece together crucial aspects of Ihsan's life during the mid-1960s. Without her, I could not have completed the arc of this book, nor could I have understood the full complexities of Ihsan's long relationship with Nasser. I am also grateful for having the chance to speak with Lobna Abdel Aziz about her experiences with Ihsan, in particular acting in his films.

Many interlocutors helped develop my thinking about this project. Special thanks go to my wonderful colleagues at Dartmouth: Tarek El-Ariss, for his brilliance and passion for all things culture and theory; Ezzedine Choukri Fishere, who patiently offered much-needed wisdom as this project took many twists and turns; Susannah Heschel, a true inspiration for her unceasing commitment to scholarship and boundless enthusiasm for academic inquiry; Kevin Reinhart, for his insight and experience in all things Middle East; Dennis Washburn, for his encouragement to expand my research beyond the Maghreb; Larry Kritzman, whose brilliance is matched only by his wit; and Barbara Will, for her support and enthusiasm for my work over the years. I am grateful to the many other colleagues who have helped make Dartmouth such a special place: Susan Blader, Jim Dorsey, Hussein Kadhim, Lewis Glinert, Jamila Chahboun, Mostafa Ouajjani, Andrew Simon, Mokhtar Bouba, Nurit Ben-Yehuda, Ehud Benor, Shaul Magid, Bernie Avishai, Jesse Casana, yasser elhariry, Dirk Vandewalle, Dale Eickelman, Levi Gibbs, Tori Holt, Michelle Clarke, Gérard Bohlen, and Jennifer Thomas. I am also thankful for the generous support of the Office of the Dean of Faculty of Arts and Sciences at Dartmouth, including Elizabeth Smith, Lynn Higgins, and Matthew Delmont. Thank you as well to the many generations of Dartmouth students who have taught me so much.

I am grateful to a number of other people for sharing feedback and thoughts on this project at various stages. Particular thanks go to Joel Gordon, who generously offered feedback on early stages of the manuscript and provided me with a number of important sources, as well as Yoav Di-Capua and Tarek El-Ariss, who also offered feedback on an early draft and helped me think through the framing of the book. My warmest thanks also go to Bill Granara, Susan Gilson Miller, and Diana Abouali for all of their support over the years. I was fortunate to be able to discuss this project with many other people, including Walter Armbrust, Mohammad Rabie, Mohamed Shoair, Ahmed Khaled Tawfik, Alaa Al Aswany, Bassem Youssef, Ashraf El-Ashmawi, Mahmoud Zibawi, and Abboudi Bou Jaoude. I am also deeply grateful for the feedback and suggestions offered by the two anonymous reviewers of the manuscript. Thank you to Kate Wahl as well as Thane Hale and the entire team at Stanford University Press. It is a true honor for this book to be included in such a distinguished list on Middle Eastern Studies. I would also like to thank June Sawyers for producing the index for this book.

I could not have undertaken this book without the support of my family. I want to thank my parents, stepparents, and in-laws for all their love and unwavering confidence over the years. My biggest thanks go to my wife, Jessica, who has been a constant source of support and encouragement, even as I was away on what must have felt like endless trips to collect material for this project. I could not have completed this book without you. This book is dedicated to our son Noah, whose creativity and joy is a constant inspiration.

# NOTE ON TRANSLITERATION AND TRANSLATION

I have used a simplified IJMES transliteration system without diacritics throughout. In the body of the text, I have adopted names based on previously published spellings (e.g., Mohammed Neguib and Khaled Mohi El Din), but I have retained the Arabic transliteration of names in the bibliography and endnotes for Arabic sources. I have used the spelling "Ihsan Abdel Kouddous" based on the wishes of his family. Unless otherwise noted, all translations are my own.

THE POLITICS OF MELODRAMA

INTRODUCTION

# ANALYZING IHSAN ABDEL KOUDDOUS

On the morning of 31 July 1954, Ihsan Abdel Kouddous, perhaps the most popular and prolific writer of fiction in the Arab world in the twentieth century, woke up in Cell 19 in Cairo's military prison. He had been arrested three months earlier by the secret police and spent the first forty-five days in solitary confinement, followed by several weeks of harsh interrogation. For Abdel Kouddous, it was a harrowing experience, a kind of psychological torture, full of insults and abuse. As he wrote soon after his release, "The initial weeks passed violently, every minute pricking my nerves. My entire body was torn apart and burned with fire."[1] When Abdel Kouddous woke up that morning, he had spent ninety-five days in prison. He had no idea when—or if—his ordeal would end.

As the guard opened the cell gate that morning, he greeted Abdel Kouddous with uncharacteristic respect after weeks of insults. "Congratulations, sir," the guard told him with a smile. "The director wants to see you in his office. We'll really miss you."[2] Abdel Kouddous was escorted to meet the prison director, who informed him that he was being released. The director gave no explanation for the decision, just as Abdel Kouddous had not been told why he was being arrested three months earlier. He only later learned that he had been charged with plotting to overturn the 23 July 1952 Revolution that brought Gamal Abdel Nasser and the Free Officers to power in Egypt. Abdel Kouddous quickly returned to his cell to take the tin inmate cup that he had used during his imprisonment as a memento of the traumatic experience. The cup, which he later had engraved with the prison name as well as his cell number and dates of imprisonment, still sits on display in the Abdel Kouddous family home.

As soon as Abdel Kouddous arrived at his apartment in the Garden City neighborhood in Cairo, the phone rang. He assumed that it was his mother calling to welcome him home. He picked up the receiver and heard the voice of Gamal Abdel Nasser. "Hi," said Nasser laughing. "Have you learned your lesson yet, Ihsan? Come have lunch with me and don't be late. I'm waiting for you."[3] Abdel Kouddous could not believe his ears. Even though he had not seen his wife and two young children for more than three months, he immediately set out for Nasser's residence. "I found myself forced to accept the invitation for a reason that I still don't fully understand," Abdel Kouddous recalled in 1975, some two decades later, when he spoke publicly about this episode for the first time.[4]

Abdel Kouddous ate lunch with Nasser, and afterwards the two watched a movie together. They chatted about the movie and other light topics but not the jailing or Abdel Kouddous's release. Nasser continued to insist that Abdel Kouddous come to his home nearly every day for a meal and a movie. During the visits, the two talked about a variety of things, but they awkwardly avoided discussing the arrest. After about a month of these forced invitations, Abdel Kouddous could no longer suppress his confusion and discomfort. He finally asked Nasser why he kept insisting on these visits. The president then looked him in the eye and said, "I'm giving you psychoanalytic treatment, Ihsan!"[5] The comment made Abdel Kouddous's blood run cold. What led up to this ominous moment? What did Nasser mean by this? Why did Nasser set himself up as analyst and Abdel Kouddous as his patient? What was Abdel Kouddous's "illness"? And how would Nasser's "treatment" impact Abdel Kouddous personally and shape his exceptionally prolific and bestselling writing, both at the time and in the years following this encounter? What was once a tight personal bond between them—one that had formed during Abdel Kouddous's surprisingly close engagement with the Free Officers in the months leading up to the 23 July 1952 coup as well as his pivotal involvement in inadvertently embedding military rule in the months afterwards—now became something more complex and troubling.

## JILTED ROMANCE

Nasser is perhaps the most important political figure in the Middle East during the twentieth century. Raised in modest socioeconomic conditions, he joined the Egyptian army and fought in the 1948 Palestine War. In the aftermath of that catastrophic military loss, Nasser founded the clandestine Free Officers, bringing together a group of fellow young men who were outraged at the corruption and incompetence of the Egyptian political and military elite. The Free Officers eventually launched a successful coup on 23 July 1952 against the monarchy, ending the dynastic line that had ruled Egypt for nearly 150 years. Nasser and the Free Officers quickly moved to uproot the old elite that had been seen as collaborators with both the palace and British colonial authorities. By spring 1955, after consolidating his control of the regime, Nasser began his meteoric rise on the global stage as an icon of anti-imperialism. In 1956, he nationalized the Suez Canal and withstood the subsequent attack of Britain, France, and Israel, solidifying himself as a masculine, militaristic figure who brought salvation, dignity, and self-respect to the Arabs after decades of colonial submission and humiliation. By 1958, Nasser orchestrated formal unity between Egypt and Syria, creating the new United Arab Republic, a stunning realization of the hopes and dreams of Arab nationalism. The Arab public's romance with Nasser reached feverish levels as massive crowds jammed into public spaces to hear him speak with men throwing themselves onto his motorcade, trying to touch and even kiss the now messianic figure of the new Arab subject.[6] While Nasser also erected a paranoid police state to repress dissent and oversaw the dissolution of the United Arabic Republic, the precipitous decline of the Egyptian economy, the shattering loss to Israel in the June 1967 war, and massive street protests against his regime in the late 1960s, Nasser was—and still is—the icon against which all Arab rulers measure themselves.[7]

Despite the massive secondary literature on Nasser, few inside or outside Egypt knew then—or know today—of Nasser's highly fraught and deeply consequential relationship with Ihsan Abdel Kouddous, the giant of Arabic fiction and popular culture. When the two met in 1950, they must have quickly recognized the uncanny parallels between them. They were born less than a year apart. Each studied law at university and got married at the same age. Each eloped because of family opposition. They both had two young children at the time. Each was reserved and shy in person, but they were both intensely driven by political convictions. It was the Anglo-Egyptian Treaty of 1936—which gave Britain the right to station ten thousand troops in the Suez Canal, among other privileges—that made both Abdel Kouddous and Nasser vehemently anticolonial, shaping their political consciousness and pushing them to participate in street protests at the time. Each was disgusted not only at the control of the British but also at the Egyptian monarchy and the collaborating elite. Each had been haunted and further radicalized by the humiliation of the Abdeen Palace incident of 4 February 1942, when British authorities surrounded King Farouk's palace with tanks and demanded the installation of a new prime minister, which the young monarch quickly and subserviently accepted. Each flirted with numerous political groups during the 1940s, including the Muslim Brotherhood, but eventually became disillusioned with them all. The loss of Palestine in 1948 dramatically escalated their political activities as each began collaborating with anyone they could find, regardless of political affiliation, to spark revolution in Egypt, end the monarchy, and eliminate British colonialism. As Mohamed Hassanein Heikal, the foremost articulator of Nasserist ideology, would later recall, "Palestine defined Nasser."[8] The same could no doubt have been said of Abdel Kouddous when the two met in 1950.

These striking parallels formed the basis of their relationship, which started sometime in 1950 when Nasser and other members of the clandestine Free Officers first visited Abdel Kouddous at the offices of the weekly *Rose El Youssef*. Abdel Kouddous served as editor in chief of the magazine, which was perhaps the most important political and cultural publication in Egypt at the time. By 1950, Abdel Kouddous was well known as a muckraking journalist and editor who was desperately searching for scandals that he could print to inflame the public and incite them to revolution. It was thanks to these meetings that Abdel Kouddous was able to break the notorious Rotten Weapons scandal in 1950. As the public would soon discover on the front pages of *Rose El Youssef*, the palace armed the Egyptian military for the disastrous 1948 Palestine War with defective rifles that shot in reverse and grenades that exploded when touched. In his fiery editorials at the time, Abdel Kouddous used secret documents leaked to him by Nasser and the Free Officers to show that the palace had purchased these "rotten" weapons at highly inflated prices, pocketing enormous kickbacks in exchange for sending unsuspecting Egyptian soldiers to their suicide on the battlefields and the loss of Palestine. Thanks to Abdel Kouddous and his secret collaborators, the shocking scandal quickly crystalized widespread disgust at the corruption and immorality of the monarchy and collaborating elite, ultimately preparing public opinion to embrace the Free Officers Coup once it arrived.

Abdel Kouddous was such an enthusiastic partner in the buildup to the coup that Nasser telephoned him during the early hours of the operation to invite him to participate in it along with the other Free Officers, making Abdel Kouddous the only civilian to do so. Abdel Kouddous felt so closely linked with Nasser and the Officers that he was terrified during the coup that he would be hanged if it failed. Moreover, in the weeks following 23 July 1952, Abdel Kouddous was so zealous in his public support for the coup that members of the old guard thought that he was the civilian official of the Free Officers. During this time, he gave radio addresses urging the public to have full trust in the Officers and called repeatedly in the pages of *Rose El Youssef* for suspending the constitution and dissolving the political parties. Abdel Kouddous took these steps because he believed that the Officers were simply acting as a pliable tool to carry out his long-standing goal of uprooting what he saw as an impossibly corrupt political system and sowing the necessary seeds for a new era of rule of law and democracy. Military dictatorship, despite the obvious warning signs, was not a concern for him, at least not publicly. As Abdel Kouddous declared in total confidence in his editorials at the time, the Officers would withdraw once they completed the necessary "cleansing" of what he saw as the corrupt political terrain.

In summer and fall 1952, Abdel Kouddous seemed certain that he would continue to guide Nasser, his handsome yet shy co-conspirator, to achieve his own political goals, just as he had in the two years leading up to the coup while inflaming the Rotten Weapons scandal in the press. Nonetheless, in the weeks after the coup, Abdel Kouddous discovered that Nasser was no longer the man he had thought he was. The quiet and seemingly servile Nasser whom Abdel Kouddous believed he had dominated before the coup now stridently pushed Abdel Kouddous aside, taking increasing steps to install military dictatorship in the country. By the time Abdel Kouddous started to rebel against Nasser and the Free Officers, both behind closed doors and in public in his editorials in *Rose El Youssef*, it was too late. By spring 1954, Nasser had not only systematically erased his recalcitrant former co-conspirator Abdel Kouddous from the official accounts of the revolution but had also imprisoned him in brutal conditions for three months to make sure that he understood who was in charge. Abdel Kouddous would not reveal his chilling "analysis" at Nasser's hands—or other critical details about their relationship—for another twenty years, well after Nasser's death.

While the story of the strikingly close personal and political ties between Abdel Kouddous and Nasser is largely unknown, the contours of their relationship might be familiar. Abdel Kouddous was far from the only intellectual or political figure before the coup to project his desires and fantasies of a new Egypt onto the masculine yet seemingly obedient Nasser, only to be disappointed by his inability to control Nasser afterwards. He was also not the only figure to feel a deep sense of ownership for a new Egypt in the wake of the coup and then be shocked and appalled at the subsequent imposition of military dictatorship. Ahmed Abul-Fath, editor in chief of the influential daily newspaper *al-Misri* (The Egyptian), served as a close confidant of Nasser in the years before the coup. Like Abdel Kouddous, Abul-Fath published articles in the buildup to the coup attacking colonialism and calling for revolution. In the weeks after 23 July 1952, Abul-Fath also went on the radio and published articles urging the public to support the Officers on the assumption that they were installing democracy in Egypt. Nonetheless, Abul-Fath quickly discovered that Nasser was no longer the manly yet subservient figure he had known before the coup. Unlike Abdel Kouddous, Abdul-Fath would spare himself years of humiliation (and, certainly, jail) by fleeing Egypt to Paris, where he would write the first tell-all insider book about Nasser, confessing his deep regret at his role in bringing him to power. As Abul-Fath wrote with tremendous guilt, "I did everything I could to push him to abandon the idea of dictatorship for democracy."[9]

Hassan Hudaybi, the Supreme Guide—or leader—of the Muslim Brotherhood from 1951 until 1973, and Sayyid Qutb, the organization's foremost intellectual during the Nasser era, believed that Nasser had sworn allegiance to the Brotherhood in the buildup to the coup. Both therefore publicly supported Nasser and the revolution through fall 1952, confident—like Abdel Kouddous—that they could direct him to install their vision of a new Egypt based on the ideology of the Brotherhood.[10] Qutb in particular surprisingly wrote a number of editorials in *Rose El Youssef* vehemently calling on the public to support the coup and the Officers. Their faith in Nasser and their confidence in their ability to push him to implement their political program once he reached power would prove to be deeply mistaken. Not only would Nasser decimate the Muslim Brotherhood after a member of the party tried to assassinate him in October 1954, but Qutb would eventually become one of the few political opponents whom Nasser executed.

Tawfiq al-Hakim, pioneer of modern Arab theater and prominent public intellectual both before and after the coup, believed that his 1933 novel *Return of the Spirit* had formed Nasser's self-image as a hero bringing liberty and freedom to Egypt through revolution. Al-Hakim saw Nasser after the coup as the embodiment not only of his protagonist in the novel, Muhsin, but also of his own vision of a new democratic Egypt.[11] For this reason, al-Hakim would later claim, "I am the prophet and the advocate of 'the blessed revolution.'"[12] And al-Hakim had no doubt that Nasser gave him appropriate credit. According to al-Hakim, Nasser admitted that "the revolution is really his revolution."[13] Unlike Abdel Kouddous, al-Hakim remained almost entirely silent about the installation of dictatorship during the Nasser era. Nonetheless, some four years after Nasser's death, al-Hakim would publish a sensational book declaring his guilt, regret, and complicity at the subsequent imposition of authoritarianism and Nasser's cult of personality.[14]

Even Jefferson Caffery, United States Ambassador to Egypt from 1949 to 1955, had a similar relationship with Nasser. Caffery met with Nasser and the Free Officers before the coup as part of the U.S. plan of a "peaceful revolution project in Egypt."[15] On the morning of the coup, Nasser even sent a note to Caffrey informing him of the move in an attempt to avoid U.S. or British intervention. While the details of the Officers' relationship with Caffrey remain murky, we know that they had dinner together on 20 August 1952 as part of ongoing consultations about foreign affairs.[16] It was in the weeks after the coup that Caffery boasted to British and French diplomats of the influence he had over the Officers, proudly calling them "my boys."[17] As with Abdel Kouddous, Abul-Fath, Hudaybi, Qutb, and al-Hakim—among others—Caffrey's naïve confidence would quickly be dashed. His romance with Nasser would end soon after the coup.

## THE LEGACY OF IHSAN ABDEL KOUDDOUS

What makes Abdel Kouddous unique among these figures is not his close personal relationship with Nasser before the revolution, his misplaced confidence that he could direct and control Nasser once he rose to power, or his later horror at feeling that he had inadvertently helped to turn Egypt into a military dictatorship. Instead, it is that Abdel Kouddous was perhaps the most popular and prolific writer in the Arab world in the twentieth century. Even by summer 1954, when he was having his lunches with Nasser, Abdel Kouddous had topped the list of the most popular authors in Egypt in a poll conducted by the American University in Cairo. He began publishing short stories in the press in the late 1930s; by the 1940s he had developed a massive following of readers who adored his unique mix of crisp and simple language, romantic melodrama, and sexual sensationalism. Abdel Kouddous was known for writing about sex, love, and romantic obsession, typically employing first-person narratives by young women as they discover their sexuality and seek love—or carnal desire—in the face of repressive social traditions. Because of the way Abdel Kouddous repeatedly broke taboos about sex and gender, his fiction had a profound impact on generations of women, who identified with the emotional and social struggles of his protagonists. In this, Abdel Kouddous helped shape the melodramatic imagination of women—as well as men—not only in Egypt but also across the Arab world. Thanks to his style and content, Abdel Kouddous's fiction appealed to much wider audiences throughout his career than the luminaries of high literature at the time, such as Naguib Mahfouz or Taha Hussein. He is widely remembered today not for his politics or his relationship with the 23 July 1952 Revolution but for the social-cultural impact of his sensational romantic melodrama.

Abdel Kouddous's fiction was also disseminated on a much wider scale than that of any other Arab writer. All of his work was first serialized in the country's most popular weeklies before it was collected in book form and subsequently reprinted in dozens of editions by multiple publishing houses over several decades. Moreover, Abdel Kouddous's novels and short stories were adapted into some of the most important and popular films in the history of Arab cinema, such as *I Do Not Sleep*, *There's a Man in My House*, and *My Father's Up a Tree*, among many others. In his seminal study of cinematic melodrama in Nasser's Egypt, Joel Gordon notes that "Ihsan's stories are lushly romantic tales of broken hearts and shattered love affairs."[18] In total, forty-nine Egyptian films were based on his work, all featuring at least one superstar of Egyptian cinema, such as Faten Hamama, Omar Sharif, or Abdel Halim Hafez. Dozens of radio plays and television series were adapted from his fiction, many broadcast over months and aired repeatedly over the years. Numerous individual works were adapted and disseminated in Egypt and the Arab world in all three media. Even though Abdel Kouddous died in 1990, his work is even still being revitalized for new audiences.[19] Considering its popularity, quantity, and reach, the fiction of Ihsan Abdel Kouddous, more than any other writer, should be considered foundational texts of Arab popular culture and the public imaginary during the Nasser era.

Despite this, Ihsan Abdel Kouddous has been almost entirely ignored by critics and academics, both in Egypt and abroad. To date, there is not a single book in any language focusing on Abdel Kouddous's fiction or his critical role in the production and dissemination of Arabic popular culture in the twentieth century, let alone the politics of his highly contentious yet little-known relationship with Gamal Abdel Nasser. And despite his unparalleled sales and popularity, it was not until late 2021, when my translation of Abdel Kouddous's classic *I Do Not Sleep* was published, that readers of English could finally discover this legend of Arabic literature for themselves.[20]

There are many reasons for this neglect. Just as Abdel Kouddous gained popularity for his scandalous fiction in the late 1940s and early 1950s, the well-known critic and writer Abbas Mahmoud al-Aqqad labeled him the "writer of the bed," dismissing Abdel Kouddous as a lowbrow writer who focused on sexual titillation instead of serious literary matters. This title stuck with Abdel Kouddous throughout his career. Although it certainly helped his sales as well as the adaptation of his work in other media, it turned "respectable society" against him.

Highlighting sexual desire—especially that of young female protagonists—was not only alluring but also disturbing for many segments of Egyptian society in the 1950s and 1960s. *Rose El Youssef* magazine, where most of his fiction was serialized, would regularly print letters of outrage about immorality in his fiction. Despite his immense popularity, Abdel Kouddous later recalled that, during this period, people would frequently not admit to reading his work for fear of being associated with questionable morality.[21] Young people—and women in particular—did not want to be caught by their parents or husbands reading his fiction. Of course, these same parents or husbands might have had their own copies of Abdel Kouddous's fiction, which they read when no one was looking.[22]

Besides at least some of the public's discomfort over the depiction of sexuality in his writing, critics dismissed Abdel Kouddous because he typically set his work in a bourgeois milieu. This is ironic because Abdel Kouddous wrote fiery editorials, especially before 1954, attacking the wealthy and their political backers in Egypt as agents of colonialism and regressivism. His fiction before the coup, which commonly depicted the excesses of the ruling class, served as a vehicle to drum up anger at the elite. As he explained in a series of retrospective interviews in 1980, "My only motivation before the revolution was to lay this class bare so that the wheel of popular revolt would turn until it arrived at what we strove for—their overthrow."[23] After the 1952 coup, popular anger at inequality helped guide the policies of the Free Officers, including the land reform program and abolition of civil titles, which sought to uproot the power and privilege of the old elite. Throughout the Nasser era, and especially after the late 1950s, the "socialist revolution" was launched, further targeting the wealthy of the previous era, including the nationalization of private companies and seizure of land and assets. In helping to build this new society, fiction—like the media—was expected to follow suit and serve a political and social role not simply by supporting the revolution but also by helping to manufacture its message. Nonetheless, almost all of Abdel Kouddous's major works during the 1950s and 1960s are set in a bourgeois context and focus on the emotional anxieties of the wealthy, almost entirely refusing to play any role in "educating" the public about Nasserist ideology. Although it is clear that Abdel Kouddous was not celebrating the wealthy in his fiction—and not all of his characters are bourgeois—critics still dismissed him partly because of the perception that he consistently focused on the lives of the wealthy of the previous era and not the aspirations and achievements of the new Egypt.

Perhaps a more important reason for the near-total critical dismissal of Abdel Kouddous as a fiction writer is his style. Unlike Nobel laureate for Literature Naguib Mahfouz, Abdel Kouddous employed simple vocabulary and sentence structure in a way that appealed to the widest possible readership—and especially to the young—but not to literary critics. As early as 1943, Abdel Kouddous was calling for the simplification of Arabic so that it could be used as a vehicle not only to build large audiences for the press but also to touch the emotions of ordinary Egyptians.[24] He developed his style under the influence of Mohamed El-Tabii, the first *Rose El Youssef* editor who popularized the magazine by employing simple, sensational language. Throughout his career, both in his journalism and fiction, Abdel Kouddous strove to democratize Arabic, moving it from the language of the elite to that of the masses, occasionally making fun of the complex vocabulary and syntax of writers like the "Dean of Arabic Literature," Taha Hussein, and Naguib Mahfouz, even though both were close friends. Seen from the perspective of the *nahda*—the nineteenth-century Arab renaissance that was forged through the simplification of classical Arabic for the newly emergent press—fiction for Abdel Kouddous was partly a tool to lure readers, who might otherwise not be interested in politics, to the next issue of his magazine, where they might come across the latest political debate of the day as they flipped through the pages to find the next racy installment of his fiction.[25]

Abdel Kouddous's focus on simplified sensational Arabic and increasing mass participation for the press was not simply a product of ideology. While it is easy to overlook now that his massive library exists in book form published in many editions over the years, all of his writing—both political and fictional—was first published in the highest-circulation magazines in Egypt. Abdel Kouddous's novels were all serialized on a weekly basis over long periods of time, sometimes for over a year. The pressures and demands of press serialization—selling magazines, keeping readers coming back week after week for the next installment—played a critical role in shaping Abdel Kouddous's content and style. Each weekly installment, which was later published as a chapter in book form, typically features some kind of sensational element and ends in a cliffhanger. Abdel Kouddous was highly attuned to the importance of sales since his magazines, at least before the nationalization of the press in 1960, depended almost exclusively on circulation, not advertising revenue, for their survival. While his clear, crisp, simple prose and sensational content were tied directly to ideological and pressing commercial concerns, these only reinforced the perception of critics that his work was popular but lowbrow, certainly not texts worthy of serious literary consideration.

Another key reason why Abdel Kouddous has not been taken seriously as a fiction writer is that he was one of the most important and influential political journalists in the Arab world, especially during the 1940s and 1950s. He called for revolution repeatedly in the press before the coup in increasingly vitriolic terms. He was particularly prolific after the coup, much more so than his peer Ahmed Abul-Fath, typically publishing a weekly political or cultural article, frequently two or three, in a wide variety of magazines and newspapers until his retirement in the 1980s. He was also editor in chief or chairman of some of the most important publications in Egypt, such as *Rose El Youssef*, *Sabah al-Khayr* (Good Morning), *Akhbar al-Yawm* (News of the Day), and *al-Ahram* (The Pyramids), the country's daily newspaper of record. Despite the obvious potential for crossover, his fiction has never been read as political. No doubt, his sexual sensationalism, romantic melodrama, simple cinematic language, and massive sales contributed to that perception, as did his total dismissal by critics.

Yet there is another important reason for why the public never understood the political aspect of his fiction. As I trace in chapter 2, Nasser and the Free Officers fully embraced their co-conspirator Abdel Kouddous during the coup and in the weeks after, but by the late fall of 1952 they had begun to distance themselves from him. The more Abdel Kouddous protested against his waning influence over Nasser and the trajectory of the revolution, both in the pages of *Rose El Youssef* and behind closed doors, the faster he fell out of favor. By summer 1953, when the Free Officers turned to producing and disseminating official histories of the first anniversary of the revolution, there was a deliberate decision to erase the insubordinate Abdel Kouddous from the narrative. No longer was the Rotten Weapons scandal cited as the prime motivation for the coup. And no longer was Abdel Kouddous even acknowledged as a co-revolutionary, participant in the coup, or friend of Nasser. Abdel Kouddous quickly went from being widely seen as the civilian official of the Free Officers—someone who had risked his life to participate in the coup and then worked tirelessly to embed the Officers in rule—to just a journalist and bestselling writer of romantic melodrama with no particular ties to Nasser. By summer 1954, after his release from jail, Abdel Kouddous stopped writing confrontational editorials entirely or claiming direct involvement to the revolution and instead turned his attention to fiction, giving the impression that he was retreating from politics to escape to popular diversion through salacious tales. Starting in fall 1954, he began publishing at least one novel as well as dozens of short stories a year for the next decade, establishing himself as the giant of popular fiction that he is known as today. His early erasure from the history of the revolution therefore helped cement for both the public and critics that his fiction is apolitical, a view that has persisted to this day.

This assumption about his work is as widespread as it is misleading. It presumes that there was no overlap between his career as a dissident political journalist and as a fiction writer. It assumes that Abdel Kouddous simply stopped being political when he wrote fiction. It assumes that his fiction was nothing more than an entertaining, prurient diversion for him and the public, a perception reinforced by his unparalleled commercial and popular success. While Abdel Kouddous typically did not address this in interviews—mostly because he was almost never asked about it—he did drop a few clues later in his career that his work was indeed highly political. In one retrospective interview in 1968, Abdel Kouddous explained, "There's something about me that you shouldn't forget. I always lived fighting in a hot political atmosphere, and I played a role in it. Fiction is one of my weapons. How could I avoid politics in it?"[26] In another series of interviews published in 1982, he said, "All romance fiction revolves around political society since a writer can't get rid of his political ideas."[27] Despite what I will show are the inseparable connections between politics and fiction in his writing, neither the public nor critics have linked these two spheres in his work. This is a deep misreading of Abdel Kouddous and his fiction, one that I will show throughout this book has led to a misunderstanding of not only his writing but also the politics of fiction, mass media, and popular culture during the Nasser era.

## THE ARCHIVE

This book is the first in any language to take Ihsan Abdel Kouddous, the neglected giant of twentieth century Arabic popular culture, seriously as a fiction writer. It is also the first to explore the impact and consequences of politics on his fiction. The new reading of Abdel Kouddous that I will offer in this book has been made possible only by painstakingly situating his fiction and editorials in the immediate context of their original publication in the press, not as they were collected in books. Everything that Abdel Kouddous wrote—including his fiction—was produced on deadline. Unlike Naguib Mahfouz, who completed his novels before serializing them, Abdel Kouddous wrote chapters of his fiction week in and week out, typically finishing each installment only days before the magazine appeared on the newsstand. As Abdel Kouddous explained once (and as others close to him have confirmed), he wrote fiction late on Friday nights after wrapping up all other work on that week's issue, rushing to meet the printer's deadline on early Saturday morning.[28] While he worked from a basic outline, he wrote without revision, except for correcting page proofs. This explains why there are no surviving drafts of his massive corpus. Writing each installment immediately before the printer's deadline meant that he was fleshing out his fiction only days before each chapter appeared. While his writing process might have led at times to less polished work as well as narrative repetition and rapid plot shifts—still more features that led to his dismissal by critics—it provides an invaluable lens through which to read his fiction. It offers a new framework to analyze how a particular installment of fiction existed in dialogue not only with other material published in the same issue of the magazine—including his own editorials—but also developments in his highly fraught personal relationship with the revolution in general and Nasser in particular. Analyzing his fiction not as published books but as serialized works coming hot off the press—putting them in dialogue with their immediate context—offers crucial new opportunities to read pulp fiction, with all its excesses and the related denigration from literary critics, as illuminating the politics of popular culture. Through this method, I show how Abdel Kouddous's writing can be read not only as romantic melodrama and taboo-breaking sexual sensationalism, which it is widely remembered as today. It also staged shocking acts of resistance in which Abdel Kouddous's regrets, anxieties, and despair about the trajectory of the 1952 revolution repeatedly erupt.

Much as I did in *Moroccan Noir: Police, Crime, and Politics in Popular Culture*, I have written the narrative of each chapter of this book by weaving together details excavated from a large archive of diverse sources.[29] This Abdel Kouddous archive, which took me years to compile and was the product of the help of many kind people and generous funding sources, is made up of thousands of magazines and dozens of audiovisual sources published over a span of some four decades. It includes all of his fiction; thousands of editorials and cultural commentaries; dozens of adaptations of his work in film, television, and radio formats; and many author interviews. I was also able to access Abdel Kouddous's surviving personal letters, notes, and other documents, thanks to the generous help of his family. His family also helped confirmed a number of critical details about his life. Hanan al-Shaykh, the famed author of *The Story of Zahra* who had a romantic relationship with Abdel Kouddous from 1963 to 1965, generously spoke with me at length, providing me with crucial background information that I would not otherwise have been able to unearth.

Despite the considerable size of this archive, it is important to stress from the outset that there are still gaps. Unfortunately, almost all of Abdel Kouddous's close friends and colleagues have passed away, leaving important holes in a researcher's ability to reconstruct what happened behind the scenes in key moments in his life. As for the written record, Abdel Kouddous wrote thousands of articles, short stories, and installments of novels, but these were almost all published under the shadow of state censorship that severely restricted his ability to write openly and directly. Moreover, nothing particularly sensitive survives in his personal papers, including information about the most difficult episodes of his career, almost as if Abdel Kouddous had been careful not to leave behind any potentially incriminating material. There is also no surviving written record of official demands for censoring his fiction or editorials, even though we know that many were made. We know that Nasser expressed his anger at Abdel Kouddous and intervened in his work many times, though, as far as we know, he never did so in writing.[30] At first, Nasser met with Abdel Kouddous in person to demand changes. Once their personal relationship deteriorated, Nasser sent intermediaries such as Anwar Sadat, a fellow founding member of the Free Officers and the future president of Egypt, and journalist Mohamed Hassanein Heikal to relay his displeasure. Time and again, the archive hints at tantalizing moments of intervention and conflict behind the scenes without clearly articulating it, echoes of which I explore throughout this book. Despite obvious gaps, the archive is without question complete enough to allow me to show the impact of the political on the fiction of Abdel Kouddous for the first time. The implications for this new reading are substantial.

## STAGING THE BIRTH OF ARAB DICTATORSHIP

First, this new reading of Abdel Kouddous transforms how we understand fiction during the birth of Arab dictatorship. There has been a widespread misconception that there was little to no dissent against Nasser in print, especially during the first decade after his rise to power. For example, after Nasser's death Tawfiq al-Hakim famously depicted the country as bewitched by Nasser's messianic qualities and incapable of criticizing him. "If someone had dared to attack 'Abd al-Nasir's view, how would the author of this dissidence publish this view? In what newspaper? In what place? The censors of the press and of broadcasting, the secret police, and the other organs of the closed absolute order would not have permitted the appearance of opposition, even of the knowledge of a dissident opinion or of its author."[31] Sadat, in his 1977 autobiography, echoed a similar view, "No one could say anything that appeared to contradict the official line of thinking (the penalty being arrest and loss of livelihood). People's passivity increased daily until one day no man felt he could be secure unless he had completely kept to himself, cut himself off entirely, both from public events and from the very stream of life around him, as though he wanted to see nothing, hear nothing, and say nothing."[32] Many others, including academics, take it for granted that there was little to no dissent against Nasser in fiction and popular culture, especially at the height of his popularity and power in the 1950s and early 1960s. Nonetheless, as I show throughout this book, Abdel Kouddous spun romantic melodrama not only to break gender taboos and boost magazine circulations. He also used it repeatedly as allegory and metaphor to frame his failed political romance with Nasser, to protest the despot currently running Egypt, and to express his anxiety, regret, and despair at what he felt was his personal responsibility for unintentionally helping to turn his beloved Egypt into a military dictatorship.

For example, in *I Do Not Sleep*, serialized in 1955-56, Abdel Kouddous retells the story of the coup by veiling himself as a young female narrator who plots to convince her father, symbolizing the Egyptian people, to divorce and expel her prim and proper stepmother (British colonialism), only to embed in her place a sexy, cunning, and devious traitor (Nasser), with the effect of destroying the household, or nation, in the process.[33] In *Girls in Summer*, serialized in 1958, Abdel Kouddous again writes himself into the fictional text, this time as a woman too weak and anxious to reveal the sexual abuse that she is suffering in secret at the hands of her husband's manly and authoritarian best friend, another thinly veiled symbol of Nasser as both a traitor and dictator.[34] In *A Nose and Three Eyes*, serialized in 1963-64, Abdel Kouddous this time writes himself as a young woman having an affair with a doctor, a not-so-subtle reference to Nasser as his "psychoanalyst," who proceeds to degrade and corrupt her, eventually turning her into a prostitute, a metaphorical reading of what Abdel Kouddous felt Nasser had done to him and the nation.[35] As I show throughout this book, romantic melodrama and sexual sensationalism repeatedly gave Abdel Kouddous the cover to transform what could not be articulated openly—regret for his failed "romance" with Nasser and the revolution—into a narrative form that was acceptable to authorities, at least most of the time. Of course, his work was not simply acceptable to the public; thanks to its mass dissemination, circulation, and consumption in multiple media throughout the Nasser years and beyond, it formed the basic backdrop—a collectively shared experience—of Egyptian popular imagination during the era.

What is this kind of romantic melodrama telling us about the relationship between the intellectual and power? What is it telling us about the advent of a new political order under Nasser? How does this fiction stage the birth of the new era of Arab dictatorship and a new role of the intellectual as dissident? By excavating this voluminous archive of material and embedding the original serialization of Abdel Kouddous's fiction in the context of its immediate publication in the press as well as its contemporaneous political and biographical backdrop, I reframe Abdel Kouddous's writing as something new. In addition to romantic melodrama helping to shape the imaginations and desires of generations of readers, I show how Abdel Kouddous's work offers a new model for understanding fiction as dissent during the Nasser era. His fiction is categorically not *iltizam*, that is, literary commitment as conveyed through high literary art, which has been the dominant model for reading the political in Arabic literary texts during this era.[36] Instead, it is one that employs the basic strategies of the *nahda*—simplified Arabic disseminated through the press to foster mass readership—to write romantic melodrama as a metaphorical vehicle to contest the fate of the 1952 revolution, condemn Nasser's betrayal of democracy, and reveal the depths of Abdel Kouddous's regret and guilt at what Egypt had become. Crucially, this new reading of Abdel Kouddous stresses the importance and inclusion of non-elite culture into the history of Nasserism.

We know that Nasser's early political imagination was formed by literature, and in particular by Tawfiq al-Hakim's *Return of the Spirit*. Nasser was so inspired by al-Hakim's novel that he began writing a novel himself, *For Freedom*, sometime in the mid-1930s, naming his protagonist Muhsin, the same name that al-Hakim used for his own hero who would rise up to bring liberation to Egypt.[37] As numerous scholars have noted, the young Nasser saw himself as playing a dramatic role, embodying the hero that Egypt had been searching for in order to lead it to freedom. My excavation of Abdel Kouddous's archive significantly complicates this depiction of Nasser's relationship to literature. I show in chapter 1 how Abdel Kouddous seemed to be well aware of Nasser's fantasy of playing the role of the liberating hero for Egypt in the two years before the coup, using this framework to construct a script for Nasser in the pages of *Rose El Youssef*, all but sending out casting calls for him to take on the role. I then read Abdel Kouddous's romantic melodrama after the coup partly as framing Nasser's affair with the nation. As Margaret Litvin has argued, Nasser had a "romance with the Egyptian people."[38] In Abdel Kouddous's metaphorical fiction, it is the Egyptian people—doubled as a young woman—who, like him, have fallen madly in love with the handsome and seemingly pliable Nasser, only to be abused, betrayed, degraded, and humiliated once he takes control of the relationship. In this, I show how Nasser went off the script of the romance that Abdel Kouddous had written. Now jilted, Abdel Kouddous's focus on sex and romance in his fiction becomes something new. It stages Egypt's relationship with Nasser and the nation's pathological obsession with his messianic qualities as a melodramatic romance and desire for his masculinity and virility.

## THERAPY

Fiction played yet another crucial role for Abdel Kouddous—it provided him with a form of therapy. On multiple occasions, Abdel Kouddous admitted in his editorials to suffering from depression, insomnia, and anxiety. As discussed in chapter 6, he also experienced panic attacks, at least in the early 1960s. Abdel Kouddous repeatedly included characters in his fiction who unsuccessfully sought solace through confession or were devastated by their inability to reveal the causes of their anxiety and abuse. At a time when Freudian psychoanalysis was in vogue, as Omnia El Shakry has shown, Abdel Kouddous regularly wrote characters who suffered breakdowns because of irreconcilable tensions between the conscious and unconscious.[39] Undoubtably, the line between fiction and autobiography was blurry for him.

Yet one more element that made Abdel Kouddous unique was the way that he sought to self-analyze in fiction through metaphors of revelation and confession. His audience was not only the broad public but also Nasser himself, who was a devoted reader of Abdel Kouddous's fiction.[40] Nasser did not read books, but he monitored the press closely, including following installments of Abdel Kouddous's fiction, even offering comments and feedback at times. Once it was no longer possible to express dissent about Nasser through editorials because of censorship or directly in person, Abdel Kouddous inserted his critiques into his fiction, which he filled with details of their relationship, known only by the two of them at the time, to protest the fate of the revolution and challenge Nasser himself. Abdel Kouddous therefore both exhibits and complicates the way that numerous writers, such as Ahmed Abul-Fath and Lutfi al-Khuli, used the press to guide Nasser's thinking.[41] In this,

Abdel Kouddous followed in the long line of authors in authoritarian environments trying to influence the ruler, seemingly writing for an audience of one.[42] I also show how Abdel Kouddous at times abandoned this strategy to rebel against Nasser in his fiction, oscillating between appeasement and condemnation. In these pendulum swings, Abdel Kouddous sometimes became a defiant, jilted patient in therapy with Nasser as his detested psychoanalyst. I show how, with each weekly installment of dissent, Abdel Kouddous tried to reveal the secrets and guilt that he had been harboring yet repeatedly failed to achieve the curative effect that he so clearly sought. While this component of Abdel Kouddous's fiction might have been opaque to the public, which could not know the details of Abdel Kouddous's personal relationship with Nasser, it was certainly clear enough to Nasser, his self-appointed therapist.

As I argue in this book, Abdel Kouddous, through his mass-consumed fiction, expressed his repressed guilt and regret through the form of romantic melodrama. Unsurprisingly, these melodramas, which were typically centered in the family, were anchored in Abdel Kouddous's relationship not only with Nasser—the self-appointed surrogate therapist—but also his mother, Fatima Youssef. Better known by her stage and publishing name, Rose El Youssef, she is one of the trailblazing divas discussed by Raphael Cormack in *Midnight in Cairo*. Youssef transitioned from stage acting to journalism when she published the first issue of her eponymous magazine, *Rose El Youssef*, in October 1925. After focusing mostly on art and theater news for the first year, the magazine shifted to political and cultural coverage mixed with a groundbreaking use of caricatures and biting political humor, establishing itself as the most important weekly periodical in Egypt by the 1930s. Abdel Kouddous had a particularly complex relationship with his mother. For him, she was not simply a stern figure of discipline and disapproval whose love he tried to gain throughout his life. She also symbolized the liberal era in Egypt, the period from the 1920s up to the Free Officers Coup, that Abdel Kouddous fought against in the pages of the same magazine. By plunging into his "affair" with Nasser and calling for revolution in the years leading up to 23 July 1952, Abdel Kouddous was also rejecting his mother and symbolically trying to kill her (and her era) off, a threat/insult she no doubt took quite personally. In a series of episodes that I cover in this book, I show how Youssef ridiculed and humiliated her son for his calls for revolution, mocking him for what she saw as his naïve support for Nasser as a democrat, his reckless involvement with the Officers, and even his fiction. As I argue, this complex triad between Abdel Kouddous, his mother, and Nasser evokes the framework developed by Lynn Hunt in *The Family Romance of the French Revolution*.[43] Hunt's basic argument, drawing on Freud, is that the individual psyche is linked to social order through collective family imagery in which the parents are eliminated and replaced by a new revolutionary figure, typically a young male. Through his writing, Abdel Kouddous provided the framework and imagery for replacing the cold, distant, and passé mother with the young, virile, and masculine Nasser, not just for himself but also for the nation. Of course, this replacement would ultimately lead to military dictatorship, much to Abdel Kouddous's regret, guilt, and horror.

## MANUFACTURING NASSERISM

Situating Abdel Kouddous's fiction and editorials at the time of their original publication in the press helps us reevaluate the history and production of Nasserism as well as what we know about Nasser himself. Abdel Kouddous, because of his unparalleled popularity, massive output, and consistent production, provides an exceptionally detailed yet unexplored case of how Nasser worked to manufacture popular culture to serve his political aims. As has been noted by many observers, even the Free Officers themselves in their memoirs, Nasser was particularly interested in controlling the media. He monitored the press closely, micromanaging not only coverage but also word choice. He regularly intervened to block the publication of articles in the press. Less than two months after the coup, he decided to work to control the message directly, launching the weekly magazine *al-Tahrir* (Liberation) and then the daily newspaper *al-Gumhuriyya* (The Republic) a year later. Within this scope, Abdel Kouddous was uniquely important to Nasser. In addition to its generalized popularity, Abdel Kouddous's fiction had a crucial appeal for women in particular for the ways that it focused on the new revolutionary woman; as Laura Bier has established, Nasser was intensely interested in overseeing precisely this demographic.[44] By unearthing Nasser's repeated interventions to shape the work of Abdel

Kouddous on a weekly basis, I show how popular fiction became a space of negotiating and contesting politics during a period that has been widely assumed to be devoid of dissent.

We know that Nasser was particularly prickly when it came to criticism, especially criticism expressed in public fora. As he read each weekly installment of Abdel Kouddous's fiction, he saw the potential for it to serve as a vehicle to disseminate his political ideology to the broader public, but he also no doubt detected the dissent aimed directly at him. As I show, Nasser took a hands-off approach to Abdel Kouddous's dissent at times, presumably viewing it as a private affair known only by the two of them, and intervened angrily at other times. Reading Abdel Kouddous's fiction in the context of its original publication in the press illuminates Nasser's repeated attempts to control Abdel Kouddous, to harness and coopt his popularity, engineer his fiction, and turn him into a mouthpiece for his political ideology and agenda. Moreover, in at least three incidents—and there were almost certainly more—I show the ways in which Nasser punished Abdel Kouddous for his dissent. The archive, read on a weekly basis in the context of its publication in the press and linked to events in Abdel Kouddous's life, offers a surprisingly detailed record not only of fiction as staging a new political order but also of the production of Nasserism, not as a top-down linear process but of the way Nasser himself repeatedly attempted to micromanage one of the most important Arab intellectuals of the twentieth century through the press. As I show throughout this book, this relationship functioned like a pendulum, with Abdel Kouddous oscillating between rebellion and appeasement. We know that Nasser punished and then resuscitated writers and members of the regime many times. Thanks to Abdel Kouddous's unparalleled production as both a journalist and fiction writer—publishing these different forms on a weekly basis, often in dialogue with each other, on deadline—his archive offers by far the most detailed record of the way Nasser attempted to manage intellectuals and shape their writing.

As is well known, Nasser left behind no diaries or any other written material that would offer an uncensored image of his views. As P. J. Vatikiotis stresses, "We can only sketch the outline of his personality by reporting what his colleagues and associates thought of him."[45] We therefore only know Nasser as a person through the composite image created by the accounts of others, such as later memoirs by other Free Officers and other figures who claimed to have particularly important influence on him, including Ahmed Abul-Fath. Moreover, as one of Nasser's biographers notes, Nasser, unlike other military dictators, did not eliminate his old comrades and co-conspirators. Instead, as detailed in later memoirs by members of the Free Officers, he kept them around, repeatedly humiliating them to render them fearful and to keep them seeking his approval. In his 1962 tell-all memoir, Ahmed Abul-Fath describes in great detail how Nasser savored humiliating the other Free Officers, especially Sadat, and then bringing them back into his inner circle.[46] When Nasser told Abdel Kouddous that he was giving him "psychoanalytic treatment," it was not the first time that Nasser sought to humiliate him, and it would be far from the last. The archive shows how each new humiliation deeply impacted Abdel Kouddous in both his personal life and his fiction, pushing him at first to try to appease and please Nasser, inevitably followed by angry acts of rebellion. Because of its scope and detail, Abdel Kouddous's archive also offers the most detailed account of the extent and impact of Nasser's micromanagement of his former co-revolutionaries, a critically important element of how Nasser managed the "friends of the past," a central part of his rule that has evaded systematic analysis to date. Through my reading of Abdel Kouddous's archive, a new picture of Nasser emerges, one that shows not only the pendulum swing of his relationship with intellectuals and members of the regime. It also highlights Nasser's unyielding obsession to engineer popular culture, to subdue and humiliate former co-conspirators, and to intervene in their personal lives in ways that have not been explored fully before.

## CAVEATS

Abdel Kouddous believed that he played a central role in laying the groundwork for the revolution, that he would continue to control Nasser after the coup as a tool to install democracy in Egypt, and that he bore a deep sense of responsibility for contributing inadvertently to turning his beloved country into a military dictatorship. It is essential to note from the outset, however, that it is entirely possible that Abdel Kouddous gave himself outsized importance in all of these aspects. Abdel

Kouddous did not discuss in public his relationship with Nasser in detail until 1974, during a time when the Sadat regime was orchestrating a process of "de-Nasserization," which included not only economic reforms but also the encouragement of intellectuals to attack Nasser and his regime. As John Waterbury has shown, the 1970s witnessed a wide array of scathing memoirs, articles, and interviews from important figures condemning Nasser.[47] Abdel Kouddous claimed at the time that he was not participating in this wave of criticism, but starting in 1974 he did give many interviews that revealed his deep sense of regret for what had happened to the revolution as well as the striking details of his troubled relationship with Nasser, even if he did so hesitantly and without the vitriol of someone like Tawfiq al-Hakim. Without memoirs or other revealing personal papers by Nasser, it is impossible to judge if Abdel Kouddous was exaggerating about his role in the revolution. Unlike Israel Gershoni in his discussion of Tawfiq al-Hakim's claims of unique influence on Nasser, I will not render judgment on Abdel Kouddous in this respect.[48] Nonetheless, I am not accepting Abdel Kouddous's claims in his interviews in the 1970s and 1980s uncritically or at face value as historical fact. These interviews show that Abdel Kouddous felt anxiety, despair, and horror for what he believed was his unique role in installing military dictatorship in Egypt. And as I show throughout this book, echoes of these sentiments and evidence of his role are clear throughout his popular, prolific, and widely disseminated writing from the 1940s until Nasser's death in 1970. In the history that I present in this book, the texts channeling the sentiments are my focus, not whether the sentiments were justified or not.

While Abdel Kouddous attacked Nasser directly in a number of editorials published between January 1953 and March 1954, this was the exception rather than the rule. Instead, as I argue in this book, Abdel Kouddous repeatedly used allegory and metaphor to express his despair over the trajectory of the revolution. It is also essential to state that I am not claiming that Abdel Kouddous was fully aware of what I read as repeated acts of dissent against Nasser in his fiction or that he always carefully constructed fictional allegory intentionally in this way. Regardless, I show throughout this book how Abdel Kouddous returned repeatedly to similar acts of rebellion against Nasser in his fiction for a period of nearly fifteen years. It is clear during this time that Abdel

Kouddous was trying to process his anxiety and despair, expressing it both to the public and to his most important reader, Nasser, on a weekly basis in his serialized fiction. Perhaps the fact that he wrote installments of his fiction so quickly and under strict deadline encouraged him to express what he was feeling in a given week without the filter of time and distance. Just as the public seemed to ignore his attempts to reveal his anger, regret, and revolt—repeatedly overlooking the political critique embedded in these mass-consumed serialized texts—it is entirely possible, even likely, that Abdel Kouddous was himself not fully aware of his own repression and acting out against Nasser. His fiction therefore can be read not only as a new kind of staging for the birth of Arab dictatorship and the oscillating, contingent relationship between intellectual and power during the Nasser era but also, paradoxically, as a slippage of repressed despair and a compulsion of revolt, not necessarily intentional heroic resistance. Nonetheless, following Fredric Jameson, I argue throughout this book that it is the political unconscious that fundamentally shaped Abdel Kouddous's work.[49]

Abdel Kouddous might be remembered today even more for the classic film adaptations of his fiction than for his written novels and short stories. For many, the endings of the films, many of which present a stark moralistic solution to complicated gender and sexual relations, are synonymous with his fiction. While many of the films faithfully followed the fiction until the climax, almost all of the endings, especially in the films during the Nasser era, were altered, sharply sanitizing the dissent that Abdel Kouddous had expressed in the original written work. Sometimes these changes were made to please the censor. Other times, they appear to be the product of the director, producers, and studio looking to maximize ticket sales. It is essential to clarify that Abdel Kouddous lost all control of these film adaptations once he signed away the rights to them. In fact, the films were a source of deep ambivalence for him. He no doubt enjoyed the notoriety and fame that followed each box-office success. Nonetheless, he was repeatedly outraged at how the films altered the endings of his fiction, sometimes even to the point of publishing complaints about them in the press. Since Abdel Kouddous had so little control over almost all of the film adaptations, I will only discuss these films when they are directly relevant to my argument.

This book offers a new history of the 1952 revolution as well as the politics and popular culture of Nasser's Egypt through the life and work of Ihsan Abdel Kouddous. In the detailed history reconstructed in each chapter, Abdel Kouddous emerges as the neglected legend of Arabic romantic melodrama, the pivotal yet erased player in the Free Officers Coup, and a tragic figure who unintentionally worked to embed military dictatorship in Egypt. He also becomes the haunted conscience of the revolution and the nation, a unique figure who lived the repeated oscillation between resisting and accommodating the dictator. He looms as a highly nuanced and paradoxical figure who struggled deeply with the contradictions, shame, and self-loathing of pleasing Nasser while being unable to repress his dissent for long, whether he was aware of it or not. Through the social-political biography that I offer in this book, I show how Abdel Kouddous comes to represent a national allegory for his beloved Egypt during the Nasser era, in its dreams and fantasies, grief and disappointment, repression and denial, and, ultimately, its degradation, submission, and defeat. By excavating the little-known yet deeply consequential relationship between Abdel Kouddous and Nasser on the level of the weekly archive and in dialogue with episodes in his personal life, this book ultimately shows how rereading Abdel Kouddous—in his anxieties, repressions, and paradoxical acceptance of and resistance to Nasser's psychoanalytic "treatment"—offers a new history of the politics of dissent, popular culture, and fiction during perhaps the most consequential period of modern Middle Eastern history: the birth and spread of Arab dictatorship.

CHAPTER ONE

**CASTING CALLS**

Men sometimes see things, including other people, through their own natures.

—*Tawfiq al-Hakim*,
The Return of Consciousness (1974)

At 9:15 p.m. on 13 November 1951, Ihsan Abdel Kouddous left the popular Armitage Restaurant, located in the historic Immobilia Building in central Cairo. At the time, the stylish art deco Immobilia was well known as the residence of movie stars and singers. Abdel Kouddous had just finished dinner with a friend who was warning him that his latest newspaper campaign attacking authorities might put him in danger. Despite the ominous tone of the discussion, Abdel Kouddous finished dinner in good spirits and left for the movies. As he approached the end of the corridor, a man hurtled out of the darkness and hit him on the back of the head with a sharp object and then fled. Abdel Kouddous, whose face was so covered in blood that he could no longer see, staggered back into the Armitage, where friends found him and rushed him to the emergency room. Abdel Kouddous survived the attack, but he could not identify the assailant. It turns out that this would not be an isolated incident, but the first of four assassination attempts against Abdel Kouddous during his life.[1] But why would anyone want to kill Ihsan Abdel Kouddous?

While Ihsan Abdel Kouddous would become perhaps the most popular and prolific writer of Arabic fiction in the twentieth century, he was well known before the 23 July 1952 coup for his inflammatory editorials and newspaper campaigns against the political establishment. Starting more than a decade before the coup, Abdel Kouddous made many enemies publishing articles calling for a total cleansing of what he saw as a collaborating and corrupt political, economic, and social elite. He looked to lay the groundwork for revolution by shaping and mobilizing public outrage, drumming up scandals that he thought would illustrate the need to sweep away the old system and establish a nationalistic democracy. During the decade before the coup, he also developed and disseminated the script for a masculine, committed, self-sacrificing leader who would rise up and act as the instrument of the people to cleanse the nation. Through the platform of his weekly editorials in *Rose El Youssef*, Abdel Kouddous repeatedly sent out casting calls for his long-awaited "hero"—based on the script—to take on that role and spark the revolution. It was Gamal Abdel Nasser who would eventually answer those calls.

By the mid-1940s, an impatient Abdel Kouddous began intervening in events, taking enormous risks to shape the path toward revolution. Abdel Kouddous used *Rose El Youssef* to put himself in contact with clandestine revolutionaries, harbor political assassins, store weapons, and issue commands to the public for mass revolt. He went to jail several times, defied censorship restrictions, and even faced the assassination attempt at the Immobilia in 1951. He acted recklessly at times, projecting the flame of revolution onto people and events that had little connection to politics. Throughout the 1940s and early 1950s, he focused obsessively on destroying the political system without planning for the future or taking the consequences of revolution seriously.

It was during these years that Abdel Kouddous would develop his deep sense of ownership and responsibility for the coming revolution, and not just because of his tireless calls to sweep away the old guard. He worked closely with the Free Officers for over two years before the coup. Collaborating secretly with Nasser and other Officers starting in summer 1950, Abdel Kouddous broke the notorious Rotten Weapons case, a sensational scandal in which the palace purchased defective weapons for the Egyptian military for the 1948 Palestine War at inflated prices, pocketing enormous profits while sending unsuspecting soldiers to their suicide on the battlefield. Behind the scenes, Abdel Kouddous pushed the seemingly pliable Nasser to leak case documents to him so that he could inflame both the public and the army to revolt over the naked corruption of the regime. Abdel Kouddous saw himself during this period as directing Nasser and the other Officers, influencing their thinking and guiding them to act. Abdel Kouddous would later believe that it was his role in breaking and disseminating the Rotten Weapons scandal that laid the basic groundwork for the revolution, preparing public opinion to embrace the coming coup.

Once the Rotten Weapons scandal reverberated in the country, Abdel Kouddous published editorials in *Rose El Youssef* chiding Nasser to step on stage and embody his role as the redeeming hero for the nation. In early 1952, Abdel Kouddous continued to use his platform at the magazine to communicate to Nasser, calling openly in the press for temporary dictatorship by a new, young, masculine leader who could perform the necessary cleansing of the political system. Abdel Kouddous saw himself as not simply a secret collaborator with Nasser and the other Free Officers but as their civilian leader, directing them to perform the roles laid out in his script. As I will show in the following chapter, Abdel Kouddous would repeat all of these crucial elements—using the press to try to influence and direct Nasser, writing editorials to support and guide the redeeming hero, seeing himself as responsible for the revolution, calling for dictatorship without considering the consequences—in the weeks after the coup.

No doubt, other writers such as Ahmed Abul-Fath, the editor in chief of perhaps the most important daily in the country, *al-Misri*, and Ahmed Hussein, the founder of the Young Egypt Society, issued calls in the press for revolution during the turbulent period of the late 1940s and early 1950s. Like Abdel Kouddous, Ahmed Abul-Fath worked closely with Nasser before the coup, echoing a number of the demands that appeared in the clandestine pamphlets of the Free Officers in his editorials at the time. Other writers, such as Tawfiq al-Hakim, would later openly declare that they were the intellectual fathers of the revolution. But Abdel Kouddous understood himself to be playing a unique role before 23 July 1952. At the time of the coup, he clearly believed that he was the civilian leader of the Free Officers, mobilizing and directing them not only to break the Rotten Weapons scandal but also to rise up and act. His sense of playing a uniquely important role for the Officers was only reinforced when Nasser called Abdel Kouddous early on the morning of the coup, inviting him to the barracks to join in. Indeed, Abdel Kouddous was the only civilian to participate in the coup, risking his life along with the Officers to eliminate the old regime. His relationship with the Officers would also explain why Abdel Kouddous had a particularly privileged status immediately after the coup and why he worked so enthusiastically to embed them in rule in the weeks afterwards. Excavating the critical period before the coup lays the foundation for understanding Abdel Kouddous's deep sense of ownership for the revolution, responsibility for bringing Nasser to power, and subsequent horror as Nasser turned Egypt into a military dictatorship.

## THE FIRST STEP

Ihsan Abdel Kouddous was born on 1 January 1919. He was the son of Fatima Youssef, better known by her stage name Rose El Youssef, and Mohammed Abdel Kouddous. His father worked as an engineer, but he was such an entertaining comedic actor that King Fuad I tried to recruit him as a court jester.[2] Mohammed Abdel Kouddous dedicated himself full-time to the theater in 1917, when he met and married Youssef against the wishes of his conservative father. Abdel Kouddous's parents divorced when Youssef was seven months pregnant. After Abdel Kouddous was born, his father returned to work as an engineer to support the family. Nonetheless, his father continued to write poetry and plays, serving as an early literary inspiration for the young Abdel Kouddous.

Fatima Youssef was not just any stage actress but one of the celebrated divas of the era.[3] Nonetheless, as Raphael Cormack explains in his cultural history of Cairo's Roaring Twenties, "actress in Egypt was coming to be seen as a byword for immorality, even prostitution."[4] Because of his parents' divorce as well as the social implications of his mother's profession, Abdel Kouddous grew up in his paternal grandfather's home in Cairo's Abbassia neighborhood, where Naguib Mahfouz also lived at the time. The two future pillars of modern Arabic fiction, who would intersect both personally and professionally many times throughout their lives, first met as children on the streets of Abbassia in the early 1920s. Abdel Kouddous's grandfather, Ahmed Ridwan, was deeply religious and traditional, frequently inviting Islamic scholars for discussion at home. Abdel Kouddous was raised by his paternal aunt, whom he was told was his mother. As a child, Youssef, whom he was told was his aunt, would visit Abdel Kouddous most weeks, but Ridwan did not permit her to enter the house, treating her as a pariah. It must have

**Figure 1.** Naguib Mahfouz (right) congratulating Ihsan Abdel Kouddous for winning the Egyptian state prize for best film in 1957. Courtesy of the Abdel Kouddous family.

been a shock for Abdel Kouddous once he discovered as an adolescent that Youssef was in fact his mother.

This was just the start of Abdel Kouddous's complex relationship with his mother. She remarried quickly, this time to a man with a family more sympathetic to the arts, and had a daughter with her new husband. Now that his mother was focusing on her new family, Abdel Kouddous felt his mother's absence deeply. That absence was only reinforced when she left Egypt to live in Paris for two years with her husband and daughter; Abdel Kouddous was nine years old at the time. Once she returned, Abdel Kouddous began to spend more time with her, becoming on intimate terms with literary giants in her circle like Ahmed Shawqi and Abbas Mahmoud al-Aqqad. She even arranged for the legendary singer Mohamed Abdel Wahhab to give music lessons to Abdel Kouddous when he was a teenager. These figures served as a stark contrast to the religious figures with whom he regularly interacted at his grandfather's house. This cultural clash—between the unapologetic liberalism of his mother and stark conservatism of his grandfather—was something that Abdel Kouddous internalized at a young age. As he explained in 1976 on the television program *Autograph*, "This contradiction became the main element in forming my whole personality, my way of thinking, and my image of society."[5] It was this clash, he said, that gave birth to his desire for revolt and overturning societal traditions.

Fatima Youssef left the stage and vaudeville scene to establish the weekly magazine *Rose El Youssef* on 25 October 1925. Just as she had devoted herself to becoming a star in the world of acting, Youssef now focused all her energy on this new enterprise, continuing to have little time for her young son. With its striking color caricatures, the magazine became widely recognized for its vibrant liberal elements as well as its populist "jihad" for nationalist liberation, supporting the principles of Saad Zaghoul, the founder of the Wafd Party who died less than a year after the magazine was launched. Building on the growing audience of readers who found its simple prose, sensational topics, humorous political caricatures, and anticolonial populist tone appealing, *Rose El Youssef* quickly became one of the most important and popular periodicals in the country. Authorities shut down the magazine—and even jailed Youssef and its editors—numerous times for its unwelcome criticisms and attacks on politicians. To escape the censors, Youssef would continue issuing the magazine during these shutdowns under alternative titles.[6]

**Figure 2.** Fatima Youssef and Mohamed El-Tabii (center), editor in chief of *Rose El Youssef* at the time, smiling on their way to prison in 1934. Courtesy of the Abdel Kouddous family.

It was only a matter of time before Abdel Kouddous sought to publish a piece in one of his mother's publications. At barely seventeen years old, Abdel Kouddous wrote a poem "I Found Her," which he submitted anonymously for publication. As Abdel Kouddous recalled decades later, when the poem appeared on 13 January 1936, he took it to his mother and asked her proudly, "Do you know who wrote this poem? Me. What do you think?" Despite his boasting, Abdel Kouddous must have known what her reaction would be. Instead of praising him, Youssef was furious. She shamed him by shouting at him, "I don't want you writing this nonsense again!" To reinforce her point, she docked his allowance for a week.[7]

This exchange crystalized an important aspect of their relationship. As Abdel Kouddous explained late in his life, "I had a big complex. My mother was a working woman at a time when women were only mothers or housewives. No one even knew anyone else's mother's name. But my mother was very famous. That became a huge motivation to make my mother leave work and become like all the other mothers. This situation made me suffer greatly and pushed me to prove myself."[8] As he said succinctly in another interview, "I did everything I could to achieve my life's desire: for my mother to stay home while I devoted myself entirely to working for her comfort."[9] Sending this poem anonymously gave him an early opportunity to try to prove to himself—and her—that he was talented enough to succeed without resorting to nepotism. It was also a first step for him to try not only to please his mother but also to demonstrate that she could rely on him to stay home. Instead of praise, however, his initiative was met with scorn, mockery, and humiliation. This early exchange is just a hint of the similar yet increasingly consequential interactions between Abdel Kouddous and his mother to come.

Despite this humiliation, Abdel Kouddous eventually managed to convince his mother to allow him to write for the magazine. On 19 August 1936, only seven months later, Abdel Kouddous published his first article, this time under his teenage nickname "Suna." Using this pseudonym to shield himself from perceptions of favoritism, Abdel Kouddous wrote about the various ways that the magazine collected news of the "highlife."[10] In the months ahead, he continued publishing pieces as "Suna," including literary portraits of wealthy young women summering on the beaches of Alexandria—a social milieu in which he would later set his fiction—as well as a number of light semiautobiographical pieces, mostly about his misadventures with young women. Despite his mother's earlier objections, Abdel Kouddous published his first short story on 18 April 1938, this time under his real name.[11] It was a first-person narrative of a girl who confesses that she found her brother's secret love letters after he returned from England. Abdel Kouddous continued publishing a number of short stories and works of drama in the magazine, none of which were collected in his later books. This early work, which he wrote as a hobby during school breaks, featured key elements of his later writing, such as epistolary fiction, accounts of real-life romantic adventures, and first-person narratives of amorous longings. These pieces gave Abdel Kouddous the opportunity to develop his fictional voice in the public sphere at a particularly young age.

The publication of his first article in *Rose El Youssef* coincided almost exactly with the political event that would become a point of focus for Abdel Kouddous's rage before the coup: the signing of the treaty between

Britain and Egypt on 22 August 1936 that granted Britain control over Egypt's defense and the right to station some ten thousand British troops in the Suez Canal and Sudan. While Abdel Kouddous himself was too young at the time to publish political protests, *Rose El Youssef* vehemently opposed the treaty, calling it a "step toward a violent death."[12] The magazine immediately framed the treaty as a repression of national sovereignty by British colonial authorities thanks to the enthusiastic

**Figure 3.** Cover of *Rose El Youssef*, 2 December 1936.

support of the collaborating Egyptian elite. Starting on 2 September 1936, *Rose El Youssef* began publishing pieces of outrage rejecting the treaty, including derisive caricatures, such as Misri Effendi, the magazine's symbol of the Egyptian everyman, bled dry by the British prime minister with the help of pliant Egyptian politicians. One prophetic cover from 2 December 1936 shows Misri Effendi angrily pointing the way toward the pyramids to rows of Egyptian soldiers with the caption "The first step to independence is to the army." Even more than fifteen years before the coup, *Rose El Youssef* had already forged the link on its cover between the Egyptian military and national liberation, framing the political through caricature.

## "WE NEED DESTRUCTION AND REBUILDING"

Abdel Kouddous's first official political mission for the magazine came in 1938, when his mother asked him to get news from the prime minister at a hotel in Alexandria. By fall 1939, at only twenty years old, Abdel Kouddous began covering meetings of politicians and reporting on the political parties. His young age was striking for his interlocutors; Abdel Kouddous mentions in several articles at the time how politicians could not resist offering him "fatherly advice" after he completed an interview. Despite his age, he became a close acquaintance of leading Egyptian political figures. In his first overtly political editorial, published on 1 October 1939, Abdel Kouddous already displayed a devotion to the abstract ideal of the nation and sharp attacks against corruption, two elements that would characterize his journalism during the decade before the coup. "All I ask is that everyone understand that partisanism is one thing and Egyptianism or nationalism is something much richer. When everyone understands that, political parties will be rid of their filth and their goals will rise up to the level of the public interest."[13] In his first political piece, published almost thirteen years before the coup, Abdel Kouddous already situated the self-interested corruption of politicians as damaging the idealized nation, pointing to the need to cleanse the system for the good of Egypt.

By August 1941—some nine years before he would meet Gamal Abdel Nasser—Abdel Kouddous had begun crafting his vision for a leader to guide Egypt to revolt in order to wipe away the corrupt political class and bring salvation to the nation. In an article in which he describes meeting with an unnamed former minister, Abdel Kouddous explains that the man was "a beacon of revolution, a revolution of reform that he calls for and works to achieve."[14] Unlike the politicians in office at the time, this former minister was not deterred by reform and "holds his nation holy." This man spoke in oppositional terms that already made sense to Abdel Kouddous—it was not the pure nation that needed reform but rather the politicians exploiting it and taking advantage of the public interest for their own enrichment: "Talking with this former minister ignited in me his revolt, a revolt against fixed governmental routine and old mentalities." In this early piece, published when he was only twenty-two years old, Abdel Kouddous included a number of the markers that would characterize his journalism throughout the 1940s and early 1950s: the need to protect the beloved idealized nation from an exploitative political class, to tear out the entrenched political system, to undertake radical reform in the form of a revolt or revolution, and to serve from his high-profile journalistic platform the inspiring leader who had the vision, outrage, and courage to carry it out.

After earning a law degree, Abdel Kouddous worked as an apprentice lawyer in early 1942, trying to strike out on his own and prove himself beyond his mother's orbit. Nonetheless, Abdel Kouddous wound up working full-time for *Rose El Youssef* in the summer, no doubt filling him with a paradoxical sense of failure and shame. He was becoming a rising star of journalism, but he was anxious that it was thanks to his mother's influence. However, as Abdel Kouddous mentioned several times, his mother struck him repeatedly at the office, calling him a failure as a writer and humiliating him in front of other journalists. It was around this time that Abdel Kouddous fell in love with Lawahez al-Mehelmy, known as Lola. When the two decided to get married, Abdel Kouddous's mother objected. Nonetheless, they eloped on 5 November 1942. While Abdel Kouddous could not achieve his dream of supporting his mother for her to retire, he insisted that Lola become a housewife. As Lola later explained, "He felt deprived of his mother because she was so busy with work and had no time for him."[15] It was at this point that Lola began to provide Abdel Kouddous with the elements he was not getting from his relationship with his mother. Abdel Kouddous later explained, "My mother was like a man. All she cared about was work. A big part of my love for Lola was being able to take refuge in her because I didn't have a mother."[16]

It was a turbulent time for Abdel Kouddous. With new financial responsibilities and family pressures—in addition to feuding with his mother for not supporting his marriage, among other reasons—Abdel Kouddous struck out on his own and took a full-time job working at a competitor magazine, *Akhir Sa'a* (Latest Hour), which at the time was edited by Mohamed El-Tabii, the founding editor of *Rose El Youssef*. El-Tabii's crisp populist style, which stood in sharp contrast to the elevated rhetoric of most other journalists at the time, laid the groundwork for the popular press in twentieth-century Egypt and had an immense influence on Abdel Kouddous.[17] *Akhir Sa'a*, with a format, political tone, and use of caricatures similar to *Rose El Youssef*, was a natural fit for Abdel Kouddous. It also gave him the chance to prove himself in a magazine that was not owned by his mother. Luminaries such as Abbas Mahmoud al-Aqqad and Tawfiq al-Hakim also wrote for it in the 1940s, which put Abdel Kouddous in good company. In his first article for *Akhir Sa'a*, published on 13 December 1942, Abdel Kouddous wrote a comedic piece in which he claimed that waiters were making more money than university graduates in Egypt, making him think about becoming a waiter until his mother angrily rejected the idea.[18] In January 1943, as *Rose El Youssef* was shut down by authorities for three months, Abdel Kouddous focused more and more in *Akhir Sa'a* on oppositional politics, establishing himself as a voice of dissent in the political world. He remained at *Akhir Sa'a* through fall 1943, when his father wrote him a letter pleading with him to go back to his mother's magazine.[19]

When Abdel Kouddous returned full-time to *Rose El Youssef* in winter 1944, he brought with him a much more confident, combative, and inflammatory tone, one that would set him on the path of political confrontation. On 23 March 1944, Abdel Kouddous declared, "We're a lying society that loves to lie, a hypocritical society that loves hypocrisy . . . a society that asks you for everything but gives you nothing, that demands that you be clean while immersing itself in filth."[20] He asks tongue in cheek if Egypt needs reform and then answers his own question by announcing, "No, we need destruction and rebuilding!" While Abdel Kouddous had discussed revolution before, this was the first time

**Figure 4.** Ihsan Abdel Kouddous, December 1943. Courtesy of the Abdel Kouddous family.

that he openly called for the end of the existing political order, which was particularly striking considering the strict censorship on the press during World War II. What mattered for Abdel Kouddous was uprooting the current political class, not addressing how the idealized nation would emerge afterwards. Focusing his early years on bringing about destruction—not how society would be rebuilt—would come to haunt him after the revolution.

By summer 1944, Abdel Kouddous continued honing his vision for revolution, arguing in particular for a leader to bring salvation to Egypt, a nation that he saw as sick with the disease of corruption. According to Abdel Kouddous, this man would not come from one of the men claiming to be leaders yet understanding nothing of what that meant. "It's not enough for you to stand among us giving a speech, imagining the pains of the nation and offering to treat them, encouraging us to cry out to you to lead us and save this sick nation. No, you have to feel these pains to treat them. And when we see the first signs of healing, maybe we'll call you a leader. Leadership is sacrifice. It's jail, self-denial, deprivation, and poverty for the sake of an idea that you strive for. You all have ideas, but you haven't struggled for them. Who among you has gone to jail or sacrificed himself or become poor?"[21] In this piece, Abdel Kouddous positions the nation as ailing and the current crop of leaders as incompetent doctors. For Abdel Kouddous, the effective leader is no physician-politician, someone who rallies crowds by proposing to treat the sick patient. Instead, the leader proves himself by performing commitment, self-sacrifice, and bravery, regardless of the consequences.

Despairing at the results of local elections in early 1945, Abdel Kouddous continued to hone his vision for a new kind of leader to guide Egypt on the path of revolt. The list of newly elected politicians only confirmed for Abdel Kouddous his loneliness in a wasteland that he saw as illegitimate and irredeemably corrupt. "I don't believe in any leader. I don't believe in any constitution, law, or government document in this country. I'm lost, lost in the desert of politics, in the desert of the future, looking for a leader, a real leader to direct me on the path and lead me through the desert, to exploit this revolt within me that is so hot that it almost makes me cry and makes people pity me. Let there be this leader among you. I'll devote to him all my faith for my pen to write for."[22] Some five years before meeting Nasser, Abdel Kouddous was already issuing a casting call for the awaited leader, someone to guide him out of the wilderness toward salvation, to take advantage of his desperation for revolt. Abdel Kouddous was pleading for the leader who would walk before him, the man who would uproot the corrupt old order and establish a new society in its place, someone for whom Abdel Kouddous could use his writing to promote in complete faith. While Abdel Kouddous had called for revolution before, this was the first time that he offered explicitly to put his journalistic platform at his leader's service. Considering the way that Abdel Kouddous would come to use *Rose El Youssef* to support the Free Officers and Nasser, both before and after the coup, this article stands as stunning foreshadowing for what was to come.

As World War II wound down and opportunity for change appeared on the horizon, Abdel Kouddous quickly went to work fleshing out the part of the actor who would play the role of his awaited leader. When the current crop of so-called political leaders went for medical examinations before traveling abroad, Abdel Kouddous was appalled. For him, this symbolized their feebleness and inadequacy: "Egypt needs a man. A man who plays the role of the doctor, not the sick person; a man who dies for his nation, not someone his nation dies for; a man who ignores himself and puts his country first, who forgets the weakness of his heart and blood pressure to remember the heart of Egypt and its blood."[23] Abdel Kouddous desperately sought a strong, virile, masculine, and courageous leader—a "doctor" who would not diagnose the nation but whose strength and self-sacrifice would stand in stark contrast to the sick politician—someone who was in complete control, with confidence and commitment. He called out for the leader as masculine, courageous, and self-sacrificing, a man so committed to the nation that he would be willing to die for it.

The 1940s was a time that Abdel Kouddous later called "the years of looking for the hidden treasure of revolution."[24] As he became more and more fanatical, Abdel Kouddous was convinced that he saw the sparks of revolution all around him. For example, in an article published on 11 January 1945, Abdel Kouddous described how he walked past a young man lying on the sidewalk, sprawled out under election posters for political candidates. Wearing the clothes of a manual worker, the man, seemingly on the verge of death, emitted a horrible stench. Abdel Kouddous could not believe his eyes as he watched people callously walk past the man as if he were a piece of garbage. For Abdel Kouddous, this man, rotting away and starving in total neglect under the slogans of corrupt politicians, represented the nation. This horror proved that "there had to be revolution."[25] It was at this point that Abdel Kouddous had an epiphany—the man must become the motivation for his writing, must push him to act: "Every page of this magazine has to be mobilized for this corpse tossed on the sidewalk. I have to write until my pen runs dry. But that's not enough. I have to get up and go to the prime minister, the minister of finance, even Abdeen Palace, and demand justice for this worker, vengeance for this corpse. The rich of this country have to starve like this worker so workers can eat their fill.... I'll sacrifice everything for this corpse." Outraged, Abdel Kouddous narrates the moment that he realizes that writing about this man—the double for the abused nation, the crystallization of the need for revolution—was not enough. He had to act, to perform his own self-sacrifice to overturn the corrupt system.

Abdel Kouddous then narrates how he inserts himself into the scene. He gives the man a cup of water, helps him to his feet, and takes him to see a doctor. Abdel Kouddous indignantly tells the doctor that this poor man, like the nation, is suffering from starvation and poverty, the ills of the era. The unimpressed doctor responds, "No, this man is suffering from hashish and narcotics!" The worker then wakes up from his drug-induced stupor and sneaks away, comically begging Abdel Kouddous not to meet any minister on his behalf. The article ends without any indication that Abdel Kouddous understands how he was using the man as a symbol for his own desires, to further his own outrage. Nonetheless, the piece shows that Abdel Kouddous was now framing his journalism to incite outrage and action—even if based on unfounded projections—and that he was becoming personally involved to achieve his revolutionary goals. If the worker was the double for the nation, Abdel Kouddous now insisted on intervening to bring it dignity. It was this kind of impulsiveness that would cast a shadow over Abdel Kouddous during his life. In a 1961 interview, he was asked what his weak point is. He responded, "My emotions. Anyone can influence me easily. All my mistakes, even in my work, were the result of my emotions."[26]

With the end of World War II, the censorship on the Egyptian press was relaxed. The impatient Abdel Kouddous decided that the time had come for himself to take on role of the leader who would go to jail to demonstrate his commitment and self-sacrifice. On 9 August 1945, he published "The Man Who Has to Go," becoming the first journalist to openly attack Sir Miles Lampson, the British consul-general in Egypt from 1936 to 1946.[27] At the time, Abdel Kouddous and other nationalists, including Gamal Abdel Nasser, were still seething over the events of 4 February 1942, when Lampson insisted that King Farouk either dissolve the Egyptian government and appoint a prime minister friendly to British interests or abdicate. Lampson ordered British tanks to surround the palace that day as a show of force, intimidating the young monarch to agree to his demands. This became known as the Abdeen Palace incident. For Abdel Kouddous, this was an intolerable insult to Egypt and its independence, an unbearable act of submissiveness and weakness that needed to be rectified: "It's Egypt's right to demand Lampson's departure from his position and to replace him with someone else since he has failed in his mission!" The incident was not simply an affront to Egypt, demonstrating the king's servility. It was an open admission that, despite the 1923 Constitution and the 1936 treaty with Britain, Egypt did not have sovereignty over its own political affairs. For Egypt to take the first step toward independence, it had to have a partner who was not stained with this crime; in other words, Lampson had to go. Since none of the collaborating politicians were courageous enough to call for Lampson's departure, Abdel Kouddous did it himself, marking a new stage of personal involvement in politics for the young journalist.

As Abdel Kouddous had clearly intended, the inflammatory article did not go unnoticed. Fearing a negative impact on British-Egyptian relations, Prime Minister Mahmoud El Nokrashi Pasha confiscated the issue of *Rose El Youssef* from the newsstands and ordered the arrest and interrogation of Abdel Kouddous. Although he was mocked in jail for his youth and idealism, Abdel Kouddous was treated well during his detention and released after only four days.[28] In the following issue of the magazine, Fatima Youssef published a letter to her imprisoned son, discussing the conflict between her commitment to the cause of Egyptian nationalism and her fear for his safety. "You're at the beginning of your path on the cause of Egypt and you've entered a noble abode on the path of principle and freedom—prison," she wrote.[29] For Youssef, going to jail was an essential rite of passage for newspaper editors, an opportunity to prove their commitment to freedom of expression and nationalist ideals.

Behind the scenes, Youssef was not pleased with the way her son had acted out, picking a fight with such a high-profile figure in what seemed like an impulsive attempt to prove himself both to the public and to her.

Moreover, she understood his escalating attacks on the political system as a rejection of her. As Abdel Kouddous explained decades later about his mother, "Our differences after that article were the differences between two generations. I belonged to the generation of revolution while my mother belonged to her generation. No matter how oppositional she was, she grew up in the middle of a political context that was different from mine."[30] As Abdel Kouddous explained in this interview, this moment represented a sharp divide between him and his mother: "I wanted to overturn the entire existing system!" The intent was clear. Along with his mother's retirement, he wanted the passing of the political system that she represented. This divide would serve as the major point of conflict between them in the years to come.

Things must have been tense between Abdel Kouddous and his mother in the weeks following his release from jail. Nonetheless, she clearly forgave him. On 24 October 1945, Fatima Youssef brought Abdel Kouddous into her office, sat him down in her chair, and made him the editor in chief of *Rose El Youssef*. Even though he was only twenty-six years old, making him the youngest editor in chief in the Egyptian press, it must have felt like a long time coming. While she gave him editorial control, she remained deeply involved in the magazine and continued to control its purse strings. She was particularly stingy in determining her son's salary, which became a source of deep friction between them. To earn additional money, Abdel Kouddous began writing articles for competing publications, something that greatly annoyed his mother and eventually forced her to pay him a livable wage.

Now at the helm of arguably the most influential political weekly in the country, Abdel Kouddous immediately took advantage of the opportunity. Upon naming him editor in chief of the magazine, his mother published a letter of parental advice in which she urged him to "fight injustice wherever it may be and stand with the weak against the powerful without asking the cost."[31] Abdel Kouddous was happy to oblige. Starting in fall 1945, he became "an adversary to power and friend to all revolutionaries."[32] It was during this time that he doubled down on looking for opportunities to incite anger at the ruling class, radicalize the public, and spark revolt. As he explained in 1980, "I believed that every piece of news would reveal a new scandal by the exploitative class and increase the number of revolutionaries, bringing the people closer to the day of eruption that would bring down their enemies."[33] Abdel Kouddous disavowed membership in any particular political party or organization, but he turned the offices of *Rose El Youssef* into a meeting place and platform for revolutionaries, regardless of their political leanings. As he later explained, "I decided that revolution had to happen... so the ideology of my editors didn't concern me. I didn't care if they belonged to the Nationalist Party, Muslim Brotherhood, or Communist Party. All that mattered was that they were revolting against the palace, the political parties, the British, and the Egyptian aristocracy."[34] Convinced that change would not come from anyone already in a position of authority, he teased the public by appearing to support a variety of revolutionary perspectives, such as publishing the agenda of the Communist Party and conducting a sensational interview with Hassan al-Banna, the founder of the Muslim Brotherhood.[35] Abdel Kouddous claimed throughout his career that while he sympathized with a variety of radical platforms and even considered someone like al-Banna a friend, he never joined a political party. As he later explained, "The revolution that I was imagining was bigger than any party or organization. It had to be a general revolution, encompassing everyone."[36]

He repeatedly railed against the Abdeen Palace incident and Egypt's lack of independence, demanding immediate abrogation of the Anglo-Egyptian treaty of 1936 and evacuation of the British from Egyptian soil. With no tangible results, Abdel Kouddous came to believe that there was no peaceful way for his beloved but maligned nation to gain independence. There had to be violence: "The only path is blood. It's a path that doesn't need ministers or negotiators, only freedom fighters, nationalists, and an entire people roaring in the face of the lion so that the whole East wakes up, shakes the world under its feet, and wipes the smile off the face of its rapists so those rapists can enjoy the sight of their own blood!"[37] This article, published on 2 October 1946, was his first decisive step toward violent confrontation. Politicians were useless because they only talked without producing results, while Britain (metaphorically) sexually assaulted Egypt with a smile of delight. It was not simply that the situation had reached emergency levels and required decisive action. Anticipating Frantz Fanon's argument that violence by the colonized against the colonizer was necessary to achieve psychological as well as national liberation, Abdel Kouddous declared that only when Britain saw its own blood shed by the hands of the Egyptian people would Egypt become an autonomous dignified nation.[38]

With the case for Egyptian independence floundering at the United Nations in the summer of 1947, Abdel Kouddous was convinced that the so-called leaders were playing with fire. Egypt had been living under colonial occupation for sixty-five years, and its coopted leaders had meekly resisted the calls for independence and supported their exploitative British overlords. Abdel Kouddous believed that, if politicians failed to achieve results at the UN, the only alternative was total armed revolt. Prophetically, on 23 July 1947, exactly five years before the Free Officers Coup, he published an editorial calling for armed squads to take matters into their own hands and lead Egypt to freedom. If the political process fails, Abdel Kouddous explained, "Egypt won't need prime ministers but military leaders. It won't need leaders of political parties but leaders of resistance fighters, squads of Stern, Hagana, and Irgun, Arab, not Zionist... that hunt down the British one by one."[39] In this, Abdel Kouddous was preparing a script for a different kind of man to bring independence to Egypt—a military leader, someone virile who would take the initiative to organize groups of resistance fighters to do the job that political leaders could not.

For Abdel Kouddous, this armed confrontation with the British would not be a guerilla war. It would encompass the entire country under the leader. The British would face "squads that include all of Egypt and all of Egypt will be the resistance fighters who open their eyes in the morning to leave their houses only to return martyred corpses, welcomed by cries of joy.... All of Egypt will be the resistance fighters who know how to hunt the British and then toss them into the sea and how to die so that Egypt is resurrected." Abdel Kouddous envisioned a clash in which the entire public became militarized, ready to sacrifice themselves to give birth to the new nation. The future would not resemble the past of party politics; instead, Egypt would become a military state in which violently overthrowing the colonizer was the basis for legitimacy: "All of Egypt will become a new generation, a generation that doesn't believe in politics, the law, the constitution, or NATO, but jihad, blood, weapons, and bombs... a generation that believes in one freedom—the freedom to get rid of the enemy. It is this new generation that will rule Egypt." Exactly five years before 23 July 1952, Abdel

Kouddous called for military confrontation, envisioning a public that was militarized under the leadership of a new generation of soldiers who would seize governance of the nation in their own hands, bringing it to freedom and liberation.

With no results by late August 1947, *Rose El Youssef* reported that three men calling for jihad in the streets of Cairo had been killed, presumably by British soldiers. Abdel Kouddous, the bomb thrower looking for revolt from any source, projected onto this the first step to revolution: "It's the beginning of an exhausting long jihad, the first step on a difficult path whose sky is sweat, ground is blood, and rest is tears!"[40] It was at this point that Abdel Kouddous began to see himself as not simply an advocate for revolution but also part of the leadership preparing for it. In his 23 July 1947 article, he imagined himself leaving his office for battle. Now, a month later, he set the ground rules for engagement, as if he himself were organizing a violent street response to the killing of the three men: "The first principle of the art of jihad is that we don't attack the Egyptian police, but we coordinate with them and protect them as they protect us. . . . The second principle is that we don't smash street lamps, but we smash the British. . . . And the third principle is that we don't attack businesses, but we attack British barracks. We won't die if we attack businesses, but we'll die if we attack British barracks—jihad is death!" For Abdel Kouddous, the country was on the verge of flames; his editorials were to serve as a guide for violent confrontation with himself as a leader. Deeply impatient and frustrated, Abdel Kouddous decided that the time had come to do more than use his platform at the magazine to mobilize the public. He had to act.

## THE FIRST NASSER

In fall 1947, a sensational murder trial gave Abdel Kouddous the opportunity to identify his long-awaited leader in the flesh, an encounter that would serve as an early dress rehearsal for his relationship with Nasser. The murder took place just after sunset on 5 January 1946, when Amin Othman Pasha, the former finance minister and a current member of Congress, got out of a taxi and entered the Victoria Club in Cairo. The doorman saw another man step out from behind the nearby trees, follow Othman into the building, and shoot him three times. Othman was rushed to the hospital but died from his wounds. The killer fled the scene, reportedly carrying a gun in each hand, firing shots behind him as he ran down Adly Pasha Street in the center of the city. He then set off a hand grenade before disappearing into the darkness.[41]

After a manhunt, the killer, identified as Hussein Tawfik, was arrested. Tawfik was a radical nationalist who believed that it was necessary to take up arms to eliminate the current political leadership and lead Egypt to independence. The details surrounding the assassination are murky, but it appears that Tawfik was recruited by the Iron Guard, a militant group that worked for King Farouk. Tawfik confessed to the killing and reportedly gave authorities details about his cell, including the names of its members. Among those implicated was none other than future founding member of the Free Officers and future president of Egypt, Anwar Sadat; Sadat was arrested and served thirty-one months in jail until he was acquitted in May 1948. Othman was targeted for assassination because militants viewed him as a long-standing agent for British colonialism and traitor to the nation. Only a few days before the assassination, Othman had been quoted as saying, "Britain married Egypt in a Catholic marriage, which knows no divorce."[42] As Sadat later explained, "That declaration was tantamount to a self-imposed death sentence."[43]

Othman, known as "the blue-eyed boy of the British embassy" who had studied at Oxford and participated directly in the negotiations that led to the 1936 treaty, was seen as close to Consul-General Lampson. In an interview conducted with Othman in 1943, very likely by Abdel Kouddous himself, the magazine *Akhir Sa'a* asked him why he was "Britain's number one friend."[44] Othman did not disagree with the premise. Littering his response with English words, he explained, "I love the British because they're 'sportsmen' in how they treat their friends and enemies. . . . They treat you with 'fair play.'" After claiming that the British hate "snobs," Othman continued, "I believe that Britain is the most refined nation morally and better than any other politically." A few months later, Abdel Kouddous openly mocked Othman for using English syntax when he spoke Arabic before parliament, showing that, as a politician, he was incapable of finding his way to the "hearts and minds" of ordinary Egyptians.[45] Predictably, *Rose El Youssef* presented Othman as a collaborator and traitor, someone so close to the British that he knew in advance what was going to happen on 4 February 1942.[46]

Uncharacteristically, *Rose El Youssef* did not initially applaud his assassination. Instead, it printed a sympathetic interview with Othman's widow, who passionately defended her husband's reputation and legacy.[47] But in November 1947, the magazine managed to interview Tawfik, who was in jail awaiting trial. It presented Tawfik firmly in the guise of the masculine, committed, and self-sacrificing revolutionary leader to whom Abdel Kouddous had been sending out casting calls. Echoing Abdel Kouddous's own condemnations of collaborators, Tawfik boasted, "If I could get out of jail now, I'd continue my struggle against the British, not only the blond men with blue eyes who've occupied our country for sixty-five years but also those people with brown skin and dark eyes who look at first like they're Egyptian."[48] Tawfik argued that none of the political parties represented the Egyptian people and that none of the current political leaders were trustworthy because they were all coopted. In committing the assassination, Tawfik had taken matters into his own hands, claiming in another interview that he had "performed a service for Egypt greater than Mustafa Pasha Kamil and Saad Zaghloul," two heroes of the nationalist movement.[49]

Abdel Kouddous was smitten. He attended the opening of the trial in early November 1947 and praised not only Tawfik but also the other twenty-five men standing trial with him for participating in other political assassinations. Although his name was not mentioned in Abdel Kouddous's articles published at the time, Anwar Sadat was among the men whom Abdel Kouddous so admired: "It occurred to me as the defendants were looking at us that they were pitying us and that they—behind bars—were freer than us. They're freer because each of them feels that he has performed his mission while we're slaves still looking for someone to carry out our mission for us!"[50] Acting with fearless courage for the good of the nation—rising up to punish traitors who were preventing Egypt from gaining independence—has led these defendants to salvation. It was Abdel Kouddous, along with the nation, that was really behind bars, waiting for someone to bring the country freedom.

At this moment, Abdel Kouddous realized that these men were something else. They were the instrument of justice for the nation, a tool for achieving its freedom: "These twenty-six young men are the executive power in Egypt. One day they might occupy the chairs of government. The presence of only one of them outside of prison would be enough to terrify every traitor, every political joker ... and every political criminal." It was these young men who had the courage and faith to carry out the punishment for the crime of treason, to execute the law. These were not the sickly Egyptian politicians who needed to see a doctor before going abroad. They were young, confident, and militant, the encapsulation of the next generation, the future leadership and government of Egypt. They represented the new Egypt coming into being. Ironically, history would prove Abdel Kouddous correct when Sadat, standing trial right next to Hussein Tawfik, became president of Egypt in 1970.

Considering how Abdel Kouddous had repeatedly positioned himself in his high-profile platform as a militant revolutionary, it should come as no surprise that Hussein Tawfik was a fan. Well aware of Abdel Kouddous's activism, Tawfik told him in court, "We were hoping you'd be here with us!" In this, Tawfik aligned Abdel Kouddous not simply as a journalist but as one of the group of radicals on trial, welcoming him as if he was one of them. Delighted to be included with these men of the future, Abdel Kouddous told Tawfik, "That's a big honor! It's an honor that you have principles and that you acted for them."[51] In this moment of mutual recognition and acknowledgment, Abdel Kouddous identified with Tawfik and his co-defendants, admiring them as men of action, driven by principles and commitment, taking matters into their own hands to put an end to a corrupt system, regardless of the consequences. Sitting in that courtroom during the trial, Abdel Kouddous realized that Tawfik was the embodiment of the way he had scripted his long-awaited leader. With his militancy, masculinity, and bravery, Tawfik served as Abdel Kouddous's first Nasser. Making good on his long-standing offer to put his pen at the service of the man who could lead him out of the wilderness to salvation, Abdel Kouddous defended Tawfik passionately in *Rose El Youssef* throughout the trial.

Their relationship—and Abdel Kouddous's commitment to revolution—would soon become significantly more entangled. On the morning of 9 June 1948, a police officer and two soldiers escorted Tawfik in a taxi to a doctor for medical treatment. When the four left the doctor's office, someone driving Tawfik's family car was waiting for them outside. Tawfik begged the officer to let him go home so that he could see his mother and have lunch with his family. Incredibly, the officer accepted. The three guards accompanied Tawfik home and, as they waited for lunch to be served, Tawfik went to the bathroom. He did not emerge again. Upon discovering that Tawfik had escaped through the bathroom window, the officer reportedly pointed his gun at his head to commit suicide, but Tawfik's father convinced him not to kill himself.[52] The officer and two soldiers were arrested later that night for dereliction of duty.[53]

On 16 June 1948, *Rose El Youssef* published a handwritten letter that Tawfik wrote to Abdel Kouddous on the day that he escaped. Tawfik explained that he was on his way to Palestine to fight in the 1948 Palestine war, which had been raging for a month, yet another marker of his militaristic masculinity and nationalist commitment. Tawfik apologized to the officer guarding him, insisting that he meant him no harm. He ended the letter by explaining that he had written to Abdel Kouddous in particular because he is "the sole journalist friend who understands me and appreciates my circumstances."[54] Abdel Kouddous apparently received the letter on 11 June 1948, but he did not inform the authorities immediately because, as he claimed, he needed time to determine the letter's authenticity. Nonetheless, *al-Ahram*, perhaps the most important daily newspaper in Egypt, speculated that Tawfik was still in Cairo and that he had written the letter to Abdel Kouddous to throw the police off his trail.[55]

The stunning escape became sensational news. Radio Cairo broadcast a notice every thirty minutes that authorities were offering a five-thousand-pound reward for Tawfik's capture. Anyone who harbored or assisted him would be considered an accomplice and would potentially be subject to hard labor or imprisonment for up to seven years. Alleged Tawfik sightings poured in to the police that week, including one of a man resembling Tawfik who then threw himself into the Nile to commit suicide. The case became so sensational that when a man stole someone's wallet on the tram in Cairo, the victim yelled out "Hussein Tawfik," leading the conductor to stop the tram and join the crowd to chase down the culprit, all of them in pursuit to claim the massive reward.[56]

In the middle of this frenzy, Abdel Kouddous continued using his platform to support Tawfik. In an editorial titled "Let Him Go," Abdel Kouddous insisted that Tawfik had to take justice into his own hands because "the law simply shrugged its shoulders and excused itself from doing anything about Othman."[57] Tawfik was a tool wielded by the people, who could not otherwise achieve justice because of the corruption of the law under colonialism. He was described in *Rose El Youssef* as an "instrument of cleansing" and an "executive power," the exact terms that Abdel Kouddous would later use to describe the Free Officers in the immediate aftermath of the coup.[58] The real criminal here was not Tawfik but British colonialism and the collaborating political elite. The real victim was not Othman but Tawfik, whom authorities illegitimately considered a criminal, not a courageous man of justice, principle, and, most important, action. As Abdel Kouddous explained the following week: "We need this resistance fighter spirit that distinguishes Hussein Tawfik. If we lose this, we'll lose thousands of resistance fighters, who are the bullets we load the gun with."[59] The stakes were therefore not simply the removal of a single collaborator. It was revolution and Egyptian independence.

It turns out that the police had reason to be suspicious of Abdel Kouddous. In January 1953, after legal pardons were issued for political crimes committed before the coup, Tawfik wrote a letter to a friend in which he explained the particulars of his escape. Subsequently published in the daily *al-Misri*, the letter included riveting details, such as a dangerous voyage on a rickety sailboat while evading man-eating sharks and an unexpected audience with the King of Jordan in Amman. Perhaps most shocking—but not surprising for astute readers—was that Tawfik admitted that he hid in Abdel Kouddous's house for four days immediately after his escape from prison. Tawfiq had nothing but praise for Abdel Kouddous, writing, "He displayed a boldness and masculinity that were rare in that era."[60]

Later, Abdel Kouddous detailed his own role in harboring Tawfik.[61] Abdel Kouddous explained that a member of the National Party called him after Tawfik's escape and asked him for advice on how to hide the fugitive. Abdel Kouddous felt that it was time to put his revolutionary ideals into practice. As he explained in a 1973 interview, "I found myself facing a difficult choice. Either I took responsibility for hiding a fugitive killer to prove to all the revolutionaries that I was one of them, or I'd duck, afraid of the punishment awaiting me if I got caught. Would I keep my safety but lose my status among revolutionaries and become nothing but a despicable salesman, someone who peddles lofty words and fake slogans in the marketplace of revolution but does nothing?"[62]

It was a dilemma that he would face repeatedly after Nasser ascended to power.

Abdel Kouddous hid Tawfik in his bedroom. Tawfik reportedly slept in Abdel Kouddous's bed next to him, hiding a gun under his pillow, as Abdel Kouddous's wife slept on a cot in the same room. Ironically, it was at Abdel Kouddous's house that Tawfik wrote the letter that *Rose El Youssef* would later publish. During the four days that he hid Tawfik, Abdel Kouddous was actually questioned by the authorities, who had grown suspicious of him and his interest in the case. Despite the incredible risks, Abdel Kouddous clearly performed well enough under interrogation to prevent the police from searching his home. When the milkman accidentally saw Tawfik, however, Abdel Kouddous, deciding that the risk had become too great, transferred Tawfik to another location. In order to disguise himself, Tawfik left Abdel Kouddous's apartment in a police officer's uniform.[63]

To anyone familiar with Abdel Kouddous's fiction or classic Egyptian cinema, these details—as well as Tawfik's case in general—should sound familiar. Abdel Kouddous used them as the basis for his 1957 novel *There's a Man in Our House*, which in 1961 was adapted into the iconic film starring future Hollywood legend Omar Sharif. I will return to this novel in chapter 4 when I discuss how Abdel Kouddous transformed the Hussein Tawfik case into fiction as part of his attempt to grapple with his regrets about bringing Gamal Abdel Nasser to power. At the time, however, hiding Hussein Tawfik represented for Abdel Kouddous an opportunity to act, to demonstrate his commitment, self-sacrifice, and courage for revolution, regardless of the consequences. He was inserting himself into his own script at tremendous personal risk to support the leader whom he thought embodied the sparks of revolution. The sequence of events provided him with a dress rehearsal of what he would later do to help bring Nasser to power.

While the confession that Abdel Kouddous hid Tawfik in his home during his escape from jail was sensational—even after the coup—he alluded to it as early as October 1948 when he published the short story "The New Generation."[64] Gesturing back to his editorial of 23 July 1947 as well as the generational split between himself and his mother, Abdel Kouddous used this story to employ fiction for the first time as a vehicle to confess political regret. As if teasing the authorities, Abdel

Kouddous begins the story with a disclaimer—that it presents the story of a friend whom he knew "from jihad, a hero of political cases whose name I heard each time a leader was attacked or a bomb was tossed." The unnamed hero is the double for Tawfik and marker for radical resistance, the eponymous example of the new generation. He committed a political crime—"if we consider every act of violence a crime," notes Abdel Kouddous in another disclaimer—because of the strength of his principles and "his complete faith that the doors of the future won't ever be opened unless a bloodstained hand knocks on them." After committing his nationalist act, which is conveniently not identified in the story, the hero is sent to hide in the home of a distant relative. In the story, as in real life, the hero quickly becomes an intimate member of the host family. In the story, it is the family's daughter that serves as the fictional surrogate for Abdel Kouddous. When the hero arrives at the door of the house, he is greeted by the daughter, in whose eyes he detects "a protest demanding the fall of British colonialism and between whose lips was the call to revolution." It was the first time that Abdel Kouddous ever wrote himself as a young female double, something that would later become a regular feature of his fiction. This strategy should not be a surprise, considering that Fatima Youssef named him after Ihsan Kamel, an Armenian actress who was with her when she gave birth, giving him what was widely seen as a female name at the time. It was also the first time he would use fiction to write political metaphor of himself having a romance with his long-awaited leader, the masculine "hero," who, according to the script, would bring redemption to his forlorn lover, a double of the nation.

As in the 1957 novel *There's a Man in Our House*, the fugitive falls in love with the daughter, depicting the "romance" between Abdel Kouddous and the revolutionary hero. In this early version, however, the hero stays in the house for twenty days and then departs. Nonetheless, he feels that he must return to the girl whom he loves. He therefore commits more nationalist crimes in order to hide in the family's house again. In stark contrast to the ending of *There's a Man in Our House*—and the fate of Hussein Tawfik, who escaped to Syria—the hero marries the girl at the end of this early version, suggesting that it is the metaphorical marriage of Abdel Kouddous with Tawfik that will propagate the eponymous "new generation." Nonetheless, the marriage "causes the hero to lose his resistance fighter spirit." Even though "he loved her because he loved his nation and he loved his nation because he loved her," the end of the story stresses that consummating this love in the form of marriage eliminates the hero's revolutionary fervor, domesticating him and putting out the fire of revolt.

If the daughter is the double for Abdel Kouddous, this suggests that, by hiding Tawfik in the house and falling in love, he unexpectedly tamed his revolutionary hero and dampened his militant impulses. In this, Abdel Kouddous hints that perhaps it was his own personal engagement with Tawfik that ultimately led to Tawfik's departure from the country, unintentionally stifling the spark of revolution and endangering the emergence of the "new generation." As a result, the story represents a confession not only of his involvement in the case but also perhaps of his own regret that by hiding Tawfik and then facilitating his escape from Egypt, he had extinguished the nationalist fire of revolt. As I will unpack in the following chapters, this kind of confession, coupled with an attempt to use fiction to work through festering anxiety, regret, and misgivings about personal involvement with the leader, would come to characterize nearly all of Abdel Kouddous's novels during the Nasser era. This story also serves as the first example of Abdel Kouddous being reckless with his fiction, not only challenging authorities and brazenly pushing boundaries but also endangering himself in the process.

Before Hussein Tawfik escaped from jail, Abdel Kouddous had published explosive editorials, challenging the authorities, welcoming revolutionaries at the offices of *Rose El Youssef*, and using his platform to inflame the public in the hopes of sparking revolution. With his involvement in Tawfik's escape, Abdel Kouddous became a man of action, risking serious consequences in order to support someone he thought might be able to play the part of his long-awaited leader. In this, he boldly took his personal commitment to revolution to a new level at tremendous personal risk. At the same time, the episode represents something else for Abdel Kouddous—it was a dress rehearsal for the coup, when Abdel Kouddous would once again risk arrest or worse to wipe the old system away. In June 1948, it was Tawfik who appeared to play the role of the instrument of cleansing on behalf of the people and the nation. Now with Tawfik gone, it would not take long for Abdel Kouddous to enter events once again to identify a new committed, masculine, and militaristic leader who could spark revolution. This time, it would put him into contact with the Free Officers.

## THE ROTTEN WEAPONS SCANDAL

On 20 July 1949, Abdel Kouddous broke a scandal that would change the course of his life as well as the history of the modern Middle East. On that day, he published a brief piece in *Rose El Youssef* titled "Prosecute the Palestine War Criminals!" He was vacationing in Italy at the time and sent the article via telegram. It read in part: "During the Palestine War, a number of huge deals . . . were made by Arab men who claimed to be representing Arab governments. When you arrive in Italy, you can smell the scent of these deals which made people rich, killed thousands of Egyptians and Arabs, and led to the loss of Palestine. I can't talk openly today, but these treasonous deals cannot pass without investigation and prosecution."[65] When Abdel Kouddous wrote this, the catastrophic Arab loss in the 1948 Palestine War was still raw. Egyptians were searching for answers. By fall 1948, *Rose El Youssef* was already publishing pieces on the bravery and valor of the Egyptian army, claiming that the loss was not the fault of ordinary soldiers. Some of these pieces were written by none other than Anwar Sadat, who started working at the magazine soon after he was acquitted of charges in the Hussein Tawfik trial.

During this time, Abdel Kouddous argued that the army was the reflection not only of the nation but also of every abused Egyptian struggling for freedom: "The army is the true mirror of Egypt. It is the mirror of the peasant who fights poverty, illness, and oppression but nonetheless lives, persists, and is victorious. It is the mirror of the laborer, who fights the plot against his rights . . . and the mirror of the bureaucrat, who suffers injustice, oppression, and abuse."[66] As early as fall 1948, Abdel Kouddous already sensed that the army had been unjustly abused like a peasant, laborer, and bureaucrat, striving for justice but oppressed by an illegitimate and corrupt elite. Pointing to his links with Hussein Tawfik and his short story "The New Generation," Abdel Kouddous then argued that the army reflected the nation's future. "The army is the mirror of the new generation—assurgent, fiery, and combative, which will live and be victorious." Despite the loss in Palestine, Egyptian soldiers, in their courage, vitality, and action, represented the victory to come.

In an editorial published on 6 April 1949, Abdel Kouddous continued to stress his support for the army, turning his projections on them: "I always was—and still am—among the most vehement believers that nations can only stand on their feet by holding onto the shoulders of their military."[67] Nonetheless, even in those heady times of support for the army, he was careful not to be seen as calling for a military coup. Prophetically, he warned, "Despite all my faith in the military, I've never believed that it's the right of any army to intervene in politics or that the military has the right to control the people, determine their fate, or administer them. I've never believed that the military leader who is victorious in war could also be victorious in politics." Growing frustration and impatience would eventually compel him to change his mind, at least temporarily.

When Abdel Kouddous reached Italy for vacation in July 1949 and heard rumors about shady deals that had enriched the elite at the expense of brave soldiers killed in the war and the loss of Palestine, he discovered that the Egyptian political elite was even more corrupt than he had imagined. For him, the loss in Palestine suddenly became a much larger case of treason against the army, the nation, and the people. This became a new fire that drove him forward to revolution. Despite the inflammatory nature of his first piece on the scandal, it did not attract widespread attention. It was the public questioning of Mustafa Mar'i, member of parliament, nearly a year later that revived the scandal. Mar'i testified that the Egyptian army had been supplied with faulty or "rotten" weapons during the Palestine War. According to Mar'i, these weapons shot in reverse, killing the unsuspecting soldiers using them. Soldiers were also provided with hand grenades that exploded as soon as they were touched. For Abdel Kouddous, this proved his suspicions that it was not the valor or strength of the Israeli enemy that had defeated the Egyptian army. Instead, it was faulty weapons, provided by traitors to the nation to unwittingly trusting soldiers. Appalled, Abdel Kouddous tapped into public outrage at the excesses of the Egyptian elite when he explained that one of the officers who benefited from the weapons sale now had a "palace" on Capri in Italy. This was where this officer "invites important Egyptian personalities to natural beauty, relaxation, and calm at the expense of the martyrs of Palestine and the noble Egyptian people whose money was embezzled in the name of Arabism and decency."[68]

It was at this point that Abdel Kouddous made a critical shift. He wrote that he would name names in the case if he had documents to prove the crime. This amounted to a call for help. Yet he was no longer issuing casting calls for someone to take on the role of the leader. Abdel Kouddous was now targeting the military in particular, asking for documents to carry out the necessary punishment. He wrote that holding those implicated in the crime accountable was essential in order to "return trust and confidence to the army. . . . When the soldier loses faith in his weapon, he has lost faith in himself and the spirit of battle. At that point, the future of Egypt has been lost!" The implications were clear. The soldiers' weapons, their symbol of virility, power, and strength, had become the tools of their death. Because of corruption and greed, the state had provided the army with the instrument of its own unwitting suicide.

As is well documented, Gamal Abdel Nasser returned from the Palestine War so furious at the incompetence and corruption of Egyptian military leadership that he formed the clandestine Free Officers. As Fawaz Gerges explains, "Nasser's own memoirs of the war in Palestine are replete with expressions of despair at the inadequate provision of supplies for Egyptian troops, their sense of betrayal, and the perceived weakness and duplicity of the political establishment in Cairo."[69] Just before the tenth anniversary of the revolution, Nasser explained to journalist David Wynne-Morgan, "As I lay in hospital [after being wounded during the Palestine War] I wondered whether I had been spared to achieve some special purpose. It was crystal clear to me now that the real battle was indeed in Egypt. While I and my comrades had been fighting in Gaza, Egyptian politicians had gotten rich on the proceeds of the defective arms they had bought cheaply and sold to the army. I knew that I had to concentrate my efforts on striking at the dynasty of Mohammed Ali. King Farouk was our main target from the end of 1948 until 1952."[70] Other founding members of the Free Officers also described their betrayal on the battlefield as a unifying force. Khaled Mohi El Din, for example, later explained, "I still vividly remember the Palestine War as a stab in the heart of each of us."[71] Mohammed Neguib wrote in 1955, "The hand grenades that we received from Italy were so poorly made that many of them blew up in our soldiers' faces. . . . [This] confirmed what we had suspected all along—namely, that several of our supply officers, in league with the King and his cronies, had been buying sub-standard munitions and pocketing the difference between what they had charged the Government and what they had actually paid."[72]

Abdel Kouddous's media campaign was exactly what the Officers were looking for. And the Officers were the partners that Abdel Kouddous needed. After Abdel Kouddous made his appeal for help, Nasser, Khaled Mohi El Din, and other members of the Free Officers contacted Abdel Kouddous and began meeting with him secretly, leaking to him critical documents about the case. After their return from the war, the Free Officers had been in touch with a variety of political figures whom they thought could lead to the overthrow of the regime. Nonetheless, Nasser, like Abdel Kouddous in his serial flirtations with political leaders in the 1940s, quickly became disillusioned with the leaders of the various political parties. No doubt, the Officers saw Abdel Kouddous at the time as a kind of leader, but he was perhaps even more valuable to them because he had the credibility of independence since he was unaffiliated with any political party. Moreover, he was the editor in chief of perhaps the most popular political magazine in the country, a particularly important platform for them since he could help shape public opinion through the press. Abdel Kouddous would also have been attractive to Nasser in particular because he was a celebrity revolutionary journalist, a type that Nasser had long admired.[73]

In the following issue of *Rose El Youssef*, Abdel Kouddous began a series on the scandal; suddenly there were significantly more details, suggesting that this was the week that Abdel Kouddous first met Nasser.[74] He explained that the Ministry of Defense had made a deal with a Swiss company to import the weapons from Spain at a massive markup. When an Egyptian soldier went to Spain to examine them and issued a report that they were not fit for use, he was ignored. Abdel Kouddous then wrote that an army officer had leaked to him the decisive document in the scandal—the contract from the Swiss company, which was represented in Egypt by King Farouk's nephew, Abbas Halim. Abdel Kouddous explained that the contract was in the name of a low-level Egyptian officer. Abdel Kouddous not only named Abbas Halim, implicating the palace in the deal, but even called on Halim to issue a statement to calm suspicions and restore trust.[75] Abdel Kouddous then reported that he had been hearing rumors from the army that massive funds had been embezzled in the names of wives and mothers. In the end, he declared, "The army has lost confidence in itself and its ministry." As Abdel Kouddous explained in the 1970s, giving himself full credit for directing Nasser and the others to collect and leak documents to him: "I was helping them with ideas, and they were helping me with news and information."[76]

The authorities were anxious. After these two articles, Abdel Kouddous was interrogated by the police. He also received anonymous phone calls threatening to kill him if he did not stop publishing his series on the case. As he explained years later, "My personal safety was the last thing I was thinking about compared to my goal of shaking the ruling system to its very foundations."[77] Undeterred and unafraid, Abdel Kouddous once again used the opportunity to demonstrate his commitment and self-sacrifice to spark the revolution, just as he had during the Hussein Tawfik case. He addressed these threats in his next article, published on 20 June 1950: "I'll quiet down but not before I calm the officers and soldiers who've suppressed their anger while accepting weapons that they can't trust.... I'll be quiet but not before I demand justice for those who were martyred, wounded, or disfigured in Palestine.... Their sacrifice is the price for a better army and a better nation."[78] Abdel Kouddous positioned himself as a leader of the abused army, using his platform in *Rose El Youssef* to take up its cause. Serving as their spokesman in the face of intolerable corruption, he presented himself as someone who not only shared their outrage but could restore their confidence and dignity. Abdel Kouddous then discussed the details of the contract that had been leaked to him. Looking to inflame resentment both inside the army and among the public over such brazen corruption, Abdel Kouddous wrote that the officer who had signed the contract officially earned only a low-level army salary. Nonetheless, he now owned a Cadillac and a Hudson, two luxury cars from America. This officer had even recently become a member of the infamous Automobile Club, where, according to Abdel Kouddous, "he always has a seat reserved for him at the baccarat table where he can lose in a single night ten times his clean salary!"

For the authorities, this third article was the last straw. In his next editorial, Abdel Kouddous joked that the ministry was finally doing something about the scandal—they issued an order to interrogate him about what he had printed over the previous three weeks. Once again,

Abdel Kouddous was willing to sacrifice himself in order to set off his long-awaited revolution. Some two years before the coup, he was clearly hoping that it would come from within the army. Abdel Kouddous wrote that twenty-eight officers of various ranks had contacted him, offering to testify in court about their knowledge of the scandal.[79] In September 1950, an order was issued to stop him from publishing on the case with the promise that the public prosecutor would investigate it. Abdel Kouddous turned his documents over to the prosecutor to aid the investigation and then bided his time. Just as he had been a trusted partner for Tawfik, Abdel Kouddous was now working at great risk with members of the army in the hopes that he had finally identified the men of action who would lead him—and the nation—out of the wilderness.

Although Abdel Kouddous could no longer print news about the Rotten Weapons case, that did not stop him from turning his attention to Mohammed Haydar Pasha, the Egyptian minister of war, to satiate the desire of the army officers for revenge. Abdel Kouddous reported that when Egyptian troops started withdrawing from Palestine, a young soldier cried out: "The Egyptian army hasn't been defeated, but its leadership has!"[80] Abdel Kouddous was outraged that, even as late as October 1950, there still had been no investigation into the devastating loss and that Haydar was still in his position. Standing up for the army and looking to mobilize outrage both within its ranks and among the public, Abdel Kouddous wrote a new series of articles in October 1950 condemning Haydar and calling for an investigation. Demonstrating his increasingly close links with the army and his awareness of radical activity within its ranks, Abdel Kouddous noted that army officers—presumably the Free Officers—had distributed pamphlets criticizing Haydar for the loss. By the time Abdel Kouddous published his fourth article calling for investigation, the news broke that Haydar had finally resigned from his post, giving Abdel Kouddous a highly public victory in his campaign to cleanse the army. At that moment, Abdel Kouddous was no longer simply a voice of criticism and revolt. He had produced results through his platform in *Rose El Youssef*, establishing himself as a high-profile leader for army officers. As he explained decades later, "I didn't want only the people to revolt but also the army."[81]

Abdel Kouddous's influence can be seen in the Officers' own clandestine leaflets at the time. The Free Officers issued their first leaflet in October 1950, right when Abdel Kouddous was attacking Haydar in *Rose El Youssef.* As Khaled Mohi El Din later recalled, using the term "defective" instead of "rotten" to describe the notorious weapons: "The main issue on everyone's mind was that of the 'defective weapons,' which had been disclosed by the press. [Our first] leaflet warned the officers against being led into another war without preparation and armaments, or with defective weapons. It also warned the King against intervening to prevent a fair investigation into the issue of the defective weapons, otherwise the throne would be endangered."[82] While I have not been able to locate a copy of this leaflet, which Mohi El Din notes was only printed in "five or six hundred copies," Mohi El Din's description of it demonstrates the influence of Abdel Kouddous on the Officers at the time. Furthermore, almost all of the leaflets that do survive call for cleansing the army and the nation of traitors and corruption. One surviving pamphlet from October 1951 refers directly to the Rotten Weapons scandal, warning officers: "Don't leave your weapons to become prey to the enemies."[83] These pamphlets suggest an important link between Abdel Kouddous and the Free Officers, and not simply because of their collaboration during the Rotten Weapons scandal. They show that the Officers, even at this early stage, were deeply concerned with shaping opinion through printed material, even if their medium was clandestine pamphlets. This early focus on media—and using it to mobilize public opinion—would later become a central feature of Nasser's regime.

Despite his highly visible victory and the display of his increasing influence and engagement with the army, Abdel Kouddous became increasingly frustrated with the lack of progress. Disregarding the dangers and flexing his confidence and commitment publicly, Abdel Kouddous returned to the Rotten Weapons in January 1951, flagrantly breaking the embargo against publishing news about the scandal. Once again, it was a public display of commitment, self-sacrifice, and principles, daring the authorities to arrest him in the hopes that it would push his fellow army revolutionaries to rise up and act. Abdel Kouddous brazenly printed a facsimile of the leaked weapons contract and then praised the army officers collaborating with him on the scandal, as if goading them directly to revolt: "Young men full of enthusiasm and fervor for their army are working with me. They have no desire except that they believe in the future of Egypt and they're working to cleanse its present. Credit for everything goes to these young men. We met secretly, getting in touch secretly, just like what we read in detective stories when we were young."[84] This is similar language, framed by literary genre, that Gamal Abdel Nasser would later use to describe his own activities during this time. As Nasser wrote in *Philosophy of the Revolution*, "Our life during that period was like a thrilling detective story. We had dark secrets and passwords. We lurked in the shadows."[85] In his article at the time, Abdel Kouddous openly admits not only to collaborating with mutinous officers in the army but also to plotting with them clandestinely to cleanse the country. Abdel Kouddous would not reveal that his collaborators were members of the Free Officers until after the coup but, as he made clear decades later, they were working together "in order to direct political opinion inside the army to prepare for the revolution."[86] At this point, Abdel Kouddous and these officers seemed to see each other as vital partners and as fellow revolutionaries. As Abdel Kouddous boasted in the 1970s: "They considered me one of them."[87]

The legacy of the case is not its accuracy or that it was a convenient way to explain away the shattering loss of Palestine. Egyptian historians have questioned its veracity, arguing that the army was simply unprepared and unequipped to fight effectively at the time.[88] That does not diminish the impact of the scandal on public perception, inflaming anger at the palace both among the public and within the army, helping to lay the groundwork for the coup. It also does not lessen the importance of the way it provided the opportunity for Abdel Kouddous to collaborate closely with the Free Officers and direct them to collect secret documents, like in a detective novel. The scandal aligned him publicly with the army and seemed to establish him as a critical partner—even a civilian leader—for the Free Officers in their revolutionary aspirations and thinking. Nonetheless, as Abdel Kouddous told the court looking into the case after the coup, its value was simply in sparking the revolution: "I publicized this case so that I could arrive at the revolution. I consider this case closed now that the revolution has happened."[89] Abdel Kouddous was even more direct in an unpublished manuscript that he wrote toward the end of his life: "My goal in breaking the Rotten Weapons case wasn't to find those responsible and put them on trial. It was to incite public opinion against the ruling system."⁹⁰

## "DOES EGYPT NEED A DICTATOR?"

Now that Abdel Kouddous was collaborating closely with the rebellious Free Officers to inflame the Rotten Weapons scandal and expose the extent of the corruption of the ruling elite, he returned once again to his script for a hero to rise up and act. He began reissuing casting calls as if using the magazine to communicate directly to Nasser in particular to take the final step and fulfill the promise of the scandal. Nasser believed as a young man that he had been cast to play the role of the redeeming hero for the nation. He had been influenced in particular by Tawfiq al-Hakim's novel *Return of the Spirit*, which was published in 1933 when Nasser was fifteen. This novel presents the emergence of an entirely new Egyptian leader, "a man from among [the people] who will manifest all their emotions and beliefs and be for them a symbol of the ultimate."⁹¹ It was this man for whom the nation would unite and sacrifice their lives in order to bring liberation from colonialism. As Israel Gershoni argued, "Hakim envisaged the dramatic appearance of a charismatic, prophetlike figure, a virtuous idealist of surpassing stature who would put an immediate end to the country's political corruption and social ills, sweeping before him the entire nation and effecting total reconstruction of the society."⁹²

On 3 September 1935, Nasser wrote a letter to a friend in which he articulated his vision of this leader. "Where is the one who will turn everything on its head and return Egypt to its first state, the day when it possessed the world? Where is the one who will create a new generation so that the silent hopeless Egyptian ... can wake up, yell at the top of his voice, and raise his head with courage to demand independence and freedom? ... We have spoken many times about an act that will wake the people up from their slumber, pound on their hearts, and rouse all the strength hidden in their chests."⁹³ It was around this time that Nasser wrote the initial chapters of a novel, *For Freedom*, which was set in 1807 and presumably would have continued to depict national resistance led by a character named Muhsin, the same name, not coincidentally, as the hero of al-Hakim's novel. As Israel Gershoni argued, "Nasser was captivated by the intense longing for a 'redeeming hero' (*ma'bud,* idol) who would emerge from the people and personify their will. Through his virtuous and charismatic personality, his redeeming hero would generate a 'miraculous revolution' that would revitalize the monumental grandeur and eternal vigor latent in Egypt, 'restore its primordial soul,' and lead it to a modern Pharaonic renaissance. There is a surprising resemblance between the young Nasser and Muhsin, the protagonist of *'Awdat al-Ruh* [Return of the Spirit], who is portrayed as an introvert seeking self-deliverance, extremely idealistic, identifying with the simple fellahin and very sensitive toward their wretched plight."[94]

Seemingly well aware of Nasser's long-standing fascination with playing the role of the redeeming hero, Abdel Kouddous published a provocative editorial on 5 September 1950 titled "Who Is the Awaited Leader?" Appearing to call out to Nasser directly, Abdel Kouddous expressed his impatience, arguing that the Egyptian people were overwhelmed by despair and anger: "Egypt needs a new leader who renews its youth and cleans its politics and morals. We can't continue on in silence and resignation for the miracle to happen and for this awaited leader to come down to us from the sky!"[95] In other words, the long-awaited leader must put aside any hesitation about remaining above the fray like an angel and act. Remarkably, this is the same language that Abdel Kouddous would later use to criticize the hesitation and inaction of Nasser and the other Free Officers in the weeks following the coup, arguing that they considered themselves as angels too pure to get involved in the mundane business of governing. In his September 1950 article, Abdel Kouddous argued that the leader who would rejuvenate the nation must be willing to sacrifice himself and, most important, represent the people. Fouad Pasha Serageddin, the minister of the interior at the time, was not pleased. Reading the writing on the wall, he considered this latest article by Abdel Kouddous "an incitement for revolution and overturning the system." He sent Abdel Kouddous to the public prosecutor, who sentenced him to fourteen days in jail but released him with a fine of one hundred pounds.[96]

Despite yet another public act of self-sacrifice to push the leader to rise up, no one in the army followed the script. As Abdel Kouddous later explained, "At that time, I was standing on the edge of the abyss staring at despair and defeat."[97] As his frustrations mounted, Abdel Kouddous published his most striking editorial from this period,

"State of Failure."[98] In it, Abdel Kouddous raged against the current political leadership. He wrote, "We in Egypt believe in failure and we worship failure. Failure is everywhere, before every step, behind every leader.... The failures are the ones who rule Egypt, who've taken it over, who drive it from one failure to the next." Abdel Kouddous condemned the political opposition as well—nationalists, communists, and other groups—as failures for not gaining the trust of the people. What was the way out of this morass? "Try out another kind of man, not one who has proven he is a failure." If this other kind of man was not one of the current politicians or opposition groups, where would he come from? It seemed to be yet another attempt to goad Nasser to take on the role. While Abdel Kouddous did not explicitly mention the military in this article, the ministry cabinet could read between the lines. It immediately issued an embargo on publishing any news about the army in the press, strong evidence that the government understood that Abdel Kouddous was targeting officers in this editorial to spark a revolution during this turbulent time.

During summer 1951, revolutionary agitation and calls for armed rebellion were all over the press. The founder of the Young Egypt Society, Ahmed Hussein, who had also drawn attention from Nasser before the coup, published a number of exceptionally scathing articles at the time with headlines like "Move, People!" and "Revolution, Revolution, Revolution."[99] It was exactly during this time that Abdel Kouddous became even more militant. He justified the political assassinations taking place at the time as "an acknowledged principle of violent struggle."[100] Led by Abdel Kouddous, the *Rose El Youssef* offices became a hive of revolutionary activity. Abdel Kouddous later admitted that during this time, he served as direct support for armed resistance fighters. "*Rose El Youssef* became a storehouse of weapons, offices were turned into arms depots, desk drawers were full of live ammunition.... During those days, I'd sit in my office with dozens of guns and hundreds of rifles around me, feeling total peace and calm."[101] As if Abdel Kouddous's editorials were not enough, *Rose El Youssef* included weekly caricatures inciting the public to attack the British. The 13 August 1951 issue, for example, includes a caricature of Misri Effendi leaping at a British soldier with a knife with the word "revolution" written on it, along with the caption: "If We Want to Cancel the 1936 Treaty."

On 7 October 1951, the Egyptian government unilaterally cancelled the 1936 Treaty. Two days later, gangs began to attack British troops in the Suez. As expected, Abdel Kouddous and *Rose El Youssef* celebrated the fighting, seeing it as perhaps the moment that the people would finally rise up to wipe the system clean. The cover of the 30 October 1951 issue, for example, shows Misri Effendi breaking out of his chains and screaming at the sky like King Kong as British soldiers look on in terror. In this issue, Abdel Kouddous called for Egyptians to organize themselves and sacrifice for the revolt to be successful. As usual, he had no faith in the government. "The people don't have an excuse if they don't move, if they don't break with the British, if they don't organize themselves into armed groups with rifles, guns, hand grenades, and Molotov cocktails, weapons which are widely available in Egypt and that people can get without the help of the government."[102] For Abdel Kouddous, this seemed at long last to be the moment of opportunity, and Egyptians had to take responsibility for it. Like Ahmed Hussein during this time, Abdel Kouddous was working openly to push the public to armed revolt.

While fighting spread in the Suez in fall 1951, it quickly became clear that it was not the cataclysm that Abdel Kouddous had for so long been dreaming of. In an effort to rally the public, on 25 December 1951, a desperate Abdel Kouddous shockingly called out: "Egyptians, head to the Suez Canal and commit suicide before the bullets of the British so that there's great hope."[103] At the same time, he was clearly anxious about whether this ultimate sacrifice was worthwhile under the current political regime. Expressing his sense of ownership of the revolt, he wrote, "I'm not calling for despair or throwing down our arms before the British or renouncing the revolution that I've spent my life writing for, beating the drum to wake us up. But I want to make sure that this revolution won't be placed in treasonous hands. I want to be sure that we die for a clearly defined goal." Some seven months before the coup, Abdel Kouddous was articulating his anxious hesitation between the need for revolution and the possibility that his efforts and the sacrifice of the people would come to serve the interests of traitors. Could the revolution take place but then betray its goals? It was a question that would haunt Abdel Kouddous for the rest of his life. Nonetheless, at the time, *Rose El Youssef* continued to push revolution in the most audacious terms. On the cover of its next issue, published on 31 December 1951, Misri Effendi stands bare-chested, raising a long sword with the word "Revolution," bringing it down toward the head of a British soldier lying on a stump with his hands tied behind him in prayer beads. His head is lying on the stone block, blood flowing from his neck forming the numbers "1952." The caption, which makes a pun of the Arabic expression for "new year," reads: "The 'Head' of the New Year!"

**Figure 5.** Cover of *Rose El Youssef*, 31 December 1951.

When riots broke out in Cairo on the night of 25 January 1952, an event known as "Black Saturday," Abdel Kouddous had an unexpected reaction—he was appalled. His concern was not the violence. And the people who participated in the riots were certainly not to blame. Rather, he was disgusted at the outbreak of leaderless violence as rioters randomly targeted buildings and property, not the British themselves. For Abdel Kouddous, these riots demonstrated how the corrupt political elite had abandoned the people, both in the Suez and now in Cairo. It was more evidence that there needed to be an entirely new kind of leader in Egypt for the revolution to succeed: "The government was incapable of leading the revolution or protecting it because it didn't believe in the revolution and it didn't believe in the people."[104] Egyptians had decisively shown their willingness to take up arms and sacrifice themselves to end British control of the country. But without a leader, their courage, commitment, and self-sacrifice were tragically wasted on property, not the British occupiers and their collaborators. This lost opportunity was yet another devastating condemnation of the corrupt political elite.

At this juncture, less than six months before the coup, Abdel Kouddous became more desperate than ever. The following week, Ali Maher was appointed once again as prime minister. Maher was an old friend of Abdel Kouddous, someone whom he believed had the principles, integrity, and spirit of self-sacrifice for the job. Abdel Kouddous seized the opportunity of having a confidant inside the system—someone he likely thought he could influence—and published an inauspicious article titled "Does Egypt Need a Dictator? Is It Ali Maher?" The failure of the Suez attacks and the 25 January riots in Cairo pushed Abdel Kouddous to focus once again on the need for his long-awaited leader to emerge and bring salvation to the nation. As he would do with Nasser in the weeks following the coup, Abdel Kouddous began to wonder openly in the pages of *Rose El Youssef* if Ali Maher could take the steps necessary to cleanse the system from within. Abdel Kouddous admitted that some people had become so desperate that they claimed that Egypt needed a temporary dictator. Perhaps, he argued, but "it has to be a dictator for the people and not against them, a dictator for freedom and not against it, a dictator who pushes freedom forward and doesn't drag it back."[105] Things had become so desperate for Abdel Kouddous that he would accept someone he knew and trusted to serve as a temporary dictator to rule without a constitution in order to cleanse the nation of corruption, all in the hope that it would eventually bring more freedom. He had reached the point where he was now willing to compromise his foundational belief in the principles of democratic governance and rule of law to embrace a transitional dictatorship, albeit one that he felt like he could influence personally, all for the sake of finally launching his cherished revolution.

All of the elements were now in place for Abdel Kouddous to embrace the coup and its immediate aftermath—years of desperate revolutionary agitation through his platform of *Rose El Youssef*; increasing personal commitment, self-sacrifice, and exposure to danger in order to ignite the revolution; collaborating with radical officers in the army to shape public opinion to embrace cleansing; and, finally, open support in *Rose El Youssef* for someone he knew and felt that he could influence to serve as a temporary dictator to suspend the rule of law to sweep away the old guard and prepare the country for democracy. Seething with years of resentment, frustration, and impatience, Abdel Kouddous stood ready to embrace revolution without pausing to consider seriously what would come next.

When Ali Maher resigned on 1 March 1952 because of what he called "obstacles to governing," Abdel Kouddous hit rock bottom. Maher, the trusted politician whom he suggested should serve as a temporary dictator to wipe the slate clean, was gone. For Abdel Kouddous, the government was entirely coopted by the British and remained in place only because of corruption and occupation. The Rotten Weapons scandal had not yet sparked the revolution. Despite his "detective novel" plotting with the Free Officers—and prodding them both publicly and privately, seemingly teasing Nasser's fantasy of playing the role of the redeeming hero—no one had risen up to lead the people and Abdel Kouddous out of the wilderness. The attacks against the British in the Suez and the Black Saturday riots only further entrenched the British in Egyptian affairs. Abdel Kouddous no doubt felt that the long-awaited leader was needed more than ever to fulfill his dream of revolution. But, in the spring and early summer of 1952, with no one stepping up to take on that role, Abdel Kouddous remained as he had been for more than a decade—lost in the wilderness, desperate for someone to exploit his enthusiasm, commitment, and platform to deliver him and the nation to salvation. When Gamal Abdel Nasser called Abdel Kouddous at 4 a.m. on the morning of 24 July 1952 to invite him to the Abbassia barracks, he no doubt felt that it was the culmination of over a decade of frustration, commitment, and self-sacrifice. His revolution had finally arrived.

CHAPTER TWO

## THE ERASED REVOLUTIONARY

> Nasser was always careful not to allow anything to cause doubt among the fellow officers about his leadership and role in the movement.
>
> —*Khaled Mohi El Din*,
> **Memories of a Revolution** *(1992)*

At 7:30 a.m. on 24 July 1952, Anwar Sadat went on the radio and announced the coup in a dramatic voice: "Citizens! Egypt, in its recent history, has been through a difficult period of bribery, corruption, and government instability. These factors have impacted the army, as the corrupt caused our defeat in Palestine. As for the period after this war, corruption has become interwoven in Egypt and traitors have plotted against the army.... We have therefore risen up to cleanse ourselves."[1] In his address, Sadat pointed directly to themes that had appeared in the Free Officers' pamphlets as well as Ihsan Abdel Kouddous's articles in the pages of *Rose El Youssef*. Corruption had led to the loss in Palestine, and there was a need for committed nationalist officers to rise up to cleanse both the military and the country in order to protect the nation.

This was how the coup was announced to the public. But it was not how Ihsan Abdel Kouddous learned about it.

At 4 a.m. that morning, some three and a half hours before Sadat's radio address, the phone rang in Abdel Kouddous's apartment. When

Abdel Kouddous picked up the receiver, Gamal Abdel Nasser declared decisively: "We have occupied Cairo."[2] Nasser then instructed Abdel Kouddous to join them at the Abbassia barracks. After getting dressed quickly and heading out, Abdel Kouddous could not help but feel a deep sense of pride. Only three days earlier, he was in Alexandria as the prime minister was facing a crisis because mid-level army officers were rebelling against leadership. Abdel Kouddous met with the entourage of King Farouk to let them know the severity of the situation, urging them to address the demands of Mohammed Neguib, one of the leaders of these officers. "I tried to convince them. I tried to warn them," Abdel Kouddous wrote in *Rose El Youssef* about the exchange only six weeks later.[3] Palace officials accused Abdel Kouddous of exaggerating and asked him mockingly: "Do you think six officers who print pamphlets and call themselves the Free Officers can do anything? These guys need someone to slap them around!" Feeling insulted, Abdel Kouddous walked out, called one of the Officers, and warned him that the palace was planning on arresting them.[4] If they were ever going to act, Abdel Kouddous urged whomever he was talking to, the time had come. Nasser immediately sped up plans for the coup from November 1952 and implemented them only two days later.

It has been assumed until now that it was Ahmed Abul-Fath, editor in chief of *al-Misri* and close acquaintance of Nasser before the coup, who learned about the impending arrests and informed his brother-in-law, Sarwat Okasha, a founding member of the Free Officers, who then relayed the information to Nasser. This sequence of events has been widely cited, by Abul-Fath and Okasha as well as other Free Officers.[5] Nonetheless, Abul-Fath is named as the journalist who tipped off Okasha only in the official celebration of the one-year anniversary of the coup. As I show in this chapter, this coincides with the period when Abdel Kouddous was being systematically erased from the history of the revolution. Excavating Abdel Kouddous's call does not disprove Abul-Fath's call. Instead, it adds yet another layer to the sense of ownership and responsibility that Abdel Kouddous felt for sparking the revolution. For Abdel Kouddous, tipping off the Officers three days before the coup no doubt reinforced his belief that he had singlehandedly changed the course of Egyptian history and played a decisive role in bringing Nasser to power. The tipoff provides even more context for why Nasser invited

Abdel Kouddous—and not Abul-Fath—to the barracks to participate in events as they unfolded. It seems that for Nasser, Abdel Kouddous was not simply a fervent nonpartisan journalist whose platform and enthusiasm he hoped to exploit. Nasser likely also saw Abdel Kouddous as a co-conspirator, a central player in the buildup and execution of the coup.

As Abdel Kouddous drove through the streets of Cairo on the early morning of 24 July 1952, he no doubt felt the release of years of pent-up frustration. Abdel Kouddous had been working for over a decade to spark a revolution that would end colonialism in the country and sweep away the collaborating elite. More than two years before the coup, Abdel Kouddous began projecting his revolutionary fervor on the members of the Free Officers in particular, directing them to help him manufacture public support for a coup and encouraging them to act. Indeed, all of the Officers, including Nasser, were regulars at *Rose El Youssef* before the coup. As Abdel Kouddous later explained: "They were so enthusiastic about every word written in *Rose El Youssef* that they participated—behind the scenes—in editing the magazine. President Sadat wrote anonymously about Palestine and other political issues. Abdel Kader Hatem wrote about finances in Egypt during the 1940s. Two other Officers volunteered as covert informants, feeding us scandals of the ruling class to inflame the public to speed up the end of the system."[6] Only six weeks after the coup, Abdel Kouddous even stated openly that the Officers had come to his house to present him with a plan to assassinate the king. Positioning himself as their advisor and guide, Abdel Kouddous claimed that he urged them not to carry out the plan on the grounds that it would only outrage the British and entrench colonialism deeper in Egypt.[7] The Officers did as he said. This brief and little-known episode is yet another example of why Abdel Kouddous believed that he was particularly close to the Officers in the buildup to the coup; it also shows how much they regarded him as a trusted advisor. As Abdel Kouddous wrote about the Free Officers in his first article after the coup, "These men were always around me, always with me, always my hope. I was writing to them and with them."[8]

On 29 July 1952, only five days after the coup, Abdel Kouddous went on the radio at the Officers' invitation and addressed the nation for the first time. He was the first civilian to speak on air on their behalf—another clear indication of his importance. As Abdel Kouddous explained in his radio address, the Free Officers had leaked critical documents to him about the "rotten" weapons because they could not launch the coup without the scandal.[9] For Abdel Kouddous, there was no doubt that his articles and activism before the coup—and especially the Rotten Weapons scandal—"led to the undertaking and success of the revolution."[10] And, to make the moment that much sweeter, Abdel Kouddous had personally intervened to save them from arrest only three days earlier. The personal triumph that Abdel Kouddous felt that morning would only be matched by his despair, regret, and anxiety as Nasser marginalized and then erased him from the history of the revolution in the months following the coup.

## "I FELT THE NOOSE AROUND MY NECK"

Abdel Kouddous had been disappointed many times by the sparks of revolution that had failed to ignite. As he made his way to the Abbassia barracks in the early morning of 24 July 1952, Abdel Kouddous was still not fully convinced that it had really happened. As he explained in his first radio address just days after the coup, situating himself as a full participant with the Officers, "We made preparations for this kind of action years ago when I broke the Rotten Weapons scandal. Public opinion was completely mobilized and I believed that the scandal would incite the Officers . . . but they didn't move."[11] Nonetheless, in his first article after the coup, written no more than one day after the morning of 24 July, Abdel Kouddous stressed that he never despaired, despite the long wait. In this first article, he focused on the Officers as masculine, strong, and committed, echoing the same language that he had used in the 1940s and early 1950s to send out casting calls for his long-awaited leader. "When I began writing years ago," he wrote, "I knew that there were men in Egypt, men with light in their hearts and hope in their arms!"[12] Abdel Kouddous explained that he had always clung to his faith that there were leaders in the country who would rise up and act: "The battle wasn't actually about corruption, but about those who believed in these men and those who didn't, between those who believed that Egypt was a nation of men or of sheep to be herded."

Even though Abdel Kouddous would be almost entirely erased from later narratives of the coup, it is clear from articles that he wrote within the first six weeks and the interviews that he gave decades later that he saw himself as playing a central role for the Officers at this decisive stage. In discussing these critical hours decades later, Abdel Kouddous explained on multiple occasions how, when he arrived, the Officers did not have any plan beyond executing the coup and looked to him for guidance on next steps.[13] On the morning of 24 July, the Officers seemed to treat Abdel Kouddous just as they had before—as a trusted fellow revolutionary who directed them to act. In his early narrative of the events of 24 July, Abdel Kouddous described how, after he arrived at the barracks, he spoke with Neguib for some two hours, debating with him the best way for Egypt to be governed now that the Officers had launched the coup. Nasser had brought the older, pipe-smoking, paternal Neguib into the Free Officers in preparation for the coup so that Neguib could serve as their figurehead, an obvious strategy to calm potential concerns among the public that the other Officers were all so young. In these critical hours of the coup, it was Abdel Kouddous who told Neguib to remove the prime minister. Abdel Kouddous then stood nearby as he listened to negotiations between Neguib and the palace about the army's demands. In several interviews many years later, Abdel Kouddous explained that he directed Neguib and Nasser not only to depose the king but also to appoint his old friend, Ali Maher, as prime minister.[14] Even in his first narrative of the coup, Abdel Kouddous described how Neguib asked him—not one of the Free Officers—to call Maher and see if he would accept the position. When he could not reach Maher on several lines, Abdel Kouddous contacted the head of the telephone system, explaining that he was trying to get in touch with Maher "in the name of the general leadership."[15] When Abdel Kouddous finally got Maher on the phone, he did not identify himself personally, even though he had known Maher intimately for years. Instead, Abdel Kouddous presented himself as one of the Officers, declaring, "This is the general leadership." Abdel Kouddous then told Maher, "Major General Mohammed Neguib wants your excellency to come to headquarters for an important matter."

Abdel Kouddous's direct participation in the coup did not stop there. Nasser designated him to ride in a military jeep with Anwar Sadat and Kamel ed-Din Hussein, two founding members of the Free Officers, to Maher's house. As Abdel Kouddous explained in an interview published in 1974, this ride filled him with tremendous pride, further solidifying his ties with the Officers and the coup: "The military jeep set out with us, forcing its way in the middle of the happy trilling masses. We met this sight with a deep sense of responsibility in our hearts."[16] When they arrived at Maher's house, Abdel Kouddous, Sadat, and Hussein were bound together by the severity of the situation. As he explained in the same 1974 interview, "We exchanged quick glances, understanding the danger awaiting the revolution if we didn't succeed."[17] Once they began discussing the situation, Maher told the three men that he needed to speak with the king. Sadat reportedly exploded, hitting his fist on the table, yelling, "What king? Wake up! We're in a revolution!"[18] It was then that Abdel Kouddous, acting as the leader of the group, intervened and pressed down on Sadat's foot under the table to get him under control. Abdel Kouddous, not Sadat or Hussein, then laid out the Officers' demands to Maher for cleansing and a new constitution "since he is an envoy of Major General Mohammed Neguib." When the three returned to the barracks, it was once again Abdel Kouddous who took the lead, relaying Maher's demand that the king appoint him as prime minister. Neguib accepted and then told Abdel Kouddous—not Sadat or Hussein— to inform Maher on his behalf.

It was only now that Abdel Kouddous seemed to realize that he was, in fact, a full participant in a coup. When a palace representative was late arriving in Cairo to meet Neguib, Abdel Kouddous became anxious. As he explained in his narrative published only six weeks after the coup, "My nerves started betraying me. I imagined that something terrifying was being hatched against the movement." Abdel Kouddous suddenly became frantic. He called the Alexandria office of *Rose El Youssef* and learned that the prime minister had told his cabinet that Abdel Kouddous was indeed a member of the Free Officers and was participating with them in the coup.[19] He then learned that King Farouk saw him as personally responsible. As Abdel Kouddous explained in an interview published in 1974: "They told me that the king held me at the top of his list of enemies."[20] In fact, when Abdel Kouddous was on a trip to France in spring 1953, he was contacted by King Farouk's personal secretary, Amin Fahim, who offered him a sensational interview with the deposed monarch in person. Sensing that something was amiss, Abdel Kouddous cancelled the interview at the last minute. Fahim would later admit that Farouk had offered the interview as a trap for his bodyguards to kill Abdel Kouddous in revenge for his role in the coup.[21]

As the coup unfolded, Abdel Kouddous came to realize that his life was in danger if it did not succeed. While he never expressed anxiety about harboring Hussein Tawfik despite the punishment of years of hard labor if caught, he now felt the stakes on a visceral level. As he explained in his 2 September 1952 article, "I felt the noose around my neck. I looked up at the airplanes in the sky, afraid that they were British planes that King Farouk sent to seize control of Cairo and arrest us."[22] Just as Abdel Kouddous conspired and collaborated with the Officers beforehand and helped guide them as the coup unfolded, he now realized that he would be arrested as one of them if the coup failed. Abdel Kouddous panicked. As he wrote, "Everyone in the leadership felt what I was feeling—the noose. He felt his life—and maybe that of his family—hang in the success of the movement." Abdel Kouddous became so anxious that he interrupted Neguib, telling him, "This silence is making me nervous. They have to be plotting something!" Nonetheless, "a voice next to Neguib," presumably Nasser, told Abdel Kouddous: "Everything's going according to plan. Relax!" His emotions and anxieties got the better of him in this critical moment, perhaps a reminder that he was not part of the military, as the other participants were. Abdel Kouddous turned to the Officers for reassurance and confirmed for his own peace of mind that these were indeed the courageous, committed, and steadfast men leading him out of the wilderness.

By three o'clock on the afternoon of 24 July 1952, Abdel Kouddous was still at the barracks. Word finally arrived that the prime minister had resigned and that the king had delegated Maher to form a government. With this act, the coup had progressed into a critical stage. Calm returned to the barracks and, after nearly twelve hours participating in the coup along with the Free Officers, Abdel Kouddous went back home to see his family, confident that their lives were no longer in danger. "I got in bed. I don't know how long I slept since I was like someone who spent ten years feeling anxious and then, finally, the time came to relax." A deep sense of catharsis washed over Abdel Kouddous, a psychological climax that cleansed him of his fears and anxieties. At that moment, he understood that his long-cherished revolution had finally taken root. At long last, he felt victorious. While the public at first had only limited information about Abdel Kouddous's involvement on the day of the coup, observant readers of *Rose El Youssef* knew enough to send telegrams of congratulations to the periodical. Published in the 4 August 1952 issue of *Rose El Youssef*, one read: "Today, you've succeeded. As a citizen, I congratulate you for what you worked so hard for despite everything and the success of your mission." Another was even more explicit: "I believe that the success of the army's movement is the victory and triumph of *Rose El Youssef* and, especially, of Ihsan." Whether justified or not, Abdel Kouddous, like some of his readers, deeply felt that he was personally responsible for the end of the old regime.

## THE CIVILIAN OFFICER

As has been well documented, the Free Officers, in the weeks and months following the coup, turned to civilian partners to help construct their message for the public. For example, under Ahmed Abul-Fath, *al-Misri* immediately aligned itself with the Officers. As Abul-Fath recounted in his 1962 memoir, "The first issue of *al-Misri* that appeared after the coup was like a revolutionary tract."[23] Mohamed El-Tabii, the first editor in chief of *Rose El Youssef* and a longtime mentor to Abdel Kouddous, was now writing uncompromising editorials in the daily *al-Akhbar* (The News), calling for acts of repression against those who stood in the Officers' way. One of the most vociferous early supporters of the Officers was, ironically, Sayyid Qutb, the foremost intellectual of the Muslim Brotherhood during the Nasser era. In his first article after the coup, which was published in *Rose El Youssef*, Qutb lamented that the army's revolution had taken place without violence. Spilled blood was needed for the people to understand that "a complete era in the life of this country has died and a new era has been born."[24] Qutb called for the revolution to move mercilessly to uproot the entire old system. "Every popular revolution in the world eradicated the old, polluted, and corrupt, and put new, young elements in their place ... because the logic of revolution requires this before change can happen in the system and the law."

No doubt, each of these writers felt that he had a special relationship with the Officers and was using the press in the aftermath of the coup to declare allegiance and try to guide them. Nonetheless, as

Ahmed Abul-Fath notes about Nasser in the initial weeks after the coup, "He possessed the talent to be able to listen to someone give opinions without revealing his own, giving the person he was speaking with the impression that he agreed with them."[25] It is in this context that Joel Gordon notes, "Some in the Left fooled themselves into thinking they could collaborate with, even guide, the new regime."[26] With his zealous support for the coup in each issue of *Rose El Youssef* and on the radio, Abdel Kouddous appears, at least at first, to be another one of these seemingly duped early propagandists. Unlike his peers, however, Abdel Kouddous was simply acting as he always had with the Officers, whom he saw as both indecisive and hesitant. As before the coup, Abdel Kouddous simply continued using his platform to try to mold Nasser and push him to follow the script. Abdel Kouddous believed that the Officers were a tool with which he could cleanse the political terrain to prepare for the emergence of a democratic Egypt. For three months after the coup, Abdel Kouddous became a fervent public voice pushing the Officers to take steps to implement temporary dictatorship, something that he argued was necessary—and harmless—to ensure the success of the revolution, clearly confident that he would be able to force them to withdraw once conditions permitted the emergence of democracy.

In his euphoric first article after the coup and expulsion of King Farouk, Abdel Kouddous stressed that the coup was simply an act of wiping away corruption and degradation, not constructing the new society. As he explained, "What happened up until today is only a 'cleansing operation' or a 'preparatory operation.' The most important thing remains—the glorious building whose plans have been traced but whose stones have not yet been placed."[27] His next step was to argue for the suspension of the constitution. On 4 August, in only his second editorial after the coup, Abdel Kouddous called for granting the Officers extraordinary powers to carry out their cleansing. For Abdel Kouddous, even though the king had been deposed, the corruption that controlled the political parties was still in place, as was extreme wealth inequality. Immediately restoring the constitution would only lead to the same corrupt results. It was therefore necessary to grant the Officers extraordinary powers to operate without a constitution in place so that they could complete their work. Abdel Kouddous was nonetheless careful to stress that he did not support suspending the rule of law permanently. "This does not mean that I'm not calling for constitutional rule or that I support the creation of a military government," he wrote, "but I want us to finish the job that has begun and has not yet been finished."[28] As Abdel Kouddous argued the following week, it was the army that needed to safeguard the road to democracy. As he explained, "The role of the army is to protect innocent, pure, political freedom."[29] The Officers—like Hussein Tawfik and his co-defendants some five years earlier—were simply the courageous, committed, self-sacrificing men who had taken matters into their own hands to shepherd the country out of the wilderness of corruption.

By mid-August, however, Abdel Kouddous was worried that the army seemed too passive, apparently waiting for the political parties to undertake reform measures on their own. He sounded the alarm that the Officers needed to take matters into their hands, fearing that feudalist enemies were creeping forward to hijack the revolution. Abdel Kouddous wanted the Officers to be decisive, to demonstrate that they were the "men" he had presumed them to be. As early as 18 August 1952, Abdel Kouddous expressed his frustrations that it was not clear whether Ali Maher—whom he quickly saw as stalling necessary land reform—or the Officers who were governing the country. For Abdel Kouddous, this hesitation and uncertainty, just three weeks after the coup, represented an existential threat. Other figures in the press were expressing similar frustrations by this time but for Abdel Kouddous, the Officers' passivity was deeply personal—it represented a terrifying risk to what he saw as his cherished, long-awaited revolution. Abdel Kouddous was anxious that the Officers were not serving as appropriate caretakers for his hopes and dreams, not implementing his vision of a rapid and decisive cleansing. Abdel Kouddous had already seen their hesitation and inaction in the months after the Rotten Weapons scandal and on the day of the coup. He was horrified to see them fall back on the same passivity. They had to be pushed.

In his 8 September 1952 editorial, written before Maher's resignation on 7 September, Abdel Kouddous wrote angrily, "I can't be silent when I see the hopes of the era placed in the hands of a group of pure angels suspended in the sky and shying away from being human, too proud to step foot on the earth.... I can't be silent as I look at the forces of regression creep forward, hatching plans to occupy what we thought in the intoxication of victory they had lost."[30] Using the same language about "pure angels" as after the Rotten Weapons scandal to try to push the Officers to act, Abdel Kouddous demanded that they get themselves dirty by facing reality and moving decisively: "I'm not calling on them to renounce their faith in the constitution. Egypt won't ever be ruled without one and I won't stop calling for one. I'm not calling on them to renounce their faith in the political party system since there's no constitution without parties. And I'm not calling on them to renounce their faith in personal freedoms. I've spent my life defending these freedoms and I won't stop. But I'm calling for the angels to come down to earth, be human, and act." Publicly pushing the Officers—as he once called on them to collect documents for the Rotten Weapons scandal—Abdel Kouddous openly cast aside any worries about military rule: "What are they afraid of? Are they afraid of being accused of dictatorship?" He was clearly so confident about his influence over the Officers and his status in the revolution that his only worry seemed to be their passivity.

Once the Officers formed their own ministry in September 1952 after strong-arming Ali Maher into resignation, Abdel Kouddous was triumphant that they were finally moving decisively, presumably because they were following his directives. For Abdel Kouddous, the Officers were simply reluctant idealists who had answered the inevitable duty to dirty themselves with events on the ground. "The army didn't want to form a military ministry," he wrote. "I don't exaggerate if I confirm that the Officers themselves don't believe in military rule. They were—and still are—honest in their faith in the constitution and parliamentary life. But conditions were pushing them to it."[31] As if looking for credit, Abdel Kouddous then declared, "They kept pushing away the idea of forming a military ministry, despite the urging of some of their advisors that they face reality and take over governing themselves." As he clarified yet again at the end of the editorial in this issue, he was not calling for permanent military rule: "We don't want from them a system of ruling Egypt. As we've said before, we oppose—and we will always oppose—that they impose on Egypt military dictatorship."

Nonetheless, the meandering and hesitancy continued, made worse by the fact that the Officers apparently had not planned, at least at first, to govern. As Sadat admitted some twenty-five years later, "It was obvious that we hadn't prepared ourselves, when we carried out our revolution, for taking over government posts. . . . We had no ambition to be government ministers. We had not envisaged that and had not even drawn up a specific government program."³² This lack of planning only pushed Abdel Kouddous to become more forceful, just as he had been on the morning of the coup. Once Neguib was appointed prime minister and the land reform law was issued, Abdel Kouddous became even more vocal about trying to guide the Officers to take total command of the political field, in the full confidence that they would withdraw once they had laid the groundwork for the emergence of a democratic Egypt.

It was during this period that Abdel Kouddous completed what he would later see as his inadvertent work to entrench military dictatorship in Egypt. For Abdel Kouddous, conditions had forced the Officers—selfless instruments of an abused, defenseless people—to undertake the coup, and conditions now forced them to step in and form a military government. In his 15 September 1952 editorial, Abdel Kouddous argued that the formation of the military ministry represented a new "period of stability" on behalf of the people. "Should we give up this decisive tool with which we're achieving our goals to return as slaves with chains of deception, hypocrisy, and plots?"³³ Abdel Kouddous had no doubt that this period would be temporary, limited only by whatever time the Officers needed to create the conditions necessary for the emergence of democracy. He declared with confidence that once the Officers completed the necessary cleansing of the political parties, "they will be forced to withdraw—even if they don't want to—because they won't find a justification to extend the period of delaying the constitution and elections. The army—as I know—is only trying to participate in preparing the people and the parties to be strong enough to protect the constitution." While others were demanding similar decisiveness by the Officers, Abdel Kouddous felt that he was at the lead. As he wrote the following week: "I was the first of those demanding the intervention of the army in order to protect the principles of the revolution before it slipped into enemy hands."³⁴

In September and early October 1952, at least publicly, Abdel Kouddous was satisfied that all was going to plan. Working behind the scenes in daily meetings with the Officers—as well as employing his platform in *Rose El Youssef* to support them, as promised—Abdel Kouddous showed no outward concern about the entrenchment of dictatorship. Basking in his apparent triumph, Abdel Kouddous now shifted to using the Officers to cultivate the conditions necessary for democratic life: the implementation of a new constitution, the cleansing of the political parties, and the withdrawal of the Officers from rule. It was during this period, Abdel Kouddous argued in his editorials in fall 1952, that several markers of democracy must be achieved. First, the people must abandon their servile mentality and, especially, fear of the Officers, stating their opinions honestly and openly in public. For Abdel Kouddous, this was a central indicator for the practice of the rule of law, freedom of expression, and healthy democratic life. He felt so passionately about this that he went on the radio again on 30 October 1952 for another national address in which he urged the public to let go of their fear of the Officers: "Brothers, believe me and trust me. Have faith that the army, when it made itself an instrument to build a new era, didn't rely on weapons, tanks, or canons. Instead, it decided to rely on strength of character, nationalism, and purity of the spirit and conscience. The leadership of the army doesn't want the people to fear it. Rather, it wants them to trust it and to rely on it and to show it their love."[35] Abdel Kouddous even stressed that freedom of speech—the freedom to criticize the Officers— was ensured. He was so certain of this that he declared to the nation, "Believe me that all freedoms are guaranteed in this era by the principles that the movement rose up for. We have to preserve these freedoms, unless we relinquish them out of fear from a false fantasy.... Know that punishment won't come to anyone simply because he expressed his opinion honestly." As he reiterated in *Rose El Youssef* a few weeks later, "What are people afraid of? Are they afraid of arrest?... I can confirm that free speech has not been a reason to arrest anyone since the rise of the army's movement."[36] In this, he would, of course, be proven tragically wrong.

During these weeks, Abdel Kouddous not only spoke on the radio supporting the Officers but also gave addresses on their behalf at large conferences, despite his deep misgivings about public speaking. In fall 1952, he appeared so aligned with the Officers that he was making people suspicious. By early November, he felt the need to declare his independence from the regime: "I repeat for the hundredth—no, the thousandth—time that I, in everything I write, am not taking direction from anyone. I don't express the view of any body, whether it be official or unofficial. I have not been at any time a voice for a master. I have never put my pen in the hand of someone else."[37] Framing his goals as simply overlapping with the Officers, Abdel Kouddous declared that he believed in principles, not people: "I might agree or disagree with officials about certain principles.... But I'm free, just as they are. That's how I've always been and how I'll always be. I say this because some think that I write under orders from the military command.... But this is not true.... They have no involvement in anything I write. And I don't have the right to express their directives."

**Figure 6.** Ihsan Abdel Kouddous, early 1950s, perhaps speaking on behalf of the Free Officers. Courtesy of the Abdel Kouddous family.

In an interview decades later, Abdel Kouddous openly acknowledged the uncomfortable link between himself and the military leadership during the initial weeks and months after the coup: "People were saying that I was the civilian official of the Free Officers."[38] To prove this point, Abdel Kouddous detailed an encounter around this time with Fouad Pasha Serageddin, the powerful former minister of the interior who had ordered Abdel Kouddous's arrest in 1949 and 1950. "After the revolution," Abdel Kouddous explained, "Serageddin came to talk with me at *Rose El Youssef*, assuming that I was on the military command, or at least influencing it."[39] Abdel Kouddous could not help but appreciate the irony of the strongman of the previous era—the same man who had jailed him—now coming to seek favor with him, assuming that he was one of the Officers. No doubt, the encounter filled him with tremendous pride.

There is a blurry line in Abdel Kouddous's editorials and radio addresses during the initial months after the coup between supporting the Officers and working to direct them. He served as a key advisor for them, meeting with Neguib and Nasser daily, pushing them to take a series of steps that ultimately laid the groundwork for establishing and entrenching dictatorship in Egypt. While this was true for someone like Ahmed Abul-Fath as well, Abdel Kouddous clearly believed that he had a special relationship with the Officers. He no doubt thought that he would continue to work with them as he always had, both behind the scenes as a collaborator and as a public voice, using his media platform and revolutionary credibility to guide them and mobilize public opinion in order to achieve his dream. In the honeymoon period after the coup, he appeared to have little doubt that his ability to influence and direct them had changed. During this period, Abdel Kouddous projected his own principles and faith onto the Officers, seemingly fully confident that they were not only the instrument of the people but also his own instrument, a pliable tool to carry out his long-awaited cleansing and to begin building the new democratic Egypt.

### REVOLUTIONARY JOURNALIST, LEADER OF THE FREE OFFICERS

Another reason that Abdel Kouddous felt such ownership for the revolution in the months following the coup was because of a film project. When he became the first civilian to address the nation on the radio on behalf of the Officers, he took the opportunity not only to urge the public to back the coup but also to put the Rotten Weapons scandal—and his role in it—at the center of his narrative. Abdel Kouddous explained on the air that the Officers came home from the Palestine War "with a deep wound, not caused by the bullets of the enemy, but by the horrible corruption that hit them as they were sacrificing their lives for religion and the nation ... after they saw their brothers killed by canons that fired backwards, rifles that shot in their faces, and hand-grenades that exploded in their hands. They returned knowing that they were the victim of weapons dealers, a toy in the hands of the lords who were amusing themselves in the cabarets of Cairo while they were getting killed in the desert.... They returned with revolution in their eyes."[40] In this very first hagiography of the origins of the Officers, it was outrage at the Rotten Weapons that had created their political consciousness, pushed them to form their organization, and spurred them to action.

In placing this kind of weight on the Rotten Weapons immediately after the coup, Abdel Kouddous was not alone. In its article on the coup, *The New York Times* also focused on the scandal: "The army coup had its origin in the Palestine war, when the Egyptian Army took a beating from the Israeli militia. The defeat was attributed in part to the fact that arms contractors, in league with senior officers, politicians and palace favorites, allegedly had palmed off unserviceable and obsolete equipment on the army."[41] This focus was echoed by *al-Misri*, which, on 26 July 1952, printed the headline "*New York Times*: The Reason for the Movement Is the Scandal of the Rotten Weapons in Palestine." In his initial statements after the coup, Neguib also stressed "cleansing" the army. When he gave an address to the king on the radio on 26 July 1954, he mentioned the scandal explicitly: "Traitors and the corrupt have found in your shadow protection, safety, and illegitimate wealth at the expense of the poor hungry people. That happened in the Palestine War and was revealed afterwards in the scandal of the Rotten Weapons."[42] The case remained on the front pages of the press in the weeks after the coup with headlines like "Shocking Documents about the Rotten Weapons Case Seized in the Alexandria Palace."[43] Even Nasser, on 1 October 1952, in his first article published in the press, pointed directly to the scandal multiple times, explaining that "the case of the Rotten Weapons exposed the disturbed minds, filthy hands, and weak souls" behind the loss in Palestine.[44] Moreover, according to Nasser, "The press played a fundamental role in inflaming the Rotten Weapons scandal and presenting the corrupt traitors for judgment. This was the first time in which the king was subject to investigation and judgment, and this sowed the seeds of national resistance and inflamed the new consciousness, especially in the army." These public declarations of the importance of the Rotten Weapons scandal in the weeks after the coup only reinforced for Abdel Kouddous the importance of his role in the movement.

Sometime in the initial days after the coup, the Officers not only asked Abdel Kouddous to deliver a national address on the radio but also commissioned him to write the story for a film that was supposed to be the first work of fiction to celebrate the coup. Abdel Kouddous hinted at this project in his radio speech on 29 July 1952. In the final moments of the speech, he declared, "When the whole story of deposing King Farouk is broadcast, you'll know that God was with us, fate was leading us, and luck was protecting us." Here, he likely used the phrase "God was with us" to link the events of the coup to the editorial that he published on 23 July 1947, discussed in chapter 1, when he prophetically called on military action to lead the country to revolt and wipe away the corrupt ruling class. The proposed film project gave Abdel Kouddous the opportunity to depict his experience acting out his detective-novel intrigues with the Free Officers in the two years before the coup. He was, unsurprisingly, enthusiastic about the task. As he recalled years later, "I believed that people needed to see all that in a story. The fastest and easiest way was to present this story as a movie."[45] While he was careful not to give himself too much credit for guiding the Free Officers in his initial editorials and radio speech after the coup, this work of fiction—something that he assumed that the public would consume quickly and widely—was his opportunity to cement unapologetically his centrality to the history of the revolution in what he thought would be its most important hagiography.

Referencing his 23 July 1947 editorial as well as his 29 July 1952 radio address, Abdel Kouddous named the film *God Is with Us*. Prominent filmmaker Ahmed Badrakhan was hired as director, and shooting began in fall 1952, exactly when Abdel Kouddous was arguably the most important civilian public advocate for the Officers.[46] The movie would not, however, be released until 1955, by which time the political atmosphere had changed markedly. Even though it was advertised as an "image pulled from the heart of Egyptian life in historical nationalist film" and described in the program printed for the film's premiere as Studio Misr's "nationalist duty to record the events of this historical period," *God Is with Us* begins with the disclaimer that the characters in the film are all fictional.[47] It then displays footage of the Palestine War, followed by images of the royal palace with a voice-over that declares, "The enemy did not vanquish the children of Egypt. Instead, it was a plot hatched against the nation here, in Abdeen Palace, by the tyrant." The film introduces Ahmed, played by popular leading man Emad Hamdy, who is tall with a mustache and a quiet manner of speaking. Clearly, Ahmed is the double of Nasser before the coup, despite several intentional biographical differences.[48] It was no ordinary role for Hamdy, who explained in the program, "I felt for the first time the greatness of a mission cast on my neck." Full of nationalist pride, Ahmed is confident of victory before leaving for the Palestine War, naïvely placing his trust in the prime minister, who has declared the army to be fully prepared and well equipped. Ahmed is engaged to his cousin, Nadia, played by Faten Hamama, a leading young actress in Egypt at the time. Her father, Abdelaziz Bey, is a wealthy businessman who has worked with the right-hand man of the king to purchase "rotten" weapons for the army. In his articles about the scandal in *Rose El Youssef*, Abdel Kouddous pointed the finger at the king's nephew, Abbas Halim. In *God Is with Us*, however, Abdel Kouddous takes the final step to depict the king himself as overseeing the deals.

Nasser was shot in the chest during the Palestine War. Ahmed is gravely wounded as well, but in the film, he loses his arm after his "rotten" cannon fires in reverse on the battlefield. When Ahmed regains consciousness in the hospital, he immediately knows that a crime has been committed against him, the army, and the nation. While Nasser was not injured by the notorious rotten weapons in the war, Ahmed nonetheless echoes Nasser's own words at the time that the real war was in Egypt, not Palestine: "We have to fight here, in Cairo. We have to fight on the interior front before going back to the battlefield."[49] The Rotten Weapons have therefore not only maimed Ahmed but also directly formed his revolutionary consciousness and commitment to cleanse the country. After leaving the hospital, Ahmed, referencing

Abdel Kouddous's editorials from 1950, tells Nadia that he is now committed to fighting the war "against the big thieves who sit in the cabarets." He then begins his quest "to uncover the criminals who imported the rotten weapons into Palestine." He meets with fellow officers as they plot their next moves around a table in a dark room, swearing on a gun and a copy of the Quran to cleanse the army from traitors, the exact "detective-novel" plotting described by Abdel Kouddous in an editorial only six weeks after the coup and echoed later by Nasser in *Philosophy of the Revolution*. Despite their efforts, however, Ahmed and his fellow officers are unsuccessful in convincing an opposition politician to pursue the Rotten Weapons case. Needing a leader to organize them, the officers turn to fiery journalist Muhsin Abdel Mawgoud, played by another leading actor of the time, Shoukry Sirhan, who immediately leaps to action full of nationalist fervor as soon as he learns the details of the case.

In the event there was any doubt who the revolutionary Muhsin is supposed to be, he works in an office with a picture of Ihsan Abdel Kouddous and his mother, Fatima Youssef, on the wall behind him as well as the iconic cover of the 30 October 1951 *Rose El Youssef*, with bare-chested Misri Effendi rising up like King Kong, breaking free of his chains. There is also a bronze statue of Fatima Youssef to the left of Muhsin's desk—a statue that, at the time of writing, resided in the entryway of the Cairo offices of *Rose El Youssef*. As if the links between fiction and reality were not clear enough, Muhsin tells his wife, played by the well-known Egyptian actress who went by the single name of Magda, that he will call his article on the case "Prosecute the Criminals of the Palestine War!," the same title that Abdel Kouddous used in June 1950 for his first series on the case. Clearly, Abdel Kouddous did not pick the name of his cinematic double by accident. By naming himself "Muhsin" in the film, Abdel Kouddous was firmly establishing himself—and not Nasser—as the real-life version of Tawfiq al-Hakim's hero from *Return of the Spirit*, the leader who has come to spark revolution among the Egyptian people. Nasser, of course, would have understood the reference, as he had used the very same name for his own double in his unfinished novel *For Freedom*. With the character of Muhsin, Abdel Kouddous writes himself at the center of the public celebration of the origins of the Free Officers. The implication is that they would have been lost in the wilderness without him.

In a pivotal scene, Ahmed and another officer—who bears some resemblance to Sadat—visit Muhsin at his office to congratulate him on his article breaking the scandal, reenacting for the public imaginary the first encounter between Abdel Kouddous and Nasser. It is Muhsin, not either of the officers, who enthusiastically leads the discussion, demonstrating not only the journalist's fervor, confidence, and revolutionary spirit but also his influence over the officers. Echoing Abdel Kouddous's own confrontations with authorities during the Rotten Weapons scandal, Muhsin declares, "We have to get the case to the courts, and the only way is for me to protect you so they investigate me. If they want to take me to jail, I'm ready." Muhsin declares that he needs documents to prove the case, recreating the moment when Abdel Kouddous called for conspirators in the army to aid him in his crusade. Ahmed and the officer resembling Sadat then declare that they will find the documents for Muhsin. Serving as their leader and guide, Muhsin gets up from his chair and stresses that he needs the papers, leaning over Ahmed commandingly and ordering the two to collect them for him. Here it is Abdel Kouddous who is giving orders to Nasser, not the other way around. In this scene, Nasser and Sadat are depicted as sheepish, needing the guidance of the strong Abdel Kouddous to prove the scandal and lay the groundwork for the coup. Ahmed may have the nationalist sentiment and desire for sacrifice, but he cannot achieve the revolution without Muhsin's direction.

As ordered, Ahmed delivers the documents to Muhsin, who prints them in the press and exposes the scandal. The film then moves immediately to the night of 23-24 July 1952, as officers begin taking over the streets in their tanks, cementing the Rotten Weapons scandal, the leadership of the revolutionary journalist, and the success of the coup. The army may execute the coup, but it does so only with the guidance, vision, and courage of their leader, the revolutionary journalist. Moreover, the climax of the film underscores the centrality of the Rotten Weapons in the execution and success of the coup. When a military jeep full of officers arrives at Abdelaziz Bey's house to arrest him, he pulls the pin of a hand grenade to throw it at them but, unsurprisingly, it explodes in his hand. It is therefore the Rotten Weapons that not only produce the coup but also kill off the corrupt ruling elite. The symbolism is quite clear.

The original story by Abdel Kouddous and screenplay by Ahmed Badrakhan unfortunately no longer survive, but we know that the existing film is far from the initial edit that was submitted to the censor for approval. As the film was shot in fall 1952, the initial complete edit included not only doubles for Nasser, Sadat, and Abdel Kouddous but also Mohammed Neguib, who was played by Zaki Talimat, Abdel Kouddous's former stepfather.[50] According to the 22 December 1952 issue of *Rose El Youssef*, Studio Misr showed scenes from the film to journalists at their annual party. *God Is with Us* was also advertised in the 31 December 1952 issue of *al-Tahrir* as "coming soon, the great nationalist film." Nonetheless, we know that this first edit did not receive a screening permit from the censor when it was submitted for approval sometime in spring or early summer of 1953. When the film had not appeared by July 1953, the one-year anniversary of the coup, a reader wrote to *Rose El Youssef* asking if it had been cancelled. The magazine responded on 20 July 1953 that "the film has been produced and will be shown in 40 cinemas all over Egypt next 23 July." Clearly, by summer 1953, Abdel Kouddous still maintained some hope that the version of history in the film—and his own centrality in it—would become the landmark cinematic celebration of the origins of the revolution. This hope would be sustained by more advertisements for the film in fall 1953, including one even in the state-owned *al-Tahrir* magazine on 23 September 1953.

Nonetheless, *God Is with Us* did not premiere in 1954 either. When it was still not released by early 1955, Abdel Kouddous frustratedly asked for help from his old friend Anwar Sadat, who arranged for a private screening for Nasser, which Abdel Kouddous attended. Nasser approved this latest edit, which now had all references to the Neguib figure cut from the film.[51] In order to give his official stamp of approval for the long-delayed project, Nasser attended the premiere on 14 March 1955 at Cinema Rivoli. As if to link the location of the premiere with the revolutionary content of the film, Cinema Rivoli was one of the locations burned during the Black Saturday riots in Cairo on the night of 25 January 1952.

As Joel Gordon suggests, the rush to produce a hagiography of the Officers' mutiny created unexpected problems. It seems clear that the film displeased the censor for two entirely different reasons, the first time in 1953 and the second when it was resubmitted for approval sometime after March 1954. As I show in the following section, Abdel Kouddous had become such a thorn in the sides of the Officers by spring 1953 that they decided to marginalize him completely. Nasser not only stopped meeting with Abdel Kouddous but also systematically minimized the importance of the Rotten Weapons scandal in the origins of the movement and erased Abdel Kouddous's personal role in the coup. As a result, the censor was no doubt given instructions to reject the first version of the film, which unapologetically celebrated the Rotten Weapons as the spark for the formation of the Free Officers and Abdel Kouddous as their leader. Shelving the film in mid-1953 certainly underscored for Abdel Kouddous that his cherished revolution had been hijacked and that his role in its buildup and execution was systematically being erased from the public.

By early 1955, after the jailing and resuscitation of Abdel Kouddous as a public intellectual, which I trace in the following chapter, Abdel Kouddous no longer represented a threat to Nasser's authority. Moreover, by that time, the Rotten Weapons and Abdel Kouddous's role in the revolution had been entirely erased by official narratives and had faded from public memory. At that point, it was not the Rotten Weapons scandal or the double for Abdel Kouddous that represented a threat; it was Mohammed Neguib, who had initially served as a calming figurehead for the Free Officers but subsequently attempted to take more and more power, which had the inevitable effect of rankling Nasser. The conflict between Neguib and Nasser escalated behind the scenes and erupted in what is known as the 1954 March Crisis, when supporters of each side struggled for control of the political terrain. Nasser emerged victorious, marginalizing Neguib and placing him under house arrest by the fall of 1954. By early 1955, Nasser was looking for ways to erase Neguib from public memory, and cutting his double in *God Is with Us* represented a welcome opportunity. Once Neguib's double was cut from the film, despite the continuity errors it brought about, the film not only passed the censor but was given the official seal of approval of Nasser himself attending the premiere. For Nasser, the film no longer represented a contestation of his authority by a rebellious former co-revolutionary journalist. This is further shown in the program printed for the premiere of the film in which Abdel Kouddous took the opportunity to criticize Nasser obliquely: "I wrote the film for its events to be memorialized so that we don't forget the days of tyranny and we don't go back." Now the film was a hagiography of a coup in which Neguib never existed.

Abdel Kouddous had been tasked with telling the story of the overthrow of the king. Given the opportunity, he wrote what he thought would become the most important work of popular culture celebrating the coup by placing himself at the center of events, directly linking the Rotten Weapons scandal and the revolutionary journalist to the origins and success of the coup. Even though the surviving version of *God Is with Us* was not screened until March 1955 after the edits excising Neguib, the film serves as a striking historical record of Abdel Kouddous's perspective on his own responsibility for the coup and his authority over the Officers in the initial days after the revolution. Clearly, when he was writing the film in the late summer of 1952, he still believed that he could guide a handsome, hesitant, and pliable Nasser, just as he had during the Rotten Weapons scandal. Like other figures who believed that they had the same influence over Nasser, Abdel Kouddous would soon be proven tragically wrong.

## ANXIETIES OF DICTATORSHIP

Despite his outward enthusiasm in editorials, radio addresses, and public fora—as well as his seeming confidence at influencing and directing the Officers—Abdel Kouddous harbored anxieties about military dictatorship as soon as he left the barracks after participating in the coup. On 15 January 1990, Ahmed Abul-Fath published a stunning article to mark the death of Abdel Kouddous titled "Ihsan Was the First to Realize It."[52] Abul-Fath revealed that he was surprised when Abdel Kouddous visited him at *al-Misri* on 24 July 1952, presumably on his way home from the barracks that day. When Abdel Kouddous arrived, Abul-Fath noticed that he seemed exhausted. Abul-Fath asked if he was happy with events and Abdel Kouddous responded, "My happiness is mixed with anxiety and fear. . . . Don't get too wrapped up in happiness and optimism. . . . We're entering military rule!" Perhaps Abdel Kouddous, in the first hours after the coup, was already projecting onto the Officers that they would have to take matters into their own hands and not leave governing to a civilian like Ali Maher. Perhaps Abdel Kouddous was indeed anxious that the necessary cleansing could lead to military dictatorship. But the encounter points to the deep ambivalence that Abdel Kouddous must have felt toward the Officers and the possibility of extended dictatorship from the start of the revolution, despite his public posture.

This early anxiety is confirmed in another source. On the evening of 11 August 1952, Abdel Kouddous met secretly with James Murray of the British Consulate in Cairo at a time when the British were still searching for basic information about the Free Officers to understand who was in charge after the coup.[53] The British recognized Abdel Kouddous as having special importance because he was their only political contact who knew the Officers before the coup. Understanding full well that Abdel Kouddous was a political advisor to Neguib, they were eager to get information from him about the Officers. Abdel Kouddous told Murray, "The army has no intention of letting things slide. If this means that there will be military dictatorship for a time, it might well be the best answer for Egypt's problems." Murray noted, however, that Abdel Kouddous "insinuated, a little ruefully, temporary military dictatorship tended to become permanent." Abdel Kouddous then asked Murray directly what the response of the British would be if a military dictatorship were to be established.

Abdel Kouddous's intentions for this meeting are open to interpretation. Perhaps he was conducting diplomacy on his own initiative, giving himself an authority that he did not actually have. This would align with his perception at this time that he was still the civilian leader of the hesitant and pliable Officers. He explained to Murray that he had advised the Officers to contact the embassies of the United Kingdom and the United States in order to keep them updated on developments, but that they turned him down. Could Abdel Kouddous have been acting impulsively, fueled by his frustrations at the Officers' inaction, which he expressed in that week's editorial in *Rose El Youssef*?[54] Or perhaps he had reason to believe that the Officers—as he seemed to be suggesting in his editorials from this time—were moving toward taking matters into their own hands and beginning to install dictatorship, and he wanted to know what the British reaction would be. Was he revealing his underlying anxieties about military dictatorship as a kind of confession, an attempt to soothe his conscience about the direction that the Officers were taking, all on the pretext of paradoxically establishing democracy?

Was he expressing regret that the revolution was already not progressing as he thought it would?

It is likely no coincidence that this meeting took place right around the first direct conflict between Abdel Kouddous and Nasser, an incident that Abdel Kouddous would not mention in public until 1974.[55] While he never gave an exact date in any of the interviews in which he discussed the incident, it could have been what drove him to meet with Murray. Abdel Kouddous explained that, having lost patience with Ali Maher in August 1952 for blocking land reform, he wrote an editorial attacking Maher, demanding that he be removed from office for not responding to the needs of the revolution. Clearly, Abdel Kouddous was disappointed that his old friend Maher, whom he had convinced the Officers to appoint, was not up to the task. Just as Abdel Kouddous had directed the Rotten Weapons case in his editorials before the coup, he expected that this editorial would compel the Officers to act once again. Abdel Kouddous clearly assumed at this point that he still occupied a privileged and influential position for the Officers. He would be in for a big surprise. As he later explained about this incident, "I didn't expect their response, which accelerated the seeds of dissent between us. The censor refused to issue a permit to publish the article."[56]

Outraged, Abdel Kouddous rushed to complain to Nasser, who coldly admitted that he—not the censor—was the one who had rejected the article out of "respect for rule and the ruler."[57] Nasser, of course, was intensely interested in the press before the coup, but it must have become clear to Abdel Kouddous the extent to which he would look to micromanage it afterwards. Abdel Kouddous protested angrily, screaming at Nasser multiple times. He explained, "I'd gotten used to meeting him as revolutionary to revolutionary, with the spirit of the revolution and faith in freedom uniting us." Only a few weeks after the coup, right when he was writing the story for *God Is with Us*, Abdel Kouddous clearly still saw himself in the guise of Muhsin Abdel Mawgoud, someone who could browbeat Nasser. Nonetheless, for the first time, Abdel Kouddous discovered that he did not have the central position or influence among the Officers that he had thought. It was also likely the first moment that he realized that he had the wrong assumptions about Nasser in particular.

Nasser told Abdel Kouddous that he agreed that it was time for Ali Maher to go. Nonetheless, he shot Abdel Kouddous a stern look, intimidating him by asking if he was with the movement or against it.[58] Nasser then explained, "I don't want to plant in peoples' minds that there's someone making a suggestion to the revolution, which it then carries out, even if he's right. I don't ever want people to imagine that there's someone pulling the strings of the revolution.... Imagine, Ihsan, if your article were published today and then we dismissed Ali Maher tomorrow, what would people say about us?"[59] Speaking about this exchange in another interview, Abdel Kouddous recalled Nasser telling him, "You're writing about land reform for you to show people that the military command is agreeing to your demands!"[60] Abdel Kouddous was not respecting the military tradition of chain of command; by going public, he represented a threat. Nasser thus felt the need to put Abdel Kouddous in his place.

Feeling this sudden and deep split with Nasser—and the revolution—Abdel Kouddous, stunned, did not respond. It was perhaps the first time that Nasser had revealed himself not as a pliable and hesitant young officer but as the figure in charge. Only a few weeks after the coup, Abdel Kouddous felt, even if briefly, that he was being displaced and decentered in the trajectory of the revolution. He suddenly sensed that his revolution—his life's work and aspiration—was being hijacked. In order to publish the article, Abdel Kouddous had to edit it in consultation with Gamal Salem, the Free Officer who headed the land reform law. The process made Abdel Kouddous feel demoted and belittled, filling him with what he would later call "internal bitterness" and quite possibly motivating him to meet with the British out of regret for bringing Nasser to power, something that he would later allude to in his fiction multiple times, as I show in the following chapters.[61] Echoing this behind-the-scenes story, the revised version of this article would not appear in *Rose El Youssef* until 8 September 1952, the day after Ali Maher resigned.

Abdel Kouddous was not the only figure to experience a starkly new version of Nasser soon after the coup. A senior member of the Muslim Brotherhood told Fawaz Gerges, "We naïvely believed we owned the revolution. We could guide these inexperienced young officers and show them the right way."[62] Nonetheless, Supreme Guide Hassan Hudaybi was shocked to discover that Nasser was not the obedient figure that he had taken him for. According to Gerges, "Immediately after Nasser and the Free Officers carried out the coup in July 1952, Ikhwan leaders considered Nasser one of their own. In their first meeting with Nasser, top Ikhwan leaders, including Supreme Guide Hudaybi, discovered to their dismay that Nasser was his own man, ambitious and unwilling to defer to their authority. From the outset, the old men of the Ikhwan were fooled by Nasser, a junior officer who brilliantly manipulated both friends and foes in order to dominate decision making."[63] It was in August 1952 that Hudaybi also confronted Nasser, demanding to be consulted on decisions. To Hudaybi's shock, Nasser reportedly responded, "I will not accept guardianship of the revolution from any party."[64]

As for Abdel Kouddous, even after his first conflict with Nasser, he clearly felt that he could still influence the Officers thanks to the resignation of Ali Maher, the formation of the military government, and the implementation of the land reform law, all steps that he had called for in his editorials. In fall 1952, Abdel Kouddous continued to meet with the Officers daily, working to guide them, trying to use them as his own instrument of cleansing so that his long-cherished democratic Egypt could emerge. Nonetheless, Abdel Kouddous soon began voicing anxieties about dictatorship in public. On 13 October 1952, Abdel Kouddous, after arguing that conditions on the ground had forced the Officers to intervene in politics and establish a military ministry, urged them to answer some basic questions: "Will the form of government be military dictatorship or democracy? Will there be a civilian ministry led by a military man or will it be purely civilian or purely military? Will a monarchy or republic be decided? Will Mohammed Neguib form a political party? Will he leave his position in the army to dedicate himself to this party?" These questions, which encapsulated nearly all of the dissent that Abdel Kouddous would express in the coming weeks and months, sought to force the Officers to establish clear guidelines for and limits on their rule.

After the 1923 Constitution was finally cancelled on 9 December 1952, Abdel Kouddous suddenly became much more anxious that the lack of clarity on the future augured permanent dictatorship. Just as he had tried to direct the Officers to act decisively and take extraordinary measures to impose their will on the political terrain, he argued that it was time for them to clarify the terms of their withdrawal. On 15 December 1952, he demanded that the Officers, without a constitution, must put in writing the rights of the people and the obligations of the rulers for the transitional period: "It was better for Egypt to live in a clear situation, in a disfigured system in which dictatorship rose up in the name of democracy and the constitution was delayed in the name of protecting it, but what is the situation that Egypt is living in now? What is the system of government in this temporary period? Is it a kind of dictatorial system? So be it. . . . But what are the binds that limit this period?"[65] Abdel Kouddous then called for guarantees for the presumably short period when Egypt would be governed without a constitution: "The first thing is to restrict this temporary period, to announce the date to declare the new constitution. . . . The leadership must confirm that it is tied to the principles of constitutional freedoms in a written document that has the force of the law, like a temporary constitution for a temporary period." As Abul-Fath noted in his 1962 memoir, "Nasser called me to his office [in late 1952] with some other journalists to convince us of the necessity to establish a totalitarian regime for three years, under the pretext that Egypt needed a period of transition."[66] No doubt, Abdel Kouddous was in the room for this discussion. Armed with his insider information, Abdel Kouddous, in contrast to Abul-Fath, who remained silent at the time, moved publicly to demand commitments from the Officers that they would not seek to extend their rule. Clearly, by December 1952, Abdel Kouddous still felt like he was in a position of privilege, authority, and influence to make these demands in print and direct the Officers. *Rose El Youssef*, despite serving as a platform of direct support and guidance for the Officers in the initial months after the coup, now found itself restored to its role of resisting, dissenting against, and even antagonizing those in power to call for democratic reform.

As Nasser gave an expansive front-page interview to friendly Ahmed Abul-Fath in *al-Misri* on 9 January 1953, Abdel Kouddous sounded the alarm about his anxieties in a daringly critical editorial that staged a pivotal moment in the birth of Arab dictatorship. Published on 12 January 1953 and written in the past tense, Abdel Kouddous positioned himself now as a former fellow revolutionary, reminiscing how he supported the Officers because of their mutually shared principles: "We believed in them because they're young nationalists indebted to a group of principles that we believe in with them. We participated with them in trying to achieve these principles. We believed in them because of these principles, their faith in them, and sacrifice for them."[67] This was an editorial of regret and anxiety, a means to excuse himself and explain how he could have been so wrong in his earlier assumptions. At this point in the article, Abdel Kouddous made a sudden shift: "We believed in them for these principles, not because they're officers in the army." Abdel Kouddous then moved to disavow the Officers as anything more than fellow revolutionaries with a popular mandate: "If the movement was military in its instrumentality, it wasn't military in its principles or goals. If its leaders are wearing military clothes, they still bear in their chests the people's principles—democracy, freedom, and the constitution, principles that they recorded themselves in their pamphlets before the movement and President Neguib supported in his speeches afterwards." Abdel Kouddous was therefore delivering a sharp critique, reminding the public—and the Officers—that he aligned himself with the military and called for them to govern on the basis of their explicit support for the principles of democracy on behalf of the people, not to establish a dictatorship.

Clearly now anxious and full of regret that he had demanded that they form a military government only three months earlier, Abdel Kouddous explained: "A few weeks after the movement, I called on these leaders to take up ministry posts under the presidency of Mohammed Neguib, but I didn't mean that they form a military dictatorship. The Officers couldn't be dictators as long as they believe in the principles that they're bound to and we know about them. I hold them completely responsible until they establish and achieve these principles and, after that, leave the ministry to return to the army or leave the army to remain in the ministry with a mandate from the people at the ballot box." For Abdel Kouddous, it was the mutually agreed upon principles of democracy and freedom that restricted the Officers and made it impossible for them to be dictators. Once democracy and freedom were solidified—once they completed their sole task as instruments of the people—the Officers could not continue to rule from the barracks.

After his actions in summer and fall 1952, Abdel Kouddous was now openly declaring his regret to the public. Adding to his horror, he clearly felt that he was the one who had pushed the Officers to take the steps toward dictatorship, based on the tragically mistaken assumption that his influence over them would continue. Not even five months after the coup, Abdel Kouddous could no longer suppress his anxieties. The possibility of the entrenchment of military dictatorship had suddenly become a stark reality. It had become increasingly clear that his ability to influence them had ended. He now articulated his opposition and anxiety about the direction they were headed, revealing his guilt and regret about what he had done, launching a desperate public attempt to influence and guide the Officers through the press perhaps one last time. As he declared at the end of this pivotal editorial, "We can finally reach true democracy if we see the road that we're traveling on." In other words, the current road was leading the country not to democracy but to permanent dictatorship. It was precisely this theme that Abdel Kouddous would take up in his 1955 novel, *The Barred Road*, which I discuss in the following chapter.

Although there is no written record of their interactions behind the scenes, the relationship between Abdel Kouddous and the Officers had clearly fallen apart by this time. Abdel Kouddous recalled decades later that the ongoing conflict between him and Nasser during this period made their relationship "truly tiresome."[68] His 12 January 1953 article almost certainly represented his final attempt to guide Nasser publicly when his efforts behind closed doors had failed. Ahmed Abul-Fath oversaw a special six-month anniversary edition of *al-Misri* that resembled the propaganda of the state-owned *al-Tahrir*; shockingly, *Rose El Youssef* did not celebrate the date at all. Two weeks later, Abdel Kouddous offered another act of dissent against Nasser when he published an editorial provocatively titled "No Dictator Is Just and No Just Person Is a Dictator."[69] Abdel Kouddous again called for the people to participate in the governing process, for more documented guarantees from the Officers, and for the formation of opposition parties. But he had special criticism for anyone contemplating dictatorship: "I don't believe in the lie that praises the 'just dictator.' The dictator can't be just as long as he is a dictator. . . . Justice only emanates from announced, clear, written principles." With this article he crossed the line. During the following months, Abdel Kouddous suddenly offered no direct criticism of the Officers, focusing instead on calling for the British to withdraw from the Suez or simply not writing editorials at all. In May 1953, when the magazine published an open letter to Nasser calling on him to welcome criticism and lift press censorship, it was not by Abdel Kouddous but by his mother, who now rarely wrote in the press.[70] By spring 1953, Abdel Kouddous's meetings with Nasser and the Officers had completely ended.[71] It was also around this time that the first edit of *God Is with Us* was refused a screening permit. Nasser had had enough of Abdel Kouddous.

Many have noted how Nasser became highly sensitive to rivals and friends in the wake of the coup. It was not only figures like Abdel Kouddous who rankled Nasser. It was also the Free Officers, many of whom, like Abdel Kouddous, felt that they had risked their lives for the revolution, only to be marginalized by Nasser. As Khaled Mohi El Din explained, "Right from the start, [Nasser] developed an acute awareness of the Free Officers who interfered in everything and spoke as if they were the makers of the movement."[72] Sadat also later depicted Nasser as quick to anger when challenged: "Nasser looked on any protests, any objection or criticism, any attempt at fact-finding or the least expression of resentment, as a counterrevolutionary reaction that must be ruthlessly crushed."[73] Clearly, Abdel Kouddous was completely out of step with the new Nasser.

As the one-year anniversary of the coup approached, the tensions between Nasser and Abdel Kouddous had become so severe that the decision was made to erase him from the revolution's history. Despite all the attention in the initial days and weeks after the coup on the Rotten Weapons scandal as well as Abdel Kouddous's emphatic promotion of his own role on the radio, in print, and in *God Is with Us*, the official celebration of the public one-year anniversary made no mention whatsoever of the Rotten Weapons or of Abdel Kouddous himself. For example, Neguib, Hussein Shafei, Khaled Mohi El-Din, and Sarwat Okasha—all founding members of the Free Officers—in their articles in the state-owned *al-Tahrir* magazine celebrating the first anniversary of the coup, did not mention the Rotten Weapons scandal at all, neither its existence during the Palestine War nor the role of the scandal in the press. Instead, both Okasha and Mohi El-Din rewrote history, claiming that it was the Officers' secret pamphlets that prepared opinion within the army and among the public for the "victory" of the coup.[74] Nasser, in his interview in the same issue of *al-Tahrir*, never mentioned the Rotten Weapons scandal, despite the importance that he had placed on it in the same magazine nine months earlier. Even the trial of the suspects in the case of the Rotten Weapons ended with a verdict of innocence on 10 June 1953, not coincidentally during this time; this ending to the scandal would not have been thinkable just months earlier.

The decision to remove Abdel Kouddous from the history of the coup is also reflected in the later memoirs and statements by the Free Officers. Mohammed Neguib never mentions that Abdel Kouddous was even present for the coup, instead claiming that he delegated Sadat to offer the prime minister position to Ali Maher.[75] Sadat and Baghdadi are the only Officers who later acknowledged that Abdel Kouddous was there, but they dismissed him as a journalist whose sole role was to show Sadat where Ali Maher lived.[76] Okasha went even further, explicitly denying that there were any rotten weapons at all: "As for what has been claimed to be the reason for the defeat of the Egyptian army in Palestine in 1948—the faultiness of the weapons and grenades that were in the hands of the army—this is something that I see as false. . . . All that happened was the explosion of four cannons by mistake as they were being loaded."[77]

Nasser himself went to great length to delegitimize both the Rotten Weapons scandal and Abdel Kouddous in *Philosophy of the Revolution*. In language that must have outraged Abdel Kouddous, Nasser wrote, "It is not true that the successful revolution of 1952 stemmed from what happened in the Palestine War; nor is it true that it was due to the defective weapons which caused the death of our men and officers. . . . These were only incidental causes."[78] As if denying the depiction of the Rotten Weapons in *God Is with Us*, Nasser also stressed that the scandal had no role in the formation of the Free Officers: "The day we conceived that idea [of the coup] was also long before the scandal of defective weapons broke upon us. The Free Officers were already in existence, and it was in fact their pamphlets which first sounded the alarm."[79] Seemingly insulting Abdel Kouddous directly, Nasser described how the intellectuals failed them before the coup: "We were not yet ready. So we set about seeking the views of leaders of opinion and the experience of those who were experienced. Unfortunately we were not able to obtain very much."[80] Stressing that they had no partners in the coup, Nasser declared: "We removed the former king without consulting anyone."[81] The final erasure of Abdel Kouddous arrived in the Egyptian Embassy biography of Nasser that accompanied the first edition of the English translation of *Philosophy of the Revolution*. This brief biography includes no mention of the Rotten Weapons scandal. Instead, it states about Nasser, "The tragedies and scandals he witnessed during his action in the Palestine war filled him with wrath against the responsible authorities, especially when he realized the Army's dire need for munitions and arms which were withheld from it."[82] In this version of events, authorities had simply deprived soldiers of weapons, not furnished them with defective arms.

By June 1953, the writing was on the wall. Abdel Kouddous had completely fallen out of favor. On 18 June 1953, the monarchy was finally abolished, and Egypt was declared a republic. Abdel Kouddous fully understood the gravity of the moment. Only four days later, on 22 June 1953, he published his final editorial during this period in opposition to the Officers, unloading his guilt at what he had done in the early period after the coup. He denied that he ever called for military dictatorship: "I didn't do that nor would I ever. I didn't ask them to take over the ministries because they're army officers, but because they're leaders of a revolution. Reality on the ground required them to take control of things, but for us to hold them completely accountable."[83] While the possibility of dissent was rapidly narrowing in his editorials, Abdel Kouddous clung to what he saw as his right to call the authorities to account: "We're still preparing ourselves for complete democracy immediately after the period of transition and the first right of democracy is to criticize ministers and guide them." With a mix of regret and anxiety, Abdel Kouddous tried to absolve himself of responsibility for the expanding military dictatorship, claiming that he had always operated on the assumption that the Officers were nothing more than fellow revolutionaries who shared his principles of freedom and democracy.

Between July 1953 and March 1954, when censorship was suddenly—and briefly—lifted, an episode that I discuss in the following chapter, Abdel Kouddous stopped almost all direct criticism of the Officers in his editorials, seemingly demonstrating to the public how the "first right of democracy" had indeed fallen. During this period, Abdel Kouddous directed almost all of his editorials away from Nasser and the Officers, writing instead about negotiations for British withdrawal and the trials of the Revolutionary Court. Nonetheless, Abdel Kouddous could not suppress his dissent. Instead of using his editorials as a means to criticize the Officers and protest the hijacking of his revolution, he turned to fiction. It was only when he infused his fiction with politics—as well as his outrage at the course of the revolution—that he became the most prolific and popular writer in the Arab world.

## I'M FREE!

Starting in the mid-1940s, Abdel Kouddous established himself as not only one of Egypt's most inflammatory and militant journalists but also as a controversial and popular writer of fiction. In most of his early short stories, which were all published in *Rose El Youssef*, he blurred the lines between fiction and autobiography, narrating the romantic adventures of an Egyptian journalist visiting Europe in the humorous style that he developed in his articles during the late 1930s and early 1940s. By the early 1950s, he began experimenting with novellas, invariably inserting a double of himself into the story. The first of these longer works, "Woman of the Salon," serialized between October and November 1950, depicts an affair between a French woman and a famous Egyptian journalist who leads newspaper campaigns against the rich on behalf of the poor. As if to underscore the confessional element of the story, Abdel Kouddous included a note with the final installment explaining that the heroine of the story had contacted him to express her concern that he might have revealed too much about their relationship.[84] In his next novella, "Dancer on Vacation," serialized between August and September 1951, Abdel Kouddous continued the confessional by depicting an affair between a German dancer and an Egyptian journalist on vacation on the island of Capri, which ironically is where he broke the Rotten Weapons scandal. This time, the links between the male protagonist and the writer were too strong for readers to ignore. Abdel Kouddous included a note with the second installment explaining that he had received dozens of letters and phone calls accusing him of being the protagonist of the story, even though he was a married man. Toying with his readers, he replied, "I don't want to deny or confirm what is said about me."[85] In his final novella before the coup, "Sunglasses," serialized between December 1951 and January 1952, he wrote himself into the narrative once again as a young revolutionary journalist having an affair with a foreign woman. In the last installment in *Rose El Youssef*,

Abdel Kouddous included a box declaring that he had suffered from "the lashes" of rumors accusing him of being the hero of the novella.[86] These early works only hint at the complex, provocative, and irrepressible ways that Abdel Kouddous would insert himself into his novels and short stories after the coup, using fiction as a medium for confession and therapy as well as to contest the trajectory of the revolution and defy Nasser.

It was on 22 June 1953—in the same issue of *Rose El Youssef* that he published his final editorial disavowing any support for military dictatorship—that Abdel Kouddous began serializing his first major fictional work after the coup, *I'm Free*. The title, whose adjective is feminine, just like the noun "Egypt" in Arabic, gestures ironically to the proclamation of the republic and Egypt's "freedom" as the one-year anniversary of the coup approached. In order to reinforce this point, each installment of *I'm Free* is framed with this ominous epigraph: "There's nothing called freedom. The one of us with the most freedom is a slave to the principles that he believes in and the goals that he's striving for. We demand freedom in order to put it at the service of our goals. Before you demand freedom, ask yourself: What goal will you dedicate it to?" In this, Abdel Kouddous suggests that freedom—the basic demand of the revolution—is not in itself an objective but only a means to an end. The revolution therefore did not end with freedom from the monarchy and the declaration of the republic. Rather, freedom is a tool that must be bound to principles in order to achieve an ambition larger than liberty. In this epigraph, under increasing pressures of censorship and restricted freedom of expression, Abdel Kouddous shifted the stakes for the revolution, resituating freedom as an instrument, not an objective. With the stage set in his editorial opening this same issue of *Rose El Youssef*, Abdel Kouddous in *I'm Free* shifted his critique from the journalistic to the fictional, suggesting that freedom without commitment to principles is tantamount to slavery to dictatorship.

As he did in *God Is with Us*, Abdel Kouddous employed *I'm Free* to establish himself as playing a central role in the origins of the revolution, protesting his marginalization and erasure in the one-year anniversary celebrations in real time. As he proclaimed in the editorial opening the same issue of the magazine, he was now turning to fiction as a "first right of democracy" to criticize Nasser and the expanding dictatorship now that the editorial was becoming barred before him as a means to do so. Fiction—and romantic melodrama in particular—became the vehicle to express his regret and guilt to the public about his own role in the coup to the public. It also provided him with a framework to interrogate his own failed romance with Nasser, how he had projected the principles and faith of democracy onto him, fully committing to him, only for Nasser to spurn him with no guarantees for the future.

Just as Abdel Kouddous inserted himself as a character into nearly all of his pre-revolution fiction, it quickly became clear that Amina, the heroine of the novel, functions as his double in the novel. Both grew up in Abbassia in the home of their paternal aunt and uncle. Like Abdel Kouddous, Amina did not know that her aunt was not her mother until she was an adolescent. Both had a mother who was a source of neighborhood rumors and remarried a wealthy older man. Both had a confrontational relationship with their surrogate parents and longed to break free of the conservatism of the childhood home. Both saw the freedom of the world of their biological parents as a sharp foil for their strict surrogate parents. Both revolted against the tradition and strict social expectations of the Abbassia neighborhood, seeking freedom based on principles. In this context, it is no coincidence that Amina's name means "faithful." Moreover, the novel begins in 1936, when both were in their mid-teens. This was not only the year in which Abdel Kouddous began writing for *Rose El Youssef*. It was also the year of the 1936 Treaty, the political event that would send both Abdel Kouddous and Nasser on the long road of revolution. As with Abdel Kouddous, so too Amina's awakening and drive for freedom originate in the same year. Finally, this was not the first time that Abdel Kouddous had played on his "female" name and had written himself into his fiction as a woman; he had employed the same technique in the 1948 short story "The New Generation" discussed in the previous chapter.

The parallels between Amina and Abdel Kouddous were so clear that Naguib Mahfouz casually mentioned in a 1956 public symposium that Amina simply was Abdel Kouddous.[87] It was an offhand comment, something that Mahfouz assumed was so obvious that it did not deserve elaboration. Nonetheless, Abdel Kouddous quickly published an angry response to Mahfouz, claiming that what he had said was a betrayal of friendship and collegiality.[88] Despite his public resistance to the association, it was around the same time that Abdel Kouddous spoke quite openly with actress Lobna Abdel Aziz about the links between himself and Amina. When he tried to convince Abdel Aziz to take on the role of Amina in the film version of *I'm Free*, Abdel Kouddous kept telling her: "You and me, we're both Amina!"[89] Decades later, Abdel Kouddous sheepishly admitted that Mahfouz had been correct, expressing his regret for the way he had publicly attacked his old friend.[90]

As the novel opens, Amina's aunt—her surrogate mother—slaps her for being late to school. This violence is the equivalent of the 1936 Treaty, the wakeup call that Amina is not free but lives under the chains of tradition and restriction, symbolized here by the generation of her aunt. The slap opens Amina's consciousness, pushing her to take the first step toward rebellion. She leaves the house and, instead of going to school, takes the streetcar into the city: "Amina clung to her revolt.... She wanted to be liberated, even if only for a single day."[91] Sitting inside the men's—and not the women's—compartment, Amina feels that she has taken revenge against tradition and seized control of her destiny by breaking strict social expectations. Nonetheless, she suddenly senses that she has undertaken her revolt for nothing: "She felt a huge confusing emptiness almost swallow her. Is freedom this huge emptiness?"[92] Amina impulsively acts out against her aunt's slap, liberating herself—at least temporarily—from the chains of Abbassia, her family, and school, but she quickly realizes that her revolt has achieved nothing.

Amina sets out on more acts of defiance and rebellion, failing to achieve freedom each time. Her aunt kicks her out of the house when she rejects an arranged marriage and insists on going to college instead. After attending the American University in Cairo, Amina regards her university degree as her "certificate of manumission.... She had become free."[93] She gets a job at an important American company, earning more money than she needs. Nonetheless, Amina again realizes that her latest revolt against tradition has failed: "She felt that there was something missing, like a huge emptiness was encircling her."[94] Like Abdel Kouddous when he repeatedly wrote in *Rose El Youssef* about his frantic struggle for freedom from colonialism during the 1940s, Amina realizes that she needs a man, a leader to guide her out of the wilderness toward salvation, to channel her revolt and compulsion for freedom. Since 1936, like Abdel Kouddous, Amina has groped for revolt; at each moment of apparent success, she believes that she has seized freedom only to be frustrated by failure. Rejecting the tradition of the Egyptian family, embracing European modernity, earning a university degree, and gaining financial independence in the workforce only bring Amina—as with the Egyptian nation under British colonialism—a false sense of freedom, one based on individualism and material success, not principles or larger goals. Like Abdel Kouddous in his *Rose El Youssef* editorials simmering with frustration during the 1940s and early 1950s, Amina has the innate drive for freedom, but she needs a leader to channel her revolt toward something bigger, to show her how to use freedom as a tool for principles. Just like Abdel Kouddous, who focused on finding his long-awaited masculine, virile leader to spark the revolution in Egypt in the years leading up to 23 July 1952, Amina suddenly realizes that she must put herself at the service of a man to achieve her independence and true freedom. "Only a man will fill this emptiness," she says.[95]

It is at this point that Amina suddenly remembers Abbas, her teenage love interest, and makes an appointment to see him. As in all of Abdel Kouddous's pre-coup novellas, a revolutionary journalist serving as his double now appears in the narrative. This time, it is Abbas, who, just like Abdel Kouddous, grew up in Abbassia, went to law school, and became a fiery journalist at an opposition magazine. The process of serialization, of writing each chapter only hours before the deadline for the magazine's print run, gave Abdel Kouddous the opportunity to write himself into the fictional text twice—first as Amina, who searches for years for freedom and revolt, and then as Abbas, the revolutionary journalist who will serve as the masculine leader whom she is seeking to bring her salvation.[96]

When Amina goes to see Abbas, she boasts to him that she is now free from the chains of their old neighborhood. Echoing Abdel Kouddous's epigraph, printed with each installment, the incredulous Abbas tells her: "Freedom is a means, not an end. I want freedom to write what I believe.... Egypt asks for freedom not because freedom is the end of the road. Not at all. But because the free state can serve its people and raise them up. If the road to freedom is difficult, the road after freedom is more difficult."[97] For Abbas—like Abdel Kouddous—freedom is not simply a goal, a tool for individual salvation. It must be put to use for the benefit of principles and ideals, to liberate Egypt from servitude.

**Figure 7.** Installment of *I'm Free* with Amina and Abbas. *Rose El Youssef*, 3 August 1953.

Freedom is an instrument, the means to struggle for justice and democracy to elevate the nation. When Amina asks him if there is no escape from slavery, Abbas tells her, "Love is the sole honorable excuse for slavery. People love their country, so they become a slave to it. They believe in a principle, so they become a slave to it."[98] Therefore, love of the nation and principle—not of the individual—represents total commitment and dedication.

Unsurprisingly, Abbas is quick to condemn the concept of freedom as slavery to a person. Echoing Abdel Kouddous's own anxieties about dictatorship at the time, Abbas tells Amina, "The slavery that has no excuse is to marry a man that you don't love and to do things that you don't believe in."[99] In this, marriage to a man serves as a national metaphor not simply for Egypt's romance with Nasser but also for the country's enslavement to him. Directly evoking his 22 June 1953 editorial, Abdel Kouddous also declares through Abbas that acting against one's principles is inexcusable. Unprincipled slavery to a person without love or conviction is therefore tantamount to embracing dictatorship. Through his fictional double, Abdel Kouddous was disavowing Nasser in plain view of the nation.

Amina leaves this initial exchange with the charismatic journalist infected by the encounter. She thinks about the various "men" who have set off revolutions in different countries and then finds herself "imagining all these heroes in the image of Abbas."[100] Predictably, now that Amina has finally encountered her long-awaited leader, revolution immediately flares up within her. She realizes that her job has oppressed her since she was simply selling herself to the capitalist interests of a Western corporation. She has become a slave to Western materialism with no nationalist purpose or goal: "She didn't believe in anything. She only believed in herself her whole life. . . . She decided to look for faith, faith in something, a faith that fills this enormous emptiness that surrounds her and establishes a cause and a goal for the freedom that she's proud of."[101] Seeing Abbas as a means to faith and a larger goal, she begins visiting him at his magazine office to talk about revolution, principles, and the nationalist mission for freedom.

With this move, Abdel Kouddous establishes himself—not Nasser—as the revolutionary leader, the man who sparks the revolution. Abbas, like Abdel Kouddous, becomes the leader who will convince the nation to put freedom at the service of a higher goal. In *I'm Free*—as in *God Is with Us*—the leader who achieves revolution is not a member of a clandestine group of mutinous army officers. Instead, it is the revolutionary journalist who becomes the long-awaited leader, guiding the nation, now represented by Amina, to strive for justice to give birth to the new Egypt. In the shelved *God Is with Us*, Abdel Kouddous depicted the Rotten Weapons scandal as producing revolutionary consciousness. In *I'm Free*, there is no mention of the scandal at all, yet another indication that it was the depiction of the Rotten Weapons and the journalist as leader of the Free Officers that led the censor to reject the initial version of the film. With *God Is with Us* stymied by the censor for the foreseeable future, Abdel Kouddous now turned to the serialized novel to re-center himself in the origins and importance of the revolution. Just as Abdel Kouddous had been erased from the first anniversary of the revolution, he returned the favor to Nasser. Shockingly, *I'm Free* elides the Free Officers entirely. Reestablishing the role of *Rose El Youssef* in the buildup to the coup, it is the magazine office—and not the barracks—that becomes the site for the outbreak of revolution.

Nonetheless, identifying the revolutionary leader renders Amina passive. Suggesting Abdel Kouddous's own anxieties about his sense of ownership of the revolution yet waiting for the Officers to act in the buildup to the coup, Amina recedes into the background and looks to Abbas to lead: "She didn't feel the need to participate with the comrades in their plots and revolution. It was enough for her that Abbas was plotting and revolting, as if every word was her word, every plot was inspired by her, every revolt was ignited by her."[102] When Amina joins an organization to help the poor, Abbas grips and shakes her, echoing Abdel Kouddous's inflammatory editorials from before the revolution by shouting, "The people have to revolt. We have to burn everything down with us. We can't build unless we destroy!"[103] Amina savors the pain spreading through her arm from Abbas's hands and submits to him, as if he were lighting a blaze within her. At this moment of violence, Abbas asserts himself on her as a man in the form of a new, young, virile masculinity.

As Tarek El-Ariss has argued, Nasser represented the emergence of a new kind of masculinity in Egypt, one that articulates a virile Arab modernity that would culminate in dictatorship.[104] Abbas in *I'm Free* would be the first time that Abdel Kouddous framed and presented this new kind of masculinity to the public through the form of romantic melodrama. Amina becomes fully aroused by this new, virile, masculine figure. Just as Nasser was the "man" that Abdel Kouddous thought he had been seeking, Amina finds her savior in Abbas: "She found her faith. She believes in this man."[105] Paralleling the nation—and, perhaps, Abdel Kouddous's own regrets in the aftermath of the coup—once Amina is convinced in the leader's principles, faith, and masculinity, she becomes submissive.

This passivity is depicted in *I'm Free* by Amina's sudden self-domestication. She performs her commitment to Abbas by taking on the role of the ideal housewife: "She felt that her natural place was the kitchen. She hoped that she'd spend her entire life there making food for Abbas. She felt, as Abbas said laughing, that she oppressed herself when she spent her life getting an education and working for an American company. The first thing she should have learned was cooking so she could make meals for him."[106] She serves Abbas, becoming a slave to him. And, thanks to this, "Abbas achieved his revolution."[107] Abbas, the revolutionary journalist—not a member of the army—succeeded in liberating the country because of Amina's self-domestication. *I'm Free* therefore presents an alternative history of the 23 July Revolution, one in which there are no Free Officers and no Rotten Weapons, only a revolutionary journalist and his romance with the self-sacrificing lover who is convinced that freedom is not a search for selfish pleasure but a sacrifice for principles to support the leader. Only through the union of the committed revolutionary leader and the people willing to sacrifice personal freedom for the nation does the journalist achieve "his revolution" and does Egypt gain its freedom.

Nonetheless, as with Abdel Kouddous's relationship with Nasser after the coup, Amina's bond with Abbas after the revolution is, to the surprise of no one, highly anxious. Like Egypt, Amina has sacrificed her freedom and independence for Abbas to achieve the revolution—she has become a slave to a man—but, like Abdel Kouddous, she receives no guarantees in return. Shockingly for the time, Amina does not live with Abbas, and they do not get married, even though Amina has sacrificed her future, career, and livelihood for him. The novel ends by explaining, "They might get married tomorrow, the next day, or next year. They might not ever get married and their love might get lost. Their story is not yet finished. Only time will finish it."[108] When people ask if they will marry, Amina gets angry and yells at them nervously, "I'm free!"

These two words form the last words—as well as the title—of the novel, but they betray deep anxiety. Amina, like Abdel Kouddous after the coup, nervously realizes that she has committed everything to the revolutionary leader, projecting principles and faith onto him, sacrificing her future livelihood, and surrendering her freedom to him so that he could achieve his revolution. By yelling nervously at friends who ask if she will marry Abbas, Amina reveals that, like Abdel Kouddous in summer 1953, she cannot suppress her anxieties, and she cannot articulate them either. Is Abbas yet another—but much more consequential—phase of a misguided revolt for freedom? Has she sacrificed her future to become a permanent slave to a man under the pretext of freedom? Is she trying to repress her anxieties—perhaps like Abdel Kouddous himself—that the revolutionary leader has betrayed the nation, compelling it to domestication by exploiting fantasies of principles and faith? Has she naïvely risked everything by projecting her desires and fantasies onto a man who will soon betray her?

With this ending—a lifetime commitment to the revolutionary leader without guarantees—Abdel Kouddous used fiction not only to stage the embedding of dictatorship through metaphor but also to demand, in his way, that the Officers provide in writing the democratic basis of their rule. By late 1952, Abdel Kouddous had been calling for written clarity for the contours of the transitional period as well as the formation of a political party that represented the principles of the Free Officers in the political arena and elections. He called for formal, written assurances—the documentation that Amina lacks at the end of the novel—from the Officers that they still shared his faith in constitutional democracy and rule of law. Amina has enslaved herself to Abbas—as Egypt and Abdel Kouddous have enslaved themselves to Nasser and the Free Officers—but Abbas has provided no formal commitment or legal guarantees to her. Up until June 1953, Abdel Kouddous was still openly calling for written commitment from the Officers that they would foster democracy, not dictatorship. When it was no longer possible to do so in his editorials, Abdel Kouddous transformed his fiction from serving as a confession of affairs with women to confessing his "affair" with Nasser, revealing his deep anxieties about the impact and consequences of their relationship for the nation.

When Abdel Kouddous finished serializing the novel on 17 August 1953, the relationship between him and Nasser—like the relationship between Nasser and the nation—was still unresolved, despite the increasing entrenchment of dictatorship. The Egyptian press was cratering under the increasing restrictions of censorship, and Abdel Kouddous, among other journalists, was forced to abandon the great bulk of political criticism in his editorials. Fiction became the only way for him not only to express his regret and anxieties but also to reassert what he saw as his centrality in the origins and trajectory of the revolution. In several interviews throughout his career, Abdel Kouddous stressed that there was no dividing line between his political editorials and his novels, even though the public never seemed to acknowledge this. As he explained in the 1970s, "I write fiction living politics and I write politics living fiction."[109] He acknowledged in one interview that *I'm Free* was indeed a "political novel," even though it has never been analyzed as such before this chapter.[110] In an interview not published until after his death, Abdel Kouddous spoke openly about the way he used fiction as a political vehicle: "When a writer in unable to express his opinion directly, he has to find another way. What could be called a distancing happened between me and the leaders of the July Revolution as a result of the difference of our opinions on principles so I devoted myself to writing novels whose heroes expressed political and national currents."[111] It was this blurred line between the two that would produce fertile terrain for his writing and turn his fiction into a vehicle for dissent when all other avenues were barred. *I'm Free* represents his first work to use fiction as political critique, attempting to subvert the censor—and avoid prison, or worse—in the process.

Abdel Kouddous knew that Nasser was a devoted reader of his work. He knew that Nasser would read his novel as a protest against dictatorship, asserting that slavery to a man—and not democracy—was unacceptable. Now that their relationship had frayed to the point that they were no longer speaking, fiction serialized in the press—not the editorial or personal communication—became the medium through which Abdel Kouddous would communicate directly with Nasser and protest what had happened to his cherished revolution. Abdel Kouddous knew that Nasser would understand that he was positioning the journalist—and not an army officer—as the novel's revolutionary hero, undoing the erasure that Nasser had performed on him. Just as the verdict on Amina's freedom was still up for grabs at the end of *I'm Free* when it was concluded in August 1953, Abdel Kouddous's relationship with Nasser had yet to be resolved. That would soon change.

CHAPTER THREE

# THE PSYCHOLOGY OF THE REVOLUTION

> [Nasser] . . . had been in the grip of "complexes" since childhood and was often motivated by them; and he, as well as many of his entourage, suffered as a result.
>
> —*Anwar Sadat,*
> In Search of Identity *(1977)*

On 24 February 1954, Ihsan Abdel Kouddous left Cairo for a trip to Saudi Arabia. Soon after he arrived, he had a private audience with King Saud. The two men drank traditional Saudi bitter coffee as they discussed the ongoing British occupation of the Suez. Abdel Kouddous was delighted when the king told him, "Make a plan and we'll stand with you on the front line. We'll sacrifice everything since life without dignity is not worth protecting."[1] Around this time, Abdel Kouddous in his editorials had been calling for the Free Officers to confront the British in the Suez in order to gain full independence. In what must have stood in stark contrast with how he saw the Officers at the time as dragging their feet in confronting the British, here was an Arab leader who recognized that dignity and principles were more important than anything else. The conversation must have inflamed Abdel Kouddous's anger and disappointment with what was happening to the revolution back home.

Abdel Kouddous tried to clear his mind by going to Mecca to perform the ritual circumambulation of the Kaaba. Nonetheless, it was difficult for him, at least at first, to focus on the divine. It was not until the sixth turn around the Kaaba that Abdel Kouddous finally became immersed in the moment. He fell down on the wall of the Kaaba and gripped its curtains with his hand. "I saw God at that moment," he wrote. "I saw Him in my heart, in my chest. What do I ask of Him? Images crowded before my eyes—my mother, father, wife, sons, friends, Egypt. As soon as I began to pray for one, the image of another jumped before my eyes before I could utter a word. Then I heard my lips say: 'Please God, justice!' That's the only thing I said."[2] Even in this moment of personal connection with the divine, it was his deep desire for justice—presumably for himself, the nation, and his cherished revolution—that rose up from within, taking precedence over family and friends.

During this visit, Abdel Kouddous also saw what he hoped would be the future. On 25 February 1954, he went with Prince Abdullah bin Faisal al-Saud, Saudi minister of the interior at the time, to the airport in Jeddah to welcome Colonel Adib Shishakli, the president of Syria who had just fled Damascus after a coup. Abdel Kouddous had seen Shishakli earlier during a visit to Cairo. "He was strong and smiling so confidently that he puffed up his chest, almost breaking his ribs," he wrote. This image of confidence, however, did not match the broken man disembarking from the plane, who at that moment was seeking refuge from his own people. Abdel Kouddous wrote, "This can't be Adib Shishakli. This man is weak and broken, his back bent and eyes wandering.... All of the Syrian people have abandoned him."[3] Here was a once bold, masculine, and fearless military ruler who rose to power via a coup now rendered feeble and forlorn because he had lost the support of his people. The symbolism for Abdel Kouddous was obvious.

The wretched Shishakli asked to visit the Kaaba. When he went to the holy shrines accompanied by his armed guards, Abdel Kouddous was appalled: "Even in the hands of God, this man could not free himself from fear. Fear of whom? Of God or the people?" Shishakli did not feel safe even in the care of the divine. After circumambulating the Kaaba and returning to the palace, Shishakli still could not free himself from anxiety. Even though the Saudi government had taken responsibility for his protection, the paranoid Shishakli insisted on posting armed guards next to him at all times. When a servant entered Shishakli's bedroom in the morning, he found dozens of cigarette butts tossed beside mounds of ash in the tray next to the bed. In order to make the symbolism explicit, Abdel Kouddous wrote, "This ash is the end of dictatorship, of every dictator! Shishakli met his end in a pile of ash, just like something you brush off your clothes." The dictator had not simply been expelled from his country after losing the faith of the people. He had internalized their rejection, becoming a paranoid, shattered man who could not feel safe anywhere, even close to God. For Abdel Kouddous, Shishakli, a double for Nasser, of justice embodied in his misery, was now just piled-up ash waiting to be dumped out and tossed to the wind.

Abdel Kouddous must have seen the fate of the Syrian dictator at that moment as a hopeful omen for the historic events that were happening back home. On 24 February 1954, the day Abdel Kouddous left for this trip, tensions between Mohammed Neguib and Gamal Abdel Nasser boiled over, prompting the Revolutionary Command Council (RCC), the governing body ruling Egypt, to accept Neguib's resignation as president. The RCC then denounced Neguib as a tyrant, leading to street protests supporting him and Neguib's return to the presidency a few days later. This sparked the March Crisis, a month-long conflict during which the supporters of Neguib and Nasser struggled against each other for control of the political playing field. Abdel Kouddous followed events as closely as he could from Saudi Arabia. During the last days of February, some thirty people came to Abdel Kouddous's hotel room to demand information. Abdel Kouddous once again had the opportunity to feel ownership for the politics of Egypt. He wrote, "They were holding me responsible for the entire revolution." After his erasure back home, he must have enjoyed the attention.

On 5 March 1954, the RCC unexpectedly announced the end of press censorship, sparking a brief, unprecedented period of freedom of expression. Abdel Kouddous rushed back to Cairo in time for the next issue of *Rose El Youssef*, desperate to seize the opportunity to air his long-simmering grievances about the trajectory of the revolution and the increasing entrenchment of military dictatorship. A number of journalists, including Ahmed Abul-Fath, published articles attacking the Officers, demanding that they take steps to implement democracy. Abdel Kouddous, upon his return, finally had the chance to reassert his authority over the revolution, to try to set it back on the road that he had originally envisioned. He had the opportunity once again to play the role of Muhsin in *God Is with Us*, to demonstrate his commitment to the revolution by directing the Officers, pushing them to act for the good of the nation and to serve as a tool of the people to prepare the way for the emergence of democracy. Like Abbas in *I'm Free*, he would argue that simply enjoying freedom was not enough. It had to be put at the service of goals and principles, not a dictator. Over the following two weeks, Abdel Kouddous published three editorials, reestablishing himself in public as the conscience of the revolution. These editorials marked a sudden yet brief return to open dissent for Abdel Kouddous, a flash of revival of his public oppositional spirit of the 1940s and early 1950s, a desperate final call to save his cherished revolution.

The three editorials that Abdel Kouddous wrote during the March Crisis stand as a turning point in his career. They resulted in his arrest in April 1954 and his subsequent three-month imprisonment, giving him a full taste of the abuses of dictatorship. They fundamentally changed his relationship with Nasser, repositioning him from a recalcitrant fellow revolutionary to an anxious subject under Nasser's rule. They led to deep soul searching about his personal role in laying the groundwork for the coup and his participation in events afterwards. When Abdel Kouddous was arrested once again in late 1954—this time seemingly at the whim of the military police—he would become utterly disillusioned with the revolution and even more disturbed by his role in bringing the Free Officers to power.

This final arbitrary arrest was the moment when Abdel Kouddous experienced a painful, deep, and permanent split from the revolution, when he fully understood that it had been irreversibly derailed toward dictatorship, sending him into a tailspin of doubt and anxiety. While he continued to write political editorials after this split, as was expected of any leading journalist at the time, Abdel Kouddous would never again publish direct political criticism against Nasser. Starting in early 1955, soon after the second arrest, he sought refuge from the censor—and indeed, avoid another jailing or even worse—by channeling his dissent to popular, serialized, romantic melodrama, resuming what he had done in *I'm Free*. In this, he used metaphor and symbolism, not the direct critique of his earlier editorials, to contest the trajectory of the revolution and, with Nasser as his devoted reader, to dissent against and try to guide the dictator himself. Abdel Kouddous also used fiction to explore his shame at vacillating between accommodating the regime and rebelling against it, to self-analyze, and to try to manage his irrepressible despair at his deep sense of responsibility for inadvertently leading to the entrenchment of military dictatorship in Egypt.

## "THE SECRET GANG THAT RULES EGYPT"

In his first article after the end of press censorship, published on 15 March 1954 and optimistically entitled "We're Moving on the Natural Inevitable Road of the Revolution," Abdel Kouddous insisted, with perhaps false optimism, that the country could only be heading toward parliamentary democracy.[4] He returned to a familiar argument from his editorials in summer and fall 1952—that by eliminating the monarchy, dissolving the political parties, cancelling the constitution, and sweeping away the old elite, the army was simply serving as the instrument for the will of the people: "The Officers acted and launched the revolution when the people felt their inability to carry it out themselves. It's therefore an executive, not a legislative revolution." Since the army is serving simply as a tool of the people, it could not do anything that opposed their will. Because of this, Abdel Kouddous declared, "The army cannot turn the parliamentary democratic system into a military dictatorship." Abdel Kouddous ended the editorial with a stark warning: "Anyone who tries to lead the revolution in this direction is a fool who understands nothing and whose efforts will only end in catastrophe." With this admonition, Abdel Kouddous pointed the finger directly at Nasser, using language that would have been impossible barely a week earlier to warn him about the consequences of dictatorship.

The following week, on 22 March 1954, Abdel Kouddous published the most dramatic and best-known article of his journalistic career, "The Secret Gang That Rules Egypt."[5] In case there was any doubt about who belonged to this secret organization, the layout of the article in *Rose El Youssef* included striking illustrations of the faces of Mohammed Neguib, Gamal Abdel Nasser, Abdellatif Baghdadi, and Khaled Mohi El Din. Dramatically escalating his confrontation with the Officers from the previous week, Abdel Kouddous begins the article by asking, "Who's ruled Egypt since the rise of the army's movement? Is it the RCC? What do you know about the RCC and what goes on in it?" He then bitterly

Figure 8. "The Secret Gang That Rules Egypt." *Rose El Youssef*, 22 March 1954.

points to his own distancing from the Officers over the previous months by asking, "What does any ordinary Egyptian know about the RCC except that either he's a close companion of its members or banished from them? Nothing, nothing at all!" According to Abdel Kouddous, the members of the RCC continued to operate exactly as they had when they were planning the coup—as a clandestine gang plotting their moves in secret. The RCC simply issued its decisions with no explanation in the same way that they distributed their secret pamphlets during the monarchy. This means that they were still a secret organization made up of military officers, working in isolation from the people, deciding what they wanted without consultation or explanation. In other words, Abdel Kouddous admits what he had denied the previous week—the RCC are operating as a shadowy military dictatorship. Abdel Kouddous is then explicit about what he had only hinted at in earlier editorials: "The only way to restore the people's trust is for the leaders to work like a governing body, not a secret gang, for the revolution to end!" The time had come to eliminate exceptional measures and implement democratic governance. Without ending the revolution immediately, its presumed fundamental goal of leading the country to democracy would be undermined, and the country would instead be entrenched in dictatorship.

On 29 March 1954, Abdel Kouddous published his third and final editorial in the series openly challenging Nasser and the Free Officers.[6] He insisted that it was impossible for men like Gamal Abdel Nasser and Anwar Sadat to go back to saluting superiors and following orders after leading the revolution, ruling Egypt, and setting socioeconomic and political policy. Abdel Kouddous also declared that the RCC could not return to the barracks because of their financial dealings: "They have set up huge commercial and semi-commercial establishments for them to supervise." The only choice was for the Free Officers to leave the army and form a political party that would be accountable to the people through the ballot box. As he had already argued in *Rose El Youssef* in fall 1952, this party would represent the principles and achievements of the revolution and include not only the members of the RCC but also allied soldiers and civilians who believed in its political, social, and economic program.[7] Without forming this party, Abdel Kouddous argued once again, Egypt would simply be a shadowy military dictatorship with tentacles extending throughout the economy. The only hope to avert dictatorship was for a new party of the Officers to contest other political parties representing other constituencies in free and fair elections. Abdel Kouddous ended the editorial by singling out Nasser, this time by name, calling on him to act on behalf of the nation: "I want him to strike a new example of sacrifice and leave the army. I want him to acknowledge reality and declare that he is a president of a political party. . . . He's the one responsible for its activities, whether he admits it or not. I want him to strike a new example and turn his organization over to the people." As he had done in the press before the coup, Abdel Kouddous, full of faith and confidence, called out to Nasser to take on the role of the hero and bring salvation to the nation. Instead of eliminating the old guard and overturning the monarchy, Abdel Kouddous was making a last-ditch effort to guide Nasser away from military dictatorship. It would be the last time that Abdel Kouddous would be so blunt.

### THE ARREST

Political uncertainty continued into April 1954, but freedom of expression did not. The RCC restored press censorship on 28 March 1954, the date of Abdel Kouddous's third and final editorial. On 29 March 1954, the RCC moved quickly to "silence independent political discourse in the media."[8] As Mohammed Neguib wrote derisively soon after this period, "The press, instead of using its freedom to enlighten the public, indulged in an orgy of misinformation."[9] Reading the writing on the wall, Ahmed Abul-Fath, whose articles during the March Crisis also called for the Officers to leave the army for civilian life and form a new political party, fled the country on 15 March 1954 immediately after meeting with Nasser at his home.[10] According to Abul-Fath, Nasser became so angry with him that he told a fellow member on the RCC that "Abul-Fath isn't directing journalists, but a gang."[11] On 4 May 1954 authorities shut down *al-Misri* for good.

Abdel Kouddous, however, had been much more direct and critical of the Officers than Abul-Fath. He was the only one to name Nasser in his criticisms and to call explicitly for the end of the revolution. It cannot have taken Abdel Kouddous long to realize that he was in trouble. As Nasser and his supporters began their clean-up operation in the wake of the March Crisis, Abdel Kouddous did not publish another editorial for four weeks, a particularly long silence for him. On 14 April 1954, the RCC dissolved the Council for the Union of the Press on the charge that seven of its members, including *Rose El Youssef*, had taken secret funds from the palace before the revolution. This was an accusation that Abdel

Kouddous would later bitterly deny, claiming that Nasser had concocted the charge out of anger at his March Crisis articles.[12] Predictably, his next editorial included no comments on Nasser, the March Crisis, or the corruption charges. Nonetheless, Nasser had not forgotten about Abdel Kouddous. By the end of April, it was time to teach his former co-revolutionary a lesson. The secret police arrested Abdel Kouddous on 28 April 1954. He then spent ninety-five days in the military prison.

While Abdel Kouddous was in jail, *Rose El Youssef* never acknowledged his absence. As an act of protest, Fatima Youssef saw to it that the magazine did not publish any news or caricatures whatsoever about the revolution or the Officers, as if they did not exist. Instead, the magazine's editorials and covers focused on the 1954 Geneva Conference, which took place during this time and centered on matters related to the end of the Korean and the First Indochina Wars. Fatima Youssef also expressed her displeasure by printing a number of provocative headlines between May and July 1954 seemingly aimed at Nasser, such as "All That . . . for Defending the Free World?" and "This Is the Only Road to a Free World."[13] The cover of the magazine marking the second anniversary of the coup was particularly inflammatory. Instead of celebrating Nasser and the revolution, like other prominent magazines and newspapers at the time, the cover instead features a stunning caricature of the exiled king on an Italian beach surrounded by women admirers with the cold description "Today celebrates two years since the expulsion of Farouk." A European officer presents him with a worn military boot as a "letter" from Egypt.

The Officers took note. First, Fatima Youssef was asked to meet with Nasser to discuss the matter but she refused, allegedly retorting that "she doesn't work for rulers, not by free will nor by fear."[14] After the Officers faced this "barred road," as Abdel Kouddous later called it, they sent the military censor of the press along with Mohamed Hassanein Heikal, who would become the foremost articulator of Nasserist ideology, to ask her to resume printing news about the revolution and the Officers. Outraged, she reportedly told them, "I won't negotiate even if the price is the freedom of my only son or his life! . . . I will not write a single word about any of you, even if you execute my son without giving me the chance to see him again."[15] It seemed that Heikal and his companion had hit a nerve.

**Figure 9.** Cover of *Rose El Youssef*, 26 July 1954.

After a month and a half of solitary confinement, Abdel Kouddous was shocked when his mother arrived suddenly to visit him in his cell. As already mentioned, he had a particularly tense relationship with his mother over the years, repeatedly trying to earn her praise only to be humiliated in return, both publicly and privately. In 1955, Abdel Kouddous wrote with surprising openness about what it was like to work for her at the magazine in the early 1940s: "She convinced everyone there that I was nothing and I wouldn't ever be anything. She insulted me and hit me in front of the editors. I passed through violent psychological crises.... All I felt was that I was oppressed, that I wasn't getting from my mother the appreciation that I deserved."[16] Yet she did not only publicly humiliate him, ridicule his creative writing, and disapprove of his marriage. With her connections to the old guard, she came to represent for Abdel Kouddous the failures of the entire political system that he was trying to overthrow. In an interview published in 2022, Abdel Kouddous explained, "I'd fight with my mother about the political direction of the country.... I called for overturning the entire political system in Egypt, beginning with the British, the king, and the political parties. But my mother completely believed in this system.... Despite our differences, I'd hug her at home, but then I'd go back to the office to fight with her about politics."[17] It seems likely that Abdel Kouddous's lifelong desire to please his mother had shifted from trying to win her praise through his writing to earning her respect by working with the youth of his generation—the Free Officers, among others—to overturn the political system in Egypt. Perhaps that was a new strategy for him to convince her to retire and to rely on him. At the same time, she must have perceived his revolt against the old political system as a personal attack against her.

Before the coup, she was certainly not pleased at her son conspiring with Nasser and the Officers. As Abdel Kouddous explained in 1983, "It got to the point that she was always telling me that my opinions were against my interests."[18] While we have no direct record of the conflict between them in the period between the coup and April 1954, it was clear that she was furious at him at the time of his arrest. Just as she had lashed out at him as a teenager for anonymously publishing a poem in her newspaper and humiliated him in front of other journalists at the magazine in the 1940s, she was ready to do it again, this time for what she saw as his naïveté and impulsiveness in helping to bring Nasser to power.

In his cell, Youssef angrily told her son about her exchange with Heikal and the censor. It must have been painful for Abdel Kouddous to hear her explain so coldly that she was willing to let them execute him. Nonetheless, he tried to reason with her, explaining that, by refusing them, she was gambling with not only his life but also the future of the magazine. He was afraid that she was blind to the dangers of the new era, arguing that "it's different this time." Youssef then gave him a mocking smile because, according to Abdel Kouddous, he "had not understood the dictatorial intentions that these friends were hiding when they spoke enthusiastically about freedom, democracy, and the will of the people before the revolution."[19] In taunting him for denying the danger of the Officers and not appreciating his own projections and fantasies about them, she was hitting him where it hurt. His arrest and imprisonment only proved her point. He had symbolically replaced her with Nasser in a way that strikingly recalls Lynn Hunt's formulation of Freud's "family romance." For Hunt, the fiction of the French Revolution reflected the collective political unconscious of the era as framed by fictional narratives of family relations. "They imagined replacing them—the king and the queen—with a different kind of family, one in which the parents were effaced and the children, especially the brothers, acted autonomously," she wrote.[20] Just as Abdel Kouddous acted out with his presumed brother Nasser, it was now Youssef's turn to reject her son. Making it clear that she valued principles more than him, she told him, "If I had to choose between my only son being executed or lowering my head in submission to the tyrant, I refuse to bow down, whatever the price."[21]

Facing her humiliation and rejection from his prison cell, Abdel Kouddous articulated his impulse to accommodate the regime rather than face jail or worse, an instinct that would reemerge repeatedly with Nasser in the years ahead. He told her, "The revolution is reality. Whether we face it with courage or we try to deceive ourselves by ignoring it, it exists." While Abdel Kouddous accepted that the Officers were here to stay, he explained how he had tried to manage that disappointment for himself: "Don't forget that the revolution is one thing and those who bear its banner or speak in its name are something else." He was splitting the abstract ideal of the revolution as he imagined it before the coup from the men now carrying it out. In this way, Abdel Kouddous continued to justify his earlier work to overthrow the old system. It was Nasser who had unexpectedly become a tyrant in the aftermath of the coup, corrupting the pure revolution. His mother was horrified. In yet another act of shaming and humiliation, she responded, "Are you that weak? Or have they succeeded in teaching you cowardice?"[22]

Abdel Kouddous spoke about his spring 1954 jailing in numerous interviews starting in 1974, but he only discussed his mother's visit to his cell and this exchange once, suggesting how sensitive and painful it was for him. It underscores how his shame at inadvertently helping the Officers hijack his cherished revolution was not simply his own guilt and regret. It embodied the shame, scorn, and disappointment of his mother, the grand dame of journalism and pillar in his life whom he could never seem to satisfy. He had risked everything to spark and embed the revolution in the dream of ending the corruption of the old era and giving birth to a democratic Egypt. He had tried to position himself as the leader of the revolution, the one who created the conditions that would permit his mother—and her generation—to stay home in comfort and retire. Now that his dream had been hijacked and he had experienced firsthand the abuse of military dictatorship, his instinct was now to accommodate the regime in order to stay alive. Thanks to his mother, that instinct for survival paradoxically became yet another source of shame and regret. Before leaving her son, Youssef could not resist one final act of humiliation. For her, not only had her son brought the dictator to power, but he was now perpetuating dictatorship by looking to accommodate Nasser. She told him, "Tyranny—any tyranny—only continues if it is confident that the ground has become sterile and can no longer produce someone who says no." It was the contradiction between his instinct to accommodate the Officers—to accept the revolution as reality—and shame at his mother's disappointment that he would carry with him for years beyond the bars of his jail cell.

When Abdel Kouddous was still not released after his mother's visit, his wife, Lola, took her demands to Nasser himself. She managed to track down Nasser's direct phone number from her nephew, who was a major general in the army. Surprising Nasser on the phone, she confronted him, wanting to know why her husband was in jail and demanding his release.[23] Abdel Kouddous finally left prison on 31 July 1954. Perhaps his mother knew about his impending release because she finally relented and printed news about Nasser—albeit a small article—in the 26 July 1954 issue of the magazine. As I discussed in the introduction, upon his return from jail, Abdel Kouddous was forced nearly every day for a month to have a meal with Nasser, who claimed that he was supplying Abdel Kouddous with "psychological treatment."

There are numerous ways to interpret Nasser's comment. First, it is essential to remember that, as Omnia El Shakry has shown, Freud and discussions of psychoanalysis were "nothing short of ubiquitous in postwar Egypt and the Arab World."[24] El Shakry traces how, partly thanks to Yusuf Murad, psychoanalytic concepts like unconscious drives had become popularized through translations of Freud's work in the 1930s and 1940s. As El Shakry shows, the Officers were so interested in psychology that they recruited Murad in the weeks after the coup "to introduce psychological and intelligence testing into the military, and to create psychological clinics alongside medical clinics."[25] Yet it was not just that psychoanalytic concepts were circulating in popular discourse and part of the reforms initiated by the Officers after taking power. In *Philosophy of the Revolution*, Nasser depicted himself as suffering from a "psychological crisis" in the buildup to the coup.[26] Sadat also later depicted Nasser as being "in the grip of 'complexes' since childhood and was often motivated by them."[27] Even Mohammed Neguib, toying with the title of Nasser's book, characterized his split with Nasser not as "philosophy" but as "the psychology of revolution."[28] Clearly, psychology and psychoanalysis were on Nasser's mind.

As mentioned, Nasser was a devoted reader of Abdel Kouddous both before and after the coup. In late 1953, soon before the March Crisis, Abdel Kouddous serialized *Where's My Life?*, his first work of fiction since *I'm Free*. In this novel, Abdel Kouddous once again utilizes a female character—this time named Aliya—as his fictional double. As a teenager, Aliya is married off to a much older man, "Uncle" Aziz, the symbol of the exploitative and corrupt prerevolutionary elite. Uncle Aziz's sudden death—the overthrow of the old guard—liberates Aliya, giving her the opportunity to reclaim her stolen youth and revolt against past abuse. Nonetheless, Aliya is unable to shake the trauma of the past and embrace the present after her husband's symbolic death. Like Amina in *I'm Free*, Aliya does not know how to use her hard-fought freedom for a larger goal until she finds her male leader. Instead of contacting a revolutionary journalist, Aliya makes an appointment with Uncle Aziz's physician, Dr. Khaled, who awakens her sexually with his youth, virility, and masculinity. As discussed in chapter 1, Abdel Kouddous had

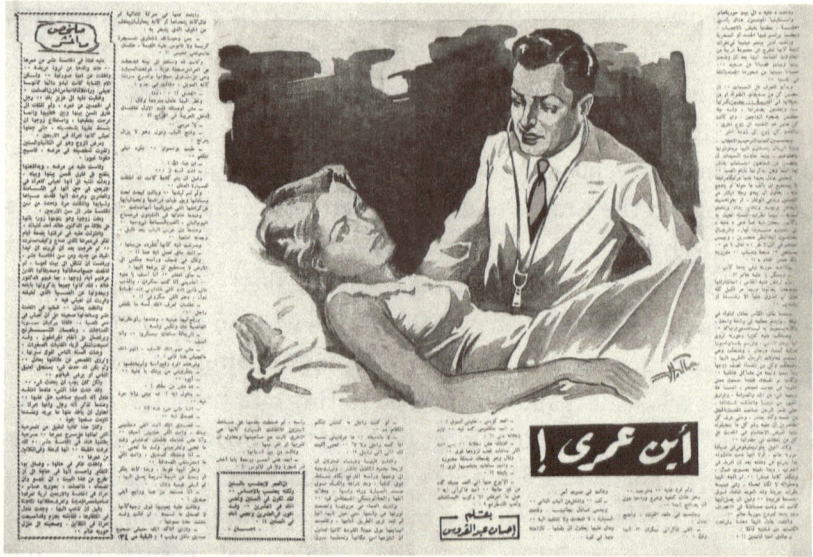

**Figure 10.** Installment of *Where's My Life?* with Dr. Khaled treating Aliya. *Rose El Youssef*, 23 November 1953.

published an article in 1945 calling for a masculine, virile, courageous man to rise up and lead the nation to redemption, a man who would serve as the country's "doctor."

Dr. Khaled immediately diagnoses Aliya's illness. She is sick with a psychological illness that prevents her from letting go of the past and accepting the present. Responding to her obvious sexual desire for him, Dr. Khaled tells Aliya, "I cannot leave you without completing your treatment."[29] At first, she angrily rejects his psychoanalytic diagnosis but soon admits to herself that he was correct. "She wants him. She wants him now. She wants him as a doctor, not as a friend or anything else, a doctor who'll calm her nerves and relieve her dark thoughts."[30] Gesturing to Abdel Kouddous's desire for commitment from and consummation with the Officers, it is only through marital—and, presumably, sexual—union with the doctor that she is cured of her illness and able to turn the page on the past. At the end of *Where's My Life?*, Aliya receives the documented guarantees that Amina is denied in *I'm Free*. In this, it is the doctor's successful psychoanalytic treatment that eliminates the trauma of the past and forges the union between the double of Abdel Kouddous and the leader of the new era.

Nasser read Abdel Kouddous's fiction closely. Could he have been referring to Abdel Kouddous's work when he suggested that he was giving Abdel Kouddous "psychoanalytic treatment"? Could he have been referencing *Where's My Life?*, published only a few months earlier, correctly reading Aliya as a double for Abdel Kouddous and the virile Dr. Khaled as a double for himself, suggesting that, by giving Abdel Kouddous psychoanalytic treatment, Abdel Kouddous would finally accept and embrace both him and the new era? After a year and a half of opposition, would Nasser's "psychoanalysis" finally push Abdel Kouddous to let go of his past obsessions?

There is another equally compelling way to read Nasser's statement. In his 1962 memoir, Ahmed Abul-Fath repeatedly describes Nasser as intentionally intimidating and humiliating journalists, editors-in-chief, and newspaper owners. According to Abul-Fath, humiliation was Nasser's favorite method of subduing the press during the initial period of the revolution. By doing this, "Gamal Abdel Nasser succeeded in transforming most of the newspapers of Egypt into real organs of propaganda at his service and the service of his politics."[31] Nasser did not humiliate only members of the press. Abul-Fath describes how, a year after the coup, Nasser began mocking Zakaria Mohi El Din for exaggerating his role in the revolution, insulting him in front of officers of lower rank. Abul-Fath also details how Nasser had a particular distaste for Sadat and would repeatedly make Sadat think that he was being expelled from his inner circle. According to Abul-Fath, Nasser had "a strange temperament inclined to humiliating people and playing on their suffering."[32] It seems likely that Nasser felt similarly toward Abdel Kouddous. In this context, when he told Abdel Kouddous that he was giving him "psychoanalytic treatment," Nasser seemed to be humiliating his old intransigent friend by suggesting that he, like Dr. Khaled in *Where's My Life?*, was analyzing an anxious, impulsive, emotionally fragile patient who refused to let go of the past.

Abdel Kouddous was shaken by the comment. When Abdel Kouddous discussed this incident publicly for the first time in 1975, he explained that Nasser then went to his office and brought out a letter on notebook paper that a schoolboy had written him in which he asked Nasser for a bicycle so that he could get to school.[33] Nasser then explained, "The ruler granting these kinds of simple desires creates the bond between him and the people, making him someone loved and close to their hearts."[34] Abdel

Kouddous understood that, like the child, he needed Nasser to grant him a vehicle to continue to write. By being allowed to write, Abdel Kouddous would "create the bond" between Nasser and the public. In other words, Nasser was telling Abdel Kouddous that he needed to serve as his personal translator or echo for the broad public if he wanted to continue to publish. It was an offer that apparently horrified Abdel Kouddous. As he explained some two decades later, "Did he really imagine that I could sink to that? Did he think that the torture of prison—or giving me psychological treatment with meals, as he told me—could make me submit to this disgraceful request?"[35] For Abdel Kouddous, this request was worse than the experience of imprisonment that he just went through. As he succinctly explained, "This is the true blow that hit me in 1954."[36]

Had Nasser spent the previous month forcing Abdel Kouddous to come for daily lunches in order to prepare him to serve as his mouthpiece? If so, why was he so interested in Abdel Kouddous? Of course, they had a long personal history, both before and after the coup. Nonetheless, Nasser gave particular importance to the press, working closely to orchestrate and manufacture it, calling newspaper editors daily, intervening in particular articles, and establishing and overseeing official titles such as the weekly *al-Tahrir* and the daily *al-Gumhuriyya* (The Republic). Ahmed Abul-Fath repeatedly depicts Nasser as obsessed with the press and in particular with *al-Misri*, the highest-circulation newspaper in Egypt before its closure in May 1954: "He tried to win it for himself to make it his mouthpiece and one of the principal organs of his propaganda. That's the only reason that pushed him to always pay so much attention to me."[37] According to Khaled Mohi El Din, every evening Nasser would go to the offices of *al-Gumhurriya* to review the following day's headlines personally. In his memoir, Mohi El Din stresses how focused Nasser was on the press: "Throughout his rule, he continued to read the first edition of all daily newspapers, revising them and issuing instructions for immediate changes to subsequent editions."[38]

Nasser was not intent simply on manufacturing public opinion and shaping the message of his policy. According to Abul-Fath, he was interested in micromanaging the media to distract the public with propaganda: "Abdel Nasser believes that a lie can become truth if the organs of propaganda take it upon themselves to repeat a truth. He believes that, submitted to a vast propaganda, the people will eventually believe what is repeated to them. That's why he has taken great care, from the first year of the movement, to organize an effective propaganda."[39] Tawfiq al-Hakim would later argue in *Return of Consciousness* that Nasser worked to coopt intellectuals and artists in order to make them "instruments of the broad propaganda apparatus."[40] According to al-Hakim, "I used to think that popularity only welled up from the heart or perhaps from the representation of hopes, promises, fancies and lies, but I did not realize . . . that it could also be manufactured, made up from start to finish."[41] Of course, al-Hakim's depiction reflects a simplistic image of the power of popular culture, but it does highlight Nasser's obsession on micromanaging the media and the arts to try to shape public opinion.

By August 1954, Abdel Kouddous represented a special opportunity for Nasser. He was a friend of the past who had already demonstrated that he preferred to accommodate the regime rather remain in jail or flee the country, as Ahmed Abul-Fath had done. He was the editor in chief of the most important magazine in the country. He was an independent populist commentator with an enormous audience built on years of political contestation, including repeatedly serving as a thorn in Nasser's side. Yet what truly differentiated him from other intellectuals and writers was his status as the most popular fiction writer of the time. By August 1954, Abdel Kouddous had already established his wide popular reach through his scandalous fiction. In a poll by the American University in Cairo in 1954, he was named Egypt's most popular author. Moreover, his most recent novels, *I'm Free* and *Where's My Life?*, had something crucial in common—both were centered on female protagonists who represented early examples of what Laura Bier has termed "revolutionary womanhood."[42] Both women represented models of advancement and "modern citizens" in the new era.[43] As Bier has shown, it was anxieties over the place of women in the new Egypt that made them a crucial focus of state engineering and planning. Omnia El Shakry also stresses the links between public discourse surrounding psychoanalysis and state feminism. It was perhaps no coincidence that Yusuf Murad published his book *The Psychology of Sex*, which focused on female psychology, in 1954. For El Shakry, "the emergence of an Arabic-language psychology of gender and sexual difference" is linked to the development of state-engineered feminism.[44] Nasser's interest in Abdel Kouddous in summer 1954 must also be seen from this angle. Nasser no doubt understood that Abdel Kouddous, through his mass-consumed romantic melodrama, could serve as a unique partner not only to disseminate his message in the press but also to help engineer the image of women and feminism in the new Egypt, not as elite high culture but as popular entertainment.

In the interviews that Abdel Kouddous later gave about this exchange, he almost always describes himself as deeply offended by Nasser's request. In one interview, however, he did admit to a much nuanced and contradictory feeling toward Nasser during this encounter. Echoing the ambivalence that he felt toward his mother in his jail cell, Abdel Kouddous described Nasser's offer as a profound dilemma: "It was a choice between life and death as an independent thinker. Do I remain a free thinker and free writer, unpolluted by servitude? Or do I content myself with the insult of subordination and servile chains, even if they are made of gold?"[45] He then claimed that he responded to Nasser in a way that would have made his mother proud: "I'll never be your man for a simple reason—since my childhood, I wasn't raised to be the voice of a master, however great that master is. . . . I have no master, I've never had one, and I never will." Rebuffed, Nasser reportedly responded, "I was imagining that Ihsan Abdel Kouddous, my friend and colleague during the years of struggle before the revolution, would welcome this opportunity to do his duty to solidify the link between me and the people for whom he struggled before the revolution."[46] Nasser then explained that he needed a translator for the people, not a loudspeaker: "This translator would be a creative artist who takes the ideas of the ruler as his raw material and then reshapes them into an attractive and exciting form that is able to charm millions and penetrate their minds and hearts." While Mohammed Hasaein Heikal had already established himself as Nasser's political mouthpiece at this point, Nasser clearly saw how Abdel Kouddous could play a unique role for him by translating his ideas for the broader public through mass-consumed romantic melodrama. The opportunity was there for Abdel Kouddous to express horror at Nasser's request, feeling like his old revolutionary partner was trying to turn him into a jester, duplicating the offer that King Fouad had made to his father years earlier. The written record, however, shows his response to have been much more nuanced and complicated.

His jailing and this exchange fundamentally changed Abdel Kouddous's life and career. Instead of simply rejecting Nasser, as he claimed numerous times, Abdel Kouddous's archive shows that he deeply internalized the conflict at the heart of Nasser's offer. And it was the contradiction between accommodation and dissent that would define Abdel Kouddous's fiction and his staging of the development of Nasser's dictatorship in his writing going forward. As Abdel Kouddous later explained, "There was a battle between me and my pen. This is something that I don't deny. . . . As for the reason for this battle, it wasn't the torture of prison, as some think. . . . The real reason for the battle that arose inside me at that time was the naïve letter written by that schoolboy."[47] Starting in August 1954, Abdel Kouddous entered a careful balancing act between maintaining his family's safety and trying to please Nasser while preserving his self-respect as a writer with the shame of disappointing his mother by not resisting authority. This balancing act—and, perhaps, Nasser's desire for him to help engineer the image of women in popular culture—explains why he moved his critical voice away from his editorials to his fiction, where he had the cover of symbolism and metaphor—as well as the scandalous way that he wrote about sex—to shroud what he wrote.

This tension between accommodation and resistance played out in nearly every installment of his serialized novels over the next decade. These novels, which rank among the most popular works of fiction in the Arab world and the basis for some of the most successful films in the history of Arab cinema, were the vehicle by which he communicated with not only the public but also Nasser, who followed for himself how well Abdel Kouddous was translating his own message to the people. Instead of serving as Nasser's uncritical echo, Abdel Kouddous commonly used his fiction—not his weekly editorials, which he now drained of political dissent—as a means to lash out at Nasser at the insult of trying to coopt him, to try to prove to himself, Nasser, and, perhaps, his mother, that he would not submit to the ruler. Just as he did in *I'm Free*, Abdel Kouddous would continue to rewrite the history of the revolution, attempting to reconcile and confess to the public his own anxieties, regrets, and despair about what he felt was his personal responsibility in inadvertently embedding dictatorship as well as unresolved tensions in his personal relationship with Nasser. There were also times when he was clearly still trying to guide the ruler, as before.

Yet as the months and years passed after his erasure from the history of the revolution, the public knew little about Abdel Kouddous's central role in the coup, his regrets and anxieties about the aftermath of the revolution, or the details of his personal relationship with Nasser. They were therefore unable to recognize the confessional elements in these texts. Nonetheless, after August 1954, when Nasser stopped his "psychoanalytic treatment," Abdel Kouddous repeatedly tried to reveal the layers of his anxiety to the public, never achieving the curative effect that he was clearly desperately seeking. The only reader who no doubt understood his confessions was Nasser, his self-designated therapist. It was in this tension between the way that Abdel Kouddous lashed out at Nasser in his fiction and the way that Nasser continued to censor and discipline him—the repeated oscillation between reward and punishment between them—that the hidden history of dissent in popular culture in Egypt during the Nasser era resides.

### WAKING UP FROM FANTASY

Soon after Abdel Kouddous left jail, famed sculptor Fathi Mahmoud made a statue of him in chains, looking up with grief in his eyes. Indeed, the carceral experience followed Abdel Kouddous after his release, not only in his "analysis" by Nasser but also in what he published in *Rose El Youssef* in the following weeks. When Abdel Kouddous published his first post-prison article on 16 August 1954, he made no mention of his absence, jailing, or lunches with Nasser. Nonetheless, public soul searching about his arrest erupted on 30 August 1954, presumably once his daily lunches with Nasser ended. That issue includes an editorial with a caricature of Abdel Kouddous scratching his head in confusion. Abdel Kouddous begins by reviewing his own history of oppositional journalism during the 1940s. Hinting at his jailing, only weeks earlier, and his anxieties about Nasser, Abdel Kouddous explained that his arrest in 1945 for his article attacking Consul-General Lampson led him to deep confusion and doubt, wondering if he had been duped into believing in former prime minister Mahmoud El Nokrashi. Seemingly drawing an analogy between El Nokrashi and Nasser, Abdel Kouddous doubted himself for projecting his principles on someone who appeared to espouse them: "It became clear that my faith in El Nokrashi's nationalism and integrity wasn't enough to believe in him as a person. . . . It's not enough to believe in a leader simply because he's patriotic, virtuous, or

**Figure 11.** Ihsan Abdel Kouddous beside the 1955 Fathi Mahmoud statue of him in chains. Courtesy of the Abdel Kouddous family.

free. I have to believe first and foremost in the leader's principles and see clearly the road that he's moving on."⁴⁸ Hinting at his current crisis but writing about the 1940s, Abdel Kouddous explained: "I left jail neither angry nor duped but confused, searching for my political faith. . . . For years, I was suffering from this confusion and oppressive doubt until I found my faith—when I believed in a principle, I didn't need to believe in people." In this way, Abdel Kouddous performed a public soul searching not about the 1940s but about his recent arrest and release, alluding to his current confusion over how he could have supported the man who ultimately jailed him and how he could move forward.

The following week, Abdel Kouddous admitted openly for the first time that he had been imprisoned for ninety-five days on the charge of working to overturn the political system. As Abdel Kouddous explained nearly two decades later, Nasser read the article in advance and unsurprisingly cut a number of lines from it, another act of disciplining and humiliating his former co-revolutionary.⁴⁹ Nonetheless, Abdel Kouddous was still the only writer at the time to discuss openly being jailed in the wake of the March Crisis, signaling that Nasser had brought him back to his inner circle after his release from jail. With a restrained and chastised tone, Abdel Kouddous did not mention the series of articles during the March Crisis or any of the criticisms that he had leveled at the Officers since the coup. There is no hint of irony that he had once been a journalist calling on the public to speak their minds about the revolution without fear of repression or arrest. He described his harrowing experience in prison, however, and hinted at Nasser's "therapy" when he confessed to the public, "I only intend to show a violent psychological experience that I had, an experience in which my patriotism was subject to examination."[50]

Only later would Abdel Kouddous explain what he meant by this. Pointing to the pain of the arrest for the first time in 1974, he said, "Imagine that you lay the ground work for a revolution, participate in it, and then as soon as the revolution happens, it jails you!"[51] In a series of interviews in 1980, he continued to stress his sense of ownership of the revolution: "When I discovered that I was being charged with overturning the system, I was filled with panic and bitterness since the 23 July Revolution took place as a realization of my labor, carried out by the Free Officers."[52] He then asked indignantly: "How could these leaders accuse me of this kind of crime?" For him, the pain of the insult and the loss of his cherished revolution were much greater than any physical pain that he endured in prison. This, however, was mixed with shame, as if he had been defeated, just as his mother suggested. As Abdel Kouddous revealed in 1975, "If I'm sorry about anything in that violent experience, it's without a doubt about how hard I was on myself for falling into the snares of weakness and submission."[53] Perhaps the most painful experience of his imprisonment was not the insults and humiliation—or, perhaps, physical torture—but the sense of shame that his mother stirred up inside him for looking to accommodate Nasser.[54]

Nonetheless, Abdel Kouddous was also deeply wounded by the realization that he had been living out a fantasy of deception about his former fellow revolutionaries: "What devastated me was that I found myself a prisoner at the order of my friends, the people who shared my principles and revolutionary thoughts. That's what I couldn't bear." The arrest forced him to confront the reality that these men did not, in fact, share his principles and perhaps never had. Had he impulsively projected what he wanted to believe on them? Was it all just a fantasy? He emphasized in particular the shock and blow of the deception: "I woke up to terrifying truths that I couldn't imagine—even imagine!— the possibility of them happening."[55] He explained that the worst thing a political prisoner could face was "the torture of the spirit, especially when he comes face to face with deception, when he discovers that he was deceived about his faith in his thinking and a person. That was my greatest tribulation." Being imprisoned by the very man he felt he had brought to power—who achieved what he had labored for—served not simply as an insult to his commitment and principles that he held so dear. It was the traumatic moment in which he woke up to his own fantasies and projections, finally grasping that he had been deluded and had even deluded himself.

In summer 1954, however, Abdel Kouddous did not elaborate on his confusion, anxieties, and regrets in his editorials. For the next year and a half, he largely avoided writing editorials, and when he did, they were about domestic affairs and international issues, devoting little space to the Officers in general or Nasser in particular. In the place of the oppositional editorial, Abdel Kouddous turned to fiction, politicizing it and employing it as a vehicle not only for dissent but also to explore his own anxieties about his relationship with Nasser, his paradoxical shame at what he saw as his own compulsion for accommodation, and his regrets about the revolution, which were now considerably more complex than before his jailing. And since he knew all too well that Nasser was a devoted reader, fiction became his medium to communicate directly with the ruler, to challenge him in some ways and appease him in others, just as he had done in his editorials in the aftermath of the coup. It was immediately after his release from prison in summer 1954 that Abdel Kouddous turned to fiction to begin working through these issues, a process that would last for more than a decade.

## CLUTCHING THE EMPTY PILLOW

In the days following his release from jail on 31 July 1954, Abdel Kouddous started work on his next novel, *The Empty Pillow*. He began serializing the novel in *Rose El Youssef* on 30 August 1954, uncoincidentally the same issue in which he broached his own confusion with principles and the previous regime. While he did not openly admit to feeling "deceived" by his fantasies and projections about Nasser until much later, he immediately alludes to it in the epigraph that framed each installment of the novel in the magazine, using the same Arabic root, *whm*. "In the life of all of us," the epigraph ran, "is a great deception [*wahm*] called the first love. Don't believe in it. Your first love is your last!" In *The Empty Pillow*, Abdel Kouddous explores the deception and fantasy of what he calls "the first love"—here, the metaphorical framing of his fervent love for the revolution—demonstrating how this illusion becomes a destructive force on the novel's main character, Salah. Read as apolitical romantic melodrama, *The Empty Pillow* appears to be an innocent depiction of the emotional torment of adolescent love. But when set in the context of Abdel Kouddous's release from jail and his anxieties at waking up to his naïve projections for the Officers while trying to accommodate Nasser, the novel instead serves as Abdel Kouddous's first attempt to use fiction to explore how he deluded himself into falling for fantasy, how he woke up to its destructive forces, and how he tried to convince himself that he had moved on. This novel became the vehicle by which Abdel Kouddous tried to let go of the destructive force of deception in order to embrace the reality of the present, just as he asked his mother to do when she visited him in jail. By the end of the novel, in a striking attempt to accommodate the ruler, Abdel Kouddous asserts for both himself and Nasser, his most important reader, that he had indeed been "cured" by Nasser's psychoanalytic treatment.

*The Empty Pillow* begins as nineteen-year-old Salah—the only time during the Nasser era that Abdel Kouddous wrote himself into a novel as a male protagonist—wanders downtown Cairo and meets Samiha. Like a teenage Abdel Kouddous suddenly overwhelmed by nationalist fervor, Salah is immediately smitten with Samiha, the double of his passion for revolution before the coup. When he finds her again, Salah quickly falls into what he calls the trap of the first love, telling Samiha, "You're mine and we belong to each other. We can't break up and no one can separate us."[56] Full of projections and fantasies, he then tells her, "We've been married since the day we met."[57] Ignoring Samiha's obvious misgivings, Salah returns home in delight, gets in bed, and looks at the pillow next to him, projecting his fantasies on it: "He saw her with his imagination. . . . He closed his eyes, took the pillow in his arms, and pressed his lips against it. He kissed the empty pillow!"[58] When Salah goes to see Samiha again, he brings two rings and puts one on her finger, explaining that it is a wedding ring.[59] Salah's love for Samiha is quickly established as an obsessive fantasy, manifested in his projections of her on his pillow and his delusions that they are married, echoing what Abdel Kouddous was trying to assert to Nasser in the novel as his own reckless delusional love for the revolution, both before and after the coup.

Predictably, reality intervenes in Salah's fantasy when Samiha reveals that her parents have engaged her to her cousin, Dr. Fouad. Once again, Abdel Kouddous writes a doctor into his fiction as a double for Nasser. In *Where's My Life?*, published before his April 1954 jailing, it is the doctor who marries Aliya, the double for Abdel Kouddous, providing the documentation necessary to let go of the past and embrace the present. While contemporaneous readers would not have understood the symbolism of the doctor in *The Empty Pillow*, it would have been obvious to Nasser, especially so soon after his told Abdel Kouddous that he was giving him "psychological treatment." Perhaps Abdel Kouddous even named the doctor Fouad as a gesture to Freud.[60] Uncoincidentally, in *The Empty Pillow*, it is the doctor who intervenes to steal the love of Abdel Kouddous's double away from him, a metaphor for how Nasser hijacked his cherished revolution. Salah is, of course, shocked and appalled, unable to face reality. In this, Abdel Kouddous writes into the fictional text his own episodes of frantic rage and denial when he realizes that he was being marginalized and erased from the revolution.

Despite this, Salah—like Abdel Kouddous once Nasser stole his cherished revolution—refuses to face reality now that his "first love" has abandoned him for the doctor. After the rejection, Salah drowns his sorrows in denial, descending into depression by drinking at bars and sleeping with prostitutes. As Samiha's wedding approaches—the formal union of the revolution with Nasser—he internalizes his grief even more. He becomes so physically degraded that "he seemed like he was leaving the grave or heading to it."[61] Once Samiha gets married and the doctor's theft of his first love is complete, the psychological becomes so overwhelming that it manifests in the physical. Drunk at the bar right after Samiha's wedding, Salah drops to the floor and falls into a coma. His refusal to confront fantasy and delusion has led to his mental and physical collapse, pushing Salah, like Abdel Kouddous, to necessary "treatment."

When Salah awakes in the hospital, he discovers that it is none other than Dr. Fouad, the man who stole Samiha from him, the double for Nasser, who has intervened to save his life. As Salah is suffering in bed after surgery, he looks at the doctor, who, not coincidentally, has a "handsome face, svelte build, strong personality, and smile overflowing with good manliness."[62] Just as Abdel Kouddous revealed two decades later that Nasser "treated" him daily for a month after his release from jail, "Dr. Fouad was always with Salah as if he was challenging death with him. He was standing day and night next to his bed."[63] As Dr. Fouad performs surgery and stands beside Salah as he was recovering, Abdel Kouddous also has the doctor heal him psychologically, emphasizing the point for his devoted reader, Nasser: "Salah was able to get control of the psychological storms that had overwhelmed him and hide the black thoughts in his head about Dr. Fouad, the man who snatched Samiha from him to marry her, the man who destroyed his life and made him a vagabond in the bars and clubs, the man who choked his dreams, made him lose his future, and tore up his being."[64]

While it was the doctor who leads to his collapse, Salah nonetheless emerges from the hospital "reborn" thanks to Dr. Fouad.[65] It seems that Abdel Kouddous was insisting to Nasser in this latest installment of the fictional text, published only a month after the end of his forced invitations at Nasser's house, that his treatment after his "collapse" and release from jail had been successful. He is not only physically and psychologically healed but, self-referentially for Abdel Kouddous, as if apologizing to Nasser and demonstrating the capitulation and accommodation he articulated to his mother in his jail cell only weeks earlier, he is now committed to letting go of the past. Salah stops drinking, succeeds at school, and, thanks to his hard work, becomes a company director. Through the weekly installments of the novel in fall 1954, Abdel Kouddous stressed to Nasser—his "doctor" after his release from prison—that he, like Salah, was indeed moving on to integration in society now that he had received successful "treatment," just as Aliya had responded to Dr. Khaled's analysis in *Where's My Life?* to enable her let go of her past.

Nonetheless, regret and resistance remain irrepressible. It soon becomes clear that while Dr. Fouad may have healed Salah's body, he has not cured him of the illness of projections and fantasy. Salah remains obsessed with Samiha, imagining her with him wherever he goes, suggesting that Abdel Kouddous could not, in fact, let go of his love for the revolution, no matter how hard he tried to repress it. His attachment to Samiha continues in the bedroom as well as he still projects her image on the pillow: "When he got in bed, he saw her with his imagination on the empty pillow. He'd see her as he saw her for the first time."[66] The "first love"—the *wahm* or delusion—is therefore a deeply embedded illness for Salah, something that the doctor cannot easily extract. It is delusion that drives Salah and fuels his imagination and identity, preventing him from letting go of the past. Now that weeks have passed since the treatment—for both Salah in the novel and Abdel Kouddous as he was writing and serializing these installments—Samiha stubbornly remains the irrepressible first love, the embedded psychological complex, that the doctor is powerless to resolve. Perhaps neither Dr. Fouad nor Nasser were effective therapists.

Even when Salah decides to marry Doreya, the daughter of an important businessman and, one imagines, the symbol of postrevolutionary Egypt, he cannot let go. At the wedding, Salah can only think about Samiha—the original idealistic love of the revolution—and imagines himself leaving the ceremony to return home to embrace her on the empty pillow. When Doreya appears in her wedding dress, Salah is shocked when he sees her as Samiha, "as he saw her the first time when she was fifteen years old."[67] The illness, the projection of the first love that is frozen in time, the teenage blossoming of Abdel Kouddous's nationalist fever for revolution, continues to haunt Salah even on his wedding night. After consummating his marriage with Doreya, Salah retreats to his own bedroom and sees Samiha's image yet again on the pillow, unable to accept his new life. Despite Dr. Fouad's treatment, he cannot embrace the reality of the present, showing how Abdel Kouddous was backtracking in his capitulations to Nasser, at least in that week's installment of the novel.

Doreya becomes pregnant but, predictably, the fetus cannot survive in this environment. Doreya has a tortured labor in which the fetus dies, symbolically demonstrating that Abdel Kouddous and postrevolutionary Egypt cannot produce an offspring. It is only in the death of the fetus—the death of the next generation—that Salah finally wakes up to his delusion: "Maybe he was the victim of a psychological complex that formed after his failure to marry Samiha and she married someone else, a complicated psychological complex that represented failure. This complex—and not the love of Samiha—is what was pushing him without him knowing to cover his feelings of failure. The image of Samiha that he traced in his imagination on the empty pillow is nothing more than the image of this complex, the image of failure."[68] The projection of failure, the inability to come to grips with it, points to Abdel Kouddous's own anxieties about his relationship with the Free Officers and the revolution. Nasser had abducted the revolution from Abdel Kouddous, destroying his vision of the free democratic nation, leading Abdel Kouddous—as he suggested in this narrative—to denial and then collapse. For Salah, the fantasy of the "first love"—a psychosis of clinging to a democratic independent nation—was destroying him and his relationship with postrevolutionary Egypt, a delusion that led to the death of his offspring right at the moment of birth.

It was at this moment that, despite his regression in the previous week's installment, Abdel Kouddous suddenly retreated and insisted to his reader Nasser that he had indeed finally woken up to the pain and suffering of his fantasies and projections for the revolution. Perhaps after a phone call from the censor—or Nasser himself—Salah now miraculously finds salvation and liberation: "He felt his chest getting wider as if a psychological complex had been resolved inside him. He raised his head and took a deep breath, filling his lungs as if his release had taken place after a long imprisonment and he went out toward freedom: freedom from fantasy, from his psychological complex."[69] Abdel Kouddous was released from jail only one month before he began serializing the novel. Like Salah, Abdel Kouddous did not recognize the fantasy that the "first love" had become for him. The novel suggests that Abdel Kouddous, in his deep confusion, which he wrote about in the 30 August 1954 issue of *Rose El Youssef*, the same issue as the first installment of the novel, did not recognize that the fantasy of the "first love" was based on delusion. The death of the fetus, the impossibility of the next generation, is the moment that Salah—like Abdel Kouddous—finally wakes up from the illness of fantasy and its destructive impact. The stillborn gestures to Abdel Kouddous asserting to Nasser that his delusions about his "first love"—the revolution, a fantasy of a democratic Egypt—were now dead and that he had to make amends with the new era of dictatorship. Abdel Kouddous was stressing that he had finally let go of his obsession, just as Salah has now let go of his first love, insisting to Nasser through Salah that he had indeed been successfully treated for his psychological illness.

As the novel ends, Doreya recovers in the hospital and Salah returns home to sleep. As before his freedom from his long imprisonment, Salah embraces the pillow next to him. This time, however, his imagination projects Doreya's face onto the pillow, not Samiha's. Relieved that he now sees his wife and not his "first love," the novel ends as Salah grips the pillow to his chest and falls asleep, a symbol of his newfound sense of calm. This is reinforced in the final words of the text: "And he slept," suggesting sleep as psychological peace, a metaphor that Abdel Kouddous would sharply reject a year later in his novel *I Do Not Sleep*, which I discuss in the next chapter. By having Salah see Doreya and not Samiha on the pillow, Abdel Kouddous was declaring to Nasser in the final installment on 11 October 1954 that he was now moving onto a new phase of fully embracing the present, using metaphor to insist that he had finally been cured from his past destructive fantasies. With this ending, *The Empty Pillow* stands as Abdel Kouddous's most apologetic and accommodating work of fiction during the Nasser era, a rush to come to grips with his imprisonment and to demonstrate—with a false optimism that reads like a post-traumatic response from the abuse of the carceral experience—that he had been "healed" of his fantasies for the revolution. It must have outraged his mother.

While remembered today as a story of the passion of the "first love" between two young people—especially how stars Abdel Halim Hafez and Lobna Abdel Aziz embodied the roles of the two characters in the classic 1957 film adaptation—*The Empty Pillow* is also a striking document of how Abdel Kouddous rushed to perform an accommodation of Nasser in the weeks following his release from jail in the same magazine where he had once attacked him. As Abdel Kouddous admitted in one of the last interviews before his death, the novel was a clear break from his earlier fiction: "There's no doubt that *The Empty Pillow* was a transition from the political of my editorials to something else. I couldn't find any way to express what I wanted to say other than through fiction."[70] In 1968, Abdel Kouddous revealed, "The truth was that the 'empty pillow' was the pillow that I clung to in prison."[71]

**Figure 12.** Ihsan Abdel Kouddous at home with director Salah Abou Seif and the stars of the 1957 film adaptation of *The Empty Pillow*, including Lobna Abdel Aziz (center) and Abdel Halim Hafez. Courtesy of the Abdel Kouddous family.

## WHISPERS OF LOVE

Although Abdel Kouddous spoke openly in the 1970s and 1980s about the burden of waking up to the deception of fantasy and projection while in prison for three months in 1954 as well as Gamal Abdel Nasser's insistence that he was giving him psychoanalytic treatment, readers did not know these details at the time. This explains why the public read *The Empty Pillow* as an obsessive love story, not as Abdel Kouddous's attempt to demonstrate to Nasser that he was embracing the present thanks to his "treatment" for the trauma of losing the revolution and inadvertently embedding dictatorship. Nonetheless, Nasser himself apparently understood the symbolism of the pillow. After finishing the novel, he reportedly called Abdel Kouddous to confirm that he had indeed let go of the past, asking him, "Did you leave prison with the empty pillow?"[72]

No doubt, Nasser had read enough to believe that he had indeed successfully treated Abdel Kouddous from his illness. Just as Abdel Kouddous was finishing serializing the novel, Nasser decided to resuscitate his former co-conspirator before the public by offering him a weekly radio program.[73] Clearly, the novel had convinced Nasser that Abdel Kouddous had been sufficiently healed to serve once again as his voice on the radio, perhaps to function as his translator for the public. Moreover, this was precisely the time when, according to Saïd Aburish, Nasser was personally involved in orchestrating a campaign to boost his importance now that Neguib was on the verge of being removed as president.[74] Immediately after the coup, according to Ahmed Abul-Fath, Nasser worked to maintain close ties with popular journalists and the editors of the main newspapers and magazines, but Neguib had focused instead on controlling the radio.[75] Giving a now successfully "treated" Abdel Kouddous, with his wide popularity as a journalist and fiction writer, a platform on the radio represented for Nasser another way to contest Neguib, eliminating any of his lingering influence there.

Although Abdel Kouddous had given two radio addresses soon after the coup directly supporting the Free Officers—also at Nasser's invitation—this new program would not be the same direct political advocacy. As if drawing attention to the toned-down volume of his new program, Abdel Kouddous gave the weekly address the name "Whisper." According to the weekly schedules of the *Egyptian Radio Magazine*, "Whisper" was broadcast most weeks from early October 1954 until late March 1955. The address aired mostly on Wednesdays at 9:55 p.m., typically after a song by Mohamed Abdel Wahhab and before a song by Umm Kulthum. While I have located a recording of only the first address, the transcripts for fourteen episodes were published in the *Egyptian Radio Magazine* at the time of their broadcast.

In the first episode, Abdel Kouddous asked the public to open their hearts to the call of love "in its high wide meaning, the love of humanity, love of your brother and neighbor, love of building your nation, love for love's sake."[76] This was not a love of oneself but of the nation, a love that encouraged self-sacrifice. In this, Abdel Kouddous reflected what Omnia El Shakry argues was the link between love and nationalism in Egypt at the time: nationalism was "the apex of social emotions and affect in humans. To be nationalist one needed, quite simply, the capacity for love and sacrifice."[77] Abdel Kouddous explained in an interview two decades later that love was simply a metaphor: "Love is not only an emotion between a man and a woman but a general feeling of life, existence, and the society that I live in. . . . I loved my people so I defended them against corruption, the political parties, and the palace. I loved Egypt so I defended it against colonialism. This is my primary motivation, not just for my literature but my entire life."[78]

The first episode of "Whisper" was so strange that it gave some listeners the impression that Abdel Kouddous had suddenly become a different person, as if he were duplicating on national radio the accommodation of Nasser that he had been performing through Salah in *The Empty Pillow*. In the second episode, Abdel Kouddous addressed this directly: "One of you wrote to me objecting, saying: 'We know you as a revolutionary. So why do you sound so weak and feeble, calling for love? What happened to you?'"[79] Rejecting this depiction of him, Abdel Kouddous argued that he has always called for love and that the men who undertook the revolution have always been full of love. Once again promoting the Officers, he suggested that these men could not have personal goals: "The revolutionary is the man who gets rid of his egotism, ambitions, and essence and becomes pure, sincere love—love of his people and nation—so that he gives his life to this love and gives it to his people and his nation." Abdel Kouddous suggested that the revolutionary is not driven by personal gain but by selfless action for the nation.

On 19 October 1954, Egypt finally signed an agreement for Britain to withdraw fully from the country. That evening, Nasser gave a speech to celebrate the achievement, telling the public, "Give your hands and take ours. Let's rebuild our nation with love, tolerance, and mutual understanding."[80] Barely a week after Abdel Kouddous performed his striking accommodation in the final installment of *The Empty Pillow*, had he and Nasser become so close that Abdel Kouddous was now writing speeches for him? In his third "Whisper," broadcast the day after Nasser's speech, Abdel Kouddous tied his radio address directly to the speech, declaring, "Love has been officially announced today." He then quoted Nasser's call for love, telling the public, "Accept Gamal's invitation and open your hearts to love." Just as Salah accepted the new era by embracing his love for Doreya, the symbol of postrevolutionary reality, Abdel Kouddous—seemingly in coordination with Nasser—was now calling on the public to embrace the present to build the future of the nation through love. *Rose El Youssef* latched on, declaring in its opening anonymous editorial that week, presumably written by Abdel

Kouddous, that Egypt, thanks to the evacuation agreement, was a new country "breathing with love."[81]

It only took a week for this optimism to crumble. On 26 October 1954, Gamal Abdel Nasser faced an assassination attempt while giving a speech in Manshiyya Square in Alexandria. In his next radio address, Abdel Kouddous was in denial: "Has the call to love failed? ... Should we despair and announce our failure because a hand of hatred fired bullets at Gamal Abdel Nasser? No, never."[82] He insisted that the people would remain as steadfast and confident in their principles and love as Nasser himself. In *Rose El Youssef* that week, Abdel Kouddous declared that, despite the attack, "I still believe in love. I believe in it as I believe in God. I believe in its strength as I believe in the strength of God."[83] This anxious insistence on love, however, only hinted at his fear about the crackdown that was already underway.

## THE SECOND ARREST

Immediately after the assassination attempt, Nasser launched an assault on the Muslim Brotherhood, decimating it as an organization. In November and December 1954, as part of this crackdown, there was also a wave of arrests of leftists and perceived opponents of the regime, including the writer Yusuf Idris. It was during this time that the secret police came to arrest Abdel Kouddous again. Abdel Kouddous did not mention his second arrest in 1954 until two decades later, underscoring the danger that he was facing at the time and the severity of the situation.[84] Abdel Kouddous was shocked and appalled when a police officer arrived at his apartment that night, asking him with a devious smile to come answer a few questions. As the horrified Abdel Kouddous arrived at the same military prison that he had left only a few months earlier, he tried to choke back his tears, thinking, "Is this what the revolution was undertaken for? ... Is this what I spent the most important part of my youth calling for?"[85] When he entered the director's office, he found Ahmed Anwar, the head of the military police, together with a number of interrogators. Anwar told Abdel Kouddous that he was accused of working to overthrow the government and plotting against the revolution. At that moment, an outraged Abdel Kouddous thought, "It was for this revolution that I spent all those years laying the groundwork?" The appalled and shocked Abdel Kouddous then thought, "I witnessed with my own eyes truth become deception and deception become justice and honor."[86] Anwar told Abdel Kouddous that his "partner," an office worker at *Rose El Youssef*, confessed that Abdel Kouddous had made him distribute pamphlets against the revolution. He also confessed that Abdel Kouddous had delivered a cache of arms in his car to an unknown man on Haram Street in Cairo.

Abdel Kouddous could not believe his ears. After he refused to dignify the charges with a response, he was taken back to Cell 19, the same cell that he had left only a few months earlier. Abdel Kouddous felt at that moment that his period of release since July had been only a temporary respite. It was at this point in the 1982 interview about this incident that Abdel Kouddous had to pause to collect himself before continuing, speaking with a voice full of pain and grief, "as if he was announcing the death inside him of the dreams of the best part of his youth."[87] Abdel Kouddous then explained that, sitting in his jail cell, he soon heard a phone ring. After a few minutes, Anwar came to bring Abdel Kouddous back to his office and handed him the phone. On the other end was Nasser, who apologized for the arrest, insisting that it had been a mistake. He then put Field Marshal Abdel Hakim Amer on the phone to apologize on behalf of the armed forces. With an uncomfortable smile, Anwar then released Abdel Kouddous.

The first arrest in 1954 lasted for three months. The second lasted for only three hours, with Nasser himself quickly intervening to save him. Nonetheless, on his way back home, Abdel Kouddous was profoundly disturbed. If, with his close connections to the leaders of the revolution, he could be arrested like that, what was happening to other people? Was Nasser's sudden personal intervention, like a deus ex machina, the only reason that he had been released? What would have happened to him if he had not had such a close connection with Nasser? "I felt a shudder shake me from my depths," he said, "as I imagined all the innocent people snatched from their houses in the middle of the night, tossed behind bars."[88]

The first arrest in 1954 woke Abdel Kouddous up to his fantasies about the revolution but pushed him try to accommodate Nasser and accept the new reality, as documented in the weekly installments of *The Empty Pillow* and the initial episodes of "Whisper." The second arrest, however, was a deep dividing point for him: "If this is the state of freedom at the beginning of the revolutionary road, what will conditions be like after ten or twenty years?"[89] The second arrest horrified him and confirmed his worst suspicions: "What I was afraid of had turned into a painful reality.... That's how I opened my eyes to what I didn't want to see was happening to the young Egyptian revolution."[90] For Abdel Kouddous, the second jailing in 1954 fully split the revolution as he envisioned it from the men executing it. As Abdel Kouddous explained in 1982, "I'm against the deviation of the revolution from its sound path to a monopoly for the benefit of a particular group."[91]

While Abdel Kouddous had written *The Empty Pillow* as a vehicle to work through the personal and psychological costs of clinging to fantasies and projections for the revolution, trying to demonstrate to Nasser that he had been cured from his psychosis, he would now take an increasingly darker turn in his fiction, trying repeatedly yet unsuccessfully to soothe and resolve his anxieties and regrets about his role in the revolution and his relationship with Nasser. Starting in January 1955, fiction would serve as Abdel Kouddous's way to explore his sense of regret for the revolution and deep feeling of responsibility for embedding a military dictatorship in the country. It also became a space to challenge Nasser himself, using metaphors of obsession, sexual abuse, rape, and degradation to protest his own abuse as well as the degradation of Egypt under Nasser's rule. It was during this period that fiction offered Abdel Kouddous the only avenue to express himself publicly because of increasingly severe censorship in Egypt after the March Crisis. As Abdel Kouddous reflected in the 1970s, once he was restricted in his political writing, he fled to fiction, where he had "wider freedoms."[92] After Abdel Kouddous's death, even Faten Hamama praised him for "his ability to express his political ideas through his fiction at a time when it was very difficult for someone to talk about politics."[93] It was in these novels that Abdel Kouddous would stage the complex relationship between intellectual and dictator for the widest audience in Egypt.

### THE BARRED ROAD

Abdel Kouddous began serializing his next novel, *The Barred Road*, on 3 January 1955, only weeks after his second arrest. Of course, the term *road* (Arabic: *tariq*) had a long history in Abdel Kouddous's editorials.

He used the term repeatedly since the coup to describe the long and difficult path that the country was traveling on toward democracy. Most recently, Abdel Kouddous had used the term in the first editorial that he wrote during the March Crisis: "We're Moving on the Natural, Inevitable Road for the Revolution." In that editorial, he insisted that the only road forward for Egypt was parliamentary democracy. With the title of his new novel after his second arrest, however, he now stressed that the road was blocked. If the road to democracy was barred, where else was Egypt moving?

The impact of the fall 1954 arrest—and Abdel Kouddous's turn toward fiction as a means to reject accommodation and express his anxieties and uncertainty about the regime's current path—become especially clear in this new work. Each installment is framed with the epigraph "Sin isn't born with us. Rather, society pushes us to it." This epigraph suggests that Abdel Kouddous, like Faiza, the main character and his double in the novel, had been innocent of "sin" in his relationship with the Free Officers and the revolution but had been pushed to it by the forces around him. By depicting Faiza repeatedly confused and wounded after projecting her fantasies of love and honor on the men around her—and then insisting on clinging to her principles when they try to exploit her sexually—Abdel Kouddous demonstrated how he had shifted considerably in his engagement with Nasser and the revolution. Unlike *The Empty Pillow* or "Whisper," there is no optimism or performance of being "cured." Instead, Faiza, like Abdel Kouddous, repeatedly stands before the barred road of honor and virtue—the marker for democracy in the novel—struggling not to let go of principles by submitting to sin and sexual exploitation, yet still utterly confused at how to move forward. Just as Abdel Kouddous described himself as wandering lost and exhausted in confusion in his 30 August 1954 article, Faiza, unlike Salah in *The Empty Pillow*, remains unable to reconcile the sinful present with her principles, uncertain at how to break through the barred road.

Faiza's father has died three years before the start of the novel—not coincidentally, at the time of the coup—leaving the family forlorn. As a result of the death of the father, Faiza's mother begins hosting men at their home for private drinking parties to support the family, teaching the two older sisters how to entertain and flirt with them, a task that they enthusiastically take on without paternal guidance. In this, the family home in the novel serves as the symbol of the nation gleefully prostituting itself in order to survive in the new era. Nonetheless, Faiza, the foil for her morally bankrupt mother and sisters who eagerly accept the new corrupt reality imposed on them, refuses to participate. Instead, she clings to memories of her upright father, dreaming of preserving the family's past reputation and honor, resisting the corruption immersing her home. This would be the first time that Abdel Kouddous expressed in fiction a sense of regret for the end of the old order. The symbol of steadfast dignity, purity, and honor defying degradation, Faiza, whose name means "victorious," is the double for Abdel Kouddous, seemingly the sole person still defiantly clinging to principles before the corruption and hypocrisy of the Nasser era.

Like Salah before his awakening at the end of *The Empty Pillow*, Faiza refuses to accept reality and flees into fantasy in order to avoid confronting the painful truths around her. A romance writer named Munir Hilmi serves as the source of her fantasies: "Nothing she saw or read could take over her imagination like the stories of Munir Hilmi. All his stories depict true love and all his heroines are honorable and pure. They all give their souls to love, protecting their bodies for it. Her imagination oppressed her to the point that she couldn't differentiate between imagination and reality."[94] Munir is the spinner of tales that have deluded Faiza, the writer who has brought out her innate desire for virtue and honor, conjuring her projections and fantasies. Munir, the thirty-eight-year-old writer of romance novels and prophet of pure love, is clearly meant to evoke Abdel Kouddous, who was, of course, speaking of love on his weekly radio program at the time of the novel's serialization. But this depiction is a decoy. Instead, Munir represents the object of fantasy and delusion, the one who has convinced the heroine through deceitful words and false appearances that he will save and protect her purity and chastity. In other words, Munir is Abdel Kouddous's projection of Nasser, before the coup and in the months afterwards, when he naïvely assumed that Nasser shared his faith in democracy. It is Faiza who serves as the double of Abdel Kouddous, the one who projects her principles onto the spinner of tales, fantasizing about his purity and ideals and taking his false words as gospel. Before the two 1954 jailings, the blurring of Abdel Kouddous and Nasser into a single character appeared in works like *God Is with Us* and *I'm Free* as the revolutionary journalist, the principled committed leader who brings freedom and independence to Egypt. After the jailings, this blurring would be put to a different purpose in the narrative, one that reveals the image of the fake savior who seeks to desecrate—not protect—the purity and principles of the main character.

One night, Faiza comes home to the usual party of debauchery in her living room and is shocked to find Munir Hilmi there being entertained by her sisters. Since he represents her projections of purity and innocence—her fantasy of the ideal man who clings to pure love and sincere principles—she cannot understand why he has come to their corrupt apartment. Locked in her delusion—like Salah in his love for Samiha in *The Empty Pillow*—Faiza cannot see the reality that is right in front of her. Even though Munir holds an alcoholic drink in his hand as her sisters entertain him, just as Nasser's intentions of dictatorship should have been obvious to Abdel Kouddous—as his mother barked at him in his jail cell—Faiza refuses to accept reality and continues to cling to fantasy, projection, and self-delusion. She talks with Munir briefly about his fiction, declaring herself a devoted fan, and then calls him the next day to set up a time to meet. As she gets ready to leave for his apartment, she convinces herself that Munir must be the "angel" that she always imagined from his stories, gesturing to Abdel Kouddous's depiction of Nasser as an "angel" in his editorials both before and after the coup.[95]

Nonetheless, right before meeting him, Faiza has a nagging feeling that something is wrong. She now imagines Munir as a doctor—yet another link between Munir and Nasser—someone who will cure her of her anxieties: "She's going to tell him her story as if she were going to a doctor to ask him for treatment."[96] Nasser clearly would have understood the reference. When Faiza arrives, she begins to tell Munir the story of her family with tears in her eyes as if in therapy. She describes her attachment to her father—the symbol of the pure but now deceased revolution in the aftermath of the coup—and how her household has fallen into disrepute since his death. The suave Munir, who repeatedly offers her alcohol and listens to her in boredom, begins playing the role of the psychologist, offering up a clumsy analysis, which no doubt irritated Nasser when he read this installment. As if Abdel Kouddous were quoting Nasser during his "analysis," telling him to let go of the past and accept the reality of the present, Munir tells Faiza, "The cause of your torture is because you see the world around you through the eyes of your father, not your own eyes. You can't see what your mother and sisters see. You judge everything through the mentality of your father."[97] When Faiza tells Munir that she understands love as he describes it in his novels, he responds, "Imagination is one thing and the truth is something else."[98] Faiza, presumably like Abdel Kouddous, still does not take the hint. As she gets ready to leave, she tells Munir that he has no idea how much he has made her feel better, as if she is a dupe, praising a quack doctor for what she thinks was successful treatment, seemingly mocking the way Abdel Kouddous, at the end of *The Empty Pillow*, had tried to convince Nasser that he had "cured" him after their meetings in August 1954.

Just as Salah—and, presumably, Abdel Kouddous—refuses to accept reality despite the obvious, Faiza returns home "in the paradise of her delusions," seeing none of the warning signs of the coming betrayal.[99] Weeks pass as Faiza calls Munir every day to confide in him, offering herself up to him for psychoanalytic treatment, yet another reference that only Nasser would have understood at the time of serialization. Faiza finally goes to visit Munir at his apartment again and, as if Abdel Kouddous were mocking Nasser directly, tells him, "I can't live without hearing your voice morning and night, as if it's medicine."[100] Feeding her fantasies, Munir tells Faiza only what she wants to hear in the hopes of exploiting her sexually: "You're the heroine of every story I write. You're my imagination. You're the truth that I'm living!"[101] He then leans in and kisses her, putting his hands under her shirt, squeezing her "innocent" breasts. Shocked and outraged, Faiza quickly jumps away. Instantly realizing that she has been duped, she tells Munir that this is not the love that he writes about in his stories. As if quoting Nasser responding to Abdel Kouddous outraged at being asked to serve as his translator for the public, Munir tells Faiza: "To hell with novels and novelists."[102] This is the moment when Faiza realizes that Munir is nothing but delusion and depravity. Devastated after she leaves, Faiza is unable to sleep the entire night. In stark contrast to Salah in *The Empty Pillow*—as if Abdel Kouddous is showing Nasser how far he has come since his late 1954 arrest—Faiza hits her pillow in anger. Munir's words have now been revealed as immoral deception, a means for him to arrive at base sexual satisfaction with no relation to the noble principles and honorable appearances that she had assumed. Munir therefore evokes a Nasser who had used fake words to excite the fantasies of Abdel Kouddous and the nation with false depictions of love and democracy, spun only for the purpose of rapacious dictatorship, here framed as sexual exploitation. Absent is any romance.

Tortured by confusion but determined to force Munir to recognize and validate her dignity, principles, and honor, Faiza boldly returns to his apartment to confront him, suggesting an outraged Abdel Kouddous defying Nasser after being asked to serve as his "translator." Munir has now dropped all pretenses and, as if mocking Abdel Kouddous's "Whisper" radio program, which aired weekly at the time, tells Faiza that he has never been in love, taunting her for believing his sweet words, insisting that she only loves "the fake images that you see in my stories."[103] Munir tries to seduce Faiza again, and he becomes enraged when she suggests that he must marry her in order to prove his love, evoking the outrage that Nasser must have felt at Abdel Kouddous with his repeated demands for formal commitment to fostering a democratic Egypt. A stark contrast to Amina in *I'm Free*, Faiza openly asks for marriage, but Munir scorns her for it, marking how any hopes for the security of guaranteed documentation for Nasser's rule had vanished by early 1955.

In her third encounter with Munir, Faiza has exposed him for the abuser he is. She has also uncovered the depths of her own delusion and projections about him, unearthed her naïveté, foolishness, and shame for thinking that he was anything but a man seeking sexual pleasure, a new framing for Nasser's now-abusive relationship with Egypt that Abdel Kouddous was developing in this novel. Munir Hilmi is therefore the marker for Abdel Kouddous's own fantasies and projections for Nasser, suggesting that Abdel Kouddous was as naïve as Faiza for believing that Nasser's sweet words about principles and democracy were anything but lies meant to provoke his fantasies to prepare him for the coming metaphorical sexual exploitation. Instead, like Munir, Nasser ultimately reveals his true nature to Abdel Kouddous, exposing his illusions, expressed in the novel through the metaphor of Munir wanting to seduce the deluded Faiza. She vows not to relinquish her honor, faith, and principles despite repeated pressure, a message of rejection that Abdel Kouddous was now sending directly to Nasser in the pages of *Rose El Youssef* with each weekly installment of the novel.

The novel then meanders through a series of episodes in which Faiza is confronted by the corruption and immorality of people who appear at first to be honorable, suggesting that Abdel Kouddous in each installment was exploring the anxieties he was feeling at the time. Grief and alienation begin to wear Faiza down, ultimately pushing her to try to play along with corruption, perhaps alluding to Abdel Kouddous's own exhaustion in navigating the regime in winter 1955. Faiza then decides to return to Munir Hilmi, "the man who dealt her the first blow in clarifying her imagination and principles."[104] Once again recycling the language from his editorials in August 1952 when he described the Officers as "angels," Faiza goes to Munir now knowing that "he wasn't an angel, but just a man like all men, a scoundrel. She was on her way to falling, falling, falling to where all men are, to the state of decay, in the mud."[105] Transferring his accommodation of Nasser in sexual terms, Abdel Kouddous depicts Faiza's return to Munir at the end of the novel as the sexual fall, the moment of self-degradation and soiling. In order to drive this point home to Nasser, Abdel Kouddous frames Faiza returning to Munir as if she were going to jail. After entering his building, she closes the elevator door "as if it were a narrow cell in the prison of sin."[106] When she enters his apartment—five years since their first meeting, which just happened to be the amount of time since Abdel Kouddous first met Nasser—she now knows Munir for who he is: "She didn't see him as she did the first time.... Instead, she felt his cunning invitation. She smiled as if smiling at the devil who was trying to appear to her like an angel."[107] As if Abdel Kouddous were mocking Nasser for marginalizing and erasing him from the revolution, Munir barely recognizes Faiza when she arrives. Nonetheless, she moves forward to give in, seemingly driven by a compulsion to submit, letting Munir grope her, employing the sexual to frame Abdel Kouddous's own submission to Nasser in fall 1954.

As hard as Faiza—and Abdel Kouddous—may try, principle and conscience cannot remain repressed. Faiza suddenly becomes cold, like a corpse, stopping Munir in his tracks. He asks Faiza why she came and she replies, "No one accepts me with my honor and dignity. Every road that I took was barred, barred by scoundrels, decay, and horrible morals. Finally, I decided that I'll be a scoundrel too, decayed, with terrible morals because it's the only road that's open to me."[108] The barred road is therefore the road to morals, principles, conviction, honor, and

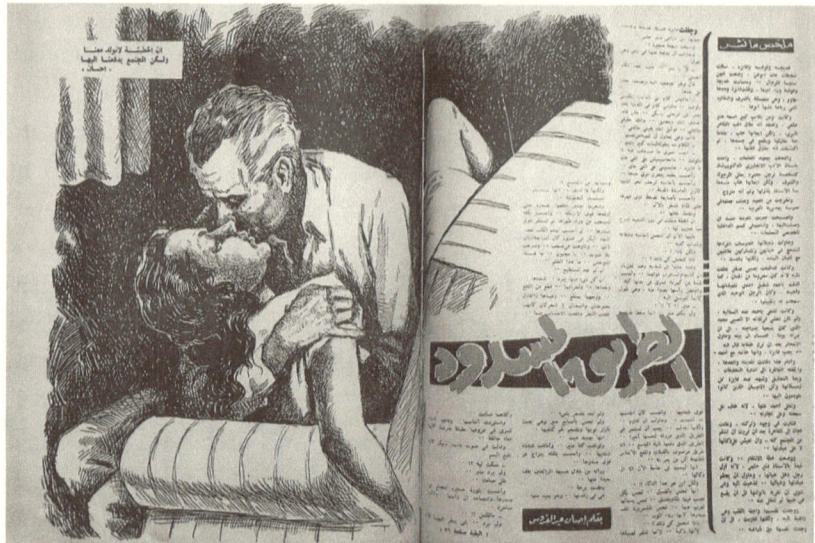

**Figure 13.** Final installment of *The Barred Road*. *Rose El Youssef*, 11 April 1955.

dignity. It is the barred road before Abdel Kouddous, with Nasser blocking the gate that leads to democracy, freedom, and rule of law. In this encounter, Faiza—like Abdel Kouddous in his encounters with Nasser after his imprisonment—feels a compulsion to compromise her morals and principles, to accept the sexual fall, to accommodate the abuses and sexual satisfaction of the scoundrel. At the time of writing, this was the only way for Abdel Kouddous to navigate the reality of such a corrupt society.

The novel does not end on such a bleak note. Surprisingly, it is Munir who suddenly saves Faiza and preserves her dignity. He tells her that she must be convinced of what she is doing and that she should remain on the same road that she has traveled her entire life, much as if Abdel Kouddous has written the validation that he had wanted from Nasser since the coup into the fictional text. He tells her, "Don't do anything against your principles. Don't do anything you'll regret."[109] He does not simply stop Faiza from the fall. He even apologizes to her, serving as another moment when Abdel Kouddous used fiction to try to guide Nasser or at least to compensate himself for what he could not receive in reality. "You're a fine, pure, honorable girl," Munir says. "Stay like that forever. Forgive me if I wronged you at first. I needed five years to understand that I abused you and that you're not like the other girls I know."[110] In this climax, Munir stops himself from sexually abusing the pure, submissive Faiza because he finally recognizes her morals and principles. In this story Abdel Kouddous was validated for clinging to the road of democracy, not succumbing to dictatorship. Even if he never received a similar apology from Nasser, fiction perhaps became the means to achieve a curative effect, at least temporarily.

Nonetheless, even though Munir encourages Faiza to hold on to her principles, he has not changed. He tells her, "I won't forgive you if you sin. If you do, you'll find me as scoundrel with you and worse too."[111] He remains the corrupt figure who uses false appearances and honeyed words to exploit and seduce women whom he has deluded. The road of freedom and democracy is still barred. Walking on the street, Faiza, like Abdel Kouddous, remains uncertain about how to move forward. The novel ends with this: "She was so confused that she almost lost her mind. . . . Is there another road beside the barred road? She didn't know. . . . She moved forward to join the great procession. The procession of confused women!"[112] Imbued with uncertainty and confusion, Faiza stands as the double of Abdel Kouddous in early 1955 as he was serializing the novel, uncertain at how to navigate a corrupt society and the entrenchment of Nasser, echoing his words of confusion in *Rose El Youssef* after his release from prison in summer 1954. While Abdel Kouddous wrote the validation of his principles and virtue into the text, he, like Faiza, concluded the novel deeply anxious and confused about the road forward in a debased country where he felt like the last person clinging to principles, morals, and honor. With the dictatorship now embedded, the end of the novel reflects the ambivalence, anxiety, and uncertainty about the path forward for Abdel Kouddous. Does he accept reality, accommodate dictatorship, and serve as Nasser's "translator" or cling to his faith in his principles in the hope that the barred road before democracy will eventually be opened? Abdel Kouddous was using the weekly deadline of each installment published in *Rose El Youssef* to explore and confess his own ambivalence and confusion.

This deeply unsettled ending did not sit well with readers. Knowing next to nothing of Abdel Kouddous's personal anxieties and history with Nasser, they flooded *Rose El Youssef* with objections, angry that they too had been left confused, showing that Abdel Kouddous was at least successful in aligning the public with his own uncertainties. Nonetheless, frustrated readers incorrectly read the impact of the autobiographical on the text. Instead of understanding Faiza as a double for Abdel Kouddous in his confusion and anxiety on how to move forward in the face of Nasser's exploitation, readers thought that Abdel Kouddous ended the novel the way he did because he needed a quick conclusion before heading to Indonesia to report on the Bandung Conference, which was held 18-24 April 1955. It was during this historic conference that Nasser began his meteoric rise as an international icon of anti-imperialism and nonalignment. Once Abdel Kouddous returned to Cairo from Bandung, he wrote a short article addressing these objections, explaining, "This 'non-ending' didn't please anyone. I returned from Indonesia to find on my desk more than 500 letters, all of them blaming me for the confusion that I left Faiza and the readers in."[113]

According to Abdel Kouddous, most of the letter writers expected virtue to be victorious over sin, for Faiza to "marry her love and then live in bliss having children, exactly as happens in Egyptian movies."[114] He explained that the way he ended the novel—with Faiza anxiously confused between clinging to principles and accommodating corruption—was the only realistic conclusion. As if arguing from personal experience, Abdel Kouddous wrote, "Reality says that virtue doesn't triumph over sin.... In every human soul is an inclination for virtue, an inclination that resists evil and sin, and makes people live confused however much they are immersed in sin." Abdel Kouddous then rejected the premise that fiction should give a clear moral lesson. Instead, he declared, "All the writer can do is put you before a mirror for you to see yourself and the society that you live in so you don't stray and become seduced by imaginary stories." As if it were not clear enough from the novel, Abdel Kouddous was no Munir Hilmi, with his sweet words and fake fiction that seduce Faiza into believing that he had principles and ideals, covering up his degradation, corruption, and insidious true intentions. Instead, Abdel Kouddous positioned his fiction for the public as a defense against the kinds of fantasies, projections, and deceptions to which he—like Faiza—had fallen victim.

As Abdel Kouddous was serializing the novel, he was still giving his weekly "Whisper" radio addresses. Nonetheless, after his brief jailing sometime after the assassination attempt, Abdel Kouddous would no

**Figure 14.** Ihsan Abdel Kouddous with Ahmed Mazhar (right), who played Munir in the 1958 film adaptation of *The Barred Road*. Courtesy of the Abdel Kouddous family.

longer serve as Nasser's "echo" on the radio. Starting in early December 1954, Abdel Kouddous began focusing on a variety of mundane topics with no political undertones. For some four months, Abdel Kouddous continued to discuss the idea of love but emptied it of any elements that might make it appear to support or oppose the regime, completely ignoring the Officers and the revolution, just as his mother had done in *Rose El Youssef* in 1954. Nasser must have been disappointed.

Nonetheless, in March 1955, exactly when Abdel Kouddous was serializing the final chapters of *The Barred Road*, he suddenly offered some dissent in "Whisper." As Faiza serves herself up sexually to Munir in the installments at this time, Abdel Kouddous clearly decided not to do the same to Nasser on the radio. On 19 March 1955, Abdel Kouddous used his "Whisper" address to offer up a critique of freedom in the new era: "True freedom is that the state provides for the citizens a dignified life . . . the freedom that guarantees for you your life, the life of your kids, and achieves the future that all of us want."[115] While no doubt mild, this kind of comment was not at all what Nasser had expected when he put Abdel Kouddous on the radio in fall 1954. Coupled with the way Abdel Kouddous was ending *The Barred Road*, Nasser had had enough. The *Egyptian Radio Magazine* lists the last "Whisper" as read on 4 April 1955, the week before the last installment of *The Barred Road*. The weekly address was removed from the radio without notice or explanation. Abdel Kouddous had once again fallen out of favor.

Abdel Kouddous would later repeatedly offer an account that had nothing to do with his 19 March 1955 address or *The Barred Road* for why the program ended. Abdel Kouddous later explained that he concluded each address of "Whisper" with the expression: "Tisbahu 'ala khayr, tisbahu 'ala hubb," which translates approximately to "Good night, good love." As Abdel Kouddous recalled in late 1956, he used the word *hubb* or "love" at the time "to make it pure and clean, to return to it its strong noble meanings."[116] According to Abdel Kouddous, his enemies saw the word *hubb* differently. For them, Abdel Kouddous was spreading licentiousness, openly inviting people to have sex at the end of his evening address. According to Abdel Kouddous, his enemies were so enraged that they took their complaints to Nasser himself, with the goal of damaging his personal relationship with Abdel Kouddous. Nasser apparently told Abdel Kouddous to replace the word *hubb* with *mahabba*, which is from the same Arabic root as *hubb* but has a meaning closer to "affection." According to Abdel Kouddous, when he refused to make the change, the show was cancelled.[117]

Although this explanation for the end of "Whisper" is widely cited, it is highly dubious. Abdel Kouddous spoke about love and apparently used the expression "tisbahu 'ala khayr, tisbahu 'ala hubb" every week for some six months, a period of time which would have been far too long if it had sparked a crisis. And when Abdel Kouddous gave a radio interview in October 1959, he did not pause when the host invited him to end the program by saying "tisbahu 'ala khayr, tisbahu 'ala hubb" with no hint of controversy surrounding the expression.[118] Instead, the record shows that the removal of "Whisper" corresponded precisely with the 19 March 1955 address and the end of *The Barred Road*. Moreover, Abdel Kouddous confirmed this in one tantalizingly brief interview in 1981. In it, Abdel Kouddous mentions that Nasser had indeed let him continue the program after he refused to change the word *hubb*. Abdel Kouddous then explained that when he was going to give a radio address on freedom, the censor, Salah Salim, intervened and rejected it. He then confirmed that it was at this point that he was blocked from the radio. Perhaps, therefore, the final address of "Whisper," the transcript for which was published in the *Egyptian Radio Magazine*, was never read on the air. Revealing his disgust at the incident, Abdel Kouddous ended the brief interview by saying, "It's enough to have censorship in the press. I didn't need it on the radio too."[119]

Just as Nasser seemingly rewarded Abdel Kouddous for his depiction of being cured of his psychological illness at the end of *The Empty Pillow* by giving him the weekly radio program and allowing the screening of *God Is with Us*—even attending the premiere on 14 March 1955—he was now punishing Abdel Kouddous for his dissent on the radio and in *The Barred Road* by cancelling "Whisper." As Munir recognizes that Faiza cannot embrace sin and corruption at the end of *The Barred Road*, Nasser clearly recognized that Abdel Kouddous would no longer be a reliable voice on the radio supporting the regime or his translator for the public. The most popular fiction writer of the era was not going to serve as his echo, at least not for the time being.

With *The Barred Road* completed and "Whisper" cancelled, Abdel Kouddous left Egypt on 9 April 1955 to cover the Bandung Conference for *Rose El Youssef*. In his articles covering the conference, Abdel Kouddous appeared to be stunned by the attention and admiration that Nasser received throughout the trip as well as his charismatic performance and political skill. No doubt, the performance showed Abdel Kouddous that Nasser was now deeply embedded as Egypt's political leader, solidifying the reality that he was still confused about how to face. In the months after Bandung, Abdel Kouddous would sink deeper into depression and anxiety about the trajectory of the revolution and his sense of guilt and shame for what he saw as his role in creating its leader. By fall 1955, Abdel Kouddous would return to fiction again, this time to write an alternative history of the revolution and his own fraught relationship with Nasser, using fiction and confession to try to ease his regret and anxieties. Nonetheless, Abdel Kouddous would become increasingly desperate and frantic, shockingly eliminating Nasser in fiction when he could not do so in reality.

CHAPTER FOUR

# THE TIME OF RESISTANCE

> There were two phases of my life with Gamal Abdel Nasser, one before the Revolution and one after.
> 
> —*Tahia Gamal Abdel Nasser*,
> Nasser: My Husband *(2011)*

In winter 1955, as he was serializing *The Barred Road*, Ihsan Abdel Kouddous could not sleep. Like Faiza, who stays up all night after exposing Munir, Abdel Kouddous suffered from terrible insomnia. For him, however, insomnia lasted for weeks. Something was clearly weighing on him, causing him great anxiety, whether he realized it or not. On 28 February 1955, he wrote an article in *Rose El Youssef* titled "Sleep and Death." He explained how, most days, he drank twenty cups of coffee and smoked three packs of cigarettes, usually working at the office until two o'clock in the morning. "Then I go home with my head heavier than the statue of Ramses II, with the taste of coffee filling my mouth and my chest tight from smoking. I try to sleep but I can't."[1] Abdel Kouddous explained how he used many methods to try to put himself to sleep, including listening to records, looking at old photographs, and getting in bed to snuggle with one of his sons. "At these moments, I'm tortured.... I feel my soul revolt against everything, against myself, my work, my lot in life. I want to relax. I want to close my eyes. I want to sleep. I want to die!" For Abdel Kouddous, sleep was a kind of temporary death, a short-lived break from his anxieties: "When we don't sleep, we're tortured by insomnia and when we don't die, we're tortured by life!" He ended the piece trying to explain away his momentary pessimism, asking readers for forgiveness: "I'm writing this after a long night of insomnia!"

It was in the context of his insomnia—of something bothering him so much that it kept him up at night—that Abdel Kouddous began developing his eagerly anticipated next novel. On 29 August 1955, he wrote in *Rose El Youssef*, "I finished preparing a novel two months ago. I set the idea and subject, traced the characters, and organized the plot. All that remained was the title—two words that I've spent two months searching for."[2] It must have been during a night of insomnia that he found the title for his next novel, which was advertised for the first time on the bottom of that page—*I Do Not Sleep*, which in Arabic is indeed two words. Abdel Kouddous published the first installment on 3 October 1955 and serialized it weekly for five months. *I Do Not Sleep* would become his longest novel to date, outraging and enthralling readers, inspiring them to send hundreds of letters of praise and condemnation.

Abdel Kouddous serialized *I Do Not Sleep* during a particularly important time in the history of modern Egypt known as the "Period of Great Victories." It was during Nasser's ascendancy on the world stage after his success at the Bandung Conference, during which he developed messianic status at home and electric popularity in the Middle East and beyond. It also marked the end of the three-year transitional period and the application of the new constitution. During this time, the state became more and more interested in not only maintaining strict censorship over the press but also harnessing the arts for political purposes. As Khaled Mohi El Din notes of this period, "The revolution took upon itself the task of carrying out a disciplined and controlled process of enlightenment—governed by comprehensive and strict control from above."[3]

In spring 1955, Abdel Kouddous framed Faiza's confusion at the end of *The Barred Road* to express his anxiety and uncertainty about how to manage Nasser as well as the conflict within himself between holding true to the principles of the revolution and accommodating the realities of military dictatorship. By fall 1955, when he started serializing *I Do Not Sleep*, Abdel Kouddous had moved on from this confusion, turning it into despair and rage. In *I Do Not Sleep*, Abdel Kouddous, as he did in *God Is with Us* and *I'm Free*, once again used fiction to rewrite the origins of the coup. Instead of asserting his centrality as the leader who sparked the revolution, as he did in the earlier works, he now retold the history of the coup through allegory to explore his deep sense of grief, guilt, and melancholy over his role in plotting to expel the king and end colonialism while inadvertently working to embed a traitor into the bedrock of the nation. It was through this reframing of the origins and early stages of the revolution that Abdel Kouddous used romantic melodrama, with all of its revelation, exposure, and excess, to try to self-analyze and soothe his anxiety and despair by once again opening his regrets and guilt to the public. Clearly, he sensed a deep connection between confession and self-purification. Memory and regret remained irrepressible.

When the self-therapy of writing *I Do Not Sleep* was ultimately ineffective at allaying his despair, Abdel Kouddous faced Nasser's ensuing "victories" in summer and fall 1956—the evacuation of British military from Egyptian soil, the fourth anniversary of the revolution, and the stunning nationalization of the Suez Canal—with growing inner anguish. It was during this time that Abdel Kouddous, like other prominent journalists, had to voice support for Nasser in editorials that became increasingly overwrought in flattery and praise. Doing so, finally serving as Nasser's echo for the public, clearly increased his despair. Abdel Kouddous would turn to fiction in the aftermath of the seemingly triumphant 1956 Suez War to try once again to extract his sense of guilt for turning Egypt into a military dictatorship. In his novel, Abdel Kouddous shockingly lashed out in anger at Nasser by killing his double in fiction, writing an alternative history of the revolution and exacting vengeance for the suffering and disappointment that Nasser had imposed on him since summer 1952.

## I DO NOT SLEEP

The beginnings of *I Do Not Sleep* do not lie solely with Abdel Kouddous's insomnia in early 1955. In 1954, an eighteen-year-old woman named Françoise Sagan published an instant bestseller in France titled *Bonjour Tristesse*. The short novel is narrated by seventeen-year-old Cécile, as she spends her summer vacation on the Mediterranean with her playboy widower father and his two love interests. The novel was striking for Cécile's world-weary, cynical, and precocious narrative tone as well as her sexual attraction for her father. At first, Cécile's jealousy for her father's love interests pushes her to explore her own sexual longings for Cyril, a handsome young man who serves as the sexual surrogate for her father. But once her father gets engaged to Anne, a woman his own age, Cécile plots to break them up by convincing her father that Elsa, his first mistress, has begun an affair with Cyril. Her father eventually falls for the lie, and Anne, furious when she sees him kiss Elsa, drives off in a rage and dies in a car accident, ending the novel with Cécile triumphant and delighted to have her father to herself once again.

It is not certain that Abdel Kouddous read *Bonjour Tristesse*, but he very likely did by summer 1955.[4] Abdel Kouddous did not read French, and it did not appear in Arabic until late 1957, when the novel was published as part of the popular *Riwayat al-Jib* (Pocket Novels) series. Nonetheless, it was translated into English, which Abdel Kouddous could read well, in February 1955, and went through at least eight printings by summer 1955. It is easy to see why Abdel Kouddous would have been struck by the novel. It was imbued with themes that had already been obsessing him—sorrow, remorse, regret, and despair as well as sexual and moral degradation—all expressed through the voice of a disillusioned young female protagonist. Cécile's plotting to overthrow a tyrannical figure who has taken over her home was also a narrative strand that clearly struck Abdel Kouddous at a time when he was deeply anxious and regretful about his involvement in the lead up to the coup and its aftermath. Moreover, *Bonjour Tristesse* blurs the lines between its seventeen-year-old narrator and its seventeen-year-old author, Sagan, suggesting that the work was more autobiography than fiction, another element that would have appealed to Abdel Kouddous. In *I Do Not Sleep*, Abdel Kouddous seems to adapt elements of the plotline of *Bonjour Tristesse* into mid-1950s Cairo for the purpose of exploring his own guilt, regret, and despair at his role in orchestrating the coup and embedding a traitor to democracy—the man who hijacked his beloved revolution—within the fabric of the nation.

*I Do Not Sleep* purports to be a confession in the form of a long letter to Ihsan Abdel Kouddous, written by a young woman named Nadia Lutfi. This kind of writing was highly familiar to readers of *Rose El*

**Figure 15.** First installment of *I Do Not Sleep*. *Rose El Youssef*, 3 October 1955.

*Youssef*. Starting in the 1940s, Abdel Kouddous regularly received letters and visits from young women asking for his advice about love, letters that he frequently included and responded to in his columns. He published epistolary fiction as early as 1949 with the short story "My Friend's in Love," in which a man writes to Ihsan asking for advice on whether he should divorce his wife.[5] In the first installment of *I Do Not Sleep*, Abdel Kouddous dedicates the work to Nadia as if she were a real person: "To "N." She gave me her story, and then went far away after she took a handful of my days and a piece of my heart." The novel begins in a similar format as the other letters to Abdel Kouddous printed in *Rose El Youssef*: "Dear Ihsan, I'm Nadia Lutfi. You don't know me, even if I did turn your head both times you saw me...."[6]

Judging from the letters that soon flooded *Rose El Youssef*, *I Do Not Sleep* seized the imagination of readers unlike any of Abdel Kouddous's previous work. Between November 1955 and March 1956, nearly every issue of *Rose El Youssef* included at least one reader letter about the novel. The form of the work—the blurring of fiction and reality—was so convincing that, throughout its serialization and even afterwards, readers sent letters to *Rose El Youssef* convinced that Nadia Lutfi was indeed a real person and that the novel was a real letter of confession to Abdel

Kouddous, asking him for advice about her "sins." *Rose El Youssef* picked up on this and began having some fun with its readers. For example, one letter published on 5 December 1955 asks the magazine to end Nadia's letter to Abdel Kouddous in the following issue, but the magazine responds that "it's Nadia Lutfi's decision." On 23 January 1956, a reader accused Abdel Kouddous of not having studied psychology, and the magazine responded that it was Nadia Lutfi who had not studied psychology and the story was after all written by her. *Rose El Youssef* published a letter on 30 April 1956, after the novel had been completed, in which the writer issued a unique offer: "If the work is a call for marriage, I'm ready to marry Nadia Lutfi immediately!"

The most striking assertion that the story was real came on 9 January 1956. In this issue of *Rose El Youssef*, Abdel Kouddous wrote that Anwar Sadat, who was minister of state at the time, had just returned from a trip during which he met with ruler of Kuwait, Emir Abdallah al-Salim al-Sabah. In the meeting, the emir surprised Sadat by talking about Abdel Kouddous and then said, "*I Do Not Sleep* can't be fiction. A writer couldn't have invented all these things. They have to be real and must have happened to the writer personally."[7] Sadat asked Abdel Kouddous to confirm for the emir if the novel was real or not. Abdel Kouddous then explained: "I wrote a letter to the emir saying that it honors me to know that his Excellency is reading my novel and that he thinks it's a real story that happened to me. That means that I've succeeded in bringing the reader into its atmosphere. I therefore prefer not to respond to his question so I don't ruin his reading pleasure!"

Abdel Kouddous was indeed trying to point to elements in the story as real, but they were not what the public—nor the emir—seemed to assume they were. In the first installment of the novel, Nadia explains that she is writing to Abdel Kouddous to ask what has compelled her to commit crimes and then regret them with horror, her devastating insomnia serving as a symptom of her repression, of how she remained incapable of soothing herself in the face of self-loathing. Instead of a real woman writing a letter of confession to Abdel Kouddous, it was Abdel Kouddous attempting to transfer his burden to the public, to confess through Nadia his regret, anxiety, and despair about his involvement in the coup and subsequent work to entrench dictatorship. Through Nadia's letter, Abdel Kouddous returned once again to his own erased

**Figure 16.** Ihsan Abdel Kouddous at his desk at *Rose El Youssef*, mid-1950s. Courtesy of the Abdel Kouddous family.

history in the revolution, rewriting events now as romantic melodrama. The novel represents a bold act of dissent and resistance, an attempt at self-analysis but also to use fictional allegory to expose Nasser as a traitor to the nation and the revolution.

Once again, Abdel Kouddous wrote himself into the fictional text as a young woman, just as he had in *I'm Free* and *The Barred Road*, using Nadia as his double and her first-person narrative as his voice to confess his "crimes" to the public. In the text, Abdel Kouddous planted a number of biographical parallels between himself and Nadia. Her parents eloped because their families refused to accept their love. Nadia's mother and father were married for only three years, and they divorced before she could remember them together. Nadia's mother, a cold and distant socialite, married a wealthy older man after their divorce while her father dedicated himself to her, sacrificing his personal life to raise her. Nadia's mother displayed little interest in her when she was a child, living in a separate social world and only visiting her weekly. The depiction of Nadia's mother must have outraged Fatima Youssef. Nonetheless, Nadia is not a simplistic fictional double for Abdel Kouddous. As Nadia divulges how she orchestrates a coup within her household and then embeds a traitor in the family fabric, she channels the anxious split within Abdel Kouddous between confession and repentance, criminality and innocence, repression and persistent anxiety and regret.

The plot begins as sixteen-year-old Nadia is picked up from boarding school in Cairo by her bachelor father, a wealthy man with large land holdings. Echoing Abdel Kouddous's own upbringing in his grandfather's home, Nadia's father has enrolled her in the school because he feels that a single father cannot adequately care for a young woman. On the way back to the house, Nadia's father announces that she will now live at home once again because he has just gotten married. Safiya, his new wife, will raise and educate her in ways that he cannot. The symbolism of the setup is obvious, even if it was not to contemporaneous readers. The father, the landowner double of Egypt, has brought the stepmother, colonial Britain, into the household, or nation, to cultivate her and turn her into an adult.[8]

When Nadia meets Safiya as she arrives home with her father, she is initially intimidated by Safiya's confidence, self-assurance, and formality: "Perhaps the most prominent thing about her was the calm that radiated from her, like the tranquilizing scent of perfume. Everything about her was calm: the expression in her eyes, her smile, her hair, her modest clothes, her walk, her low voice, and her relaxed, sedate way of talking. This calmness pushed you to respect her, feel at ease with her, and trust her."[9] Now the "mistress of the house," Safiya as colonial Britain immediately takes control, looking to leave her mark everywhere as if it were a colonial worksite: "She'd turned the house completely on its head without adding anything new. She'd moved pieces of furniture from one place to another, rugs from one room to another, and reorganized the flowerpots and all the beautiful porcelain so that the house looked as if it had been refurnished, as if everything in it were bought just for her, on the occasion of her marriage."[10] Safiya installs a new "system" in the house, directing dinner with excessive formality, ceremony, and pleasantries; she seats herself at the head of the table as her father looks on with appreciation and respect. In order to reinforce her image as colonial overseer, Safiya also dedicates herself to training and disciplining the servants—the natives—so that they know how to do their work properly: "She was the one who put strawberry juice into the refrigerator. She was the one who taught Abdou to present it before dinner. This was a new world that she built for me and my father to live in—a world I couldn't have offered him when I was mistress of the house."[11] When the servants prove difficult to train and repeatedly forget or neglect her instructions, Safiya spouts colonial stereotypes in her annoyance, accusing them of ignorance and laziness.

Predictably, Nadia, like the teenage Abdel Kouddous, is appalled by the intrusion of the colonial foreigner into the household and immediately resists. She first thinks about the special love and close relationship that she has for her father, the double of Egypt. With Safiya's arrival as stepmother, however, Nadia is devastated that her father has brought this intruder into her house. Nadia is horrified that she has been displaced, becoming a second-class citizen in her own house, an unacceptable demotion: "I wanted to revolt, to destroy something, to pounce on my father and shake his shoulders, to wake him up to my existence, to make him remember me, to make him remember that I was everything in his life."[12] Colonial displacement does not lead immediately to revolt for Nadia. Instead, pointing to the sexual repressions of nationalist ardor, it rouses deep incestuous desires in Nadia for her father. When Nadia's uncle, who also lives in house, tells Nadia that she should get married too, she responds bitterly, saying, in earshot of Safiya, "Ever since I was young, I wanted to marry Daddy!"[13] Nadia watches obsessively and jealously as Safiya and her father giddily treat each other like newlyweds. Alone in her room, Nadia tortures herself by imagining her father and Safiya having sex. It is this jealousy that awakens her sexuality: "My imagination persecuted me. It wasn't only dripping those images into my head, it was also dripping its poison into my body. . . . It was the most intense physical feeling I had experienced in my life."[14]

Nadia's incestuous fantasies soon become embodied when she hears moans coming from her father's bedroom. Her horror at her father having sex with another woman turns to pleasure as she becomes addicted to listening to their whispers and nightly moans of pleasure. As Nadia eavesdrops from the adjoining balcony, she channels the thoughts and sensations of Safiya: "Something even more perverse happened. My imagination, stirred up by the whispering in my father's bedroom, evolved and began to overwhelm my pure, chaste body. I started imagining myself every evening in the arms of a man: my father. Yes, I was imagining myself in my father's arms, his arms around my body, his breath heating my face, hearing from him the same words that he whispered to his wife. I whispered in his ears the same words that she whispered to him, the words popping in the air like soap bubbles. I was in agony, intoxicated, rebuking him in delight, repulsed yet pleading for more. I was being tortured. I knew how deviant my mind was."[15] Like Gloria in Freud's work, Nadia experiences a masochistic sexual longing for her father. Masochistic, incestuous desire becomes the framing for Abdel Kouddous as he explored his own repressions, delusions, and fantasies of nationalist love for Egypt. It is these urges for the father that uncoincidentally become the staging ground that pushes Nadia, like Abdel Kouddous in his 1940s *Rose El Youssef* articles, to find a man to lead her to revolt and to serve as both the surrogate of an Egypt free of colonialism and the transferential object of love for the nation.

When the family goes to the famed Mena House Hotel for brunch, she sees a playboy, Mustafa, the double of the pre-coup Nasser, the man whom Abdel Kouddous had been calling out to: "I examined a lot of men until I found him. I found the man. The first man in my life!"[16] Mustafa is the same age as Nasser when the novel was serialized—thirty-six—and clearly resembles Nasser with his brown skin and short, black, frizzy hair and "small eyes" that "emitted a razor-like intelligence."[17] Nadia is immediately smitten. That night, she fantasizes not about her father but about Mustafa, transferring her incestuous desires onto him, just as Cécile does to Cyril in *Bonjour Tristesse*. At the same time, she imagines herself directing him, as he plays the role of the handsome, pliable lover: "I pictured myself with him. I saw him bow down at my feet. I saw myself point to him. He got closer to me, kissed my cheek and lips, and enveloped me in his arms, whispering in my ear the same words that my father whispered to his wife."[18] Just as Abdel Kouddous began anxiously engaging in "detective-novel" meetings with Nasser and the Officers in the early 1950s, so does Nadia feel the same thrill as she tricks her stepmother—the colonial authority—to sneak out for secret meetings with Mustafa: "I was frightened of the adventure and I had little confidence in myself. I didn't know exactly what I'd do. Despite that, I felt I was being driven on a path paved with happiness."[19] Like Abdel Kouddous when he began meeting with Nasser and the Free Officers in 1950, Nadia feels elation that she has found her masculine, virile, handsome hero: "Yes, he's a man, a strong man, but he's *your* man. . . . He's become the secret you're graced with."[20]

Their clandestine affair continues for over a year, just like the detective-novel plotting between Abdel Kouddous and the Free Officers during the time of the Rotten Weapons scandal. One night, when Nadia, her father, and Safiya go to a party, she sees Mustafa there. Mustafa meets Safiya, and Nadia is enraged when she sees him flirting with her. This unleashes Nadia's rage and fear that her stepmother could steal Mustafa from her, as if Abdel Kouddous were alluding to Nasser and the Officers delaying their coup in the months after the Rotten Weapons scandal, somehow becoming allured and coopted by colonial authorities. Echoing Abdel Kouddous's frenzied calls for violence in late 1951 and early 1952, Nadia frantically imagines laying waste to everyone around her: "An oppressive desire had taken hold of me to destroy—to destroy everything, to destroy my father's wife, my father, Mustafa, and myself. I was thinking like a crazy person."[21]

It is at this moment in the text that Abdel Kouddous rewrites the critical moment when he spoke with King Farouk's entourage about the Free Officers on 21 July 1952. Nadia suddenly decides that she will attempt to befriend her stepmother and reveal her relationship with Mustafa to soothe her anxieties and rage. As Nadia haltingly confesses to Safiya that she is in love, Safiya quickly interrupts her to complain angrily about the servants in the house, reenacting the master's colonial obsession with disciplining the natives: "'It's no use,' she said. 'These servants—no matter what you teach them, you have to stand there right next to them.'"[22] Just as Abdel Kouddous was appalled when the palace official insulted him when he began to tell him about the Free Officers three days before the coup—perhaps hinting at his own "affair" with them—Nadia is outraged by her stepmother's dismissal. Nadia is then full of relief that she did not fully confess her relationship with Mustafa and, like Abdel Kouddous after the palace officials mocked him that day, feels a new urgency to move forward in her plot to destroy the stepmother. Writing from the perspective of the end of the novel, Nadia frames the encounter through the regret and guilt at the aftermath of embedding a traitor in the household: "I wonder today what would have happened to me if Safiya had listened to everything I said, if she'd shared my secret with me and learned about my love for Mustafa. Maybe she could have saved me, my father, and herself. "[23] Abdel Kouddous discussed his pivotal exchange with palace officials in the days before the coup only once, in his first radio address to the nation on 29 July 1952. Here, now that his role in the coup had been fully erased, he uses his fictional double to reenact it, to reveal it again to the public, and to try to soothe his anxieties about this moment when he could have changed the course of Egyptian history. As with Abdel Kouddous on 21 July 1952, this insult is the critical moment that pushes Nadia toward her "crime," taking the final step to spark the coup.

Nadia decides that she must expel the colonizer from house. She confronts Mustafa about her disgust for Safiya to try to push him to action. When he refuses to condemn Safiya, Nadia realizes that Mustafa is not committed to her and that she cannot rely on him: "I didn't cost him anything. I was just a pretty girl who had thrown herself on him and whom he had taken to please himself with. . . . At that moment, I thought he kept me a virgin not because he was afraid for my future or out of respect for my reputation or because he was a refined man who believed in virtue. No, he kept me a virgin so he didn't have to bear the responsibility of turning me into a woman. . . . He was a coward fleeing from responsibility."[24] It is at this moment that Nadia moves forward with her plan to orchestrate a coup on her own, abandoning hope that Mustafa will help her, much like Abdel Kouddous must have felt waiting for the indecisive and hesitant Nasser to act in the aftermath of the Rotten Weapons scandal.

Nadia decides to plot to convince her father that Safiya is having an affair with her uncle Aziz. Aziz is a hedonist bachelor who lives on the second floor, above the others, without taking any interest in the household. He spends his nights drinking at hotel bars and lazily sleeps in until the afternoon. He is a freeloader, completely unengaged in the management of family farm, which pays for his opulent lifestyle. Safiya, colonial Britain, goes up to Aziz's living quarters each day to look after him, clean up, and make sure that he is presentable to come down to see Nadia and her father. When Nadia's father is angry at Aziz, he ridicules him by using second-person plural pronouns, mocking him for acting like royalty.[25] Clearly, Aziz is the double for King Farouk in the novel. And uncoincidentally, it is the relationship between him and Safiya that Nadia decides to exploit, seeking to convince her father, the double for Egypt, that the two are having an illicit affair and to manipulate him to expel them both—colonial Britain and King Farouk—from the household.

Nadia begins by planting doubts for her father about Safiya and Aziz's faithfulness. As if Abdel Kouddous needed to be any clearer about the metaphor for her coming confrontation with Safiya, Nadia declares, "I felt every drop of my blood howl like stray dogs running forward and barking as if I announced the revolution!"[26] One night, Nadia storms off from the dinner table, trying to draw attention to herself. She then goes to her father's study and writes a letter to her mother, detailing the affair that Safiya supposedly is having with Aziz: "I can't be quiet anymore or I'll go crazy. Imagine, Mother, that I'm living in a house that consists of nothing but cheating, that I'm witnessing betrayal with my own eyes but I can't speak. Imagine that the traitor is Auntie Safiya and that she's betraying my father! Who's she cheating on him with? My uncle! Yes, Mother, she's cheating on Daddy with Uncle Aziz. It's a betrayal that's been going on for months."[27] Nadia then leaves the accusation of treason out for anyone in the house to read. The written document, of course, is fake, suggesting that Abdel Kouddous is revealing here through his fictional double that his articles in *Rose El Youssef* before the coup that sought to push the public to revolt were fake as well, left out for the public to read, to convince them to revolt based on fabrications. As Abdel Kouddous himself explained multiple times after the coup, the purpose of the Rotten Weapons scandal was to incite revolution, not to bring anyone to justice.

Nadia leaves the "poison letter" on the office desk, wondering if her father will read it.[28] She watches as he passes by the letter several times and then finally picks it up. As if Abdel Kouddous is revealing his own contradictory emotions about the Rotten Weapons scandal in the buildup to the coup—in contrast to his public bravado in *Rose El Youssef* at the time—Nadia is immediately overwhelmed by regret: "I wanted to run to him, throw myself at his feet, wash his shoes with my tears, and confess...to plead with him not to believe me, not to trust the letter he'd read, and go back as he was."[29] Nonetheless, conscious regret is no match for repressed compulsion. "All those feelings couldn't save me from my crime or push me to save my father and his wife, to save the whole house. It was as if I had two people inside me. One who felt things and was tortured under the whips of her conscience and another who didn't feel anything, who wasn't tortured at all, but was a deformed criminal standing coldly frozen, the blood of her crime dripping between her fingers. The criminal was victorious, the one ruling my being."³⁰ Despite her awareness of the crime and its consequences, Nadia does nothing as she watches her devastated father discover the supposed treason being committed under his roof.

Perhaps like Abdel Kouddous in the wake of the Rotten Weapons scandal, Nadia is now locked in the lie. She knows that she must move forward with her crime and prove the treason to her father or she will lose him forever. The next morning, Nadia watches in horror as her father begins his revolt, lashing out angrily and irrationally at both Safiya and Aziz. Now that her plot has been hatched, it is moving forward beyond her control. Nadia reveals, "I felt the entire house shake and myself shake with it. I felt that its foundation would collapse and that it would collapse on me, but what could I do?"³¹ It is the crumbling foundations of the house, the beginning of her wish fulfillment, that arouses Nadia sexually, pushing her to want consummation with Mustafa, framed in the text as a "a rougher and more exciting adventure."

That evening, when her father, stepmother, and uncle all leave for dinner, Nadia manipulates Mustafa to sneak into her house. The typically confident Mustafa is shaken and insecure, full of anxiety and fear yet unable to control his sexual desire for Nadia. He finally takes Nadia's virginity in a frantic climax of desire: "He couldn't bear my resistance. He lifted his lips from mine and a terrifying look sparkled in his eyes. With both hands, he ripped off my robe as if he was crazy. He then grabbed me by my hair and pulled me violently to the ground."³² Despite the suggestiveness of the scene, Abdel Kouddous makes it clear that this is not the coup. Overwhelmed by fear and anxiety, Mustafa flees immediately, abandoning Nadia and rejecting any responsibility for what he has done. Nadia has brought Mustafa into the household and given herself fully to him, but he runs off terrified, abandoning her, proving himself to be a coward at the moment of consummation.

It is at this point that Nadia must take control of matters herself, gesturing to Abdel Kouddous's sense of directing the officers in the buildup to the coup. After orchestrating one final suspicious encounter between her uncle and stepmother, Nadia's emotional and easily manipulated father snaps. When he returns to the house in a rage, screaming at Safiya and tossing her clothes to the ground, Nadia knows that her plot has finally succeeded and that the coup has begun. Instead of delight, however, she feels panic, like Abdel Kouddous on the afternoon of the coup: "The feeling of the gambler left me and terror took its place. I felt a terrifying fear that almost tore out my heart."³³ Even at the moment of victory, when Egypt has finally risen up to expel colonial Britain and the king, Nadia realizes that she has the opportunity to relent, hinting at the anxieties that Abdel Kouddous felt watching the coup unfold that day in the Abbassia barracks: "I found myself thinking seriously about aborting my plan before it was completed. What was I doing? Oh God, what was I doing?"³⁴ Nonetheless, she cowers as the events unfold before her eyes. Nadia's father tosses his brother out of the house for betraying the family and divorces Safiya on the spot, accusing her of being a traitor. Nadia tries to intervene and stop Safiya from leaving, attempting to confess what she has done: "'She's innocent, Daddy!' I said. 'Auntie Safiya is innocent and—.'"³⁵ Nadia then throws herself on her father and sobs: "'Don't believe it, Daddy! . . . I'm a liar. I'm the criminal. Your daughter is the criminal. I—.'"³⁶ Despite articulating her guilt and regret, her father pushes her aside, refusing to listen.

Once Safiya and Aziz leave the house and the coup has been completed, Nadia collapses on the ground, gesturing to Abdel Kouddous's own moment of collapsing in sleep after returning home on the afternoon of the coup. Possibly, this moment of climax for Abdel Kouddous had become the wellspring of regret. Just as Salah collapses in the bar after the symbolic coup in *The Empty Pillow* when Samiha marries her doctor fiancé, Nadia, unable to face the reality of what has happened in the metaphorical house, falls to the ground and passes out: "My fainting was real. There was no fabrication or acting. The ugliness of my crime had overwhelmed me until I could no longer bear myself. The intensity of the crime had become greater than I could handle."³⁷ As for Salah— and, perhaps, for Abdel Kouddous on the afternoon of the coup—this is the moment of melodramatic rupture. According to Peter Brooks, melodrama "refuses to content itself with the repressions, the tonings-down, the half-articulations, the accommodations, and the disappointments of the real."³⁸ This helps explain why melodrama was so attractive to Abdel Kouddous. It was the literary mode of openly acting out repressed confrontations.

By giving emotions full-throated articulation, melodrama resists censorship and accommodation, which was clearly of great appeal to

Abdel Kouddous. As Brooks argues, "The genre's very existence is bound to this possibility, and necessity, of saying everything. If we can sense its appeal (as well as its limitations), it must be because we are attracted to (though perhaps simultaneously repulsed by) the imaginary possibility of a world where we are solicited to say anything, where manners, the fear of self-betrayal, and accommodations to the Other no longer exert a controlling force."[39] According to Brooks, melodrama, which emerged during the French Revolution, is fundamentally democratic. While focusing on the way the genre articulates repression, Brooks identifies a crucial paradox: "Melodrama so often, particularly in climactic moments and in extreme situations, has recourse to non-verbal means of expressing its meanings. Words, however unrepressed and pure, however transparent as vehicles for the expression of basic relations and verities, appear to be not wholly adequate to the representation of meanings, and the melodramatic message must be formulated through other registers of the sign."[40] Clearly, this is Nadia's collapse. At the moment of the coup—the expulsion of the stepmother and uncle—words cannot articulate the weight of the climax.

It seems like not a coincidence that the installment of the novel that depicted the coup was published on 26 December 1955, the last issue of *Rose El Youssef* before the end of the three-year transitional period. Betrayal was clearly on Abdel Kouddous's mind. A week earlier, the magazine published a stunning editorial titled "We Want the Constitution Because We Believe in Democracy" under the pseudonym "The Egyptian Citizen," no doubt written by Abdel Kouddous.[41] It was a shocking act of protest against the lack of democracy in Egypt as the three-year transitional period drew to a close. It seems that Abdel Kouddous went one step further by timing the installment of the novel with the metaphorical coup to appear as another stark reminder of the lack of democracy in the country. Just as Abdel Kouddous appeared to be doing in this installment, Nadia tries to confess her regret and guilt to her father—Egypt—but to no avail: "I was at the point of screaming at them, telling them that they were all idiots, that they didn't know . . . they didn't know that I was a criminal."[42] Even if contemporaneous readers did not pick up on the allegory of the novel in the aftermath of Abdel Kouddous's erasure from the history of the revolution, Nasser would certainly have understood the link between

Nadia's trauma during the fictional coup and the end of the three-year transitional period.

Now that her stepmother and uncle have been expelled, Nadia cannot shake her regret at what she has done. Alluding to how Abdel Kouddous contacted the British consulate in Cairo in August 1952, as discussed in chapter 2, Nadia calls Safiya. "'I don't care about my health,' I said as if apologizing for something she didn't know about. 'All I care about is that you come back home. Without you, the house is worthless. It's empty, with no feeling. Please, Auntie!'"[43] Just as Abdel Kouddous spoke with James Murray, possibly expressing regret soon after the coup for his own role in helping to install dictatorship in Egypt, Nadia articulates her own regret and guilt by begging Safiya to return to the house. When she demurs, Nadia knows that there is nothing that she can do to convince Safiya to return. Gesturing perhaps to Abdel Kouddous's own anxieties and horrors in August 1952, Safiya now haunts Nadia, coming to represent a specter that she cannot shake. "Unable to sleep, I'd spend the night wandering the house like a sad ghost.... I'd drift from room to room, feeling like I was fleeing from Auntie Safiya chasing me. I could almost see her image on the walls. I almost felt her breath behind my ears. I almost heard her footsteps following me. She was everywhere in the house.... I felt afraid, to the point of terror."[44]

As many close to him experienced, including Abdel Kouddous in August 1952, Nasser became a different person in the aftermath of 23 July. Predictably, with the coup complete, Mustafa, who represents the double of the pre-coup Nasser, now exits the novel. Once Nadia recovers from her illness after the expulsion of Safiya and Aziz, Mustafa symbolically loses all attraction for her: "Mustafa was no longer a drug that I was getting more and more addicted to. Instead, he became a man occupying my life. A man who couldn't move my emotions."[45] The climax of the coup wakes her up to the fantasy that she has projected onto him: "It became clear that I used to love Mustafa irrationally, unconsciously, and I now felt that I'd woken up. It was as if the blow I suffered after committing my crime was like the electric shock they give patients to jolt them out of their insanity. I woke up."[46] Like Abdel Kouddous in the weeks after the coup, Nadia realizes that Mustafa has been nothing more than an excuse for her to move forward in recklessly expelling Safiya: "My love for Mustafa wasn't the motive, rather it was a piece of evidence that I used to convince myself to commit this crime."[47]

Nonetheless, Nadia goes to see Mustafa one last time. Once again gesturing to Nasser as his therapist, Abdel Kouddous depicts Nadia as going to Mustafa hoping to "find a doctor to treat my psyche."[48] When she arrives, she realizes, "I'm here to present my problems to Mustafa. I'm sick and Mustafa is the doctor. Mustafa, with all his experience and all his philosophical ideas, could be my doctor."[49] Abdel Kouddous mocks Nasser not only with his usual depiction of him as a doctor offering psychoanalysis but also as a philosopher, with *Philosophy of the Revolution* published only weeks before this installment. Predictably, Nadia immediately feels that he is incapable of giving her treatment. Instead of receiving Nadia as a doctor, Mustafa, echoing Munir in *The Barred Road*, looks for sexual pleasure, suggesting that exploitation and humiliation had been behind the exchange when Nasser declared that he was giving Abdel Kouddous psychoanalysis. As if stressing to Nasser how he has now lost all magic for him, Abdel Kouddous wrote that Nadia feels none of the attraction of the past as Mustafa kisses her: "His lips opened and found mine. No, it wasn't a kiss. Despite all of Mustafa's skill, I didn't feel the intoxication of a kiss. It was simply two lips on mine—a kiss to which I submitted, thinking about when it would end."[50] As with Nasser after telling Abdel Kouddous that he was giving him psychoanalysis, Mustafa quickly notices Nadia's coldness. Echoing the end of *The Barred Road* and Abdel Kouddous's exchange with Nasser about the schoolboy's letter, Mustafa apologizes to Nadia for misunderstanding her. Instead of leaving their final encounter in confusion—as at the end of *The Barred Road*—Abdel Kouddous repositions Nadia in a position of strength and defiance, an act of clear dissent against his reader Nasser: "I felt that I'd gotten a heavy weight off my chest, that I'd recovered from the drug I'd been addicted to, and that it had been only a dream between me and Mustafa."[51] And with this, Mustafa, the pre-coup Nasser, is erased from Nadia's life.

Nadia now has her father to herself, but the reality of the post-coup household is, of course, not at all what she had imagined. Nadia is horrified at her father's transformation in the aftermath of the expulsions, pointing directly to Abdel Kouddous's own anxieties about the Egyptian public's erratic behavior after the coup: "My father became a different person. He was no longer dignified, calm, responsible, or tender. He became miserable—an unbearable drunk who could not get enough to drink. It didn't happen gradually but all of a sudden, as if, when his wife left the house, she took with her my father's mind, conscience, and will, and left him as an empty box."[52] In the aftermath of the coup, the father-nation is incapable of assuming responsibility for himself, descending instead into denial and self-destruction. Hoping to leave the ghosts of the past behind and end her father's deviance, Nadia arranges for them to move to a new apartment in the upscale Zalamek neighborhood, a symbol of the country's transition from the old era into the modern age. Nonetheless, suggesting once again the indifferent response of the public to the transition from the old to the new, the move to modernity does little to alter the father's behavior. Nadia now finds that her father is sleeping with prostitutes and discovers that he has been selling their land to finance his new profligate life.

With her father becoming increasingly lost and miserable, Nadia decides that she must "look for a wife to compensate him for the one he'd lost, so as to return his happiness, dignity, and feeling of responsibility and to bring him back to the house."[53] It is at this point that Abdel Kouddous writes his post-coup fictional double for Nasser, Kawthar, into the novel. Once again easily manipulating the gullible father, Nadia arranges meetings between the two and he quickly falls in love: "Kawthar's smiles wiped the suffering from his heart and made him forget the blow that had crushed him.... My father became as I wanted him.... I felt that I'd regained my father."[54] Through Nadia, Abdel Kouddous reveals how relieved he was at Egypt's increasing delight at Nasser, as if Nasser in the months after the coup had been able to restore the nation's happiness and dignity. Nadia soon realizes that Kawthar compensates her for the guilt of her crime: "Not only did I need her to preserve my father, but I also needed the life that she gave me. Her free spirit diverted me from my suffering, distracting me from the sickness of my psyche, from my sins, from my crimes. I decided to keep her at any price."[55] Like Abdel Kouddous working to wed Egypt to Nasser in the months after the coup, Nadia becomes convinced that she must arrange her father's marriage to Kawthar. Through Nadia, Abdel Kouddous now began the process of confessing to the public why he worked to embed Nasser into the nation after the coup. Orchestrating the marriage between Egypt and Nasser served as a way to compensate for his guilt and horror at his responsibility for plotting the coup. This time, Nadia works to bring the lover into the household instead of expelling one, just as Abdel Kouddous no doubt felt personal responsibility for orchestrating Egypt's romance with Nasser in the aftermath of 23 July. Her father and Kawthar are quickly married with rushed formalities, seemingly like Egypt's marriage to military dictatorship. With her father married and happy thanks to her, Nadia, feeling that she has now cleansed her conscience and atoned for her sin, will be able to sleep once again.

Predictably, the outcome is not at all what Nadia—or Abdel Kouddous—anticipated. As early as the engagement, Nadia becomes suspicious that Kawthar is having an affair, suggesting that Nasser had already turned to treason against the nation at the earliest stages of his marriage to Egypt, just as Fatima Youssef had insisted in Abdel Kouddous's prison cell. At first, Nadia, like Abdel Kouddous, does not heed the warning signs as Kawthar sneaks off to talk in whispers on the phone when her father is absent. Only a few weeks after orchestrating the marriage, Nadia, like Abdel Kouddous, discovers the truth, realizing that she has inadvertently embedded a traitor into the family home: "Yes. She was betraying my father, robbing him of his honor, bleeding him of his dignity with another man. I had kicked the faithful wife out of his life and put a cheating one in her place. . . . Everything around me was filthy. Everything around me was hypocrisy, lies, deception."[56] Horrified at what she has done, Nadia is overwhelmed by a new kind of regret and anxiety. She knows that she could reveal the treason to her father—just as Abdel Kouddous could have revealed Nasser as a traitor to the public through his platform *Rose El Youssef*—but decides that the consequences are too great: "I could crush her. I could kick her out of the house like a dog . . . [But] no, my father must not know. Kawthar had to stay in his life at any price. Whatever it cost. Whatever this charade, this hypocrisy, this deception cost me."[57] Not exposing the traitor is therefore a new form of abuse for her, one that compounds the horror of plotting and executing the coup: "I, alone, was being tortured. I, alone, smelled the scent of betrayal, a bitter heavy stench entered my lungs."[58]

Just as Abdel Kouddous vocally supported Nasser in the aftermath of the coup despite knowing that he was betraying Egypt by installing dictatorship instead of the democracy that he promised, Nadia begins to cover up Kawthar's affair, concocting stories to her father to explain Kawthar's trysts with her lover. And just as Nasser knew that he had control over Abdel Kouddous, who was willing to concoct lies for him to the public to cover up his treason, Kawthar exploits Nadia to cover up her cheating: "She knew she had me by the neck and that I wouldn't be able to do anything about her treachery. She knew I was drinking the poison silently and that I was letting her trample my dignity, that she could whip me whenever she wanted and I wouldn't moan or complain. She knew I'd cover up for her, not out of love for her but to preserve my father's happiness. She knew I'd sacrifice everything—my dignity, my comfort, my entire life—for this love, the love of my father."[59] Through Nadia, Abdel Kouddous confesses to the public his anxieties about being trapped into executing the cover up for Nasser's turn to dictatorship, his committing treason against Egypt: "I was tortured horribly. I was tortured by the wound from having my own dignity trampled. I was tortured by the deception of my father. I was tortured by my hatred for Kawthar, a hatred branding me, burning my heart."[60] Like Abdel Kouddous before the public, Nadia is careful to disguise her disgust before her father, despite her hatred for Kawthar and her self-loathing. Like Abdel Kouddous, Nadia is forced to pretend before her father that she loves the new stepmother, whose romance with the father she secretly orchestrated, knowing full well that she is engaging in dissimulation.

Kawthar becomes more and more impudent, savoring humiliating Nadia by forcing her to orchestrate more elaborate cover-ups of the cheating. When Kawthar arranges for her lover to meet her and Nadia at Groppi's café, Nadia is shocked. To Nadia's horror, her father happens to walk by at that moment and comes into the café to find Kawthar's lover there with them. Abdel Kouddous makes the symbolism of his fictional double serving as national metaphor explicit: "I had to say something to save this situation, to save my father from death as Joan of Arc saved her nation, and then was burned alive."[61] Kawthar is delighted when Nadia concocts a lie on the spot to cover up the affair.

In a radio interview in October 1959, Abdel Kouddous explained, "When I write, I act. . . . When I write a girl, for example, I find myself when I write that I feel that I'm playing the role of this girl, I live inside her. . . . It's a very exhausting emotion. . . . It's an internal performance, not a performance on a stage."[62] Writing Nadia's latest cover-up must have been particularly painful for Abdel Kouddous. As if Abdel Kouddous could no longer repress the rage that he felt toward Nasser for savoring his humiliation, he shockingly depicts Nadia fantasizing about taking revenge against Kawthar: "Fear turned into violent revolt building up inside me. I dreamed I had a knife in my hand and I was ready to stab Kawthar. I stabbed her until she fell to the ground and I was washed my feet with her blood. Then I cut her body into pieces and tossed them to the dogs."[63] Abdel Kouddous writes the taboo of murdering Nasser as a form of catharsis when he felt the most oppressed and humiliated. The metaphor of fiction provided him with the framework not simply to dissent but also to articulate the unacceptable to the public.

Nadia's father not only is oblivious to the treason taking place in the household but is in the thrall of love and devotion, reflecting Egypt's frenzied infatuation with Nasser at the time of the novel's serialization, a period that Saïd Aburish calls "the golden age Nasser."[64] Nadia's father tells her, "You can't imagine how much I love her. I never thought I could love someone this much."[65] Echoing how Abdel Kouddous must have felt watching the euphoric crowds greeting Nasser wherever he went by this time, Nadia feels pity for her father: "He seemed like an overgrown child who didn't know anything about what was going on around him. He was a child I loved: my child. Should I open his eyes to see the world as it was.... Should I put a stop to the beautiful dream he was living? No.... He won't ever wake up.... At any price, no matter what happens."[66] Despite the obvious, Nadia's father remains in bliss, blinded by his love for his adulterous wife: "His love for Kawthar had swallowed up everything, even his past."[67] To Nadia's horror, her father, the double for the easily duped Egyptian people, is the only happy person in the house, the nation, that is now governed by a traitor. Nadia fails to cope with the misery and emptiness of living in the same house as the happy father, totally ignorant of his wife's treason, which Nadia bears responsibility for.

The novel ends with Nadia, like Abdel Kouddous, utterly devastated, confessing "crimes" through the written text but incapable of finding catharsis: "I live in boredom and emptiness. I hate my mirror, my bed, and my house. I don't know what's good and what's evil. I don't try to know.... I'm a person of nonexistence, of emptiness. Nothingness, nothing."[68] It is only her hatred for Kawthar that proves that she is alive. Nonetheless, in the final lines of the novel, Nadia stresses that while she may still be alive, she is like the walking dead. Echoing what Abdel Kouddous wrote about himself in his article "Sleep and Death" in February 1955, Nadia ends the novel in limbo between sleep and death: "I don't sleep. Maybe because to sleep, I'd have to be awake. And I'm not awake. Today, there's no waking up or sleeping in my life. I'm dead. I move like the dead and I sleep in my bed like the dead, a dead person with open eyes. I want to close my eyes so I can sleep. When will I sleep?"[69] Becoming the waking dead is the way that Abdel Kouddous now framed himself as someone who cannot sleep, not just because of regret for plotting the coup and embedding a dictator in nation but also for being forced to continue to cover up Nasser's obvious treason to keep the easily duped nation happy in its marriage to him.

This is how the first edition of *I Do Not Sleep*, which was published some six months after the final installment in the magazine, concludes. This ending, however, was not the one that Abdel Kouddous wrote for the original serialization in *Rose El Youssef*, demonstrating a rare example of him editing his own work between the original serialization and the first edition of a novel. The final installment of *I Do Not Sleep* in *Rose El Youssef*, published on 12 March 1956, ends as follows: "This emptiness and boredom which surround me push me fully to evil. This evil is what only the law of heaven punishes or the judge of the court of the soul. I don't sleep when I commit my crimes. I don't sleep out of regret for committing them. Yes. I don't sleep. When will I sleep?"[70] The final installment of *I Do Not Sleep* in *Rose El Youssef*, unlike the first edition of the novel, makes no mention of death. Instead, Nadia does not sleep because she is tortured by regret not only for what she has done but also for continuing to lie to cover up the treason of Kawthar and the deception of her father. It is the feeling of regret—for expelling the stepmother, embedding the traitor in the house, and continuing to dupe the father—that the final installment stresses. The first edition of the novel, however, ends with Nadia catatonic, in a permanent state between sleeping and death, suggesting that Abdel Kouddous had moved from regret to an even deeper despair and desperation several months after he finished the novel, taking the opportunity of publishing *I Do Not Sleep* as a book to express his shifting perspective on his depression.

Instead of concluding in a state of confusion and uncertainty about the future, like *The Barred Road*, *I Do Not Sleep* ends, in both versions, with the main character—the double for Abdel Kouddous—devastated, imprisoned, unable to sleep, and without hope for the future. Spanning five years, the timeline of the novel carefully frames Abdel Kouddous's own history with Nasser, from when the two met sometime in 1950 until early 1956, when Abdel Kouddous, like Nadia at the end of the novel, was overwhelmed by anxiety and regret at what he saw as his personal responsibility for embedding Nasser. With its despair and melancholy, *I Do Not Sleep* represents a stark retelling of the revolution, a novel in which Abdel Kouddous attempts to reveal his grief over the permanent entrenchment of the military regime in Egypt through family melodrama. The military regime was no longer simply barring a road. The marriage considered at the end of *I'm Free* has finally happened, but it is a false marriage, one based on treason maintained and perpetuated by the dissimulation of Abdel Kouddous himself. As if stressing to the public the link between himself and Nadia Lutfi, Abdel Kouddous even published a piece the week after he completed serializing *I Do Not Sleep* in which he again described himself as suffering from insomnia.[71] Abdel Kouddous had ended *The Empty Pillow* with the words "and he slept," insisting to his reader—Nasser—at the time that he had finally found solace and comfort in the new era. The irrepressible insomnia that both Abdel Kouddous and his double Nadia were now suffering represented a stark rejection of that accommodation.

*I Do Not Sleep* was Abdel Kouddous's first sensational novel, but it was not the novel's shocking rewriting of the revolution as a family drama of plotting, treason, regret, and despair that caught the duped nation's attention. Not understanding the confessional nature of the text or Abdel Kouddous's personal relationship with Nasser, readers instead sent letters to *Rose El Youssef* accusing Abdel Kouddous of spreading degradation and immorality and, even worse, of being an existentialist.[72] Many of these letters denounced Abdel Kouddous for "poisoning" the youth. Despite the desperation in the novel, the public did not understand that it was Abdel Kouddous's own confession, not that of a young woman named Nadia Lutfi. Instead, the public insisted on reading it as a work of sexual deviancy. Since the novel was written on a weekly basis, Nadia's despair at the end of *I Do Not Sleep* therefore reflects not only

Abdel Kouddous's grief over his responsibility for embedding a traitor into the nation but also, perhaps, his anguish at the public's refusal to read his confession for what it was. At the end of the novel, Nadia, like Abdel Kouddous, must live with the knowledge that she alone knows and understands her crime, despite repeated attempts at confession and self-exposure.

Public anger at the perceived immortality of *I Do Not Sleep* reached the point that Abdel Kouddous, in his despair over the novel's reception, went to consult with the "Dean of Arabic Literature," Taha Hussein. Hussein reportedly fully supported Abdel Kouddous and encouraged him to continue serializing the novel.[73] Abdel Kouddous defended himself in the press against charges of immortality, arguing that the novel was what he called the "realistic trend" in literature, a new kind of fiction in Egypt that sought to expose reality instead of covering it up. In addition, he explained, "I was condemned before the revolution for my faith in it and people said then what they say about my fiction today. They said then that I was a communist just as they say today that I'm an existentialist.... Despite that, I clung to my faith until the revolution happened and the unbelievers came to believe. I'll kept clinging to my faith in the literary path that I'm going on."[74] In other words, Abdel Kouddous remained hopeful that the public would eventually read his texts as they are—not just daring romantic melodrama but confessions of regret and despair alluding to—if not revealing—the tragic fate of the revolution.

Some, however, understood enough of what Abdel Kouddous was getting at with the conclusion of the novel that the ending was completely changed for the film adaptation, which is widely considered to be among the most important works in the history of Egyptian cinema. The film was directed by Salah Abou Seif and starred an all-star cast, including Faten Hamama as Nadia, Yahya Shahin as her father, Omar Sharif as Aziz, and Emad Hamdy as Mustafa, once again playing a Nasser double in an Abdel Kouddous adaptation. In announcing the film on 9 January 1956, as the novel was still being serialized, *Rose El Youssef* reported that, in order to prepare for the role of Nadia, Faten Hamama was reading books on psychology, presumably because it was the first time in her long career that she would play an "evil" character. The film version of *I Do Not Sleep* was finally released on 31 October 1957. In the climax of the film, Nadia confesses to her father that Kawthar is having an affair. After Nadia passes out in bed in grief—a moment of melodramatic rupture—a candle falls on the carpet and lights her on fire. In a striking shot, Nadia is then seen screaming with the flames of the fire dancing across the frame, emphasizing her punishment. While divine justice has reached Nadia, Kawthar runs off to escape punishment. Nadia's father and uncle rush into her bedroom to put out the fire, and then Nadia, with her eyes closed and on the verge of passing out, confesses that Safiya and Aziz are innocent: "I was jealous of her and God took revenge against me." Unlike the novel, which suppresses Nadia's attempts to admit her role in expelling the stepmother and uncle, the film places her confession at the moment of climax, right after the intervention of divine punishment. Nadia has been permanently maimed—a perpetual visible marking and warning of her inner criminality—but she will survive. Nonetheless, both her father and uncle forgive Nadia and stand by her side, ending the film at the nexus of divine punishment and forgiveness.

With this ending, the film concludes along clear moral lines that do not exist in the novel, demonstrating that evil is punished and virtue is triumphant in the end. The film eliminates the melancholy at the end of the novel. Instead of sitting catatonically in her bedroom awash in horror and regret at secretly plotting the coup, permanently embedding a traitor, and being forced to continue to cover up the treason to the duped father in order to maintain his delusional happiness, the film ends with her maimed and voicing a full-throated and regretful confession. Instead of leaving the immoral and adulterous plotter permanently embedded in the household to the ignorant bliss of the father, Kawthar, having been exposed, flees, restoring the moral integrity and cohesion of the Egyptian home and, consequently, the nation. The film version of *I Do Not Sleep* therefore eliminates any reason for despair—the plot has been revealed and punished, the traitor has been expelled, and the nation has returned to its integrity and virtue. And with this, Abdel Kouddous's attempt to use fiction as a vehicle to confess his own plot, to reveal his own regret, and to soothe his feelings over embedding a military dictator into the nation has been fully suppressed. The repression imposed on him, which is broached through the metaphor of family melodrama in the novel, is therefore restored in the film. Abdel

Kouddous would need to turn to even more desperate measures in his fiction to soothe his anxieties, to relay his guilt to the public, and, perhaps, to correct the wrongs of the dictatorship.[75]

## THE ECHO OF NASSER'S VOICE

As if performing Nadia's dissimulation to cover up Kawthar's treason to keep her duped father happy, as if trying to compensate Nasser for his obvious dissent in *I Do Not Sleep*, Abdel Kouddous immediately—and strikingly—transformed his editorials after the final installment of his latest novel. In the months after *I Do Not Sleep*, Abdel Kouddous published a number of editorials full of bombastic, exaggerated praise of Nasser, the tone of which would have been unthinkable for him even a year earlier. While Abdel Kouddous had rejected Nasser's request to become a translator of his ideas through fiction for the general public, these editorials represent a stunning submission to Nasser, a stark swing in the pendulum of their relationship toward accommodation, something that must have appalled his mother. On 21 May 1956, for example, Abdel Kouddous published "The Man We Believe In."[76] In it, he explained that before the revolution, Egyptians did not believe in any of their earlier nationalist leaders as people. Instead, "we believed in abstract principles and theories. All we wanted was the revolution. And perhaps the revolution would be revealed in a man who embodied the principles we believed in." Once the revolution happened, it became increasingly clear that Nasser was that man: "Our principles became embodied in Gamal's steps. In each step, one of our dreams was realized. The principles and dreams that we were jailed for became the official principles of Egypt." Now, the dream has been realized: "We found the man who represents our principles—the principles of the people—so we confess to him that we believe in him." In this, Nasser represented not a traitor whom Abdel Kouddous helped embed into the fabric of the nation but the embodiment of his dreams and principles before the revolution. As if publicly disavowing his rebellion against Nasser in *I Do Not Sleep*, Abdel Kouddous then explained that he gave a copy of *The Barred Road*, which had been just published as a book, to Nasser with the dedication "To my faith ... Gamal Abdel Nasser." As he explained in his editorial on 21 May 1956, "These are words that I never thought I'd write to a man." Considering the way that he defied Nasser in his two latest novels, it was a striking act of dissimulation. It was at this point, as Abdel Kouddous hinted multiple times, that his political editorials, with their hyperbolic praise of Nasser, became fiction, just as his fiction had become political dissent.

When Nasser announced the nationalization of the Suez Canal on 26 July 1956, four years after the coup, Abdel Kouddous was ecstatic. In "This Man Is the People," his editorial published on 30 July 1956, Abdel Kouddous began by refuting what he saw as the American attempt to separate Nasser from the Egyptian people, suggesting that they could not attack Nasser without attacking the Egyptian people: "22 million Egyptians came together in a single heart, a single mind, and a single desire and they were named Gamal Abdel Nasser. Gamal Abdel Nasser is the people. His heart is the people's heart, his mind is the people's mind, and his will is the people's will. He who wants to reach Gamal Abdel Nasser will only reach him through the millions of individuals who compose the people. . . . We're all Gamal. We're all this man."[77] In this move, Abdel Kouddous echoed Nasser's famous words after the Manshiyya assassination attempt, when he cried out, "You're all Gamal Abdel Nasser!" In this moment Abdel Kouddous elided any line between the ruler and the people, arguing that Nasser had been simply disseminated throughout the nation, with each Egyptian representing him. He continued his gushing praise: "The people appreciate the enormity of the step that Gamal Abdel Nasser took to restore for them their pride, dignity, and resources. . . . We'll protect this step with our lives." As Israel Gershoni argues, Nasser during this period was "imbued with a prophetic mission to extricate his flock from the 'humiliating and dark past' and lead them to 'the brilliant and glorious future.'"[78] In his editorials from this time, Abdel Kouddous, participated in constructing this image of Nasser.

As with other commentators enthralled by the nationalization of the Suez, Abdel Kouddous's naked enthusiasm for Nasser continued throughout the summer. On 6 August 1956, as the crisis expanded, Abdel Kouddous argued that Britain would have to work with Nasser because "there is no one other than Gamal Abdel Nasser in Egypt." Nasser and the Egyptian people were now fused to the point that "the people insist that they're Gamal and Gamal is the people. . . . The people will never let go of Gamal and Gamal will never let go of the people."[79] Egyptians therefore had no independent consciousness beyond Nasser. Abdel Kouddous then elided the lines between Nasser as a person and the principles that he believed in: "Gamal is not a person but a principle. He's a battle, a battle that doesn't concern Egypt or the Arab world alone but a battle that all of humanity has entered. Gamal will be victorious because humanity will be victorious." Nasser therefore transcended Egypt, coming to represent the struggle of humanity for justice.

Abdel Kouddous's praise of Nasser became even more histrionic when he covered Nasser's press conference the same week. He began, "You can all close your eyes and picture yourself having become an ideal leader, a complete person whose nerves don't shake as half the world announced war on him and whose insight doesn't betray him as the representatives of fifty-two countries gather to question him, and whose intelligence isn't disturbed as he knows the future of his country hangs in his every word. . . . This image could be a dream or a fantasy, but Gamal Abdel Nasser achieved it all." After describing the packed room with frantic journalists holding enormous cameras, Abdel Kouddous quoted parts of Nasser's speech of resistance, marveling at his calm, confidence, and strength. He declared that Western journalists were now discovering that Nasser was stronger than they had thought or their leaders had told them: "This is Gamal. This is Egypt. Hands clap in amazement!"[80]

The following week, Abdel Kouddous took it on himself to defend Nasser from the charges coming from Western leaders that he was a dictator. Pointing to the widespread love for Nasser in the streets of Egypt and other countries that he visited, Abdel Kouddous wrote, "Yes, we have dictatorship. This is true. But it's not the dictatorship of Gamal Abdel Nasser and it's not a dictatorship on Egypt alone. It's the dictatorship of the people, the entire Arab people and the entire Arab world. . . . All Gamal Abdel Nasser did was awaken the dictatorship of the people, clear the road for them, and lead them. It's the dictatorship of the people that the West is facing now."[81] Nasser's strength was the Arab people coming together to discover their strength and position in the world. The following week, as pressure continued to build, Abdel Kouddous ended his editorial by declaring, "The Western countries are calling on God to remove Gamal Abdel Nasser, but he won't be removed. He'll remain forever because God won't listen to the calls of the infidels. God is with the believers. With us."[82] Despite this confidence, despite his public hyperbolic performance of allegiance in these editorials, Abdel Kouddous would soon show in his fiction that Nasser would not, in fact, remain forever. Perhaps Abdel Kouddous was compensating for what he knew was coming in his fiction.

## KILLING GAMAL ABDEL NASSER

It was in the context of the British withdrawal from Egypt, the election of Nasser as president of Egypt, the euphoria over the nationalization of the Suez Canal Company, and the ensuing attack by Britain, France, and Israel, also known as the tripartite aggression, that Abdel Kouddous prepared his next novel, *There's a Man in Our House*. While the exact timeline of the novel's development is unclear, it was likely a letter that Abdel Kouddous received in early May 1956 that inspired it. The letter came to him from a Syrian jail, written by none other than Hussein Tawfik, the first of Abdel Kouddous's long-awaited "men," his first version of Nasser before the coup. As discussed in chapter 1, Tawfik assassinated Amin Othman Pasha and Abdel Kouddous hid him in his house for four days after he escaped from prison. Now in jail in Syria for participating in a plot to assassinate President Shishakli—the same military leader whom Abdel Kouddous met when he sought refuge in Saudi Arabia—Tawfik wrote to Abdel Kouddous that he was now suffering in the Lataqqia prison.[83] Abdel Kouddous received at least one more letter from Tawfik, this one in early July 1956, that must have again stirred up his feelings of the years of sacrifice leading up to the coup, helping to frame his thinking about his next novel. This time, Tawfik wrote about the withdrawal of British troops from Egypt, mimicking the same bombastic praise of Nasser that he must have read Abdel Kouddous using at the time in his editorials: "Finally, the dream has become reality. Gamal Abdel Nasser achieved it and returned to Egypt its freedom, dignity, and self-confidence as a deep majestic nation. . . . I want to be in my nation to smell its air after it was cleansed of the British. I want to walk on the soil of my nation after it was purified from the filth of colonialism."[84] As we saw in chapter 1, Tawfik was the first manifestation of the kind of leader that Abdel Kouddous had been dreaming of before the coup, the fantasy that would eventually become embodied in Nasser.

He was no doubt writing to Abdel Kouddous hoping to have his letter published, performing his own public allegiance of Nasser in the hopes that he would be transferred from Syria to Egypt, perhaps as part of the celebrations of the five-year anniversary of the revolution. If the first letter had not jarred Abdel Kouddous's hopes and dreams of the 1940s, reminding him of the link between Tawfik and Nasser, this one clearly did. For Abdel Kouddous, Tawfik was the pure, manly, self-sacrificing revolutionary of the past, whereas Nasser was the treasonous actualization of the fantasies of his youth. Tawfik was the prerevolutionary double of Nasser, his earlier embodiment before Abdel Kouddous's revolutionary project became hijacked and corrupted, supported by his own dissimulation. This letter made the link between the two men explicit, suggesting that Nasser had ultimately achieved Tawfik's revolutionary dreams, despite Abdel Kouddous's tremendous anxieties and regrets.

In his next novel, *There's a Man in Our House*, Abdel Kouddous would return to the story of Hussein Tawfik but tighten the link for himself even more between Tawfik and Nasser, ultimately blurring the line between the two. During summer 1956, after the unprecedented success of *I Do Not Sleep*, letters poured in to *Rose El Youssef* eagerly asking when Abdel Kouddous would begin serializing his next novel. On 15 October 1956, with tensions over the Suez high, Abdel Kouddous wrote about meeting Queen Dina of Jordan and describing his new novel to her. Abdel Kouddous explained, "The hero—or leader—doesn't make himself, but his nation makes him, the people surrounding him and the society he lives in."[85] When the queen disagreed, Abdel Kouddous replied, "Whatever the leader's talents, he can't lead or become a hero unless there's a public that creates his leadership or heroism, that makes him from their faith and conviction." This position is echoed in the epigraph for the novel: "The hero doesn't make himself. Rather, his nation makes him." As the clouds of war gathered over the Suez, Abdel Kouddous suggested that, at least at the time when he was planning the novel and preparing the initial chapter, it was the people that formed Nasser's legitimacy, echoing his editorials from the summer. By the time he completed the novel, he would arrive at a very different perspective on Nasser.

The first chapter of *There's a Man in Our House* was published on 5 November 1956, the first issue after the tripartite attack, but it was immediately discontinued because of what the magazine described as paper shortages during the crisis. Nonetheless, Abdel Kouddous later explained cryptically in one interview that the censor immediately intervened, demanding changes to the plot.[86] Once paper shortages were over—or, perhaps, once the censor was now satisfied after two months of reshaping the plot—Abdel Kouddous returned to the novel when the Suez crisis passed and serialized it between 7 January and 10 June 1957. The first installment in *Rose El Youssef*—as well as the first edition of the novel—included these words: "This story could have happened in the ten turbulent years before the revolution," hinting at the element of verisimilitude in the narrative, especially since, by late 1956, readers would likely not have remembered the Hussein Tawfik affair or known about Abdel Kouddous's direct connection with it. In the novel, through the character of Ibrahim, Abdel Kouddous fictionalizes the real-life events of Hussein Tawfik's involvement with the Iron Guard, turning the assassination of an Egyptian minister seen as a collaborator with the British and his arrest into nationalist acts of resistance and courage. Also through Ibrahim, the novel narrates how Tawfik faked an illness to leave jail, befriended his guards, and managed to escape from them. Like Tawfik, Ibrahim takes refuge in a house with a family for four days as authorities blanket the airwaves with offers of a five-thousand-pound reward for his arrest and sneaks out of the house in an officer's uniform. Like Tawfik, Ibrahim writes a letter to express his regret over how the officer he escaped from was punished. Abdel Kouddous, of course, had firsthand knowledge of these details since Tawfik wrote the letter of regret to him to print in *Rose El Youssef* and it was Abdel Kouddous himself who hid Tawfik in his house with his family for four days. The novel even includes Abdel Kouddous's own justifications for Tawfik's assassination of Amin Othman Pasha, printed from late 1947 through June 1948, when he argued that Tawfik had simply carried out the verdict of the people on the traitor Othman and that the killing was justified just like a killing in war.[87]

Through the basis of the real-life story of Tawfik, however, Abdel Kouddous transformed reality into fiction. First, he blurred the lines between Tawfik and Nasser, lines that must have been blurry for Abdel Kouddous himself. While the real-life Tawfik was outgoing and talkative, Ibrahim in the novel is quiet and unassuming, like Nasser before the coup: "Maybe he himself didn't ever consider that he was a hero...."

He didn't even consider himself more courageous than other young men or more nationalistic than them. . . . He felt that he couldn't face the masses and give a speech."[88] Abdel Kouddous, like others, had said in numerous interviews that Nasser before the coup was unassuming and quiet, offering no premonitions of his political future. Like Nasser, Ibrahim organizes in the shadows and listens more than he speaks: "Little by little, his friends started to consider him a silent leader."[89] Also like Nasser, Ibrahim becomes more and more politically conscious and active during the 1930s, but without becoming linked to any particular political party. While he does not go to military school, Ibrahim loves his gun: "In his love for it was a naked masculinity, boldness, and resistance spirit."[90] With his quiet masculinity, Ibrahim becomes increasingly active, moving toward revolution. "He wants to carry out a positive nationalist act to rouse the people, wake them up, bring them together, and open the doors of the battle for them all."[91] Like Ibrahim, Nasser was involved in political assassinations in the 1940s, something that he wrote about openly in *Philosophy of the Revolution*. After Ibrahim assassinates the collaborating minister, he manages to escape from the hospital by putting on the coat of a doctor—a fictional element that Abdel Kouddous added to the story, winking once again to his reader Nasser through the symbol of the doctor in his fiction. To underscore the link between Ibrahim as a doctor symbolizing Nasser, when Ibrahim walks out of the hospital, another doctor sees him but does not identify him as a fake. Having Ibrahim successfully pass as a doctor in his escape from the authorities, Abdel Kouddous solidified the link between Ibrahim and Nasser.

Ibrahim decides to go to the house of Muhi, picking him because he has no political leanings and will therefore not attract the attention of the authorities. Through his powerful magnetism, naked masculinity, and inspiring nationalist spirit, Ibrahim serves as the "man in the house," the man who wakes up all of the members of the politically detached household, the double for the nation, to the spirit of the revolution. In this, Abdel Kouddous is explicit about the symbolism of the house as the nation as Ibrahim "felt that all of Egypt is this house, simple, good with peace and calm surrounding it."[92] Thanks to his magnetism, Ibrahim transforms each member of the household, waking up their latent nationalism and political consciousness, turning them all into participants of the revolution. Each member of the family is scared to give Ibrahim refuge at first, pointing to their lack of political consciousness and courage, but the father ultimately agrees, "as if he were submitting to something stronger than himself, to a force that is coming from his chest, that he can't resist."[93] Scared, hesitant, and insecure at first, Muhi quickly develops an intense attachment to Ibrahim, later refusing to confess to the authorities after his arrest that he has been hiding him despite facing horrendous torture and imprisonment. Through his ordeal, Muhi, like the Egyptian masses by the end of the novel, is transformed, becoming a participant in the revolution, "melting among the millions."[94]

The father, who has been politically paralyzed by memories of the 1919 Revolution, develops such a strong bond with Ibrahim in only a few days that he considers him to be his own son. Instead of mourning Muhi's imprisonment, the father is proud of his son's sacrifice, feeling like a new human being who has entered into a synergistic relationship with Ibrahim, clearly echoing Abdel Kouddous's own editorials from this period: "He felt that Ibrahim wasn't simply a nationalist youth who took refuge in his house. There was something of himself in Ibrahim, as if he was participating in creating Ibrahim, in creating his heroism, his nationalism, his adventures."[95] Thanks to Ibrahim, even the mother, who remains in the background for most of the novel, discovers a new Egypt, one in which nationalists courageously face torture for their faith and political activities. This spirit of nationalism was something that resonated strongly for the audience of *Rose El Youssef* during the novel's serialization. For example, the magazine published a reader's letter on 15 April 1957 that praised the novel for its "nationalism and masculinity," calling it "an entirely new school for nationalism." The end of the novel also echoes Tawfiq al-Hakim's classic *Return of the Spirit*, as it is the redeeming hero who brings the family together in *There's a Man in Our House*, inspiring their self-sacrifice as well as the sudden uprising of the nation as a "fiery mass."[96]

The most important relationship in the novel, however, is between Ibrahim and Nawal, Muhi's sixteen-year-old sister. It is Nawal who opens the door to Ibrahim when he arrives, serving as the person who brings the hero into the metaphorical nation, just as Abdel Kouddous had done with the real-life Tawfik and as his fictional double does in the 1948 short story "The New Generation," discussed in chapter 1. When Nawal wakes up the next morning, she discovers that she is alone with Ibrahim. Struck by his magnetism, she looks at his Nasser-esque "brown face like the face of a peasant who lived his whole life in the field without leaving once for the shade of the city, at his big honey eyes that he doesn't rise out of fear that they'll reveal his feelings, at his big nose as if it were the head of an arrow heading to the chest of his enemies, and at his silent fine lips that hang over his strong wide chin as if he were hiding in it his entire will."[97] In less than a day, Nawal falls in love with Ibrahim, mirroring Abdel Kouddous's early impulsive romance with Tawfik and then with Nasser. Echoing Abdel Kouddous's own defense of Tawfik, Nawal insists to her sister that Ibrahim is no criminal: "The government should make a statue of him. He's a hero. He killed someone British, not to steal or because he's a criminal. He killed for his country."[98] She has fallen in love with Ibrahim not as a nationalist hero or a symbol of the revolution, however. Predictably, Nawal has fallen in love with him as a man, "the first one to come pry open the cover of her virginal heart."[99] The next day, when it becomes clear that Ibrahim is on the verge of leaving the house, Nawal cannot bear being separated from him: "She tried to convince herself that her emotions were only fantasies . . . but she failed."[100] As Ibrahim leaves, this time dressed in his officer uniform—yet another wink to Nasser—Ibrahim and Nawal confess their love to each other, and Ibrahim proposes that she come to a public square every Monday and Wednesday for them to meet.

The real-life Hussein Tawfik left Abdel Kouddous's house after hiding there for four days and escaped Egypt to Syria. In *There's a Man in Our House*, Ibrahim sneaks out to flee to Greece but, unlike the real-life Tawfik, he backtracks, deciding that he cannot abandon his country and the cause. He then decides to attack the Abbassia barracks, a location that had particularly poignant symbolism for Abdel Kouddous since it was the place to which Nasser summoned him on the day of the coup. Ibrahim goes to the barracks to spark the revolution, sets off a number of bombs, and starts a gunfight. When he raises his gun to shoot an Egyptian soldier, he is paralyzed. Rendered impotent by his inability to kill an "innocent" Egyptian, the soldier in return shoots and kills Ibrahim. In this moment of climax, the novel not only makes a radical break from the history of the real-life Hussein Tawfik. Here, Abdel

Kouddous rewrites the history of the coup, killing off Nasser at the moment of its inception, as if stressing that the Nasser who entered the Abbassia barracks to spark the revolution was killed off from the start. While Abdel Kouddous could not change history or declare his regret for the coup in the editorial pages of *Rose El Youssef*, he used *There's a Man in Our House* to write an alternative history and kill Nasser before the revolution ignites in the barracks. Fiction gave him the opportunity, at least when he wrote this part and published it in the 20 May 1957 issue of *Rose El Youssef*, to take control of his regret and kill the source of his anxiety and despair. It was a moment of revolt, a stark contrast to the ongoing public mood of adoration for Nasser in the aftermath of the Suez crisis, that must have made his mother proud.

Abdel Kouddous admitted at the time that he had been living through the suffering of the characters in the novel. On 3 June 1957, he explained in *Rose El Youssef*, "When a writer writes a novel, he lives its events, emotions, and characters. He suffers when he describes pain, laughs when he describes laughing, and loves when he writes about love."[101] In the installments leading up to the killing of Ibrahim, Abdel Kouddous had been also narrating how Muhi, Nawal's brother, was suffering in prison, sacrificing himself through his arrest, like Muhsin in Tawfiq al-Hakim's *Return of the Spirit*, for the redeeming hero. Abdel Kouddous explained in the same article, "In recent weeks, the heroes of my novel were being tortured. Muhi was arrested and the jailors were beating him. As I was writing, I was living in the darkness of the jail and then feeling the slaps on my face. I felt that I was sleeping on the cement and tears were swelling in my eyes as I was writing about Muhi's tears. . . . The days when I was writing these chapters, my heart was always seized. I was nervous, irritated, agitated. I had terrifying dreams and then I'd stay up all night without sleeping."

In a rare moment of directly addressing the political and personal echoes of his fiction, Abdel Kouddous underscored the link between his own imprisonment in 1954 and Muhi's torture in jail in an interview published in 1975. He said, "*There's a Man in Our House* is an image for what a power that has deviated from the people—with its own interests—can do. This might have happened for real before the revolution in the time that the novel is set but it might also be an indirect expression of what some citizens faced after the revolution at the hands of the enemies of freedom."¹⁰² Writing the torture of his character, Muhi, was particularly provocative because it seemed to force Abdel Kouddous to relive his own imprisonment in 1954 at the hands of Nasser.¹⁰³ It was in this emotional state that Abdel Kouddous took the ultimate revenge—he finally had the opportunity to lash out and kill Nasser, not only for the abuse that he had suffered but to change the trajectory of the revolution, if only in fiction. Abdel Kouddous had briefly depicted Nadia's fantasy of killing Kawthar, Nasser's post-coup double in *I Do Not Sleep*, stabbing her to death, cutting up her body, and throwing the pieces to dogs. In *There's a Man in Our House*, he once again depicted killing Nasser, but he made it central to the plot, perhaps on the assumption that his earlier articles of bombastic praise had bought him leeway in his fiction. In this environment of heavy censorship and authoritarianism, popular fiction became the way for Abdel Kouddous to articulate the unacceptable and transform it from taboo into something apparently unrelated.

While I have found no evidence that anyone at the time explicitly equated the killing of Ibrahim with the killing of Nasser, readers of *Rose El Youssef* immediately sensed that something was very wrong. On 3 June 1957, Abdel Kouddous wrote that he had received dozens of phone calls after the 20 May 1957 issue, demanding to know how he could kill Ibrahim. A furious colleague, Abdel Sattar Tawila, went to his office to protest the killing. A woman wrote to the magazine in outrage: "Why did you kill him, Ihsan? Shame on you!" Sensing that perhaps he had gone too far, Abdel Kouddous tried to excuse himself: "I can't do anything. I set Ibrahim's end from the first chapter of the novel. The plot is like fate that has to be followed!" Two weeks later, even after he finished serializing the novel, which raised the circulations of *Rose El Youssef* even more than *I Do Not Sleep*, Abdel Kouddous was still receiving dozens of letters demanding to know why he had killed Ibrahim.¹⁰⁴ He had some explaining to do. On 17 June 1956, he made another attempt to justify the killing: "Ibrahim had to die to prove that heroism is not limited to an individual, but that it's the heroism of a people, a heroism embodied in individual after individual. Ibrahim died, but heroism didn't. The revolution didn't stop with his death."¹⁰⁵ Abdel Kouddous therefore explained the killing by decentering the importance of an individual leader in the revolution, showing that the leader was a spark for every person to achieve the goal of freedom.¹⁰⁶ This explanation was clearly not satisfying. The angry letters kept coming. More than two months after Abdel Kouddous finished serializing the novel, on 19 August 1957, *Rose El Youssef* published another one of these letters, which declared, "Ihsan has no right to kill the martyr Ibrahim!" The magazine responded, perhaps tongue in cheek, as if once again teasing with the lines between fiction and reality: "Ihsan is innocent, I swear!"

When *There's a Man in Our House* was published as a book in early 1958, Abdel Kouddous still had some explaining to do. On a visit to the Gamal Abdel Nasser Museum in Cairo in October 2018, I found the copy of *There's a Man in Our House* that Abdel Kouddous had personally given to Nasser among the other books in Nasser's office. Abdel Kouddous's handwritten inscription reads: "To the hero whom Egypt made from its pains and dreams. To my faith, Gamal Abdel Nasser. Ihsan Abdel Kouddous, 15 January 1958." This inscription offers rare insight into how Abdel Kouddous tried to manage Nasser behind the scenes. Breaking with the stand that Abdel Kouddous had taken on Ibrahim in the pages of *Rose El Youssef*, Abdel Kouddous suggests in his inscription that Nasser was the hero produced by the struggles and aspirations of the Egyptian people during the revolution. In this, he harkens back to what he told Queen Dina before he began serializing the novel, an act of denying that he killed off Nasser in the novel at the inception of the coup. Just to ensure that Nasser read the novel through the lens of his recent bombastic editorials and not his murder in the novel, Abdel Kouddous echoed what he wrote in his *Rose El Youssef* in May 1956, calling Nasser "my faith." In this, he blurred the lines in the inscription between his political pieces full of inflated praise and his fiction of protest and regret. It was this vacillation between dissent and accommodation that would characterize their relationship in the years after Abdel Kouddous's arrests in 1954.

As Abdel Kouddous the novelist angrily killed Ibrahim in revenge as a reaction to painful memories of his own incarceration, his fictional double in the novel, Nawal, is utterly devastated when she learns of Ibrahim's death. This contradiction underscores the deeply paradoxical relationship of love and hate that Abdel Kouddous had for Nasser. When Nawal first reads about the killing in the newspaper, she screams out in grief. Nawal remains in denial, insisting on going with her sister to the square where she had planned on meeting Ibrahim. The loss is so traumatic that it leads to a split within Nawal: "She felt like there were two girls inside her, one who knows that Ibrahim is dead. And her dreams died with him. And another girl who refuses to believe that he died.... Neither girl could convince the other. One is a sad, exhausted by despair, unable to resist, while the other is crazy!"[107] Instead of simply repressing her loss, Nawal's consciousness has split into two personalities, one that is overwhelmed by grief and another that refuses to accept that Ibrahim has been killed, echoing the similar psychological splits seen in Aliya in *Where's My Life?*, Faiza in *The Barred Road*, and Nadia in *I Do Not Sleep*. In this new novel, the splitting suggests that Abdel Kouddous had entered a new phase of his mourning for the revolution. On the one hand, he was grief-stricken at its trajectory but, on the other, he refused to accept that the Nasser whom he knew and loved, the Nasser who sparked the revolution, was dead and gone.

The two split selves inside Nawal enter into conflict. The exhausted grief-stricken self manages to gain control long enough to tell her sister, "I have to go out. I know he's dead. But I don't know where he's buried so I can visit him. I feel like going to visit him where we used to meet."[108] Clearly hoping that the visit will bring closure for Nawal, her sister agrees to accompany her. As they approach the location on the bus, however, Nawal becomes absorbed in the second self: "She kept thinking until he became embodied before her, until she felt Ibrahim by her side and she felt his breath. She heard the sound of the beats of his heart. She almost touched him with her hand but the other girl awoke in her chest, the crazy girl who didn't want to believe that Ibrahim is dead."[109] Nawal imagines a domestic life with Ibrahim—the life that they had together in the early version of the story "The New Generation"—saying goodbye to him in the morning as he leaves for work and welcoming him home at the end of the day with a hot dinner. As they approach the meeting place, the self that refuses to accept Ibrahim's death takes over and Nawal tells her sister that they will meet Ibrahim there.

The inner conflict between the self that is exhausted by grief and the self that refuses to accept the loss continues for Nawal. Two years pass—uncoincidentally, the timeframe between Abdel Kouddous's own jailing and when he began preparing the novel—during which she pays no attention to her appearance and is overwhelmed by depression, like Nadia at the end of *I Do Not Sleep*. Nonetheless, she comes to feel that Ibrahim has become embodied in her, "as if the hero was living in her chest and speaking with her tongue, as if Ibrahim was always with her."[110] On cue, a doctor—the persistent symbol of Nasser in Abdel Kouddous's fiction—comes to propose to her. Even though she is still fully devoted to Ibrahim, the pre-coup double for Nasser, she decides to accept the proposal of the doctor at the encouragement of her family: "Society pushed her to marriage, not to love. The family was waiting for her to marry, not to fall in love!"[111] Accepting the doctor's proposal is therefore a duty, an obligation on behalf of her family and society, a compromise that represents settling on a bitter reality. This acceptance echoes the work of Yusuf Murad, who, according to Omnia El Shakry, uses a female case study to show the tensions between the conscious and unconscious self, tending "toward masochism and the denial of her own pleasure. This tension has manifested in the splitting off of the two aspects of love, the bodily and the spiritual or affective."[112] Before marrying the doctor, she takes Ibrahim's shirt from her room and gives it to Muhi in tears, suggesting that she might be able to let go of her attachment and devotion to Ibrahim. Nonetheless, she keeps a note that Ibrahim wrote to her before he left the house and puts in a gold locket on a necklace, "carrying it above her chest ... as if she is still waiting for Ibrahim."[113]

The ending of the novel therefore suggests Abdel Kouddous's position in postrevolutionary Egypt—an identity split between grief and denial, despair and acceptance of reality, clinging to the internal embodiment of the now-dead hero while marrying the "doctor" as a duty to family and obligation to society, refusing to let go of the past as a deluded hope that the original leader-hero will return one day to complete her. By killing Ibrahim in the novel, however, Abdel Kouddous lashed out at Nasser, extracting revenge for his own imprisonment and torture, expressing his dashed hopes for a different trajectory for the revolution. At the same time, the symbolic killing of Nasser also provided Abdel Kouddous with the pathway to explore his own psychological splitting, to show how the trauma of loss led to his own grief and repression. Like Nawal in the new era, Abdel Kouddous decided to move forward somberly with his obligation as a journalist by praising Nasser in his editorials but continuing to cling to hope that the real leader-hero—the pliable democrat—will return one day.

Confessing his plotting and regret in *I Do Not Sleep* might have been soothing while Abdel Kouddous was writing and serializing the novel in *Rose El Youssef*, but, as is clear from the revised ending he wrote when it was published as a book, it only made him even more melancholic. This, in turn, led him to more extreme measures to try to calm his anxiety—killing Nasser in *There's a Man in Our House* and writing an alternative history in which the nation rose up in revolution without him. Despite the shift from confession and despair to vengeance and erasure, Abdel Kouddous unsurprisingly did not manage to alleviate his repressed guilt and anxiety during the process of writing and publishing *There's a Man in Our House*. This would lead him to an even more frantic cry to the public through a confessional mix of pleasure, compulsion, and self-loathing in his relationship with Nasser. His next attempt would be an even more frantic attempt at self-analysis. In the process, Abdel Kouddous would reach the brink of exposing his own abusive relationship with Nasser and Nasser's betrayal of the nation, putting himself on the verge of catastrophe.

CHAPTER FIVE

## THE GREATEST SPLENDOR OF VICTORIES

> All the fiction that I wrote was under political pressure. I was always a victim of this pressure.
>
> —*Ihsan Abdel Kouddous (1981)*

Sometime in late September 1958, Mohamed Hassanein Heikal once again paid a visit to the offices of *Rose El Youssef* with a message of displeasure from Gamal Abdel Nasser. He had previously come to see Fatima Youssef, Ihsan Abdel Kouddous's mother, in the same offices in June 1954 when she stopped publishing news about Nasser and the revolution out of protest for jailing her son. At the time, Heikal, who was well on his way to becoming the intellectual "echo" that Nasser sought to use to disseminate his political message to the public, relayed the request that she relent and end her boycott. Of course, Youssef angrily refused. When Heikal arrived in summer 1958 with another message from Nasser, this time he came to visit Ihsan Abdel Kouddous. By fall 1958, Nasser was no longer an untested leader rushing to consolidate power in the aftermath of the March Crisis. He was now at the peak of his popularity. Not only had Nasser become a revolutionary icon on the international stage, he had also achieved the withdrawal of British forces from Egyptian soil, nationalized the Suez Company in a historic defiance of the West, resisted the subsequent joint attack by Britain, France, and

Israel in fall 1956, and, most recently, orchestrated the creation of the United Arab Republic, a stunning realization of the hopes and dreams of Arab nationalism. He was no longer to be denied.

As soon as Abdel Kouddous learned from Heikal that Nasser was unhappy with him, he must have known that something ominous was at hand. Abdel Kouddous no doubt immediately thought back to Heikal's earlier visit. It must have evoked his mother, who had died only months earlier on 10 April 1958, a loss that filled him with such grief that he frantically fought against people who tried to move him away from her death bed. With her death, Abdel Kouddous was now alone to face the regime, alone to decide whether to accommodate or resist. Heikal's visit must have stirred up charged memories and emotions of his jailings in 1954, inflaming his feelings of anxiety, regret, and despair about the "road" of the revolution, feelings that erupted when he wrote installments of fiction alone in his office the night before the printer's deadline.

With the increasingly repressive censorship of the mid- to late 1950s, Abdel Kouddous regularly faced objections to words, phrases, and even entire articles that appeared in his magazine. It was this atmosphere of escalating censorship that pushed him to transfer his political dissent from the direct discourse of the editorial to the metaphor of fiction. As he later explained: "My fame as a fiction writer started after the revolution, after the intensification of censorship, as fiction was expressing political opinion indirectly."[1] Nonetheless, as far as we know, Heikal had not visited Abdel Kouddous to express Nasser's displeasure when he was serializing either the highly inflammatory *I Do Not Sleep* or even when he shockingly killed Nasser's fictional double in *There's a Man in Our House*. By late September 1958, right before this visit, Abdel Kouddous clearly believed that fiction was still a space of freedom to express his regret, guilt, and dissent about the course of the revolution in general and about Nasser in particular, even if direct critique in his editorials was now off-limits.

One reason Abdel Kouddous remained in Nasser's good graces after those two wildly popular novels was because he had been so careful to publish submissive and obsequious editorials about the president, almost as if he were paying off a debt for lashing out against him metaphorically in his fiction. Abdel Kouddous began writing these editorials immediately after he completed *I Do Not Sleep*, performing his allegiance to the president in the same magazine that he published installments of his fiction. Abdel Kouddous became even more creative and bombastic once he finished *There's a Man in Our House*, perhaps anxiously compensating for going too far against Nasser in the novel. For example, after the referendum approving Egypt's union with Syria and Nasser's presidency of the new United Arab Republic on 21 February 1958, Abdel Kouddous wrote a piece titled "The Leader and the Principle" in which he developed his earlier depictions of Nasser in his editorials. Instead of situating Nasser as simply an instrument carrying out the will of the people, Abdel Kouddous now shockingly placed him—not the people—as the one responsible for the revolution: "There was a revolution in his chest. Not a new or foreign revolution, but the same revolution that the chests of millions bore. Gamal achieved the revolution."[2]

In this editorial, Abdel Kouddous also began a strategy that he would develop in the months to come, transforming Nasser from simply a "man" and a "leader" into the transcendental embodiment of hope, principles, and the nation, something organically connected to all of Egypt: "People turned and saw a face that they hadn't seen before, even though they knew it. They knew it in the fields, the factories, offices, and army ranks. It's the face of the people." With his victories, Nasser became something greater than a familiar and comforting mirror for the Egyptian people: "Gamal became a leader, a president. More than that, he became a faith, a faith that doubt or hesitation doesn't intervene in. Faith in Gamal Abdel Nasser isn't simply faith in a person, but faith in a people. Not only the Egyptian people, but the Arab people. Faith in him is faith in a group of liberated ideas, principles turned into reality, and ideas that have become truths." In his editorials at the time, Abdel Kouddous elevated Nasser from the human to the abstract embodiment of principles, faith, and the nation.

When Abdel Kouddous traveled with Nasser to Bandung in April 1955, he was stunned at Nasser's incredible popularity. Starting in late December 1957, Abdel Kouddous began following Nasser on more trips as a reporter, both inside Egypt and abroad, and was repeatedly confronted by mass hysteria in the streets for the president. His accounts of Bandung were comparatively sober compared to the bombast with which he now described people swarming the president. For example, on 26 December 1957, Abdel Kouddous depicted the crowds in Port Said as unable to control themselves when Nasser came to town.³ Underscoring his subservience, Abdel Kouddous described himself as having to run to keep up behind Nasser, who walked as if he were superhuman, taking one step like it was five. Abdel Kouddous marveled at the massive crowds of adoring men, women, and children chanting and cheering, rushing Nasser's car, trying to touch and kiss him as if he were the messiah. When Nasser gave a speech, the crush of humanity overwhelmed the public square with people hanging on poles and crowding on balconies and rooftops, ecstatically jubilant and emotional as they celebrated their leader.

In Damascus in March 1958 after the declaration of the United Arab Republic, Abdel Kouddous reported from the presidential palace as the massive ebullient crowds waited outside demanding that Nasser come to them and give a speech. Watching delegation after delegation visit Nasser, Abdel Kouddous again depicted his former co-revolutionary as a kind of prophet, a messianic figure that produced an overwhelming transcendental experience for all who encountered him: "Gamal Abdel Nasser isn't a person. He's a hope. All the delegations met their hope. An old man was standing and speaking, his voice trembling with enthusiasm. It seemed like he wasn't directing his words to Gamal but to himself, to his hope, to the dream that he was living for, to his faith. Another old man couldn't bear his happiness at seeing his hope and he fell silent, tears running down his cheeks."⁴ As Tawfiq al-Hakim later wrote about the depictions of Nasser during this period, "This was perhaps the first time in the modern history of Egypt in which it happened that an idolized person had appeared who wanted his will to have, throughout the Arab countries, a degree of holiness, greatness and power which not even God's prophets and messengers possessed."⁵

When Heikal came to visit *Rose El Youssef* to relay Nasser's displeasure in late September 1958, Abdel Kouddous would have known that it was not because of his editorials. He learned instead that Nasser was angry about his latest work of fiction, *Girls in Summer*. While we have no direct record of the conversation, Abdel Kouddous quickly understood that he was on the verge of losing Nasser's support, which would have had dire consequences. Ever since he left jail in summer 1954, Abdel Kouddous felt that he had been living under Nasser's protection, who

**Figure 17**. The only known photograph of Ihsan Abdel Kouddous (right) with Gamal Abdel Nasser, taken with Syrian leaders in Damascus in early 1958. Originally published in *Rose El Youssef*, 16 January 1989.

after all allowed him expansive freedom in his fiction that no other writer enjoyed. Besides their tightly interlinked past in the buildup to the coup and its immediate aftermath—as well as Abdel Kouddous's attempts to please Nasser after his release from jail and his bombastic displays of allegiance in his editorials—there seemed to be another reason for Nasser's unusual support. When Abdel Kouddous visited Saudi Arabia in late February 1954, he learned about a plot to assassinate Nasser on his upcoming trip to perform the Hajj. Abdel Kouddous later reported that he relayed documents proving the plot to Nasser, who subsequently cancelled his trip. According to Abdel Kouddous, Nasser was forever grateful. As Abdel Kouddous revealed years later, "I lived during all of Nasser's life in his personal protection. Many people tried to get rid of me, but Nasser was my savior from them."[6] This protection, of course, did not save him from jail in the aftermath of his editorials during the 1954 March Crisis, but it perhaps helped him avoid an even worse fate. It also helps explain why Abdel Kouddous, unlike any of his peers, felt such confidence to explore his regret and despair about the revolution through the metaphor of fiction, challenging Nasser in the pages of *Rose El Youssef* and protesting the trajectory of the revolution unlike any other writer at the time.

When Heikal came to visit him in late September 1958, it was yet more evidence that times had changed. As editor in chief of *Rose El Youssef* and one of the most prominent and important public intellectuals of the era, Abdel Kouddous faced the pressures of censorship on a daily basis, navigating how it became increasingly severe and restrictive in the 1950s and early 1960s. While written evidence of demands for changes to Abdel Kouddous's fiction are conspicuously absent from his personal papers, we know that he faced these pressures regularly, and not only because of what he said in later interviews. For example, *Rose El Youssef* began serializing Mahmoud al-Saʿadani's novel *Until the Moon Returns* in March 1961. That novel follows a journalist who travels to Ismailiyya in 1951 to cover the guerilla battles against the British at the time. When the fifth part of the novel was published on 24 April 1961, the censor was not happy. On the same day that the issue appeared on the newsstands, the censor prepared a report on official letterhead and included a hand-marked copy of the published installment, including the annotation that the author had written "some sexual incidents, depicting them explicitly and with shameful outside-the-bounds expressions."[7] The same copy includes a section of the chapter highlighted with the accompanying words: "For shame, Ihsan!" In order to stress the seriousness of the situation, the censor sent another note to Abdel Kouddous the following week with the request to "please pay close attention to the novel." While this incident took place in spring 1961, it is rare written evidence from this period of how closely the censors read fiction, at least during this period, and involved themselves in its production, looking to alter language, content, and plotlines. Nonetheless, the description of the scene that inspired the censor's objection—an encounter in bed between an unmarried man and a woman—is certainly no more daring than the typical depiction of sexuality in Abdel Kouddous's own fiction. If the censor was intervening about this chapter of *Until the Moon Returns*, it seems likely that he would have objected to Abdel Kouddous's own work, which was much more popular.

Nonetheless, because of his dutifully performed editorials and regular accommodation of the censor, Abdel Kouddous must have assumed that the audaciousness of his latest work of fiction, *Girls in Summer*, would be ignored, just as it had been in his previous novels. He must have assumed that thanks to his increasingly bombastic editorials, he had continued to buy himself a space of freedom of expression in his fiction, to use his latest novel to continue contesting Nasser and to perform therapy in public. He quickly learned from Heikal, however, that he had crossed a line in his latest metaphorical depiction of Nasser in his fiction. Nasser had intervened in Abdel Kouddous's editorials to demand changes and cuts many times before, even blocking the publication of a number of pieces. Sending Heikal to relay his anger about *Girls in Summer* was the first time that we know for certain that Nasser intervened in Abdel Kouddous's fiction, confirming that, by September 1958, fiction was now no longer a safe space of dissent for Abdel Kouddous.

Nasser's anger at his latest novel set off a panic for Abdel Kouddous as he realized that his safety—as well as that of his family and the existence of his magazine—suddenly hung in the balance. Perhaps it stirred up the horrors of imprisonment in 1954 and conflicted memories of how he had sought to please Nasser in *The Empty Pillow* and "Whisper" upon his release from jail. Abdel Kouddous immediately changed the narrative of *Girls in Summer*, directing it away from the metaphor of the consummation of the revolution and the embedding of dictatorship as an act of sexual assault. This move, however, was clearly not sufficient to get back in Nasser's good graces. Through a close reading of Abdel Kouddous's archive, both contemporaneous issues of *Rose El Youssef* and later interviews, I show how Abdel Kouddous rushed to begin his next novel, his magnum opus *The Sun Never Sets*, in the shadow of anxiety about losing Nasser's support and oppressive pressure by the censor. He began the novel clearly intending to please Nasser and compensate for what he had done in *Girls in Summer*. Nonetheless, through a close reading of the original installments of *The Sun Never Sets* in *Rose El Youssef*, I show how Abdel Kouddous moved from accommodation to ambivalence and then, once again, to shocking dissent as the serialization dragged on for months. By excavating the politics of censorship and the tensions between accommodation of and resistance to Nasser in *The Sun Never Sets*, I demonstrate how Abdel Kouddous finally served as the fictional "translator" that Nasser so desperately wanted between himself and the public while, at the same time, paradoxically exposing the absurdity of censorship and comical expectations of servility by intellectuals at the time. Abdel Kouddous became so disgusted by the suffocating pressures of censorship and demonstrations of bombastic fealty that he made a public call for the nationalization of the press, ultimately offering up his family's media legacy to state takeover. Only through this latest, most exorbitant act of accommodation would Abdel Kouddous be able to remain in Nasser's good graces, at least for the time being.

### RISE AND SHINE

In summer 1957, soon after he had completed *There's a Man in Our House*, Abdel Kouddous was experiencing terrible anxiety. He had suffered from insomnia and anxiety regularly since the revolution—and perhaps much earlier—but this most recent spell was particularly harsh. He wrote in September 1957 that, for two months, "I've been trying to flee from myself . . . because I want to relax from my work, thoughts, and emotions. For a brief time, I want to be another person, a person without a past, who doesn't live in this present, and doesn't bear anxiety about the future, a person not occupied by a nation. . . . I want to take a break from the 'I,' even if for a single week."[8] As he explained, the only place where he could find relaxation from anxiety was in his office writing fiction: "I take the pen as if I'm taking a bottle of medicine, psychological medicine, and I begin writing fiction." Judging by his voluminous fictional production that erupted soon after he wrote this piece, Abdel Kouddous was feeling a tremendous amount of anxiety in the late 1950s and early 1960s, turning to fiction more and more for therapy and self-medication. During this time, Abdel Kouddous published at least one piece of fiction—either an installment of a serialized novel, a short story or both—nearly every week, just as censorship of the press was reaching its most suffocating levels.

Between 28 August and 6 November 1958, Abdel Kouddous serialized a new novel, *Girls in Summer*, this time in his second magazine, *Sabah al-Khayr* (Good Morning). This new magazine was launched in January 1956, at the end of the three-year transitional period. In the inaugural editorial in the first issue, Fatima Youssef explained that she was a morning person: "I always feel with each morning that I'm strong, happy, radiant. . . . The morning for me is the symbol of victory and hope."⁹ With this seeming optimism for a new era, for the new Egypt, Fatima Youssef situated the magazine as a wish of a "good morning" for a happy new day, a buoyant marker of strength in the post-transitional period. In his inaugural editorial in the same issue, Abdel Kouddous claimed that Fatima Youssef received the permit to launch the new magazine back in 1951, but that they decided to wait to launch it because the ensuing period was a time of "preparing for the revolution and participating in it and we didn't have surplus energy."¹⁰ The appearance of the magazine in January 1956, right at the end of the three-year transitional period, therefore suggested that the political domain had finally stabilized into a new dawn for Egypt, even though Abdel Kouddous clearly saw this new era as, tragically, the installation of dictatorship and authoritarianism.

The magazine differentiated itself from the more elevated *Rose El Youssef*, which largely featured articles on politics together with serialized fiction and cultural reviews, by focusing on the modern urban Egyptian family. As Fatima Youssef wrote in the fifth issue, "To that family, we present *Sabah al-Khayr*. We present to the father and mother serious subjects, images and studies about the youth so they can understand their children. We present to the son and daughter who are completing their education a simplified literary and political culture. And we present to their sister who is waiting to get married topics about marriage, how to treat her husband and furnish a nice house."¹¹ The magazine disseminated an image of a progressive Egypt, focusing largely on the aspirations of a young middle-class audience with its drawings of midcentury modern furniture and household schematics, as well as articles on psychoanalysis and the liberation of young women from traditional religious and cultural restrictions. Although the magazine featured the same journalists and illustrators as *Rose El Youssef*, Abdel Kouddous explained on the second anniversary of *Sabah al-Khayr* that it was a social and artistic magazine that "had to be published to speak with the generation that owns the future."¹²

It was no coincidence that *Girls in Summer* appeared in *Sabah al-Khayr* and not *Rose El Youssef*. The novel features a number of heroines who represented the magazine's target audience with their focus on chic modern appearance and materialistic consumption, navigating the contradictions between the desire for a liberated sexual life and the pressures of a conservative and restrictive society. Set on the beaches of Alexandria, the novel was serialized at the end of the summer, just as *Sabah al-Khayr* readers were heading back to their urban routines after vacations and summer flings. Moreover, in the environment of increasingly onerous censorship of the late 1950s, *Rose El Youssef*, with its focus on political commentary, had become a more and more fraught vehicle for publishing daring and controversial fiction. *Sabah al-Khayr*, by catering to a younger audience with open aspirations for joining the new era, seemed to offer Abdel Kouddous something of a respite from the micromanagement of the censor.

### THE BRINK OF DISASTER

*Girls in Summer* as published is divided into five sections, each focusing on a different "girl."[13] While the first two sections were daring for their depiction of adultery and sexuality, it was the Third Girl that inspired Nasser's displeasure and led to a crisis for Abdel Kouddous. It begins as nineteen-year-old Wafiya sits outside a beachside cabin with her flabby thirty-year-old husband, Omar, and Omar's best friend, the manly, virile, and dominating thirty-four-year-old Ismail. Ismail suggests that they cook dinner that evening and orders Omar to leave to buy groceries. With her husband gone, Wafiya immediately senses Ismail's eyes all over her body, feeling that "she did not dare confront him. Did not dare. Something inside her was afraid, trembling, shrinking."[14] Wafiya gets up and goes into the cabin "as though extricating herself from the chains cast by his eyes."[15] She is furious that her husband, oblivious to the coming sexual assault, has abandoned her, gesturing back to the image of Nadia's duped father that Abdel Kouddous depicted at some length in *I Do Not Sleep*: "That decent husband had no idea, was incapable of knowing."[16] As Wafiya paces nervously around the cabin in the horror of anticipation, she is confronted with her own vulnerability and inability to defend herself, echoing Abdel Kouddous's own paradoxical anxieties of shame coupled with accommodation: "She sensed the weakness of her personality, which only made it worse and her more neurotic and awkward."[17]

Looking at herself in the mirror, Wafiya sees Ismail's reflection as he comes into the room and walks over to embrace her: "A bout of weakness engulfed her. She felt her nerves melting, dissolving. She had to resist. Help me, Lord. Just this time. Help me resist."[18] Once he kisses her, her resistance dissolves immediately. She cries and tries to escape, but once his lips touch hers, she not only submits to him but actively participates, stressing the contradiction between weakness and fear yet, paradoxically, a masochistic desire to be assaulted by her oppressor: "She responded and kissed him back. Kissed and cried."[19] As he lays her down on the bench inside the cabin, Wafiya cries more and more: "Tears of weakness. Tears of ecstasy. Tears of shame."[20] This mix of insisting on resisting, yet being overwhelmed by weakness when confronted, feeling horror and degradation at being assaulted together with desire and intoxication solidifies the obvious triad established in the opening scene of the story. Wafiya, in her weakness, repression, and habituation to abuse yet intoxicated participation in the assault once it begins, stands as the double of Abdel Kouddous in his evolving relationship with Nasser. Ismail, the manly, charismatic, and deceitful best friend with a tiny mustache who sexually assaults Wafiya behind closed doors is the double for Nasser. His name even echoes that of Abdel Kouddous's previous Nasser double, another interloping "man in our house." And the husband, the docile, subservient, eager-to-please dupe who is oblivious to the treason of the dictatorial beloved friend against his wife because of blind faith, is the nation. With this triad, Abdel Kouddous gestures back to *I Do Not Sleep* but, in this story, becomes even more daring and desperate to expose the cheating and abuse taking place behind closed doors.

Wafiya was married to the flabby and meek Omar through an arranged marriage two years earlier. Nonetheless, Ismail, Omar's best friend, has been a constant presence with them, rather like the police state surveilling its citizens. In order to underscore this point, Ismail has unapologetically participated in all aspects of their engagement, dominating decision making, organizing their activities, and confidently speaking for the three of them. After the marriage, in contrast to the weak personalities of Wafiya and Omar, Ismail orchestrates their family life, arranging their day, picking some friends and rejecting others, serving as an apparent source of safety and protection for Wafiya in his seemingly constant presence beside her and surveillance of their domestic life. In addition to the secret police, he represents the dictator

**Figure 18.** First installment of the Third Girl from *Girls in Summer*. *Sabah al-Khayr*, 25 September 1958.

whose orders cannot be questioned or opposed, brought into the family home, embedded gradually and without resistance by Wafiya and Omar due to their relief, at least at first, at his control over their lives. Echoing Lynn Hunt and gesturing to how Abdel Kouddous replaced the old generation, symbolized by his mother, with the young, virile, Nasser, Ismail becomes everything for Wafiya: "[He] took the place of her mother.... She felt safe next to him, as if next to her mother.... Ismail had become everything. Life itself. Laughter. Talk. Action.... He knew everything."[21]

During this initial period, despite the obvious, Wafiya does not notice that anything is amiss, just as Nadia seemingly does not notice Kawthar's cheating at first in *I Do Not Sleep* or Abdel Kouddous, as his mother accused him, naïvely overlooked Nasser's dictatorial intentions before and immediately after the coup. About a year after getting married, however, Ismail suddenly comes to visit Wafiya at home while Omar is away. At first, she is not surprised because "she was used to him coming round to the house at any and every time."[22] When he kisses her, however, she feels his mustache brush against her for the first time, making her aware of his masculinity and sexual desire for her. Wafiya initially insists to herself that she must resist him, but she quickly capitulates. After he leaves, Wafiya is in shock, feeling "disgust at her body, as though it would never be clean again."[23] This first sexual assault transforms her, soiling her for the first time, producing her weakness combined with false hope for resistance, fear with shame, and self-loathing: "In an instant, she had become aware of a new world. A world full of sin, evil, and deceit. A world that Ismail rules!"[24]

Wafiya, whose name ironically means "faithful"—yet another gesture to her status as the fictional double for Abdel Kouddous, echoing the way he depicted himself as Amina in *I'm Free*—now desperately tries to defend herself against Ismail's manipulations to isolate and soil her while, at the same time, repressing the horrible secret that only she and Ismail know. In *I Do Not Sleep*, Kawthar tortures Nadia with a secret as well, forcing her to participate in covering up the crime of cheating. Making the torture more painful and violent, Nasser's fictional double is now sexually assaulting Abdel Kouddous's double, pointing to the escalation in their relationship since *I Do Not Sleep*. It is now no longer simply the attempted sexual exploitation of *The Barred Road* but rape. Underscoring Ismail's dominance over Wafiya—and the seeming willful ignorance of her husband, the fictional double for the nation—Ismail easily finds ways to isolate and assault her whenever he wants: "The husband's trust in his best friend and the friend's sway over the husband thwarted her efforts."[25] And when she has found herself alone with Ismail, she has been unable to resist him, perhaps gesturing to Abdel Kouddous's own capitulation to Nasser in his *Rose El Youssef* editorials since *I Do Not Sleep*: "Her weakness, hatred, and fear combined and came welling out of her eyes as tears while she surrendered."[26] As she becomes more and more accustomed to the shame and masochistic pleasure of the assaults, her relationship with the abuse and the abuser changes: "She was addicted to these moments. Addicted to those tears. Addicted to her weakness. It was no longer Ismail who was making her sin; the sin welled up from inside her."[27] Through Wafiya, Abdel Kouddous alludes to how Nasser's escalating assaults produced not only self-loathing and disgust, but also debasement, rendering him addicted to humiliation and abuse, explaining through Wafiya his own seemingly compulsive relationship with Nasser that oscillated between submission and resistance in the aftermath of the installation of dictatorship.

Because of her guilt, self-hatred, and weakness, Wafiya is unable to confess the sin to her husband, just as Nadia in *I Do Not Sleep* cannot reveal Kawthar's treason to her father and Abdel Kouddous remained unable to expose to the public his own abuse. While Wafiya paradoxically both detests and desires Ismail, she soon develops a deep hatred for Omar, the nation, a radical new development within Abdel Kouddous's fiction. Omar is entirely incapable of protecting her from Ismail or herself, willfully ignorant of the betrayal taking place in the house because of his delight and gratitude for the embedded dictator, Ismail. Moreover, Wafiya's inability to reveal the betrayal and abuse only produces more self-loathing, isolation, and desperation: "She no longer hated just Ismail. She hated herself too. She hated her weak husband, who could not protect her from Ismail and from herself." In direct contrast to the way he articulated love of the nation and Egypt in his radio program "Whisper," Abdel Kouddous was now revealing how this love had shockingly turned into disgust: "Life itself became hate."[28]

As in *I Do Not Sleep* and *There's a Man in Our House*, Abdel Kouddous's loathing for Nasser boils over into a fantasy of killing the traitor: "In her hand she held a knife formed of her antipathy. In her imagination she stabbed Ismail with it. Stabbed her husband with it. Stabbed herself with it. How she hated. Hated everything. She hated God too. She no longer feared Him. No longer prayed to Him. Because she hated Him. Hated Him because He too could not protect her."[29] This murder fantasy, however, had developed significantly from the two earlier works. Here, it is not simply Abdel Kouddous's hatred for Nasser that leads to the fantasy of stabbing him to death. Ismail—the double for the now-messianic Nasser—has become so powerful and manipulative that even God cannot protect her from him. This leads to the fantasy of revenge that turned into a murder suicide, ensnaring not just Abdel Kouddous and Nasser but also the nation. Abdel Kouddous's despair had reached new lows.

After the assault in the cabin that begins the story, Wafiya decides that she must act. She must rid herself and her husband of Ismail, just as Abdel Kouddous fantasized about expelling Nasser for betraying the principles and ideals of the revolution: "She would kick him out of her house, never to return."³⁰ Infused with sudden confidence and strength, she writes an anonymous note to her husband on a typewriter: "Beware your friend Ismail. He is seducing your very, very virtuous wife and trying to ravish her. You have to kick him out of your house immediately if you want to protect your wife and your honor."³¹ In this, Wafiya resorts to writing—like Abdel Kouddous and his fictional double Nadia in *I Do Not Sleep*—to reveal her anxiety and suffering, to urge her husband—Egypt—to expel the traitor from the metaphorical house. She imagines Omar reading the letter and learning the truth, then becoming enraged and attacking Ismail, finally protecting her honor and soothing her weakness, sin, and tears. Nonetheless, when Omar reads it, he calmly tells Wafiya that it is just an advertisement. Unlike the fake letter in *I Do Not Sleep* that compels Nadia's husband to believe that his wife was cheating on him, this letter has no impact whatsoever, even though it confesses adultery that is indeed taking place, suggesting how much deeper Nasser had become embedded into the fabric of the nation, gesturing to the unflappable faith the nation had in him by the late 1950s. Distraught and stunned, Wafiya wonders, "Did he trust Ismail so much that even such a letter could not shake or diminish his belief?"³²

In shock that her husband could simply disregard her veiled confession, Wafiya is convinced that Omar must have secretly decided to keep watch on Ismail so that he can confirm the betrayal for himself. She decides that she must trick Ismail into coming on to her while her husband is watching in order to prove the abuse to him. When they arrive at a club, she asks Ismail to walk her to the garden, where she kisses him, leaving her lipstick on his cheek, a marker that Omar ignores. Her husband once again represses what is happening before his eyes, sending Wafiya into a rage and gesturing to the disgust that Abdel Kouddous must have felt when the public did not understand his fiction as a metaphorical confession of Nasser's betrayal of the nation and the revolution: "She looked at her husband. He was stupider than her. He was a dope. She hated him. She hated him more than Ismail."³³ Abdel Kouddous then further underscored the doubling of Nasser as Ismail by depicting him as imprisoning Wafiya after she attempts to warn her husband about the betrayal, gesturing to his own imprisonment after his series of editorials in 1954 warning the nation of dictatorship: "Ismail left her at the door of the house. He was like a prison guard taking her to prison and shutting the cell door behind them."³⁴ Enraged, Wafiya fantasizes about exposing the assaults openly to her husband—as well as her addiction to them—but she cannot find the courage: "Every part of her was silently screaming in exasperated fury."³⁵

Nonetheless, Wafiya does not give up. She tries to expose Ismail again through writing, this time even more explicitly, sending a second letter to Omar: "Your wife is cheating on you with your friend Ismail. If you want to make sure of their betrayal, pretend that you are going to leave them alone for a half hour, then come back in after five minutes and you will see the disgrace with your own eyes."³⁶ Like Nadia in *I Do Not Sleep*, Wafiya feels a compulsion to destroy her abuser, but she cannot bring herself to reveal the betrayal directly. Gesturing to Abdel Kouddous and his allegorical confessions in his fiction—including this story—Wafiya can only reveal the crime indirectly, pushing her husband to uncover the treason himself: "All she wanted now was to destroy Ismail and her husband. Destroy the vast deception that bound them, which they call friendship. She wanted to take revenge on them both. Over her dead body."³⁷ When Omar reads the second letter, he once again claims that it is an advertisement, ignoring it, stunning Wafiya once more with his blind faith in Ismail. Nonetheless, Omar goes to make a phone call outside of the cabin, inadvertently making Wafiya think that he is leaving only to return quickly to catch Ismail in the act, just as she has instructed him to do in the letter. In order to reveal the treason, Wafiya then lets Ismail assault her as a final desperate performance of addiction to degradation, self-loathing, and masochism. But Omar does not return until after the assault, demonstrating again that Omar's faith in Ismail, like Egypt's faith is in Nasser, is unshakable.

Wafiya revolts in disgust and rage, fleeing to her parents' house in Cairo, demanding a divorce, and refusing to see either Omar or Ismail but unable to explain why. Like Nadia at the end of *I Do Not Sleep*, Wafiya locks herself in her dark bedroom, catatonic at her grief, despair, and self-loathing. It is at this point that Abdel Kouddous radically complicated the two endings that he wrote for *I Do Not Sleep*. Instead of concluding the story here, as in *I Do Not Sleep*, Wafiya is overwhelmed by disgust and self-hatred, but she is also pulsating with desire to taste once again the feeling of submission to Ismail: "She was crying with longing for her weakness. She was like a drug addict deprived of their fix. She was in agony. In pain. At times she almost went mad as she knew the secret behind her agony and what she needed. But she resisted. Resisted. How long, though could she resist? How long?"[38] After Ismail's repeated assaults, she has become habituated to desire self-destruction, self-loathing, and degradation, like the downward spiral of drug addiction. She is trying to flee from herself, just as Abdel Kouddous wrote about himself in September 1957, showing that the act of writing this story—of once again confessing through the metaphor of widely consumed fiction—served as a soothing drug, at least for a while.

Wafiya's friend Effat calls, accusing her of staying in the "prison" of her bedroom. Wafiya emerges to go visit Effat, where she finds Ismail waiting for her. Thinking that she is resolving a marital dispute, Effat leaves Wafiya alone with Ismail, and Wafiya is once again incapable of resisting him. In the final act, Ismail, after assaulting Wafiya yet again, takes her back to Omar to continue performing the role of the dutiful wife who is addicted to sexual abuse, just as Abdel Kouddous needed to continue to return to the press to publish his obsequious editorials as a form of humiliation and self-loathing. There is no escape now, no matter how hard either tries.

Wafiya returns to Omar's house as a kind of compulsion, a drug addict unable to break the habit, "crying over her weakness."[39] As they enter, Omar, the double of Egypt, looks at Ismail with gratitude, squeezing his hand, like an Egyptian on the street clamoring to touch Nasser in jubilation, grateful for restoring his dignity and pride. The story ends with Omar saying, "Thank you, Ismail. Thank you so much. I don't know how to thank you enough."[40] Abdel Kouddous therefore shows how Omar will remain the dupe, just like the father in *I Do Not Sleep*, and the traitor-dictator Ismail will continue abusing Wafiya. But the ending also suggests that Abdel Kouddous is no longer Nadia, isolated and paralyzed by regret and melancholy for plotting to embed a traitor into the house and her inability to confess her crime and reveal the truth. He is now Wafiya, living an addiction of degradation, relentlessly soiled by Ismail and Omar, Nasser and Egypt. He cannot stop himself from submitting to the dictator-traitor, cannot overcome the addiction of humiliation, regret, anxiety, weakness, and failure, regardless of any revolt or attempt to flee. This ending suggests that Abdel Kouddous, like Wafiya, might resist through writing notes to Egypt, trying to use fiction to reveal the abuse to the public, to orchestrate moments in which the traitor will be exposed. Nonetheless, these acts are futile. Egypt, like Omar, will never understand the message, no matter how direct and obvious it is. The nation will continue living in repressed denial at the abuse happening to its most "faithful" love. Like Wafiya, Abdel Kouddous will continue to submit to the dictator in the house with the contradictory feelings of weakness and self-loathing, addicted pleasure, and intoxication. This ending is not the tortured despair and hopelessness of Nadia at the end of *I Do Not Sleep*, an admission that the traitor has been embedded never to be revealed, forcing her into the dark despair of isolation. It suggests that Abdel Kouddous's relationship with Nasser—who was at the height of his power and popularity after the creation of the United Arab Republic, the formal union of Egypt and Syria in 1958—has now become a masochistic addiction of sexual assault, degradation, and subjugation.

The Third Girl section of *Girls in Summer* was much more brazen than *I Do Not Sleep* or *There's a Man in Our House*. And Nasser, unlike the public, saw through Abdel Kouddous's confession in the story. Considering the increasingly stifling censorship at the time and the escalated audaciousness of the story, it should come as no surprise when Heikal arrived to tell Abdel Kouddous that he had gone too far. Perhaps finally drawing Nasser's attention, even anger at his fiction was what Abdel Kouddous wanted after all. Abdel Kouddous had been able to suppress his need to lash out at Nasser since June 1957, when he finished serializing *There's a Man in Our House*. He had been behaving himself by avoiding Nasser in his fiction for the past fifteen months while continuing to publish fawning editorials. Perhaps something happened behind the scenes on one of Abdel Kouddous trips with Nasser in 1958. Perhaps it was the increasingly stifling censorship that Abdel Kouddous was facing at his magazine—or something else that we have no record of—but it is clear from the Third Girl that Abdel Kouddous could not restrain himself anymore and gave into his compulsion to resist, confess, and despair, a contradictory intoxication coupled with self-loathing.

Despite the crisis behind the scenes once Heikal arrived at Abdel Kouddous's office, there was no obvious indication of it in print. There was also no indication that the public understood the symbolism of the story either, suggesting that readers—like Omar—remained in repressed denial about the abuse taking place before their eyes. It was not until 1980 when Abdel Kouddous revealed Heikal's visit and Nasser's objections in a collection of short stories that he published under the provocative title *Sorry, I Can't Anymore*. The first piece in the collection is a letter that Abdel Kouddous wrote to Nasser right after Heikal's visit. Abdel Kouddous explains in his introduction to the letter that censorship had become so severe in the late 1950s that it had fully gripped the political pages of *Rose El Youssef*, as if "newspapers had actually been the possession of the state."[41] Abdel Kouddous recounts that they put up with the censor in the political pages of the magazine because, at the time, Nasser, after nationalizing the Suez Canal, resisting the joint attack of Britain, France, and Israel, and forming the United Arab Republic, was "at the greatest splendor of his victories," something that compelled many to "give him the right to do anything, even impose this severe censorship. Indeed, success justified all mistakes."[42] Abdel Kouddous explained that Nasser was fanatical about word choice, even outside the political context. At the time that Abdel Kouddous published *Sorry, I Can't Anymore*, a flood of memoirs criticizing Nasser and his era as part of Sadat's "de-Nasserization" project had already appeared. According to Abdel Kouddous, by publishing this letter, he was not participating in that wave: "I don't have memoirs to publish since I already published everything I have to say. What I couldn't publish in an editorial, I put in fiction wearing the clothes of another person."[43] This is perhaps the most direct Abdel Kouddous ever was in print about the way he used his fiction not only to say what he could not in political editorials but also to indicate that he himself embodied various characters in his work, gesturing directly to the Third Girl.

In the letter, Abdel Kouddous explained that Heikal relayed Nasser's displeasure about *Girls in Summer*, something he had also heard from the director of censorship, Hasan Sabry, who demanded an immediate redirection of the novel's narrative. In particular, according to the letter, Nasser was not happy about the depiction of "what might be happening in the cabins on the beaches of Alexandria," pointing directly to the opening of the story of Wafiya, Ismail, and Omar.[44] As Abdel Kouddous explained in a later interview, "Sometimes I was forced to comply with what was said, especially if it was said by Gamal Abdel Nasser. I had to comply with Nasser in the Third Girl of *Girls* *in Summer."*⁴⁵ Abdel Kouddous had written about adultery many times before, so why would the Third Girl in particular have upset Nasser to the point of sending Heikal and Sabry with demands for changes to the rest of *Girls in Summer*? Abdel Kouddous had simply become too transparent in his allegory of dictatorship in Egypt as embodied in the three characters. In his letter to Nasser at the time, Abdel Kouddous ignored the suggestiveness of his dissent and instead tried to explain away the objection by focusing on the story not as allegory but as an honest and accurate picture of what was happening behind closed doors in society at the time.

Abdel Kouddous once cryptically suggested that the censor intervened in the plot of *There's a Man in Our House* after he published the first installment. In his letter to Nasser, Abdel Kouddous openly admitted for the first time that he changed his fiction at the demand of the censor: "I agreed with Sabry to alter the direction of the novel."⁴⁶ This explains the sudden shift *Girls in Summer* takes after the Third Girl. In the Fourth Girl, a middle-aged man is sexually obsessed with his housekeeper, but after she rejects him, he frames her for theft to justify firing her. The Fifth Girl tells the story of a narcissistic young woman who ruins her relationship with a sincere suitor from her neighborhood by chasing after a wealthy playboy who abandons her after she sleeps with him. Both of these stories have striking sexual overtones of "what might be happening in the cabins on the beaches of Alexandria," but neither features a fictional double for Abdel Kouddous or Nasser, strongly suggesting that it was the allegory of dictatorship in the Third Girl that Nasser objected to, not the depiction of adultery and sexuality.

The adaptation of the Third Girl in the film *Girls in Summer* underscores this point even further. Premiering on 28 March 1960, only fifteen months after the original serialization, the film presents three parts from the novel—the Third, Fourth, and Fifth Girl. Each vignette has a different director, with Ezzedine Zulficar directing the adaptation of the Third Girl, which leads off the film. Maryam Fakhreddine stars as the anxious, insecure, and tearful Wafiya; Kamal El-Shennawi, a former leading romantic hero in Egyptian cinema, plays the lecherous, confident, and dictatorial Ismail; and Adil Khayri plays Omar, the symbol of an Egypt that is both submissive and fawning, easily pushed

**Figure 19.** Poster for the 1960 film adaptation of the Third Girl from *Girls in Summer*.

around and in repressed denial about the abuse taking place in his house right in front of his eyes. The film was advertised by three separate posters, one for each vignette. The poster for the Third Girl beautifully fronts the precise dynamic of the story that Nasser purportedly objected to. Against a red background suggesting sin, the masculine and strong Ismail grips Wafiya by both arms, burying his head in her hair, closing his eyes in sexual satisfaction. Wafiya, with the strap of her dress falling off her shoulder, looks off in weakness and despair, longing for a savior yet masochistically submitting to her abuser. Omar is marginalized in the bottom corner of the poster, distant from the two, looking forward with a worried, impotent expression on his face, demonstrating that he knows the abuse is happening despite his attempts to repress it and is incapable of doing anything to stop it.

While there are small changes to the plot leading up to the climax, it is exactly "what might be happening in the cabins on the beaches of Alexandria" that is emphasized in the film adaptation, with Ismail repeatedly sexually assaulting Wafiya while Omar remains in denial. As usual, the climax "fixes" the objections of the censor or, in this case, of Nasser himself. After Effat brings in Ismail to take Wafiya back to Omar and leaves the two alone, Ismail once again begins assaulting her, just as in the novel. In the film, however, Effat brings Omar into the room so that he can witness the betrayal with his own eyes. Wafiya, now pregnant and uncertain who the father is—a detail unique to the film that stresses the theme of adultery and sexual degradation even further—openly shames Omar for abandoning her to Ismail's abuse. Omar, however, cannot overcome his repression. He looks away, shaking his head in denial, squeezing his tearful eyes shut, turning his back to Wafiya and Ismail, incapable of facing them. Omar, like Egypt, is in such denial that he cannot acknowledge the cheating, even as it takes place openly. Reaching new depths of desperation, Wafiya grabs a letter opener and stabs Ismail in the back as her repressed and impotent husband looks on, exacting the vengeance that he cannot. Wafiya then runs out of the cabin and commits suicide by throwing herself off a cliff.

With this ending, the film fixes not "what might be happening in the cabins of Alexandria" but the moral ambiguity, the ongoing abuse, and the allegory of dictatorship in Abdel Kouddous's Third Girl. In the film, instead of submitting to Ismail's ongoing abuse as a form of masochistic addiction of pleasure and self-loathing, Wafiya finally rises up and kills Ismail, dishing out the punishment that the adulterer and abuser justly deserves. Thanks to her revolt, Ismail meets his end along clear moral lines. Moreover, murdering Ismail in the film is a way to stress that he is not a double for Nasser. This is reinforced when Wafiya flees the murder scene and immediately commits suicide, carrying out the necessary punishment on herself for her own participation in the relationship. The vignette therefore ends in harsh, stark moral lines—just like the film adaptation of *I Do Not Sleep*—lines that the novel refuses, punishing both participants in the ongoing immorality and erasing any doubt that the story could serve as an allegory of the abuses of dictatorship. Abdel Kouddous's confession to the public of the sexual and psychological abuses of dictatorship is recast into moral clarity and richly deserved punishment. Unsurprisingly, this film adaptation appalled Abdel Kouddous. After the premier of *Girls in Summer*, he wrote in *Rose El Youssef* how a friend criticized him for the film: "He held me completely responsible for it without taking it on himself to read the novel."[47]

When Abdel Kouddous sat down to write his letter to Nasser after Heikal left his office, he was clearly in a panic. He fully understood the danger. Perhaps he wrote the letter to demonstrate that he was not his uncompromising mother, who sharply rejected Nasser's demands for accommodation back in June 1954. To prove his pliability, he wrote that he agreed to change the plot of *Girls in Summer* going forward, as requested. But, more important, he also pleaded with Nasser not to abandon him. Abdel Kouddous closed his letter by explaining, "All I mean to say with this letter is please keep your faith in me since I need you as a pillar and as a brother."[48] Abdel Kouddous suggested that he needed Nasser's protection not only to ward off another arrest—or worse—but also to continue to write and publish fiction, his only presumed space of freedom, even if with increasingly restricted margins. Without Nasser as a pillar of support, he would also no longer have his much-needed "drug," his method of self-analysis and therapy. As he explained in a radio interview recorded in mid-October 1959, perhaps thinking of this episode, "I can't manage without writing fiction."[49] The stakes therefore could not have been higher. Without fiction, Abdel Kouddous would have had no medicine, no way to treat his illness, no outlet to self-soothe, even if the revolt in his fiction was repressed in the subsequent film adaptation.

## NASSER EX MACHINA

As Abdel Kouddous admitted in a 1980 interview, the crisis surrounding *Girls in Summer* made his relationship with Nasser even more distant.[50] While we do not know exactly what happened behind the scenes, thanks to whatever he told Heikal and the censor, as well as changing the narrative of *Girls in Summer* after the Third Girl and writing his letter to Nasser, Abdel Kouddous survived the crisis in fall 1958. As he explained in an interview about this episode toward the end of his life, "Nasser didn't impose any punishment or prevent me from writing fiction."[51] This is clear from the fact that Abdel Kouddous continued serializing *Girls in Summer* after the Third Girl, publishing the remaining installments from 9 October until 7 November 1958, never missing an issue even as he had to alter the plot of the novel rapidly to please Nasser and the censor.

The crisis, however, was still clearly hanging over his head once he finished. Abdel Kouddous typically took a break of several months before even starting to plan a new novel. This time, however, he scrambled to begin preparations for his next novel within only a few weeks after finishing *Girls in Summer*.[52] This exceptional haste suggests that Abdel Kouddous felt pressure to return to the novel, perhaps to demonstrate to Nasser that he would indeed use his fiction to accommodate the regime and compensate for what he had done in the Third Girl. If he needed any inspiration during this short window for how to please Nasser in this next novel, he did not have to look far. In November and December 1958, just as he started planning his new novel, Egypt was celebrating the second anniversary of the Suez War, culminating in the "Holiday of Victory" on 23 December. The celebrations no doubt reminded him of the euphoria over Nasser's speech in which he nationalized the Suez Canal as well as the sense of pride and dignity that the conflict brought the nation. During summer 1956, as events were unfolding, Abdel Kouddous seemed to feel tremendous nationalist enthusiasm for how Nasser navigated the crisis and war. In fall 1956, not only did Abdel Kouddous publish editorials heaping praise on Nasser, but he went back on the radio, even after the schism surrounding the end of his 1954-55 program "Whisper," to urge Egyptians to flock to the Suez Canal to defend their country. Under Abdel Kouddous, *Rose El Youssef* was a bastion of militant support for the conflict, publishing weekly centerfolds of art celebrating the bravery and sacrifice of Nasser and average Egyptians on the battlefield.

If not the celebrations in November and December 1958, something pushed Abdel Kouddous to turn his thoughts back to summer 1956 as he began planning for his next novel. In August 1956, he published a short story titled "The Return of Character."[53] This brief story focuses on an unnamed man who becomes weak, insecure, and lost after getting married. As a result, his wife does not consider him "the man of the house," and his children do not respect him as a father. The man fantasizes about confronting his wife to restore his dignity and self-respect, but he cannot bring himself to do it: "He's weak, weak at home, at work with his colleagues, everywhere." One day, however, as he sits in a café, the man hears Nasser's 23 July 1956 speech in which he nationalized the Suez Canal: "The man felt something revolt within him, something that he hadn't felt before. He felt it fill his chest and flow in his limbs. He felt strength that he hadn't felt before. He wanted Gamal Abdel Nasser to continue giving the speech his entire life so he could feel this strength forever. But Gamal's speech stopped." The man needs more Nasser, like a drug, in order to feel strong: "Why doesn't Gamal delegate to him something to do, something from which he could derive this strength, something that makes him feel that he's a great man who could play an important role in the affairs of his country?" The man realizes that he can achieve this by volunteering for the National Guard. When he returns home in his National Guard uniform, his wife is stunned: "She looked at him as if he was a new man, a man whom she hadn't met before, a strong man." When his children see him in the uniform holding the rifle, they are full of admiration instead of their usual mockery and scorn. The story ends with the declaration "Their father is a hero!" It was simply in hearing Nasser give his speech on the radio that the man was radically transformed, eliminating his weakness, insecurity, and anxiety. In this story, Nasser functions not as a human being but as a deux ex machina figure who swoops in suddenly to bring salvation to an irresolvable tragedy.

Simply by hearing Nasser articulate nationalizing the Suez Canal, the unnamed protagonist resolves his mysterious and intractable crisis of weakness, insecurity, and emasculation. Like the nation during the Suez conflict, he completes his quest for dignity and self-respect, ultimately achieving transcendence. Just as in Greek tragedy, this "Nasser ex machina" requires the suspension of belief, providing a simplistic and convenient resolution to an unsolvable crisis.[54]

It was to this story that Abdel Kouddous, in the immediate aftermath of the crisis surrounding *Girls in Summer*, turned. Perhaps it was because the story reminded Abdel Kouddous of a period of personal enthusiasm for Nasser and the mass sense of restoration of national dignity and strength through confrontation with the West, a sentiment that could have made the necessary accommodation that he was clearly expected to perform in his new novel more palatable. Perhaps Abdel Kouddous thought that the image of a weak, aimless man miraculously brought salvation through the arrival of Nasser like a deus ex machina would be an acceptable—if not excessive and parodying—way to express remorse for *Girls in Summer* and demonstrate obedience to the regime through his fiction. Perhaps the image of a Nasser ex machina provided him with the literary technique to transfer the bombastic praise of Nasser in his editorials into the space of his fiction. Regardless, Abdel Kouddous quickly began planning his new novel around the two basic storylines of "The Return of Character." In the first, a family is set adrift because of the intractable weakness, anxiety, and insecurity of its male head. In the second, the male head—and, consequently, the family and nation—miraculously finds dignity, self-respect, masculinity, and salvation through the sudden, astonishing arrival of Nasser as deux ex machina.

As Abdel Kouddous was developing the novel in December 1958, barely a month after he finished serializing *Girls in Summer*, he began polling colleagues at *Rose El Youssef*—as well as Abdel Halim Hafez and the composer Kamal El-Tawil—on a list of titles for his new novel. When he continued hesitating picking one into January 1959, Ahmed Bahaa Eddine, close colleague and editor in chief of *Sabah al-Khayr*, took the liberty of deciding for him by printing in the 15 January 1959 issue of *Sabah al-Khayr* that Abdel Kouddous's next novel would be called *The Sun Never Sets*.[55] Since the cryptic meaning of the title—the transformative power of Nasser arriving as a deus ex machina—would only become clear in the final installments, Abdel Kouddous must have known from the earliest stages where he would be taking the plot. He used the word *sun* likely to gesture to the most famous example of a deux ex machina, the sun god Helios saving Madea in Euripides's tragedy. Perhaps Abdel Kouddous was also hinting at Louis XIV, known as the Sun King, who is well known for the expression "I am the state," or that, like the British Empire, the sun never sets on Nasser and his presumed influence. In addition, the title of the novel shifted narrative focus from the weak male central figure in "The Return of Character" to the sun, which would only be revealed after months of installments as Nasser, like Helios, appears suddenly as a deus ex machina in the novel to resolve an intractable crisis.

Only four months after completing *Girls in Summer*, the shortest gap between novels during the Nasser era, Abdel Kouddous began serializing *The Sun Never Sets* on 2 March 1959 and continued for fifty-nine weeks uninterrupted, finishing on 4 April 1960. The novel is by far his longest work, his magnum opus, totaling over fifteen hundred pages in the first edition of the book. As Abdel Kouddous wrote in the issue of *Rose El Youssef* in which he published the first installment, "I am trying to write a symphony after I'd gotten used to writing light songs."[56] The sweeping novel begins by introducing the various members of the Zuhdi family, an expansion of the family in "The Return of Character." At twenty-five years old, Ahmed is the oldest male and head of the family after his father died some ten years earlier. Strikingly handsome, manly, and broad-chested, Ahmed is in the prime of life, seemingly the manifestation of a strong, masculine, and fearless Egypt at the height of Nasser. Nonetheless, his impressive physical appearance "hid under it his confused nervous self, his trifling personality that he can't define and hasn't traced yet."[57] Tortured by the contradiction between his handsome appearance and inner anxiety, insecurity, and aimlessness, Ahmed is incapable of bearing the weight of social expectations, leading him to crumble repeatedly in the face of familial and societal responsibility. For example, when Ahmed discovers his sister, Nabila, holding hands with a man on the corniche in the opening installment of the novel, he is filled with such an urge to flee from confronting her that he experiences a panic attack: "A fog crept over Ahmed's eyes until he was no longer able to see a thing. . . . Confusion paralyzed him to the point that he could no longer move."[58]

Throughout the novel, Ahmed takes refuge at the Gazeera Club, which is depicted as teeming with aimless young people like him trying to fill the emptiness of their lives. There, Ahmed steals looks at the nineteen-year-old Shahira. Despite his manly appearance, Ahmed is a "coward and virgin" since he is incapable of bringing himself to make direct contact with her even though he goes to the club every day to stare at her nervously from a distance.[59] When their eyes finally meet, Ahmed is destabilized and gets up to run away. It is Shahira who eventually breaks the silence between them, forcing Ahmed to confront his impotency and anxiety, at least briefly. When Shahira later tells Ahmed that she is in love with him, Ahmed is in disbelief. He confesses to her, "I don't believe in myself. I don't believe that I deserve your love. I'm a failure, Shahira. A failure in everything. I can't believe that you love a failure."[60]

The initial installments meticulously chart how Ahmed's anxieties, insecurities, and cowardice destabilize his family, with catastrophic results. Mamdouh, Ahmed's optimistic and confident younger brother, is the life of the house, exuding the mettle, poise, and tenacity that Ahmed lacks. Without any guidance from Ahmed, however, he wastes his enthusiasm, courage, and boundless energy by rejecting university for a variety of menial jobs, horrifying the family as he appears to be dropping down in class. Conflict over his career choices eventually enrages Mamdouh, causing him to flee the house in anger and tragically die in a moped accident. Ahmed's inability and failure to serve as head of the family also paves the way for Layla, his beautiful and vulnerable eighteen-year-old sister, to have an affair with her thirty-nine-year-old married piano teacher, Fathi, who serves as an emotional and sexual surrogate for her dead father. The affair quickly becomes an addiction for Layla, ruining her prospects for marriage and leading her to attempt suicide. Without paternal guidance, Fifi, Ahmed's oldest sister, also endangers her future by toying callously with perhaps her final suitor, now on the verge of ruining her last chance to get married. Nabila, the middle sister, meanders without a family pillar as well. In love with the manly yet poor Mahmoud, she is unable to recognize the class divisions between them, imperiling her future. All of the sisters are rudderless,

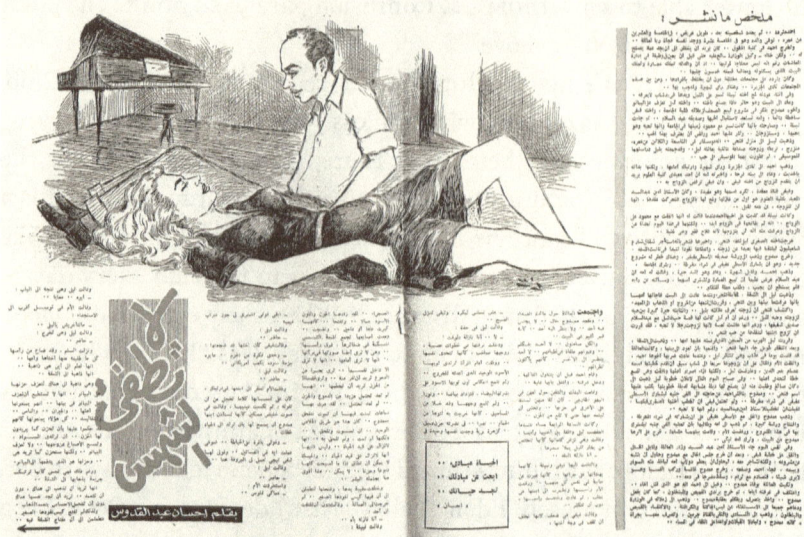

**Figure 20.** Installment of *The Sun Never Sets* with Layla and her piano teacher. *Rose El Youssef*, 24 August 1959.

flirting with self-destruction as they are abandoned without paternal guidance to navigate the turbulence of love alone.

The condemnation of Ahmed and his family is so devastating that the novel can be read as a bitter critique of the failures of Nasserism at the time. This is especially true in the first three months of serialization, when the temporal setting of the novel was clearly intended to be contemporaneous with its publication, even though a date is never given. For example, in the second installment of the novel, published on 9 March 1959, Mamdouh tells Ahmed about his plan to sell newspapers and novels on the streets to make money. He tells Ahmed that he is also making money by selling copies of the novel *There's a Man in Our House*, which was originally published in 1957, but it had been reissued in late January 1959 and would have been sold on the streets exactly when Abdel Kouddous wrote this chapter. This detail would later be corrected in the first edition of *The Sun Never Sets*, which lists the novel that Mamdouh was selling as *I Do Not Sleep*.[61] In the third installment of the novel, originally published on 16 March 1959, Fathi tells Layla that he cannot believe that he loves someone so young, someone "who knows the Russian rocket, not someone who reads about it or sees its photograph not being able to believe it. My love for you is like the Russian rocket."⁶² Clearly, Abdel Kouddous is referring here to Luna 1, which was launched in January 1959, soon before this installment was published. Another piece of textual evidence that Abdel Kouddous assumed a contemporaneous timeline when he began serializing *The Sun Never Sets* is in a scene in which Ahmed's mother reads an old letter from her lover. In the installment of this scene in *Rose El Youssef*, published on 25 May 1959, the date of the letter is 1931. The mother was seventeen years old at the time that she received it, and she was forty-five at the start of the novel, establishing the temporal setting as 1959. Abdel Kouddous would later correct the date of the letter in the first edition of the book to change the temporal setting to 1956.⁶³

The depiction of Ahmed and his family, especially in the context of these details that confirm a contemporaneous temporal setting, must have greatly annoyed the censor at the time of the original serialization. Abdel Kouddous likely explained the full plot to the censor, perhaps arguing that he needed to display the failures of the family in order to demonstrate the need for Nasser's salvation but, as the weeks and months passed, this was clearly not enough. Tensions with the censor behind the scenes are the most likely explanation for why, in the installment published on 1 June 1959, three full months into serializing the novel, Abdel Kouddous suddenly inserted a clunky scene in which a young man asks Ahmed at a party for his opinion about the Bandung Conference. Considering that the novel was being serialized in the aftermath of the formation of the United Arab Republic, harkening back to Bandung at this point—which must have seemed to readers like a distant memory—only served the purpose of providing a jarring anchor for establishing the temporal setting of the novel for readers as 1955 and not 1959. Correcting the temporal setting of the novel as opening before Bandung, especially when the novel had clearly assumed a contemporaneous temporal setting for three months, also helped to clarify that the failures of the family could not be linked to the contemporaneous period—the height of Nasser's fame, Arab nationalism, and the United Arab Republic—but to the long shadow of the monarchy period and the uncertain meandering of the country before Nasser's meteoric rise. Bandung was the beginning of Nasser's success on the world stage and electric popularity at home, allowing the story to suggest that Ahmed and his family represented no condemnation of the current era but were rather damaged leftovers from the monarchy period and had not yet been transformed by Nasser. The awkward and heavy-handed reference to Bandung almost certainly represented a blatant concession to the censor, a way for Abdel Kouddous to buy himself time to continue his "symphony."

Despite this blunt accommodation, Abdel Kouddous did not move quickly to deliver salvation to the family. From the beginning of June 1959 until the end of the year, Abdel Kouddous meandered in the plot, continuing to highlight the failures of Ahmed and his family with no clarity within the novel for how the family would find salvation. Moreover, the installments during these long months continue to betray the author's ongoing tensions and frustrations with the censor, as the challenges of serialization during this period played out in full view of the public. For example, Mamdouh's death appears at first to be the spark that will transform the family. For several installments, Ahmed seems to have internalized Mamdouh's courage, subsequently embracing the principles of the revolution. Nonetheless, he quickly regresses to his old self, full of social anxiety, insecurity, and aimlessness. In the installment published on 7 December 1959, in what reads like another concession to the censor, Abdel Kouddous depicts Ahmed listening to Nasser give a speech on the radio about the principles of the revolution: "In Nasser's voice was something that excited Ahmed. He felt as if this voice was waking him up, pushing him to work, to produce, to be something."[64] It seems, at first, that Nasser has arrived to rouse Ahmed and bring him salvation. Nonetheless, in the following installment, Ahmed once again collapses into instability, insecurity, and anxiety, getting drunk to flee responsibility for Layla's affair with Fathi. His regression after hearing Nasser's speech must have irritated the censor greatly. On 11 January 1960, Ahmed once again encounters Nasser, this time through a speech printed in the newspaper. Shockingly, the novel is explicit about how the speech is powerless to change Ahmed: "All of Egypt was moving quickly and decisively. Despite that, Ahmed was sitting in his place not moving. He couldn't do anything. He couldn't be decisive about anything. He was still looking for himself."[65]

The period covering late 1959 and early 1960 was clearly a difficult time for Abdel Kouddous. The heavy-handed inclusion of these encounters with Nasser in the novel suggest that he was fighting regularly with the censor behind the scenes, writing what appeared to be the long-awaited moment of salvation one installment only to backtrack the next. These repeated false starts perhaps show how he was toying with the censor, frustrated at what felt like constant intervention in his work. They could also reflect a deep anxiety and hesitancy by Abdel Kouddous at moving toward the blatant propaganda and absurdity of incorporating Nasser as a kind of deus ex machina at the climax of his magnum opus. Perhaps Abdel Kouddous was also under pressure to keep the colossal novel going in order to boost circulation at a time when he was growing more and more concerned with the financial viability of his magazines.

The novel was also creating unexpected personal problems for him. On the morning of 10 December 1959, Abdel Kouddous received an anonymous letter at the offices of *Rose El Youssef* from a reader threatening to kill him if he did not kill off a particular character in the novel. Instead of taking the letter seriously, Abdel Kouddous chalked it up to just another emotional fan reaction. That same morning, however, the man who wrote the letter went to Abdel Kouddous's apartment, delivered a second letter to his butler, and then pulled out a gun, threatening the butler and telling him to move inside. The butler managed to escape and alert nearby doormen. When they all returned to confront the assailant, he had disappeared. Abdel Kouddous wrote in *Rose El Youssef*, "I informed the police. I can stand an isolated crazy person, but I can't stand one with a gun. If I'm killed, know that I went as a martyr of the crazies!"[66] With a wife and two young children at home, the incident must have deeply disturbed him. When another man came to Abdel Kouddous's office in mid-January 1960 accusing him of destroying his family when his wife divorced him after reading the novel, his must have thought about the possibility of another outraged reader looking for revenge.[67] Between these incidents and ongoing tensions with the censor, it was time to start moving the novel to its conclusion.

Nasser finally arrives as a deus ex machina on 1 February 1960. As Ahmed listens to the radio broadcast of the speech nationalizing the Suez Canal, he is suddenly transfixed, completely unlike his previous encounters with Nasser in the novel: "He felt as if the voice of Gamal was piercing the pores of his body and flowing in his blood. He felt as if it were lashes calling him to rise up, yelling at him to carry out his duty.... Gamal spoke confidently, strongly as if he was the strongest man in the world, as if behind him were the strongest people on earth."[68] Like the unnamed man in "The Return of Character," Ahmed jumps up, suddenly on fire with nationalist pride, pulsating with purpose, and overwhelmed by the need to join in and act, erasing his personal anxiety: "One problem swallowed up all the others. The problem of participating in this important event. The problem of searching for something to undertake, to rise up to the level of his nationalist feeling."[69] Ahmed felt that Nasser was speaking to him personally, ordering him to perform his duty, "as if there were millions of people in his chest, all of them calling out to Gamal.... He wanted to join the people. He wanted to find himself among the millions, to go with them on the path of the great event. So he went out."[70] As Abdel Kouddous had written many times in his *Rose El Youssef* editorials, Nasser was strong because he embodied the Egyptian people. Ahmed becomes one of the millions who embody their leader, the individual who serves as the double of the nation. After hearing this latest speech, Ahmed feels a compulsion to stand with Nasser: "He and the people can't leave Gamal alone these days. Gamal is strong with him, strong with the people. The people have to gather to put themselves in Gamal's fist to hit their enemies."[71]

Like the hero of "The Return of Character," Ahmed suddenly decides to volunteer for the National Guard, which erases his ego and generates a feeling of solidarity with others in the struggle. When Ahmed grabs a rifle, "he feels rebirth, new blood pulsating in his veins, a new strength collecting in his muscles with hunger."[72] With a sudden new militaristic masculinity, Ahmed undertakes the volunteer training and, instead of imagining himself shooting at the British, French, and Israelis, he pictures himself killing a different foe: "He was aiming his rifle at himself, at things in himself. He was aiming at his hesitation, confusion, and aimlessness.... And when he hit the target, he felt happy, a happiness of victory, victory over the enemy that lives within." As if Abdel Kouddous could not resist gesturing once again to Nasser as his therapist, the novel continues, "Ahmed felt a psychological calm after these trainings.... He felt as if he had ended sessions with a psychologist who made him feel calm about his worries."[73] The transcendental encounter with Nasser ex machina not only miraculously produces strength, decisiveness, and self-respect but, as in *The Empty Pillow*, successful psychoanalytic treatment.

Eradicating his former self and enjoying productive therapy with the leader is not enough for Ahmed to break with the past. Continuing where "The Return of Character" ends, Ahmed now registers to join the resistance fighters going to fight in the Suez. Once he arrives, Ahmed sees these men as a new family and a new house, replacing the failures of his own home: "He looked at them with love. He felt as if he was with them his whole life. They weren't simply friends or colleagues but more than that. They were living in his house. All of them lived in a single house, eating together, sleeping together. They were his family."[74] Nasser ex machina has not only produced new men but also new identities and social bonds. Ahmed marches with others in the streets before heading to the battlefield, feeling that it was the fight of the entire Egyptian people. After his training, erasure of ego, successful therapy, and fusion with the resistance fighters, Ahmed finally exudes confidence: "He wasn't hesitating or confused. He found himself now. He found himself in his depths after he washed off the dirt that had piled up on it, the dirt of the past, the dirt of the environment that he grew up in, the dirt of the complexes that tore up his character. He found it. He found himself. He found himself strong and stable. He knew what he wanted."[75] In this transformation, Ahmed has achieved what Nasser called for in his 23 July 1956 speech: "We're turning back to destroy the traces of the past, the traces of tyranny, servitude, exploitation, dominance."[76] Before leaving for battle, Ahmed returns home in his military uniform to say goodbye and even his uncle, the symbol of the displaced, corrupt, previous generation in the novel, suddenly voices support for him. Ahmed has become the conduit that proves Nasser's organic connection and transformative power for the Egyptian people.

Now taking on the fictional translation of Nasser's socialist project, the novel predictably shows how the war presents opportunities to elide social class. Mahmoud, Nabila's love interest, also volunteers for the resistance fighters and serves with Ahmed in the battle. In war, the two are the same class as they sleep in trenches beside each other. They fight alongside each other and demonstrate equal valor and bravery. As Abdel Kouddous wrote in his editorial published on 2 November 1959 to celebrate the third anniversary of the Suez War, just as he was serializing *The Sun Never Sets*, "Nasser was the force that emanated in all the individuals of the people.... This is a burning force, a force that enemies cannot defeat.... And after the aggression, we moved forward with faith, the faith of the president, our faith in the president and our faith in our principles. Believers are always victorious." After Ahmed crosses the Canal and passes out from his wounds, he wakes up four days later in the hospital in Ismailiyya next to Mahmoud. Juxtaposed sharply throughout the novel because of privilege, their class difference has now been eliminated through collective sacrifice. Ahmed loses significant blood on the battlefield, and it is the Egyptian people—of all classes—that provide it to him. Mahmoud informs Ahmed that he received a "popular cocktail" of blood as part of his treatment: "He let his imagination picture the masses as they were filling him with life. He saw in his mind millions of faces. He imagined that he knew each of these faces, knew them personally.... The blood of the people was flowing in his veins, millions of people, everyone. He really felt it, hot and pulsating."[77]

As Abdel Kouddous wrote on 20 July 1959 in an editorial celebrating the seventh anniversary of the revolution, "The Arab citizen has become a different person, different in his way of thinking, in his discussions, nationalist feelings, understanding of his rights; a person proud of his dignity and strength, his head raised. The revolution has settled in his blood."[78] What is the secret of the newfound strength of the Arab citizen, the man who has eradicated colonial submission and subjugation from inside himself and his country? According to Abdel Kouddous in his seventh anniversary editorial, "The secret hides in the personality of the leader of the revolution, Gamal Abdel Nasser; in his faith, in his way of thinking, his political style, the goal that he wants to reach. We could say that the secret of the success of the revolution hides in the strength of the people and their unity, but the strength of the people could have surged and come to nothing, and their unity could have shattered. The waters of the Nile surge forward in tremendous strength, but what sets the path of this strength and protects it and makes it good for exploitation are the two shores, which Gamal Abdel Nasser made for us, exhausting himself so they don't crumble." Indeed, Nasser is not simply the banks of the Nile, helping to direct the raging waters of the Egyptian people: "The secret of the strength of Gamal is that he believes in the principles that he calls for. His principles aren't just sweet words or slogans that he gives to excite the dreams of the people. They're a true faith. Principles are everything. They're before everything. When he calls for liberation, strength, and national dignity, he truly means it. Every word expresses principles that are fixed in him."

The epigraph for *The Sun Never Sets* that accompanied every installment in *Rose El Youssef* reads, "Life is principles. Look for your principles and you'll find your life." After nearly a year of installments depicting his failure, aimlessness, and anxieties, Ahmed has suddenly found his principles thanks to Nasser ex machina. With his new strength, faith, and identity, Ahmed returns home ready to correct the past and unleash Nasser's revolution within the family. First, he integrates Mahmoud into the family home. Class lines and poverty have barred Mahmoud from stepping foot inside the house, but Ahmed's transformation thanks to the miracle of Nasser has now eliminated those divisions. Ahmed brings Mahmoud home with him when he returns after war. He introduces Mahmoud to Nabila as if he is introducing a new person to her, not the man she loves. Ahmed presents Mahmoud to the entire family, explaining that he saved his life in battle and donated blood to him afterwards, declaring to his mother, "That means he's my brother and your son!"[79] Mahmoud is initially anxious and uncomfortable, but the barrier of class that had separated them throughout the novel has been permanently breached. Thanks to Ahmed integrating Mahmoud into the family, Nabila has found purpose: "She felt that her love was taking on a new meaning, a new taste and new responsibility."[80] Mahmoud will now seize his dream job as a radio announcer and, presumably, marry Nabila, marking the dawn of a new era in the family.

As Ahmed looks at the family at the dinner table triumphant at this radical change, another speech by Nasser comes on the radio. This time, after the triumph of the Suez war, the line between Ahmed and Nasser has fully melted, just as Abdel Kouddous suggested in his editorials at the time that Nasser was simply an amalgamation of the people: "Ahmed felt the voice as if he was the one speaking. He thought that if he opened his lips, the same words that Gamal was saying would come out. He's a piece of Gamal. He is Gamal. He is fighting the same battle, believes in the same faith."[81] Finding his manhood and purpose on the battlefield, returning home with the blood of the people pulsating through his veins and breaking class barriers within the home, Ahmed has fully eliminated his past confusion, anxiety, and self-torture, not only to become the man of the new era but to be transformed into Nasser himself.

It is Ahmed—now embodying Nasser—who saves Layla. Instead of trying to imprison her in the house or marry her against her will, Ahmed decides to bring Layla with him to the Gazeera Club to meet Shahira. Earlier, Layla felt abandoned, giving up piano and isolating herself in the darkness like Nadia at the end of *I Do Not Sleep*. By liberating Layla from behind closed doors and introducing her to the Gazeera Club, Ahmed integrates her into a society of peers, bringing her out in public and treating her as an equal. In the sunlight of the new world—light provided by Nasser, of course—Layla finally lets go of her destructive love for her married piano teacher: "She feels that her life has begun anew, a life without Fathi.... She feels as if her heart was beating again, a new heart rising up as if it was drinking from life."[82] Proving that she has finally been healed from illness, Layla is delighted when she hears that a handsome young man at the Gazeera Club is now interested in her, suggesting that she has indeed been rehabilitated for the new era.

Thanks to Ahmed, the two other women in the house, Fifi and the mother, now feel the confidence to exercise their will. Fifi has been wavering about marrying her suitor throughout the novel. Now that Ahmed is back from the war, Fifi realizes that she has been making decisions for her life only in consideration of others. She decides that she wants to marry her longtime suitor out of her own desire, not because of anyone else. As for the mother, she decides not to remarry, not because of her children but because she decides that she does not want to. In this, the two women who have exercised little will throughout the massive novel join the new era as active participants, demonstrating how Ahmed, thanks to the transcendental power of Nasser, has transformed the home by inspiring them to exercise their agency. The women of the novel have uncoincidentally become the revolutionary women of the Nasser era.

The novel ends as Ahmed decides that the stately old family home is no longer suitable for the new era. With heavy-handed symbolism of the nation moving to the modern era, Ahmed proposes selling the house to buy an apartment in a newly constructed building and furnishing it entirely with new furniture—something out of the midcentury modern illustrations published weekly in the magazine *Sabah al-Khayr*: "Everything in the apartment will be entirely new. We'll live a new life."[83] In the closing scene in the novel, Ahmed suggests to his mother that he will marry Shahira, and the mother is delighted. It is in the final lines of the novel that Abdel Kouddous finally makes the meaning of the title explicit, as if it had not been already clear after the sudden arrival of Nasser as a deus ex machina. Ahmed returns to his room and looks out the window: "He can see the night. He can see all the way to the last days of his life. He knows his life as if it is lines drawn on paper. He knows that the sun is rising tomorrow. The sun rises every day. It is like a light that never sets."[84] At the end of the novel, Ahmed has found not only salvation but clarity, thanks to the sun, Nasser, which will burn forever. There is no more confusion, anxiety, or despair as at the end of Abdel Kouddous's previous novels. Ahmed knows what his life will bring and has certainty that, even at night, the sun will rise the next day and illuminate the world—just like Nasser.

Back in 1952, Abdel Kouddous was given the opportunity to write the first cinematic hagiography of the 23 July Revolution, *God Is with Us*. As discussed in chapter 2, instead of representing a national celebration of the 1952 Revolution, the film became an afterthought once it was finally released in April 1955. As Abdel Kouddous was serializing *The Sun Never Sets*, he knew that it was going to be adapted for cinema. He must have thought his fiction would once again serve as the basis for a national hagiography, this time of the Suez War. Directed by Salah Abou Seif and featuring an all-star cast of Faten Hamama, Shoukry Sirhan, and Emad Hamdy, *The Sun Never Sets* premiered on 25 December 1961. Even though the film focuses less on Nasser himself—it is not his voice that Ahmed hears in the nationalization speech on the radio—and emphasizes Ahmed's military experience instead, the basic trajectory of the novel's plot is kept fully intact in the film. Ironically, the film is the only cinematic adaptation of Abdel Kouddous's novels from the Nasser era without an altered ending, showing perhaps that he had finally written a climax that was so pleasing to the censor that it would work even for cinema. Considering his frustration at the extent to which his novels, especially their endings, had been changed in the film adaptations, Abdel Kouddous must have found this a bittersweet victory.

Nonetheless, such heavy-handed depiction of salvation by Nasser ex machina did not age well, even after a few years. A ten-part television series of *The Sun Never Sets* was produced in late 1964 and aired in Ramadan 1965. It was directed by television pioneer Nour El-Demerdash and starred Karam Motawea and Madiha Salem.[85] The television series radically changes the plot of the novel by removing Nasser as a deus ex machina and the Suez War entirely, setting the story instead in contemporaneous time. After Mamdouh dies in his moped accident at the end of the penultimate episode, Fifi, the oldest sister, accuses each member of the household of being responsible for his death. She demands that each of them stop fleeing from their responsibilities, thereby producing the transformation that Nasser achieves in the novel and film. The series ends as the newly unified and confident family leaves the house for the Gazeera Club, a marker of them entering the gates of modernity. On their way out the door, Ahmed and his mother stop to look at a photograph of Mamdouh over the mantle. The two embrace, looking longingly at the photograph, grateful for the transformation that Mamdouh has inspired in the family. The title of the series then appears over the photograph, shockingly emphasizing that it is Mamdouh—not Nasser—who now serves as the symbolic sun that never sets.

No doubt, television was a much more conservative medium than cinema in Nasser's Egypt. It is therefore striking that the climax of the television series of *The Sun Never Sets* was corrected to remove the intervention of Nasser as a deus ex machina. On the one hand, the corrected ending—Mamdouh's death serving as the motivation for change within the family—shows that the story could not end with the typical pessimistic climax of Abdel Kouddous's fiction. On the other, it demonstrates that the intervention of Nasser as providing such sudden and complete salvation was too heavy-handed and blatantly propagandistic for 1965, even for television officials, as if acknowledging a new era of Egyptian cinema in which criticism of Nasser could be broached.[86]

The appearance of Nasser ex machina in the novel could, of course, be read as propaganda, the fictional translation of what Abdel Kouddous had been writing in his editorials about Nasser since *I Do Not Sleep*. It had been five years since Nasser originally asked him to serve as his "echo" or "translator" in his fiction to the public. Now, in the aftermath of the crisis of *Girls in Summer*, with his incredible popularity as a fiction writer and the massive audience of *Rose El Youssef*, Abdel Kouddous finally seemed to be performing the task. Nonetheless, the sudden, dissonant, sharp, and all-too-convenient arrival of Nasser as a deus ex machina, after eleven months of weekly installments focusing on Ahmed's failures and anxieties, is so absurd and over the top that it does more than require the typical suspension of belief, as with any deus ex machina. It suggests that Abdel Kouddous was trying to draw attention to the suffocating levels of censorship at the time and the demands on him for public performance of praising Nasser. It is therefore possible to read the depiction of Nasser ex machina and his impact on Ahmed and his family not as salvation but as a striking act of resistance and dissent, a form of mockery and parody, a defiant undermining of Nasser's messianic cult of personality right at the height of his power. Indeed, there is strong evidence from the 1 February 1960 issue of *Rose El Youssef*, the same issue in which Nasser ex machina first appears, to support this reading.

### NATIONALIZING THE PRESS

As if revealing to the public that censorship had imposed itself on all aspects of his writing at the time, in such a way as to provide a framework for readers to understand the absurdity of the arrival Nasser as a deus ex machina, the 1 February 1960 issue of *Rose El Youssef* led off with a striking editorial by Abdel Kouddous in which he called for the nationalization of the press.[87] In this piece, Abdel Kouddous explained that the basic mission of the National Union, the sole political party in the United Arab Republic, is "to spread consciousness and the tools for this are speeches, personal communication, cinema, mass media, books, schools, and the press." Abdel Kouddous argued that the press had played the role of the onlooker and occasional commentator while the National Union had monitored it with either pleasure or anger: "The National Union is concerned not only with what is published about the decisions of its committees but everything that is published in the press—political articles, foreign news, sports news, and literary production." By adding literature to the concerns of the National Union, Abdel Kouddous tied this editorial directly to the hyperbolic depiction of the arrival of Nasser as a deus ex machina in the same issue, highlighting the impact of the censor on fiction. As Abdel Kouddous would later claim many times, perhaps giving himself an outsized role, he was the first to call for the nationalization of the press in this article because the censorship had become so stifling that the press already had little freedom. Including Nasser ex machina in this particular issue was perhaps his way of showing through mockery and parody that censorship and the demands of praising Nasser had become infused throughout the entire magazine. Nationalizing the press would simply make it transparent that the state owned the media. As he later stated bluntly about this period, "I resorted to that because censorship wore me out."[88]

It was particularly shocking that Abdel Kouddous called for the nationalization of the press because he was the owner of both *Rose El Youssef* and *Sabah al-Khayr*, two of the most important and bestselling magazines in Egypt. He was therefore demanding that the state seize his own assets and family legacy. As he admitted years after the nationalization, "I didn't think at that time about the results. And I was among those who paid the biggest price."[89] He later explained that he felt that *Rose El Youssef* needed to change significantly since politics was the main focus of the magazine and writing about politics had become nearly impossible due to the censor.[90] The magazine therefore needed an infusion of funds to transition its coverage to something new. He did not, however, have the personal resources to make these changes on his own. He admitted that Nasser had offered him funds secretly, but he refused, insisting that any state support must be made public. Once his mother died, Abdel Kouddous started thinking seriously about nationalization. If she had been alive, he later explained, "this solution could not have been executed. She would never have let the magazine become the possession of the government."[91] Calling for the state to seize his magazines therefore also represented yet another rejection of his mother and impulsive embrace of Nasser without thinking through the consequences. According to Abdel Kouddous, Nasser read his 1 February 1960 editorial and decided to move forward with the plan.

The last installment of the novel *The Sun Never Sets* was published in *Rose El Youssef* on 4 April 1960. When he finished writing the novel, Abdel Kouddous wrote a short piece in the magazine about how he felt tremendous loss, imagining himself parting from his characters with tears in his eyes.[92] Only a month later, the press was nationalized, ending the charade that Egyptian newspapers and magazines were independent from state control. *Rose El Youssef* was even specifically mentioned in the law issued on 24 May 1960. In his speech to newspaper and magazine editors four days later, Nasser explained that "the press has to be a message more than it is a product or a business." As if pointing directly to a novel by Abdel Kouddous, Nasser then complained that the press had reveled for too long in scandals such as women cheating on their husbands: "If we're going to limit the thinking of the press to this deviance that doesn't represent us, we won't ever find the means to make the press express our country.... Is it the role of the press to write about evenings out at the Hilton?" For Nasser, the mission of the press was to participate actively in building and representing "respectable" society, not smearing it with sexual sensationalism. Lecturing the editors, who were suddenly employees of the state, Nasser gave them a specific order: "I'm asking you to cooperate with us in tracing the image of the society that we want to make. It's required for you too to participate in working to build this society that will be the society of your children. Don't leave it just to me, or five or six people with me to do it."

Once nationalization of the press was announced, Abdel Kouddous projected enthusiasm at the confiscation of his magazines. He wrote that he was overjoyed, as if continuing to prove in public that he was a reliable partner for Nasser: "I yelled out on the phone in delight: Congratulations! Congratulations! My happiness was shaking my body, the same happiness that I felt when the phone rang in my house at dawn on 23 July 1952 and I was told that the army had announced the revolution."[93] Nonetheless, as I discuss in the following chapter, it would not take long for Abdel Kouddous to regret what he had done, just as it did not take long for him to regret laying the groundwork to help bring Nasser and the Free Officers to power. Moreover, even though the law specifically states that the owners of the press would be compensated for the value of the property, neither Abdel Kouddous nor his family ever received any money for the magazines, intellectual property, building, or equipment that the state confiscated. Indeed, Abdel Kouddous's bombastic editorials and newfound role as Nasser's "echo" to the public in his magnum opus were not enough. Nasser had now seized his family's heritage and assets, finally putting an end to the resistance of the grand dame of Egyptian journalism, Fatima Youssef.

In the aftermath of the nationalization, Abdel Kouddous became an employee of the state. He had proven himself to be such a reliable partner during these months that Nasser named him chairman of the board of *Rose El Youssef*, making Abdel Kouddous the only pre-nationalization editor appointed at the same publishing house. While this was a point of pride for Abdel Kouddous, the whole situation would have horrified his mother, whose statue sat next to his desk during this period, as if keeping a critical eye on what he was writing and how he was managing the magazine.[94] After paying such a high price to get back into Nasser's good graces, Abdel Kouddous increased his bombastic praise of Nasser in his political editorials. The most sycophantic of these articles typically came on the anniversary of the revolution. On 25 July 1960, for example, Abdel Kouddous once again pointed to the organic link between Ahmed in *The Sun Never Sets* and the transcendental leader of the revolution: "Gamal Abdel Nasser didn't produce himself, but history did. Gamal Abdel Nasser isn't forty years old, but four thousand, the age of the Arab people since they began to revolt. The experiences of Gamal Abdel Nasser aren't his alone, but that of a people, dozens of leaders, thousands of martyrs, and millions of the oppressed. This is the secret of the success of our revolution, of our leader.... And the secret of the success of Gamal Abdel Nasser is that he is the people.... The people aren't outside of Gamal Abdel Nasser, but they're inside him, in his being, in his blood."[95] For four thousand years, "we were looking for a leader until we found him." Nasser is therefore the embodiment of the centuries old spirit of the Egyptian people, a spirit of resistance and triumph.

On 24 July 1961, Abdel Kouddous wrote about the widespread nationalization of companies in Egypt with delight and wonder: "How were we able to apply socialism so simply? By faith, faith in ourselves and in the people. This faith is what Gamal Abdel Nasser gave us and spread from his heart to ours, from his will to ours."[96] The naysayers are the ones who lacked faith in the people, who did not recognize the victory of the people inspired by Nasser, as if he were a real-life deus ex machina who descended to restore the nation's dignity: "The people are victorious because behind them is a leader who knows how to be victorious.... The head of the peasant, the worker, and the bureaucrat will rise up and we'll see a new peasant, worker, and bureaucrat, those that the revolution, socialism, and justice produced, who Gamal Abdel Nasser produced." By summer 1961, with the press nationalized, Abdel Kouddous no longer depicted the people as producing their leader, as he had in *There's a Man in Our House*. Shockingly, it was now Nasser who had forged the people and the revolution.

A year later, on 23 July 1962, Abdel Kouddous marveled at how quickly the previous ten years had gone, as if the revolution had taken place only yesterday: "The happiest years of life are the ones that you don't feel."[97] He gushed at how the achievements of one hundred years have been made in only ten. How did that happen, he asked? "The personality that produced the revolution is the personality of the hero . . . a personality that has entered every home, every heart, every mind. . . . We've all come to live in Gamal Abdel Nasser. Gamal Abdel Nasser has become each one of us. . . . It's love. A great love." According to the article, it was an emotional day for Abdel Kouddous: "It's the day of my birth, your birth, the birth of a people. I feel my head reaching into the clouds. I feel my chest expand with strength and my eyes seeing the farthest green future. I feel the entire world looking at me in surprise, expectation and envy as my smile fills my lips, a smile of confidence, insistence, and loftiness, which I get from Gamal's smile." Incredibly, Abdel Kouddous now placed himself in the position of Ahmed in *The Sun Never Sets*, someone transformed physically by Nasser, a man who has gained transcendental confidence and strength thanks to his personal savior. With these pieces, Abdel Kouddous had become such a reliable partner during this period that Gamal Abdel Nasser awarded him the Order of First Merit on 16 December 1962 in recognition of his service as chairman of *Rose El Youssef*.

And with that, it appeared that Abdel Kouddous had become a fully coopted intellectual, that his past dissent had been entirely eliminated, that the rebellious Abdel Kouddous had become yet another victory for Nasser during the era of the "greatest splendor of victories." Indeed, Abdel Kouddous's fiction in the three years after *The Sun Never Sets* does not hint at any resistance. During this period, he wrote dozens of short stories, none of which gestured to the resistance and rage of his earlier work. And in his next novel, *Holes in Black Cloth*, serialized in *Sabah al-Khayr* from 18 January to 26 March 1962, nearly two full years after he completed *The Sun Never Sets*, Abdel Kouddous could not bear to face the Egypt that he helped create. This novel, which is highly unusual in his oeuvre, is a first-person narrative of an Egyptian psychologist who travels to Bamako, where he meets a Lebanese man who suffers from a split personality complex. After the doctor treats him with enactment therapy, the Lebanese man is cured of his illness, suggesting optimistically that psychological complexes are fully manageable and can be diagnosed, unraveled, and, eventually, cured, with the doctor-psychologist providing salvation. It was a message echoed in another work by Abdel Kouddous during this period, *The Well of Deprivation*, which presented first-person accounts of the psychologist treating—and curing—various illnesses through talk therapy and intervention.[98] With Abdel Kouddous's move away from writing his anxieties, regret, and guilt about the revolution during this period, these works suggested that Nasser the therapist had finally been successful at treating his long-standing and once-stubborn patient. But as with other figures in his inner circle, Nasser could not resist the urge to humiliate Abdel Kouddous once again, an insult that would subsequently push his former co-revolutionary to his most shocking and defiant act of revolt yet.

CHAPTER SIX

## THE TIME OF DEFEATS

> Because I'm disgusted with myself, all else sickens me.
> —*Naguib Mahfouz,*
> The Beggar *(1965)*

Before setting off to Europe for his summer vacation in 1963, Ihsan Abdel Kouddous, now an employee of the state, performed yet another job as "translator" of Nasser to the public. On 22 July 1963, he published his obligatory editorial in *Rose El Youssef* celebrating the anniversary of the revolution. He began, "On 23 July 1952, a systematic process of discovery was begun—the discovery of the Egyptian people. The people were present, but their spiritual treasures were buried under the dust of years of colonialism, exploitation, and oppression." As he had done many times in his editorials since the mid-1950s, Abdel Kouddous depicted Nasser as a prophetic leader with messianic qualities, this time as an archaeologist who had unearthed the Egyptian people, whose true self had been buried for centuries. The most important factor in this discovery was, unsurprisingly, Nasser's character: "It is a purely popular character whose roots reach the deepest depths of the people, whose elements extend from every peasant, laborer, and bureaucrat.... This character has become all the people and all the people have become Gamal Abdel Nasser." Concluding his piece, Abdel Kouddous declared,

"We can't stop wondering: How did we achieve all this in eleven years? It's a miracle. Our miracle." And with that, Abdel Kouddous bought himself some time away from the burdens of writing as perhaps the most prominent employee of the state. According to a box published on the same page as this editorial, he traveled to London "to see the latest printing equipment and to buy some of it for *Rose El Youssef*."[1]

Abdel Kouddous did not go directly to Europe. On his way, he stopped in Beirut to pick up his eighteen-year-old Lebanese girlfriend, Hanan al-Shaykh, who would go on to become one of the most important Arabic novelists of the twentieth century thanks to works such as *The Story of Zahra* and *Women of Sand and Myrrh*. As a precocious high school student, al-Shaykh began publishing pieces in the Lebanese press. When she arrived in Cairo in early January 1963 for boarding school, armed with a letter of introduction from Georges Khoury, the owner of the Dar al-Sayyad publishing house and editor in chief of the well-known Lebanese magazine *al-Shabaka* (The Network), she went to *Rose El Youssef* to meet the famed Ihsan Abdel Kouddous in the hopes of seeing her work published in his magazine. Al-Shaykh's first and only article to appear in *Rose El Youssef*, "Don't Betray Me," published on 21 January 1963, overflowed with youthful enthusiasm. Al-Shaykh employed floral language to describe how a girl gets dressed and puts on perfume to go to the Omar Khayyam Club on Hamra Street in Beirut, hoping to see her lover, whom she knows is betraying her. "But no matter," she wrote. "Men are like that, at least most of them. They trample on women's emotions and ignore their hearts as they cling to their tight waists."[2] Soon after this piece was published, al-Shaykh started dating Abdel Kouddous. When al-Shaykh brought a poem to him to consider for publication soon after, he told her that he did not mix work with love. If she wanted to continue dating him, he would not publish anything else by her. Surprised at his response, al-Shaykh chose Abdel Kouddous.[3]

Even though Abdel Kouddous was married and a celebrity, he did not hide his affair with al-Shaykh. He took her regularly to public places in Cairo such as the Semiramis and the Hilton, refusing the hypocrisy of married men who cover up their relationships with younger women behind the closed doors of bachelor apartments. According to al-Shaykh, "Ihsan was a free spirit. He did not comply with any rules. He was like a teenager, falling in love again and again. He was so courageous in defying society. He was a great rebel."[4] In July 1963, after they had been dating in Cairo for six months, Ihsan Abdel Kouddous met al-Shaykh in Beirut and took her to Europe. They visited London, Paris, and Rome. One night, in the ancient part of Rome, they had dinner in an underground restaurant which had a stone ceiling and walls that looked like catacombs. Abdel Kouddous suddenly gave her a strange look and then explained that he was suffering from his "azma," or crisis. At first, al-Shaykh did not understand what he meant. She initially thought that he was suffering from an asthma attack. He was having trouble breathing and could not speak. She quickly rushed him outside to get him some fresh air. Abdel Kouddous lay down on the ground in a square near the restaurant in an attempt to recover. Panicked and confused, al-Shaykh ran around frantically, using her broken English—she did not speak the language fluently at the time—to ask passersby for help. After several minutes, Abdel Kouddous revived himself and told her that he was fine. It happened from time to time, he explained, and it was nothing to worry about. He told her that a doctor had diagnosed him with what he called a "confused vein," something that occasionally caused him difficulty breathing.[5] It was a diagnosis that made no sense to her then—or when she told me about the incident in May 2019. Did the experience

**Figure 21.** Hanan al-Shaykh, taken in Beirut by Ihsan Abdel Kouddous, 1963. Courtesy of Hanan al-Shaykh.

of being in a tight underground space cause the eruption of anxiety, a repressed trauma of regret, anger, and guilt, bringing on a panic attack that even the pleasure of being in Rome with his girlfriend could not alleviate?[6]

In August 1963, Abdel Kouddous returned to Cairo while al-Shaykh went back to Beirut. As soon as she arrived, her older brother angrily confronted her with rumors from the Lebanese press that she had been traveling in Europe with the famous writer. Despite her denials of any romantic involvement with Abdel Kouddous, her family refused to let her return to Cairo. Al-Shaykh wrote a letter to Abdel Kouddous, frantically explaining why she had not come back yet and how much she missed him. She received no reply. Abdel Kouddous's secretary then called and told al-Shaykh to send any letters to her instead. Al-Shaykh later learned that a man had gone to *Rose El Youssef* asking to see Abdel Kouddous about a private matter. Once alone together, the man showed Abdel Kouddous the letter that al-Shaykh had sent, explaining that he was a member of the secret police and that her letter had touched him so much that he had decided to deliver it personally. The man did not want Abdel Kouddous to think that his girlfriend had broken up with him in silence when she was really being kept home against her will, pining for him. It was at this point that Abdel Kouddous discovered not only that he was being monitored by the secret police but that they were confiscating letters from his lover. If not for the empathy and personal intervention of this officer, he would have assumed that al-Shaykh had broken up with him without even the courtesy of informing him. Abdel Kouddous was furious. Why were the secret police monitoring his private life?

Al-Shaykh managed to convince her family to let her return to Cairo in September 1963. Her relationship with Abdel Kouddous continued, but so too did the interventions to break them up. According to al-Shaykh, sightings of them together in Cairo and rumors of a European vacation between the famous Abdel Kouddous and his teenage Lebanese girlfriend made their way back to Nasser. She said that Nasser disapproved of the way Abdel Kouddous had been flaunting standards of public conduct with her, acting as if social conventions did not apply to him. Sometime in early fall 1963, with Abdel Kouddous continuing to flout his relationship with al-Shaykh in Cairo, Anwar Sadat called

Abdel Kouddous and asked him to go for a walk along the Nile. As the two strolled, Sadat did not directly address the affair with the young Lebanese woman. Nonetheless, after some light conversation, it soon became clear to Abdel Kouddous why Sadat had wanted to meet with him. Sadat told him that he "should stop eating tabbouleh."[7] The outraged Abdel Kouddous, of course, understood what Sadat meant by the famous Lebanese dish.

Nasser had intervened in Abdel Kouddous's work many times. At the very least, we know that Nasser rejected his article calling for the resignation of Ali Maher in August 1952, removed words from his first article after his summer 1954 jailing, rejected his fall 1954 article protesting being named as one of the editors accepting money from the palace, canceled his weekly radio show "Whisper" in spring 1955, and demanded changes to the plot of *Girls in Summer* in fall 1958. There were, no doubt, other interventions, for some of which no record survives. The possible displeasure of Nasser at his work was an ever-present reality for Abdel Kouddous, a constant threat hanging over his professional life and personal safety. By the early 1960s, Nasser has confiscated Abdel Kouddous's magazines and Abdel Kouddous had become a government employee with little space of freedom or independence left in his professional life. This could explain why he refused to hide his relationship with the much younger al-Shaykh. His personal life was the final space of freedom left to him. And perhaps that is why Nasser objected. Nasser already controlled Abdel Kouddous in his political editorials and fiction. He was now looking to discipline his personal life as well.

Ahmed Abul-Fath, the former editor in chief of the daily *al-Misri* who fled Egypt for Paris during the March 1954 Crisis, published his tell-all insider book about Nasser in 1962, less than a year before Sadat took Abdel Kouddous for their stroll along the Nile. In his book, Abul-Fath detailed at great length how Nasser savored humiliating the people closest to him as a way to establish his dominance over them and make them dependent on him. In particular, Abul-Fath writes how Nasser would employ his "domestic affairs methods" to monitor the other Free Officers for trespasses in their personal lives. According to Abul-Fath, "He exploited them to submit them to his mercy."[8] Nasser also used this technique as a form of blackmail with foreign ambassadors. Abul-Fath described how Nasser secretly collected information on a closeted gay ambassador in Cairo, blackmailing him in order to control his reports to his home government. Nasser confronted another ambassador with clandestine photographs of him with a young Egyptian woman, lecturing him about traditional Egyptian family values and threatening to leak them to his family if he did not follow orders.[9] In each case, according to Abul-Fath, Nasser was able to exploit these trespasses thanks to "his irreproachable personal life."[10]

We do not know exactly how Abdel Kouddous responded to Sadat during their stroll along the Nile, but the conversation did not go well. According to al-Shaykh, Abdel Kouddous was outraged. Unlike the members of the Free Officers or the ambassadors in Cairo, he would not accept any intervention into his private life. He refused to stop seeing al-Shaykh or taking her out in public. Perhaps falling in love with the young Lebanese woman made him throw caution to the wind. Perhaps at forty-four years old and now more than eleven years removed from the revolution, he was experiencing a midlife crisis. Perhaps the confiscation of al-Shaykh's love letter and Sadat's comment stirred up previous moments of humiliation by Nasser—some of which we might not know about—and Abdel Kouddous had simply had enough. He had already seemingly surrendered everything to Nasser—his editorials, his fiction, his magazines, his financial assets, his cherished revolution, his dignity—and his love life was, perhaps, that one final demand that went too far. Perhaps after four years of increasingly contrived public declarations of devotion with no dissent in his fiction, Abdel Kouddous could no longer repress his desire to lash out at Nasser and once again use writing as a form of therapy to soothe his despair at what his cherished revolution had become. Perhaps he simply could no longer bear the self-loathing of having to prostitute himself publicly to Nasser in the pages of *Rose El Youssef* and *Sabah al-Khayr*.

Regardless, Abdel Kouddous suddenly revolted. In October 1963, he immediately ceased any mention of Nasser in his editorials, let alone writing any of his typical pieces full of messianic images of the president. And his new novel, *A Nose and Three Eyes*, which he began serializing that month, was a reckless return to the antagonism of *Girls in Summer*, a defiant flouting of orders, an angry revolt against the way that Abdel Kouddous had increasingly prostituted himself to Nasser in the press since the mid-1950s. In *A Nose and Three Eyes*, Abdel Kouddous wove together elements of his earlier novels in which he condemned Nasser and the trajectory of the revolution, unearthing once again his regret and despair at its aftermath but framing them with a deep sense of grief, melancholia, and anxiety for selling himself to the regime. The novel is a shocking act of dissent, a defiant rejection of Nasser. It is Abdel Kouddous's most daring, explicit, and controversial work. While scholars of Egyptian cinema have noted hints of dissent against Nasser in the lead-up to the June 1967 defeat, *A Nose and Three Eyes*, serialized 1963-64, is by far the most critical work of fiction during this period.[11]

Abdel Kouddous would eventually pay a heavy price for his latest public revolt and act of disavowal. By spring 1964, a crisis erupted over the novel behind the scenes, leading to charges brought against him in parliament for harming public morality, as well as demands that installments cease immediately and that the novel be banned and prevented from ever being adapted into a radio play, film, or television series.[12] Nasser, easily seeing through the novel's thinly veiled rebellion against him, would abandon Abdel Kouddous, finally withdrawing his long-standing support of his former co-revolutionary, sparking a scandal that touched legendary writers such as Tawfiq al-Hakim, Taha Hussein, and Naguib Mahfouz. Unlike the crisis surrounding *Girls in Summer*, when Abdel Kouddous rushed to accommodate Nasser and the censor, he would not back down this time. Abdel Kouddous wove the escalating crisis into the plot of the novel in protest as he was writing and publishing the final installments, recklessly defying his accusers and Nasser himself.

In spring 1954, the last time Abdel Kouddous revolted against Nasser so openly, Abdel Kouddous was imprisoned for his defiance. This time, some ten years later, jail was no longer punishment enough. By June 1964, Abdel Kouddous was once again painfully humiliated, this time by becoming the first writer brought before the Egyptian parliament on the charge of harming public morality in his fiction. He was subsequently interrogated by the public prosecutor, the morals prosecutor, and the police. He was disgraced by being unceremoniously fired from both *Rose El Youssef* and *Sabah al-Khayr*, his family's former magazines that were now owned by the state, and then exiled from public life. The scandal sparked a deep psychological and emotional crisis for Abdel Kouddous, ending his relationship with Hanan al-Shaykh and plunging him into a deep depression, leading to his collapse and breakdown. It was in his catastrophic defeat that Abdel Kouddous's personal life came to mirror his fiction, the internal degradation and dissolution reflecting the crumbling foundations of Nasserism that would soon collapse with the shattering defeat in the 1967 Arab-Israeli War.

## NASSER THE SCOUNDREL

Sometime in spring 1963, Hanan al-Shaykh was walking in Cairo and saw Ihsan Abdel Kouddous drive by, laughing in delight with a young woman sitting next to him in the front seat. When the devastated al-Shaykh confronted Abdel Kouddous, he insisted that he was not dating the young woman. He explained that he was with her because she had an incredible story to relate. According to Abdel Kouddous, this young woman came to see him at the office, as many women did, to ask for advice about love. This particular woman told him that she had been forced to marry a much older man and that she was very sick with a heart problem. Abdel Kouddous explained to al-Shaykh that he felt terrible for this young woman and that he wanted to help her. He mentioned that they had noticed al-Shaykh as they drove by and saw the look of devastation on her face. The young woman next to Abdel Kouddous, instead of commenting about how upset al-Shaykh looked, casually mentioned to Abdel Kouddous that the color of al-Shaykh's hair was so nice that it must have been tinted. When al-Shaykh heard this offhand remark, she was appalled and told Abdel Kouddous that it was cold and callous. He replied that women all saw him completely differently. He explained that he sometimes felt as if he was a nose, which the women close to him perceived through their own eyes. He then told her that he should write his next novel about that.

On 14 October 1963, Abdel Kouddous began serializing *A Nose and Three Eyes* in *Rose El Youssef*. As he had suggested to al-Shaykh, the novel centers on a "nose," or a man named Dr. Hashim 'Abd al-Latif, and three "eyes," his female lovers, who each narrate their relationship with him in starkly divergent ways. The novel is divided into three sections, each narrated by an "eye." The novel is Abdel Kouddous's most modernist work, with Dr. Hashim never given the opportunity to speak for himself. Instead, he is constructed as a collage through the perceptions of the

**Figure 22.** Ihsan Abdel Kouddous with admirers, early 1960s. Courtesy of the Abdel Kouddous family.

three lovers. While the text is broken up into the three eyes, the overall narrative is mostly linear, as Dr. Hashim dates each woman sequentially, spanning from the pivotal year 1950, when Abdel Kouddous met Nasser, through the contemporaneous period. There are brief flashes of intersection between the lovers, but the narratives remain mostly distinct from each other. To emphasize the point that each woman sees Dr. Hashim in entirely different ways, the end of each section of the novel summarizes the basic perception each woman has of the doctor: for the first narrator, Hashim is a "scoundrel"; for the second, he is "incredible"; and for the third, he is "weak."

As he had done in earlier works, Abdel Kouddous used *A Nose and Three Eyes* to narrate his own romance with Nasser and the Egyptian revolution, intersecting the personal with the political, stressing how Nasser became a different person during subsequent phases. The First Eye covers the period leading up to the coup and its aftermath, when, for Abdel Kouddous, the masculine, alluring Nasser betrayed him and became a "scoundrel"; the Second Eye covers the "Period of Great Victories," when the now messianic Nasser was "incredible"; and the Third Eye covers the formation and breakup of the United Arab Republic, showing how an insecure Nasser chased after union with a fickle and rebellious Syria, becoming "weak." In *A Nose and Three Eyes*, Abdel Kouddous rejects the accommodation that he had performed in his fiction since fall 1958, returning to the dissent of works such as *The Barred Road*, *I Do Not Sleep*, and, especially, *Girls in Summer*. Once again, Abdel Kouddous used fiction not only to explore his regret, guilt, and anxiety about his role in the revolution but also to protest directly to his devoted reader Nasser, refusing to accept this latest humiliation of being told to "stop eating tabbouleh."

In June 1953, as Abdel Kouddous and the Rotten Weapons scandal were being erased from the official history of the revolution, he began serializing *I'm Free*. With this novel, Abdel Kouddous wrote himself back into the narrative of the buildup and execution of the coup. *I'm Free* tells the story of Amina, who serves as the double of both Egypt and Abdel Kouddous himself for the first half of the novel. Like Abdel Kouddous in the 1930s and 1940s, Amina sets off on a long series of acts of defiance and revolt to gain her freedom from the oppression of the old era. She realizes that she has been wasting her efforts at revolt when she reconnects with Abbas, her childhood love interest who is now the editor in chief of an oppositional magazine. Thanks to Amina's support, Abbas—a dissident journalist, not a military officer—becomes the leader who sparks revolution. Through this move, Abdel Kouddous shockingly returned the favor of erasure, eliding the Free Officers and framing the magazine office—not the barracks—as the site for the outbreak of the revolution.

Pointing to Abdel Kouddous's own rhetoric in his editorials in 1952-53, Abbas convinces Amina that there is no freedom without principles, conviction, and love. Now that she has found Abbas and believes in him, Amina domesticates herself for Abbas, learning how to cook and clean the house for him, sacrificing her freedom to serve the revolutionary leader. In the controversial and ambivalent ending of the novel, Amina surrenders everything for Abbas—she willingly turns herself into a "slave" to him, as the text suggests—but she receives no commitment or guarantee from him in return. They do not live together, and they do not get married, underscoring the lack of legal guarantees for the relationship. As discussed in chapter 2, this lack of commitment from Abbas suggested a bitter critique of Nasser and the Free Officers—Abdel Kouddous himself had sacrificed everything to spark the revolution and embed the Officers, "enslaving" himself to them on the assumption that he would gain his freedom, but—a year after the coup—they had not yet provided any commitment to democracy to him or the nation. Did the controversial and ambiguous ending therefore suggest that Abdel Kouddous, like Amina, fooled himself into thinking that Egypt had become free? Was her faith in Abbas naïve self-delusion that would lead her and the nation to disaster?

It took Abdel Kouddous over ten years, but he finally returned to Amina to clarify this ambivalent ending, rewriting *I'm Free* as the First Eye. Making the connection with *I'm Free* explicit, the narrator of the First Eye is also named Amina. Uncoincidentally, the narration begins not from the perspective of the heady days of revolutionary fervor but from the disillusionment and despair in the aftermath of a disastrous love affair. Amina opens the novel by declaring, "There's no such thing as love. I scoff at the foolish girls who go crazy at the sighs of 'Abd al-Wahhab and the wails of 'Abd al-Halim Hafiz. They pour their youth out into the lines of romance novels and movies and then hitch their fantasies to the first guy they meet, tearing up their hearts with their fingernails proclaiming 'We've fallen in love!' No, girls. No, deluded girls. There's no such thing as love. Believe me. I know. I'm an expert. I have long, bitter experience."[13] With this melancholic beginning, Abdel Kouddous seemed to be insisting that his past faith in love, expressed for years in his editorials, fiction, and, especially, radio program "Whisper," was simply a delusion: "What we call love is only, how to put it, habit. Yes, just habit. You get used to a man and habit takes root deep inside you until you think it's love. Or what they call love.... What was between me and Hasim couldn't be more than that. Simply habit. I didn't love him. It couldn't have been love.... I only got used to him."[14] In these initial pages, narrated from the perspective of the time of publication and looking back on the detritus of delusional love, Abdel Kouddous reveals that his relationship with Nasser—as narrated through Amina's ruinous affair Hashim—was a gradual process of habituation that led to torment and suffering.

From this opening of cold, detached disillusionment, the new Amina launches into narrating the history of her catastrophic affair with Hashim. Like the heroine of *I'm Free*—and Abdel Kouddous himself—the teenage Amina in *A Nose and Three Eyes* is a rebellious product of divorced parents. Writing colonial abuse in Egypt as romantic melodrama, the sixteen-year-old Amina is engaged to the gluttonous and slothful thirty-six-year-old 'Abd al-Salam, the symbol of the old, corrupt pre-revolutionary era. As in *I'm Free*, Amina rebels against social restrictions and her sense of emptiness, this time defying her family's attempt to subdue and chain her to the past through the engagement. She tries to attract men from the neighborhood and forces 'Abd al-Salam to take her to popular restaurants, which she scans for handsome men. One night at the Semiramis, she spots Hashim, a renowned and wealthy doctor. Of course, Abdel Kouddous had written Nasser into his novels as a "doctor" many times before, first in *Where's My Life?* before his 1954 arrest and subsequently in *The Empty Pillow, The Barred Road, I Do Not Sleep, There's a Man in Our House*, and his more recent psychoanalytic dramas. Writing Nasser as a doctor in his novels after summer 1954 was Abdel Kouddous's way of gesturing to Nasser, his devoted reader, toying with the way he claimed to be giving Abdel Kouddous "treatment." While Nasser would have immediately understood the reference, the details of their fateful encounters in summer 1954 were not publicly known until 1974. Nonetheless, it was not a stretch to read Nasser as Hashim throughout the novel. In the First Eye, which retells Abdel Kouddous's delusional romance with Nasser before and immediately after the coup,

Hashim is described as tall and strong with broad shoulders, brown skin, thick lips, a long straight nose, and enticing movie-star looks, just like the virile Nasser of the early to mid-1950s. In the Second Eye, set during the "Period of Great Victories," Hashim takes on messianic deus ex machina characteristics, just as he had in propaganda in the mid- to late 1950s. In the Third Eye, Hashim becomes weak, insecure, and prematurely grey as he chases after a young Lebanese woman, paralleling Nasser's physical and psychological decline in the early 1960s during the dissolution of the United Arab Republic.[15]

As soon as Amina sees Dr. Hashim for the first time, she is, of course, immediately enthralled: "He was the kind of person you found yourself looking at for a long time because there's something that sets them apart from everyone else."[16] Yet her attraction for Dr. Hashim is not simply because he was magnetic and handsome. Harkening back to Abdel Kouddous's columns calling out for a "man" to lead him—and the nation—out of the wilderness, stressing the sexual as a metaphor for consummating his desire to revolt with a "man," Amina immediately senses a physical desire for him: "Looking at him brought strange feelings to my body, to my body and not my mind. With an involuntary movement, I found myself pulling my dress over my knees and lifting my palm and covering my arm with it, as if I was protecting myself from him."[17] Amina compares Hashim's masculinity, confidence, and virility to the obese and loathsome 'Abd al-Salam—paralleling the striking dichotomy between the manly Nasser and the gluttonous Fouad Serageddin or King Farouk before the coup—and she immediately feels disgust and hatred for her fiancé, the double for the old era in the novel. It is this first encounter—and striking dichotomy—that quickly turns Hashim into an obsession, producing reckless fantasies of expelling her slothful fiancé for the manly doctor with movie-star looks.

Soon, fantasy is no longer enough. Like Abdel Kouddous in the 1940s, Amina decides that she must take matters into her own hands in order to meet the man who will bring her salvation. Just as Amina in *I'm Free* calls to make an appointment with Abbas at his magazine, Amina in *A Nose and Three Eyes* calls Dr. Hashim's office to make an appointment for an examination. Like Abdel Kouddous in his first meetings with Nasser, Amina is struck by Hashim's silence and reserve as they meet for the first time. Nonetheless, tremors of sexual desire run through her as his fingers touch her body during the examination. The sexual tension of their initial encounter boils over as Dr. Hashim soon invites Amina to his bachelor apartment. Perhaps gesturing to tensions with his mother during the 1940s and early 1950s as Abdel Kouddous searched for the man who would spark revolution, Amina tricks her mother in order to sneak out of the house to begin her affair with Hashim, just like Nadia in *I Do Not Sleep* when she leaves to meet Mustafa. Amina's daring determination with Hashim—as well as her adventures sneaking out to see him—also echoes Abdel Kouddous's own risky detective-novel plotting with Nasser and the Free Officers in the two years before the coup. Told from the later, contemporaneous perspective of disillusionment at her affair with Hashim—reverberating with Abdel Kouddous's own bitter regrets at his relationship with the revolution and Nasser—Amina pauses her retelling to stress the reckless abandon of the initial stages of the affair: "The confidence that we felt at that time was strange. A huge, incredible confidence, a confidence of optimism, of being alive. We moved in life like the waters of a small stream, bubbling happily past rocks that were in its way, not even noticing they were there. At the end of the road, the big ocean would swallow it. We didn't see the big ocean or hear it. We rushed forward joyfully, scoffing, confident in ourselves until it swallowed us, that big ocean."[18]

Abdel Kouddous returned once again to the launch of his relationship with Nasser by narrating the buildup to sexual consummation, but he updated it from the perspective of his latest stage of malaise, regret, and despair. Instead of a compulsion based on projections and fantasies of love, principles, and devotion, he now focused on violence, masochism, and sexual satisfaction as way to frame the beginning of his "affair" with Nasser. When Amina goes to Hashim's apartment for only the third time, he slaps her across the face for being late. It is this act of violence that sparks their first sexual encounter: "He then pulled me by my hair and dropped me to the ground. I found him on top of me. I no longer knew what was happening. It was faster than I could take in. His lips were on mine and then on my neck. I felt his fingers opening the buttons of my blouse. A piece of my flesh was uncovered and then another piece. He was crazy, ravenous. I was resisting, but my body was thirsty. From that day, I got used to inflaming him. And he got used to hitting me. We only met like that, both of us crazy."[19] With this scene,

**Figure 23.** Installment of the First Eye with Hashim and Amina from *A Nose and Three Eyes*. *Rose El Youssef*, 28 October 1963.

Abdel Kouddous reframed the initial stages of his relationship Nasser through the lens of 1963, looking back some thirteen years. Instead of the dominance of Muhsin in *God Is with Us* or the insecurity of Nadia in *I Do Not Sleep*, here he frames the beginning of his affair with Nasser through the metaphor of Amina goading Hashim into an eruption of frantic sexual violence, with her savoring his response, despite her initial resistance, gesturing to the depiction of Wafiya in *Girls in Summer*.

The warning signs of their relationship are obvious, even as Amina impulsively represses them. When she tells Hashim of her impending marriage and asks him to marry her instead, he refuses, telling her bluntly that he has decided not to get married and that she has no future with him. Like Abbas in *I'm Free*, Hashim enjoys the sexual benefits of his relationship with Amina, but he refuses to make any commitment to her. And pointing to the end of *I'm Free*, Amina briefly realizes, "I was sacrificing everything while he was sacrificing nothing."[20] Nonetheless, she plunges forward with Hashim, ignoring the obvious catastrophe on the horizon, just as Abdel Kouddous's mother accused him of naïvely believing that Nasser was a force for democracy. Once Amina marries the loathsome 'Abd al-Salam, she sneaks off only six days after the wedding to sleep with Hashim, a clear taunt to Nasser for his purported objection to *Girls in Summer*, when he objected to "what might be happening in the cabins on the beaches of Alexandria." Like Abdel Kouddous before and immediately after the coup, Amina continues the affair despite the obvious, sneaking away from the watchful eye of the old generation—her mother and husband—to sleep with Hashim, inciting him to hit her and habituating her to violence, self-loathing, and emptiness. In a bit of heavy-handed symbolism, Amina soon becomes pregnant without knowing who the father is. Predictably, Hashim disavows responsibility, telling Amina that she must get an abortion, yet another stark warning and metaphor for the future.

It is in this context that Amina decides to set in motion her delusional coup. Echoing Abdel Kouddous's own actions in 1952, she risks everything to divorce her husband on the deluded hope that Hashim will finally marry her once she is free. She is compelled forward, no matter the consequences, recognizing only the scale of the disaster as she writes in 1963. Amina explains, "I was deluded of course. My love for Hashim was filling me with delusion and resolve. I couldn't appreciate the danger of what I was embarking on."[21] It is this period of heady excitement, passion, and misplaced confidence, which Amina, like Abdel Kouddous, would only recognize was false from the contemporaneous perspective: "Why am I saying this now? We are still at the beginning of my story, but I see it from the end. However much it was filled with tears, there was sweetness to those times, the sweetness of my youth, the sweetness of hope, the sweetness of self-confidence, of only seeing half of the truth. And then we grow up, and we see more of the truth until we see it all. The half-truth is more beautiful and more terrifying. Like the moon, half of it is exciting and beautiful while the other half is dark and terrifying. I live now in the dark, terrifying half. I was still in the illuminated half as I thought about divorcing my husband. The light around me was the light of pride in myself, of my infatuation with my beauty and youth. I couldn't see how disgusting my thinking was."[22] Full of regret, horror, and revulsion more than ten years after the coup, Abdel Kouddous, through Amina, looked back on the buildup, scorning his false self-confidence and deluded faith in carrying it out. Nonetheless, in her impulsive desperate hope to be "free," to divorce her husband, the double of the corrupt, gluttonous colonial system, Amina recklessly launches a coup from inside her mother-in-law's house without considering the consequences. She symbolically "lit the house on fire," fabricating hysterical violent fights, locking herself in her bedroom and throwing herself off a dresser in an attempt to self-abort.[23] When she tells 'Abd al-Salam that she will cheat on him if he does not divorce her, he slaps her, accusing her of having no principles, divorcing her on the spot. Of course, within the timeline of the novel, the metaphorical coup takes place in 1952. With the divorce secured, Amina, like her 1953 predecessor, triumphantly declares, "I had become free."[24]

Soon after the divorce, Amina, like Abdel Kouddous in the early hours and days after the coup, experiences a rush of remorse, wishing that her husband had intervened earlier to snap her out of her delusion: "A volcano of emotions erupted in my chest, contradictory, dark, and painful. 'Abd al-Salam's slap still burned my face. Unlike Hashim's many slaps, it tore up my dignity. It was a slap of anger, not desire. It revealed a truth that I had not seen before: he was a man, a strong man. I felt a violent wave of regret. Oh, Lord! Why hadn't he slapped me before? Maybe I would've woken up from this madness. Why did he spoil me so much? Why was he so permissive? Why did he leave me to Hashim?"[25] Just as Nadia calls Safiya after the divorce in *I Do Not Sleep* in horror at what she had done, hoping for Safiya to return, Amina is full of regret at her coup: "The torture of my conscience pressed down on me. I even entertained reconciling with 'Abd al-Salam. I even called him. I tried to be gentle with him. I talked to him about the approaching birth, trying to stir up his sympathy. He was cold with me and I gave up that hope. I submitted to fear, torture, and loss."[26] As discussed in chapter 2, we know that Abdel Kouddous met with James Murray of the British Consulate in Cairo soon after the coup, seemingly expressing his regret about the embedding of military dictatorship. The repeated inclusion in his fiction of the sudden horror at the recklessness of the plot—coupled with the frantic attempt to get the expelled spouse back—suggests that Abdel Kouddous was indeed acknowledging this meeting, at least through the metaphor of fiction, even if he never acknowledged it elsewhere.

Amina has chased an obsessive violent love for the masculine "hero" to achieve her freedom by ending the loathsome past, all in the deluded fantasy that Hashim will marry her. Like Abdel Kouddous before the coup, she has only planned for the divorce, not what would happen afterwards. She tells Hashim that she has not thought about what will come next: "I'll get divorced first and then I'll figure it out."[27] Predictably, Amina becomes the jilted lover who has wagered her future on her "man" and lost. Like Abdel Kouddous in the months after the coup, Amina feels increasing weakness, fear, and jealousy for her lover. She becomes furious and humiliated when Hashim begins avoiding her, jealous that he is devoting his time behind the secrecy of his clinic, the symbol of the clandestine committee meetings of the Free Officers in the novel. Framing memories of Abdel Kouddous's heated attempts to attract and hold Nasser's attention after the coup, Amina frantically chases Hashim around Cairo, desperately forcing her way into the clinic, demanding validation from him. Hashim repeatedly tells her that they have no future and that they should split up, but she insists on clinging to denial, spreading a false rumor that they are, at least, engaged. Amina explains, "I insisted. I insisted on living a big lie."[28] Through this confession, an echo of Salah in *The Empty Pillow* when he refuses to let go of his fantasy of the first love for Samiha, Abdel Kouddous framed himself, the jilted revolutionary, as Amina, the unhinged discarded lover, desperately demanding attention and guarantees from Hashim in the aftermath of her divorce. Amina knows that her relationship with Hashim is false—he repeatedly tells her that their love has no future—but she frantically insists on continuing anyway.

Hashim refuses to give Amina the guarantees or love that she demands, but he begins giving her money. At the end of his life, Abdel Kouddous admitted that Nasser secretly offered him cash in the years after the coup to fund *Rose El Youssef* and *Sabah al-Khayr*, an offer that he claimed he refused.[29] The First Eye, however, suggests otherwise. As if Abdel Kouddous was confessing to receiving funds from Nasser with all of its corresponding requirements and loss of dignity, Amina thinks, "It didn't occur to me that this money would get me used to a life that I couldn't sustain without him, and would set me on a path of holding out my hand to men. I didn't imagine that I was selling my body since I'd given my body to Hashim for free for so long. I didn't feel that I was selling my dignity. Hashim had already trampled on my dignity. I no longer had any left to sell. None of that occurred to me. I felt strong, so strong that I'd dismissed my entire family and everyone else."[30] From the perspective of 1963, full of regret and digging up the past to understand the ruined present, Abdel Kouddous framed Amina taking money from Hashim as not simply a loss of dignity but a deluded sense of confidence and strength, rendering her more dependent on Hashim and turning her increasingly frantic that she will lose his support, like Abdel Kouddous once he discovered Nasser's displeasure at *Girls in Summer*. Unable to marry anyone else because of her ruined reputation, Amina realizes in the aftermath, "I sold my future . . . but he didn't give me anything except those brief moments together and his money."[31]

Just as Amina quickly gets used to his money, she becomes habituated to his brutality. When Hashim begins to treat her gently, with a cold and distant respect, she is disgusted. Like Wafiya in *Girls in Summer*, she represents the double of an abuse victim addicted to masochism: "I didn't want him respectable. I wanted him violent, as I'd gotten used to, like he used to hit me, tear me up, or give me a look that would terrify me as if he was going to choke me."[32] She lashes out at him, inciting him until he hits her, pushing him to violence to prove that he loves her. This, of course, suggests that by 1963, Abdel Kouddous was reframing for himself the way that he had been attacking Nasser repeatedly in his fiction since 1955—not as dissent, but as "acting out," a desperate call for attention from his most important reader, attention that, as far as we know, he only got with the *Girls in Summer*. Despite repeated moments when Amina seems to wake up from the toxic relationship and tries to leave Hashim, she ultimately cannot resist returning to him, as if he is an addiction. With each return, Amina becomes more reckless, begging for his masculinity, only feeling strong when she sleeps with him and commands his attention: "It was a feeling that destroyed me, destroyed what remained of me. . . . I didn't know if this feeling of victory was only a reflection of my defeat, my defeat in front of myself."[33] Driven by Hashim's increasing neglect, she seeks to debase him by sleeping with multiple men, suggesting that the novel itself was for Abdel Kouddous yet another form of revenge against Nasser.

Decisively answering the ambivalence at the end of *I'm Free* in mid-1953, it is the freedom through staging a coup against the past—marked by the gluttonous 'Abd al-Salam and, not coincidentally, her mother—that destroys Amina. The more freedom Amina achieves, the more destructive she becomes: "I became free. I plunged into my freedom until the end."[34] The repressed anxiety at the end of *I'm Free* now erupts to the surface as Amina is appalled at what freedom and independence have done to her: "[Hashim] didn't try to save me from myself. He didn't try to intervene to limit my freedom, my freedom that was killing me. My nerves were becoming more frayed.... I felt as if I wanted to take off my skin, as if I needed a knife to cut off the skin from my body. Maybe after that I could be free, as if my skin was a jail choking my body."[35] By the end of the First Eye, self-loathing has become a compulsion for self-mutilation.

Despite Amina's frantic attempts to keep Hashim, the oscillation in their relationship suggesting the pendulum swing of Abdel Kouddous's own relationship with Nasser, he finally cuts her off, giving her money for two years of expenses and changing his phone number. Like Abdel Kouddous as he was confronted by Nasser's displeasure at *Girls in Summer*, Amina panics as she now faces the reality of losing Hashim. The public, of course, did not know that Abdel Kouddous wrote a letter to Nasser during the *Girls in Summer* crisis to plead with him to keep his protection. Once again using the fictional text serialized in the press to communicate with Nasser himself, Amina—like Abdel Kouddous in fall 1958—attempts to keep Hashim by writing him a letter:

Hashim, my love,

You know I love you. I still love you. More than my soul, more than my daughter, more than anything in the world. I sacrificed everything because I love you. I sacrificed my daughter, my family, my future, everyone. Then I made a mistake. I admit that I made a mistake. Please be merciful and remember that you're the one who pushed me to it. I've forgiven you for what you did to me, so forgive me for what I did to you. I promise you that as soon as I return to you, I'll atone for my mistake. You'll find me as someone else, a girl who loves you more, who desires you more. The saying goes: the broken plate lives longer. Our love was broken, but it will live longer. I beg you. Let me come back to you."[36]

Just as Nasser did not answer Abdel Kouddous, Hashim does not respond to Amina. Nonetheless, this act of begging only fills Amina with resentment, with the horror that she has only prostituted herself to Hashim, suggesting Abdel Kouddous's own feelings after he sent the letter to Nasser in fall 1958: "My torture got worse after I sent him that letter. I felt he was sucking my dignity, that he was degrading me more now that I humbled myself to him. I felt a torture set out with the fire of rage, rage at the greatest of scoundrels, the doctor of despicableness."[37]

Hashim "the scoundrel," uncoincidentally the same accusation that Faiza levels at the Nasser double Munir at the end of *The Barred Road*, finally abandons Amina. She then lives with her second lover, Muhammad, pretending to be his wife. As at the end of *I'm Free*, Amina deludes herself into thinking that the formality of marriage is unimportant: "I didn't need to marry him or anyone else. It was better that way. I wasn't lacking anything. I had a house and a man. All I lacked was a piece of paper, a piece of paper with no value."[38] Drawing a parallel between the final pages of *I'm Free* and *A Nose and Three Eyes*, Abdel Kouddous suggests that both Aminas remain in denial, repressing the reality that freedom and independence have brought only self-destruction and debauchery, ultimately turning them into social pariahs.

Nonetheless, Abdel Kouddous takes the ending of the First Eye even further. When Muhammad marries another woman and pays Amina off to avoid a scandal, Amina knows that a respectable future is now fully barred. As the First Eye ends, Amina faces what Hashim has done to her, clearly echoing Abdel Kouddous's own grief at the time of writing: "I no longer felt anything except my hatred for Hashim, the stone that he left in my heart. . . . I hate Hashim, the scoundrel, the doctor of despicableness. I detest him."[39] Starkly rejecting the accommodation of *The Sun Never Sets*, there is no salvation at the end of the First Eye, no Nasser ex machina to save Amina miraculously from the fall: "I had paid the entire price. I hated him. Hatred consumed me to the point that I wished he were dead."[40] She moves in with a female friend and meets a pimp who introduces her to foreign clients. As Amina notes, "This is better than getting used to just one man."[41] The narrative trails off as Amina coldly describes the way they dance at the club, echoing Nadia's emotional death and isolation at the end of *I Do Not Sleep*.

As in *I'm Free*, Amina's relationship with Nasser's fictional double led to her "freedom," but in *A Nose and Three Eyes*, freedom is ultimately catastrophic and debasing. Like Abdel Kouddous with Nasser, Amina bet her family, reputation, livelihood, and future on her delusional projections of Hashim—despite the obvious—only for him to abuse her sexually and habituate her to violence, without any consequences. Their relationship has become so toxic, compulsive, and addictive that Amina plunges forward in her descent into instability, co-dependence, and self-destruction. As the final page of the First Eye stresses, her liberation through a steamy yet violent affair with Hashim finally turns her into a prostitute. In turn, this frames not only Egypt's debased romance with Nasser "the scoundrel" in the aftermath of 23 July 1952 but also Abdel Kouddous's own relationship with Nasser. For freedom and liberation from the corruption of the monarchy era, Abdel Kouddous impulsively wagered everything on his projected fantasies of Nasser, despite the obvious warning signs, as his mother told him in his jail cell in July 1954. Once liberation arrived, their relationship became more and more toxic and degrading until Abdel Kouddous arrived at the point of obsession, addiction, and self-loathing, losing all dignity by increasingly lashing out and then prostituting himself before the nation in editorials and fiction, culminating at encouraging Nasser to nationalize the press and confiscating his family's magazines. As Amina writes to Hashim in her plea for him to return: "I sacrificed everything because I love you."

The First Eye therefore does not simply rewrite *I'm Free* and provide clarity for the ambiguity and ambivalence about the depiction of freedom and revolt at the end of that pivotal novel. The First Eye is Abdel Kouddous's most desperate attempt to expose the scandal of the trajectory of the revolution to the public, a shocking declaration in fall 1963 that he would no longer repress his abusive past with Nasser and continue to prostitute himself as he had been doing since late 1958. It is a devastating condemnation of the degradation of the relationship between Egypt, Nasser, and Abdel Kouddous himself, a powerful foretaste of the shattering catastrophe of June 1967 some three and a half years beforehand. While Egypt—like Abdel Kouddous—might have descended into prostitution to Nasser as a result of its deluded desire for him and clinging to "freedom" regardless of the consequences, Abdel Kouddous serialized the First Eye as a defiant and stunning act of protest and lashing out against Nasser, a revolt against his latest humiliation, showing that, unlike Amina, he and his dignity were no longer for sale.

### NASSER IS INCREDIBLE

When Abdel Kouddous began serializing the Second Eye on 17 February 1964, the first installment included a hint of regret that he might have gone too far. As with the First Eye, the Second Eye begins as a retrospective first-person narrative. This time, Nagwa, the narrator, introduces herself by disavowing bleak pessimism on love, as if Abdel Kouddous was backtracking, at least momentarily, from his bitter rejection of Nasser in the First Eye: "Love is everything: happiness, well-being, comfort. It is intelligence. It is success. I'm amazed at the girls who deny the existence of love. Love is the one firm truth in life."[42] Narrating in retrospect, Nagwa then explains that she discovered love through the arrival of a deus ex machina figure when she was at the peak of despair: "I found this man. A strong man. A marvelous man. I found my love, Hashim. Doctor Hashim 'Abd al-Latif. I found him while standing on the edge of hopelessness. He returned life and love to me. He returned my faith, faith that life could include men like him. I gave up hope. I lost my confidence in life and love, in myself, until Hashim came."[43] As if stressing the links between herself and Ahmed in *The Sun Never Sets*—foreshadowing how Nagwa would find her own salvation through the sudden arrival of Nasser ex machina—Nagwa continues, "He lit the light in my heart and my mind. He returned life and love to me. He returned my faith."[44]

With this declaration of a doctor returning her faith in life and love after the trauma of crisis, Abdel Kouddous once again circled back to the wellspring of his early post-revolution fiction, this time rewriting his second major work after the coup, *Where's My Life?* That novel, which he serialized in early 1954, begins with Aliya, a fifteen-year-old girl, married to the much older "Uncle" Aziz, the symbol of the corrupt monarchy era in Egypt. Uncle Aziz robs her of her childhood not only through marriage but also by isolating her on his farm for twelve years, until he becomes sick. Aliya is woken from her depression when she meets one of Uncle Aziz's doctors, Dr. Khaled, the double for Nasser who awakens sexual desire inside her for the first time. When Uncle Aziz dies suddenly—the symbol of the coup in the novel—Aliya revolts. Instead of mourning her husband, the now thirty-year-old Aliya rejects her mother for selling her off to the much older Uncle Aziz, a fictional disavowal that must have enraged Abdel Kouddous's own mother. Aliya also takes refuge in her lost childhood, dressing and acting like a fifteen-year-old again, plunging into an illness of stunted growth, serving as the double of an Egypt incapable of productively navigating the new era of freedom of late 1952 and early 1953.

Aliya then meets Adil, a virile nineteen-year-old, and acts out with him her fantasy of reliving her teens. She cannot face Adil's sexual desires for her and loses consciousness when he forces himself on her sexually. Confronting her split personality that results from the trauma, Aliya decides to visit Dr. Khaled at his office for an examination, a scene that Abdel Kouddous would rewrite some ten years later when he depicted Amina visiting Dr. Hashim at his office at the beginning of the First Eye. Like Dr. Hashim, Dr. Khaled invites Aliya for a rendezvous. Instead of treating a physical illness, Dr. Khaled diagnoses her psychologically—as Nasser would do with Abdel Kouddous after his release from prison in summer 1954—explaining that Uncle Aziz, the symbol of the corrupt past, had controlled her for so long that she cannot embrace the present. Dr. Khaled confesses his love for Aliya, sending her into delight, presumably healing her from the psychological abuse of her marriage to Uncle Aziz. While Aliya might have been cured from the repressed anxieties of her marital past, she is still haunted by shame over her sexual relationship with Adil, the outcome of her illness since the divorce, the marker of Abdel Kouddous's own rebellion against Nasser after the initial months of the coup. She tries to confess her anxieties to Dr. Khaled, but he refuses to listen, explaining that she can tell him in five years, giving her a transitional era that parallels the one that the Free Officers gave Egypt at the same time Abdel Kouddous serialized the novel.

Unlike *I'm Free*, Dr. Khaled marries Aliya and provides her with commitment for that love—a marriage certificate, the symbol of Abdel Kouddous's demands for documentation for the transitional period. It is this marriage certificate that presumably protects Aliya—and Egypt—from the anxieties of past. With this ending, Dr. Khaled is the answer to the book's title, of Aliya asking, "Where's my life?" Nonetheless, like *I'm Free*, *Where's My Life?* ends with deep ambiguity, suggesting that Nasser sees Abdel Kouddous as an idealistic projection, refusing to acknowledge his anxieties and regrets about the coup and its aftermath. Does Dr. Khaled see Aliya simply as a projection of purity and faithfulness or does he accept her for who she is, embracing her anxieties and regrets over her behavior since the "divorce"? What will happen when Aliya finally articulates her anxieties and regrets to Dr. Khaled? Will Aliya's relationship with Dr. Khaled survive once he finally learns the truth about her?

In the Second Eye, Abdel Kouddous rewrote *Where's My Life?* for his latest revolt against Nasser, once again returning to the questions lingering at the end of his early post-revolution fiction to provide decisive answers after the experience of some ten years after the coup. As with the relationship between the First Eye and *I'm Free*, the parallels between the Second Eye and *Where's My Life?* are clear from the start. The narrator, Nagwa, was raised by her aunt, whom she thought was her real mother until discovering the truth as an adolescent, just like Abdel Kouddous. Echoing *Where's My Life?*, Nagwa's father is almost entirely absent. He is not dead, as in the earlier novel, but, metaphorically, he is paralyzed and mute, lying in bed as an impotent onlooker to the increasing degradation of his household. Nagwa's adoptive mother, Aziza, like Aliya's mother in *Where's My Life?*, stands as the symbol of the outmoded, controlling, and oppressive past, gesturing to Abdel Kouddous's own mother. As in *Where's My Life?*, Nagwa faces sexual abuse followed by psychological breakdown with two separate men—the younger and virile Adil, whose name is recycled from the first novel to reinforce the links between the two novels, and the much older Uncle Abdou, the reincarnation of Uncle Aziz. In order to provide some daylight between the two texts, Abdel Kouddous flips the appearance of the two men in the Second Eye, as Nagwa faces her sexual trauma with Adil before getting married off to Uncle Abdou.

Paralleling Aliya's sexual encounter with Adil in *Where's My Life?*, Nagwa collapses after she sleeps with Adil in the Second Eye and becomes bedridden. She then meets Dr. Hashim, who comes to treat her. As Aliya is struck when she first encounters Dr. Khaled in *Where's My Life?*, Nagwa immediately feels that Dr. Hashim is not simply a man but a soothing force. Like the messianic figure that Nasser represented in Abdel Kouddous's editorials starting in the mid-1950s, Hashim's touch alone is enough to heal Nagwa: "My pain fled under his slender, gentle fingers. Wherever he touched me, I felt that part of me was healed. I was confused about what to tell him. I'd tell him about the pain in one spot, but then I didn't feel it anymore after he'd examined me there."[45] Just as Dr. Khaled offers Aliya a psychoanalytic diagnosis in *Where's My Life?*, Hashim tells Nagwa that that she has only suffered a nervous breakdown. Directly pointing to his release from jail on 31 July 1954, Abdel Kouddous mocked his devoted reader Nasser by having Hashim tell Nagwa, "I can be your psychologist. Talk to me."[46] Nagwa has spent a month in bed, but Hashim, like a prophet, raises her up on her feet, providing her miraculously with the strength to walk again. Nonetheless, like Aliya, Nagwa does not reveal to Hashim the source of her anxiety—shame at her sexual encounter with Adil. Nagwa is aroused by Hashim but, unlike Amina in the First Eye, she understands that her feelings for him are only a fantasy. In a reference to *The Barred Road*, Nagwa thinks, "Hashim is a barred road with no hope. He's a clean love that my imagination has stirred up. He's only an illusion."[47] Like Dr. Khaled in *Where's My Life?* after he first encounters Aliya, Hashim then disappears from the narrative.

It is at this point that Abdel Kouddous inserted another key difference between the Second Eye and *Where's My Life?* Nagwa's adoptive mother does not simply oppress and control her, like Aliya's mother in *Where's My Life?* Instead, in the mother-daughter relationship, Abdel Kouddous continues toying with the theme of prostitution as central to the 1960s rewrite of his early post-revolution fiction. Alluding to the morally bankrupt mother of *The Barred Road*, Nagwa's mother inserts her daughter into a social network of older men, enthusiastically trying to prostitute her. Nagwa's mother is pleased when she finds 'Abd al-Fattah Bey, whom Nagwa calls "Uncle Abdou." The counterpart to Uncle Aziz in *Where's My Life?*, the wealthy Uncle Abdou is some thirty years older than Nagwa and is married with children, including a daughter who is older than Nagwa. Their relationship reaches a climax when Nagwa's mother manipulates her into signing a contract for an *urfi*—or temporary—marriage to Uncle Abdou. Desperate to rid herself of her mother's dominating control and pressure, Nagwa signs the contract without reading it. 'Abd al-Fattah writes her mother a check for two thousand pounds ostensibly as the dowry, but it is the purchase price for sexual rights over her daughter.

With Nagwa's adoptive mother waiting in the living room, delighted and satisfied, and her father paralyzed in bed seemingly oblivious to the abuse taking place in his house, 'Abd al-Fattah follows Nagwa into her bedroom. Needing to protect herself from the horror of the moment, Nagwa is overwhelmed by the feeling that she wants to watch 'Abd al-Fattah have sex, observing the process of splitting from her body as a way to suppress her trauma, duplicating the splitting that happened in *Where's My Life?* when Aliya is raped by Adil. In this scene, Nagwa tracks his eyes and hands as he gropes her body: "Then a violent feeling took

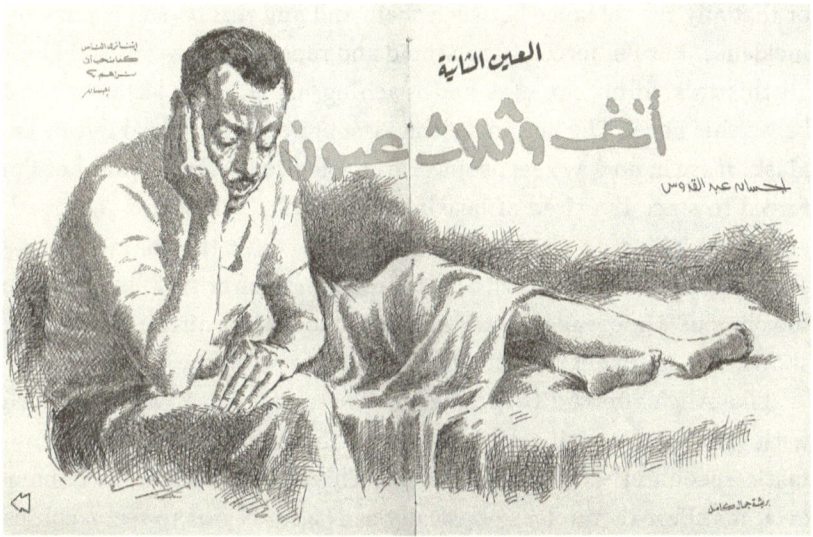

**Figure 24.** Installment of the Second Eye with Uncle Abdou and Nagwa from *A Nose and Three Eyes*. *Rose El Youssef*, 30 March 1964.

hold of me. I wanted to watch 'Abd al-Fattah Bey Ra'fat, the rich, famous man, the man with influence. I wanted to watch him as he was making love. So, I watched. I watched his lips as they moved onto mine with a violent, greedy lust. I watched his eyes sparkle and then I watched his eyes close. I watched his thick dry hands as they picked spots to grope on my body. I watched as he took off his clothes in a comical rush. I watched his face as it got red and flushed. I watched him as he hissed and panted. I watched. I felt I was watching a movie, a movie for adults only, and that this body wasn't mine, everything that was happening wasn't happening to me. I was far away."[48] Amplifying the horror of the scene, Abdel Kouddous had 'Abd al-Fattah, after finishing with Nagwa, get dressed and leave her room to have coffee with Nagwa's mother, who has been waiting outside the bedroom, listening to what was happening, underscoring the morally bankrupt dominance of her daughter.

Abdel Kouddous clearly anticipated that this sequence between Nagwa, Uncle Abdou, and her mother would be a problem. In a highly unusual move, when this scene was published on 30 March 1964, Abdel Kouddous included a disclaimer in a separate box on the same page depicting the sexual assault: "I feel the stupidity of the writer when he's forced to say that the characters of his stories aren't particular people or that any resemblance between them and any real person is pure coincidence. But I'm forced to be stupid and repeat these words so I block all this talk filling my ears and reaching me through letters since I began this novel. The heroine of the First or Second or Third Eye or Dr. Hashim are in no way real people. . . . I apologize for saying this, but I'm forced to since I'm tired of hearing all the talk."[49] It seems that readers were picking up on the obvious links between the characters and their real-life doubles. As with *Girls in Summer*, the critique had become too obvious. Unfortunately for Abdel Kouddous, his disclaimer for this shocking installment did little to quell the storm on the horizon.

Like Aliya after Adil rapes her in *Where's My Life?*, Nagwa is filled with grief mixed with cold indifference in the aftermath of her traumatic encounter with 'Abd al-Fattah. This shame and disgrace, however, manifest themselves physically as Nagwa begins to feel stabbing pains in her chest, becoming bedridden with cardiac rheumatism, as her heart symbolically threatens to end her life. Just as Aliya in *Where's My Life?* contacts Dr. Khaled to save her miraculously from the crisis of her trauma, Nagwa contacts Dr. Hashim, who returns, at least initially, as her own deus ex machina. Once again, Nagwa feels Hashim's magnetism and purity as he soothes her pain simply by touching her skin. Like Aliya in *Where's My Life?*, Nagwa is disturbed in her second meeting with the doctor, overwhelmed by the shame of her recent sexual encounter coupled with a compulsion to cleanse herself from sin so she can be united with the messianic savior as a pure woman.

Thanks to Hashim's arrival as a deux ex machina, Nagwa emerges suddenly healed, just as Aliya is transformed by her encounter with Dr. Khaled after having sex with Adil in *Where's My Life?* Both women rediscover their femininity and fall in love with their savior doctors. In the Second Eye, Nagwa is unable to repress her feelings for Hashim: "I couldn't stand it anymore. I loved him. I didn't care if I went to university or not. I didn't care if he married me or not. All I cared about was that I loved him. I wanted us to go out alone, a world just for us."[50] Like Dr. Khaled for Aliya, Hashim is Nagwa's life. But just as Aliya at the end of *Where's My Life?* is anxious that Dr. Khaled does not know the reality behind her facade, Nagwa becomes increasingly anxious that Hashim loves her as a projection, something pure and innocent, not as a woman soiled by the past: "I couldn't reveal the truth to him. I couldn't lose his love. But if I built my love on deception, Hashim would break it off after he discovered the truth."[51] When Hashim, seemingly preparing to propose to her, tells Nagwa that he feels like he knows everything about her, she is horrified: "I felt a knife was cutting into my heart. He didn't know anything about me. He didn't know I wasn't an innocent girl who loved him."[52]

At the end of *Where's My Life?*, Aliya tries to reveal her anxieties and regrets to Dr. Khaled—as if Abdel Kouddous were symbolically confessing his true feelings to Nasser at the time—but he stops her, marrying her regardless, saying that she can tell him in five years. In the Second Eye, Nagwa cannot resist. The time has come for her—and Abdel Kouddous—to confess the truth to the doctor, to reveal who they really are and what they have been repressing. Nagwa demands that Hashim take her to his apartment, setting up yet another climactic scene in Abdel Kouddous's fiction between the female protagonist and her lover in his bachelor apartment: "I decided to put an end to this farce that I was living. I decided to shine a light on myself so I could appear before my love as I really was, no matter what that truth was, no matter how much of a risk it was, no matter my fate. I couldn't bear this deception anymore, this deceit, this lie."[53] Reflecting Abdel Kouddous's revolt against Nasser during fall 1963 and winter 1964, Nagwa thinks, "I could no longer play the role of the virgin, of the angel. I'm a woman. He had to know that and forgive me."[54] As she has sex with him, the climactic moment of revelation, Nagwa is in bliss. She has finally confessed: "I felt love at its peak, its climax. I felt love flowing in my body, calm and beautiful. My tears rushed out, silent tears, perhaps tears of happiness, a happiness that I hadn't felt before."[55] Hashim, however, is stunned to learn the truth that she is not a virgin, a stark contrast to his projections of purity and faithfulness upon Nagwa. Nagwa then reveals her relationship with 'Abd al-Fattah, completing the act of revelation. Just as *A Nose and Three Eyes* represents a public exposure of Abdel Kouddous's revolt against Nasser, Nagwa has finally revealed all of herself to Hashim.

As the First Eye offered closure to the ambiguity at the end of *I'm Free*, this is the moment that the Second Eye begins to answer the questions left at the end of *Where's My Life?*, reflecting the crisis that was spiraling behind the scenes about the novel. Predictably, Hashim cannot handle the truth. Stunned at Nagwa's confession, Hashim tells her that he feels that he does not know her at all. Nagwa declares that she will leave 'Abd al-Fattah, but Hashim refuses any responsibility, saying that she should not leave 'Abd al-Fattah for him and that she would have to do it without his help. Nonetheless, Nagwa leaves Hashim's apartment with newfound strength and confidence—confession and revelation therefore eliminate anxiety, regret, and shame, at least for Abdel Kouddous when he wrote this installment. Unlike Faiza, who leaves Munir's apartment confused at the end of *The Barred Road*, Nagwa is strong and confident, as if Abdel Kouddous was reframing the pivotal exchange when Nasser asked him to serve as his "translator," asserting to Nasser now that their earlier exchange filled him with strength, not confusion: "I held my head up high. I felt strong, that I wasn't ever as strong as I was at that moment. I felt whole. I felt as if I'd been liberated, that I'd been released into a new world which I was controlling. I was its master."[56] As Nagwa walks out of Hashim's apartment confident, this is the moment that the backlash against the novel that had been brewing behind the scenes began to intervene in the plot. Abdel Kouddous began taking the opportunity of writing each installment on a weekly basis, right before the printer's Saturday deadline, to declare his defiance against the backlash against the novel as it was unfolding.

Instead of simply ending the Second Eye with Hashim's rejection and abandonment of Nagwa, the plot takes a sudden turn that only makes sense within the context of the crisis now raging about the novel. With the installment published on 4 May 1964, the week after the climax in Hashim's apartment, Nagwa becomes emboldened. Echoing Abdel Kouddous's own angry clash with those stirring up a scandal around the novel at the time, Nagwa suddenly refuses to live immersed in corruption and degradation. She confronts 'Abd al-Fattah and her mother, insulting 'Abd al-Fattah and accusing her mother of selling her off like a pimp: "The road to a clean life was difficult. I plunged into battle. 'Abd al-Fattah and my mother were on one side. And I was on the other, all alone. Hashim refused to stand beside me, refused to intervene, refused to do anything that would lighten the burden. He insisted that it was my battle alone."[57] The scandal raging at the time of writing and serialization has therefore suddenly repositioned the characters in the novel, transforming them from the parallels of *Where's My Life?* into fictional doubles of the actors in the crisis playing out as each installment went to press. Now, Nagwa represents a defiant Abdel Kouddous, full of strength and confidence, defiant and unashamed of his past "sin," ridiculing those oppressing her. Nagwa's mother and 'Abd al-Fattah now take on the roles of those repressing Nagwa, doubles for the people stirring up the scandal at the time to oppress and corrupt Abdel Kouddous. And Hashim is now a new depiction of Nasser, a weak man who cannot handle the truth of the real Abdel Kouddous and has abandoned him to face his accusers alone.

Nagwa sneaks out to see Hashim at his bachelor apartment, as if Abdel Kouddous is narrating secretly meeting Nasser about the scandal inflaming the novel. While Nagwa has remained resolute and steadfast in the battle, Hashim is now overwhelmed by weakness, unable to look at her directly, a condemnation of both the symbolic and real-life Nasser. Nagwa complains to him about her oppressors, echoing what Abdel Kouddous likely told Nasser at the time, declaring, "You don't know what they're doing to me."[58] When Nagwa tells Hashim that she plans to stay at his apartment and live there with him, Hashim rejects her and tells her to go home. Hashim meekly tells Nagwa, "I don't know if I love you or not. I'm not confused about you, I'm confused about myself, confused about every day that's passed since I met you. I love the you I thought you were, a strong, innocent, young girl. That girl is the one I love. But all of a sudden, I found another girl in front of me.... Now, I don't know who I love. Do I love the innocent girl or the woman who has another man? It's driving me crazy."[59] Nagwa pleads for Hashim to remain by her side, perhaps gesturing to Abdel Kouddous's latest panic over losing Nasser's support: "I love you, Hashim. I can't do without you. I don't want anything from you but your love."[60] Despite this plea, the weak, unstable Hashim feebly rejects her, telling her that the real Nagwa is not the one with whom he fell in love. Abdel Kouddous was protesting in real time to Nasser through this week's installment of the novel, lashing out at him yet again, this time for his weakness and not supporting him against his accusers in the crisis.

Abdel Kouddous wrapped up the Second Eye in a way that makes sense only within the context of the scandal engulfing the novel in May 1964. Despite all indications to the contrary before the final two installments of the novel, the suddenly strong, defiant Nagwa quickly conquers her opponents, convincing her adoptive mother to tear up her *urfi* marriage contract, end her relationship with 'Abd al-Fattah, and let her go to university. Her adoptive mother suddenly and inexplicably respects Nagwa's freedom. Throughout the novel, Nagwa's adoptive mother is depicted as obsessed with appearances and money as well as controlling Nagwa. Now, she happily accepts that they will no longer receive money from 'Abd al-Fattah, who has moved them to a luxurious new home with servants, and that they will now move into a modest apartment near the university where Nagwa will go to school. She is even "proud" of Nagwa for going to college, which metaphorically serves as a strong repudiation of Abdel Kouddous's accusers, even if only in the fictional text.

Nagwa is now confident that she has regained her life, like Aliya at the end of *Where's My Life?* The crucial difference, however, is that Nagwa has confessed her anxieties and regrets about her past and the doctor has rejected her for it, abandoning her in the process. Harkening back to how Abdel Kouddous took refuge in the idea of love in his radio series "Whisper" as a means to cope with his jailing in summer 1954, Nagwa declares that it is love that has saved her from the abyss, suggesting that Abdel Kouddous was resorting to an abstract love of the nation—and not how Nasser perverted it—to serve as his crutch through the crisis. Even though love has turned Hashim weak, insecure, and suspicious—a clear condemnation of an increasingly unstable Nasser at the time of serialization—Nagwa remains grateful because he is the one who has motivated her to defy her oppressors: "Before, I was weak. I couldn't choose the kind of love that I wanted. But all of life is love. Every road is love. What's important is that I choose the road that I want and that I'm convinced of where I'm going. Hashim came and gave me this love, a love that I wanted. I regained my strength, the strength of who I was. I could choose my road. I could free myself from 'Abd al-Fattah and my mother. It was Hashim that did this. Hashim was incredible. He was a real man."[61] This optimism at the end of the Second Eye—the assertion that Nagwa has defeated her oppressors despite Hashim's abandonment—did not match the way things would play out.

As early as February 1956, as he was serializing *I Do Not Sleep*, Abdel Kouddous wrote in *Rose El Youssef*, "There are now dozens of journalists trying to install themselves as public prosecutor and, whenever I publish a novel, to direct against me the charge of 'harming public morality and insulting religion.'"[62] In May 1964, as he was confronting a new group of accusers both in person and in fiction, it finally happened. A representative of parliament, Abdel Samad Muhammad Abdel Samad, raised the charge that *A Nose and Three Eyes* was harming public morality with its graphic sexuality, demanding that serialization cease immediately, that the novel be banned, and that the work never be adapted into any other format, including radio, television, or cinema.[63] The details of the campaign against Abdel Kouddous are murky. Abdel Kouddous did not discuss the scandal directly with Hanan al-Shaykh, but he did tell her in spring 1964 that someone wanted to replace him as chairman of *Rose El Youssef*. Abdel Kouddous claimed at the time that it was this person who had pushed Abdel Samad to raise the charge. A full decade after the case, Abdel Kouddous explained instead that the charge was motivated by political—not literary—reasons; indeed, Abdel Samad later confessed that he had not even read the novel.[64] As with *Girls in Summer*, it seems almost certain that the novel's graphic sexuality was just a cover for attacking Abdel Kouddous for his temerity in daring to oppose Nasser.

Anwar Sadat was serving as president of parliament at the time. He called Abdel Kouddous to explain to him that he had received the charge and that he would move it to the floor for discussion. Sometime in late May or early June, a meeting of the High Council for Arts and Literature was held with Tawfiq al-Hakim as chair and Naguib Mahfouz in attendance. Abdel Kouddous was present as they discussed the novel and defended the freedom of writers to express themselves. Tawfiq al-Hakim reportedly declared, "I read this novel, and there isn't anything in it that violates morality. Rather, it's the highest form of literary creation."[65] Yet when Abdel Kouddous asked him and the others present to record their support in the minutes of the meeting, al-Hakim refused, explaining that he had to wait to hear what the government wanted in the case. As Abdel Kouddous explained nearly a decade after the incident, pointing the finger at the network of people around Nasser, "They knew that the centers of power were the ones who launched the whole campaign against me."[66] It would, unfortunately, take another decade—some four years after Nasser's death—for al-Hakim to stand up to Nasser publicly when he published his scathing critique in *The Return of Consciousness*. Abdel Kouddous claimed on numerous times that he was the one who had originally proposed to Nasser to create this Council years earlier. As if representing his own alienation and isolation from the regime, a final rejection by the revolution which he had helped spark, it was this very council that refused to support him once Nasser had abandoned him.

On 7 June 1964, one day before the charges were debated in parliament, Abdel Kouddous wrote a letter to al-Hakim as Hanan al-Shaykh sat beside him. He explained to al-Hakim that he attended the Council "because of a psychological crisis that I'm suffering and a horrible feeling of loneliness. I'm alone, alone to a terrifying degree."[67] Just like Nagwa at the end of the Second Eye, Abdel Kouddous wrote to al-Hakim that he had felt strong in his solitude and had been able to wage all of his political and literary battles alone. But now, he wrote, "I don't know what's happened to me. Maybe I'm tired of all the conflicts that I've plunged into."[68] Nonetheless, for Abdel Kouddous, relenting was tantamount to "cowardice and fear . . . and this is my crisis."[69] Abdel Kouddous explained that he believed in his fiction and how he writes: "I can't renounce any part of my fiction unless I renounce it entirely and stop writing. . . . Simply feeling that I'm avoiding a particular direction is a hypocrisy that paralyzes my pen and makes me hate myself, my writing, and the entire world. And self-hatred is my poison."[70] While Abdel Kouddous forced himself to incorporate blatant praise of Nasser in *The Sun Never Sets*, *A Nose and Three Eyes* shows how he could not repress his sense of hypocrisy forever. As he told Hanan al-Shaykh, "If I give up my freedom, I've lost my soul."[71]

Abdel Kouddous wrote this letter only about three weeks after he finished the Second Eye. Unlike his fictional double, Nagwa, Abdel Kouddous was ultimately unable to face his crisis with strength and defiance. He explained to al-Hakim that he would not attend the next session of the Council to continue pleading his case: "What's important is to save myself from being torn apart by my psychological crisis."[72] It was time to withdraw. Abdel Kouddous ended his letter to al-Hakim by explaining, "I'll leave everything and travel far away after finishing the last two chapters of this novel that has caused all this controversy. I'll try to collect myself once I'm away and get back to writing again."

## NASSER IS WEAK

As the crisis over the novel was in full force, Abdel Kouddous began serializing the Third Eye on 25 May 1964. In the first and second parts of the novel, Abdel Kouddous wrote two previous lovers as his fictional doubles in the text, depicting their relationship with the doctor as a metaphor for the way Nasser had degraded and betrayed both Abdel Kouddous and the nation since the coup. In the Third Eye, however, as if trying to downplay his own role in the text, Abdel Kouddous removed himself as a female fictional double in the narrative. Instead, he turned to his current lover as the basis for Rihab, a teenage Lebanese woman modeled on Hanan al-Shaykh. In late May 1964, Abdel Kouddous was deeply disillusioned that Nasser had abandoned him and that the complaint against the novel would be brought forward in parliament. In the Third Eye, Abdel Kouddous used the relationship between Lebanese Rihab and Egyptian Hashim as a metaphor for the collapse of the United Arab Republic, the union of Syria and Egypt, angrily heaping scorn on Nasser for being old, weak, and delusional.

In the Third Eye, nineteen-year-old Rihab, like al-Shaykh at the time, is an existentialist with a black bob resembling an *Elle* model. She is depicted as hedonistic, flighty, and dominated by emotions, quickly giving in to her feelings without understanding them, a metaphor for Egypt's relationship with Syria in the United Arab Republic: "The reality was that my feelings controlled me. No one could control me, not my father not my mother, not my brother, only my feelings. . . . I'd always submitted to my feelings. Yet, most of the time, I was incapable of explaining them because I was incapable of understanding them or expressing them."[73] Overwhelmed by boredom, she decides to escape Beirut, going to Cairo on a whim. As Hanan al-Shaykh arrived in Cairo with a letter of introduction to Ihsan Abdel Kouddous from Georges Khoury, Rihab receives a letter of introduction to Dr. Hashim from her uncle. Once she arrives in Cairo, Rihab lives with extended relatives and mixes with the Lebanese community. When she decides that she needs an Egyptian guide to Cairo, she contacts Dr. Hashim, who is forty-five, the same age as Nasser at the time of publication.

For Rihab, Hashim is not simply a doctor. Echoing Abdel Kouddous's repeated editorials between 1955 and 1963 about Nasser as a metaphysical embodiment of Egypt, both its people and its physical space, she thinks, "I felt like there was a drop of the Nile in Hashim. There was the strength of the Nile in his prominent nose. There was the goodness of the Nile in his calm eyes. There was the arrogance of the pyramids in him. There was the faith of the call to prayer in him. There was the tumult of

'Ataba Square in him and the calm of Gabalaya Street. Hashim was all of Egypt walking on two feet."[74] Nonetheless, Hashim is not the strong, masculine figure whom Amina and Nagwa initially encountered. Instead, he is weak, insecure, and unstable, as Abdel Kouddous left him at the end of the Second Eye in protest over the way Nasser had abandoned him in the crisis. Once Rihab begins dating Hashim, their relationship becomes a metaphor for the formation and collapse of the United Arab Republic. As Nasser quickly became infatuated with Syria, trying to control it despite repeated resistance, Hashim falls in love with Rihab, becoming jealous and possessive of her, compulsively seeking to control her and rein in her independence, fickleness, and emotions. Trying to convince her of their union, Hashim explains, "'All I'm trying to do is for us to live in the same world, to bring your world closer to mine so that they become one world. . . . This won't be easy, since what separates my world from yours isn't just friends and interests, but my country and yours. You're in Beirut and I'm in Cairo. I'm afraid, afraid of us failing in building our single world. This fear is making me hate your friends and hate Beirut. I hate everything separating us. But we have to pass the test.'"[75] Hashim humiliates himself by inviting himself to tag along with her and her teenage friends. Compared to her young Lebanese friends, Hashim looks old and weary, wearing out-of-date clothes and comes off as a parental chaperone, not a peer. Abdel Kouddous mocks Nasser's attempts to dominate Syria by depicting Hashim trying to assert himself among Rihab's friends in a series of cringeworthy scenes, leaving Rihab horrified that her friends will make fun of him behind her back: "There wasn't anything he could do to make himself one of us. He was the only one there with white hair."[76]

Rihab soon learns that her host family is furious that their aluminum factory has been nationalized. The family convinces Rihab that Hashim is so well known and important that officials at the airport will not search his bags, arguing that he would be able to smuggle money for them out of the country. They convince Rihab to travel to Beirut, leave a suitcase with secret pockets full of cash behind in Cairo, and ask Hashim to bring it to her, the implication being that Nasser was simply an unsuspecting fool being manipulated by Syria.[77] In turn, Rihab feels that she has come to represent the hero of the Lebanese community that has become prisoner to Nasser and Egypt, working secretly to save it.

Further symbolizing Syria, she plays a role with Hashim, trying to convince him that she loves him, yet seeking to exploit his possessiveness, jealousy, and weakness.

With her departure imminent, Hashim becomes more and more insecure and possessive: "Hashim became even weaker toward me. I could see weakness in his eyes, in his trembling lips. I felt weakness in his kisses where it seemed he could no longer breathe except through my lips."[78] Overcome with insecurity, Hashim suddenly proposes that they get married in a frantic final attempt to maintain their union, a proposal that she declines with alacrity. Amina and Nagwa, symbols both of Egypt and of Abdel Kouddous, desperately wanted to marry Hashim but were callously rejected. Instead, Hashim proposes to the young, flighty Lebanese, driving home the critique that Nasser abandoned and degraded Egypt because of a delusional, vain desire for glory on the international stage. As Abdel Kouddous explained about Nasser years later, "The fundamental mistake that happened was that he was interested in Egypt's international situation—unity with Syria—more than its domestic, even though I myself asked him to wait until finishing building Egypt internally."[79]

Rihab prepares the suitcase with a secret compartment full of cash and jewels and then takes it to the Hilton, where she spends the night with Hashim. She goes to the airport with Hashim, who is devastated at her departure. He tells her, "I've never given in like I have with you, given in to the point of weakness. I feel so weak it's like a kind of impotence, the same thing I feel when I can't diagnose a patient."[80] At the airport entrance, Rihab runs away from Hashim, fleeing his weightiness, pressure, and responsibility. The relationship with Hashim is over, as if Abdel Kouddous was not simply narrating a metaphor of the weak, possessive, controlling Nasser unable to accept the breakup with Syria but also declaring his own breakup with Nasser. Rihab thinks, "I didn't want to marry him. He was a big responsibility that I didn't want to bear.... He was the kind of man who wanted everything. I didn't want him to be weak with me or to exploit his weakness. And I didn't want him to be strong, as he could overpower me. It was better for both of us for us to end it."[81]

Hashim accuses her of fleeing, suggesting that she is committing suicide, a metaphorical depiction of the end of the United Arab Republic and a theme that will resurface in the literary affair between Abdel Kouddous and al-Shaykh. When Rihab returns to Beirut after the relationship has ended, she finally feels calm. She writes Hashim a letter, starting by explaining that she is controlled by her feelings and emotions, which even she does not understand. She was attracted to him more than to any other person, but now she is resisting him. The letter suddenly shifts from the focus of the Third Eye—the love affair and subsequent split of Syria and Egypt—to Abdel Kouddous's own crisis at the moment as he wrote the final installments of the novel. As if Abdel Kouddous were speaking to Nasser through Rihab's words to Hashim, rejecting Nasser while echoing the language of the letter he wrote to Tawfiq al-Hakim only days earlier about his crisis and need to get away, Rihab continues, "I can see the truth of my feelings now that I'm far from you. When I was in Egypt, I was really convinced that what was between us was friendship. But now, no, I know it was love. Despite that, I had to resist this love. I kept resisting. I was feeling that the wind pushed me despite myself to the edge of the abyss. But I had to resist so that I didn't fall into the abyss. Sorry, you're not an abyss. You're a mountain. You're a strong tree that casts its shade on people to protect them from the Cairo sun. But I had to resist you because I didn't want this love. I still don't know what this future holds, but it's not you. Your love isn't in my future."[82] Just as Abdel Kouddous told al-Hakim that he was leaving Egypt to find himself, Rihab explains, "I have to look for another world to live in, no matter how much confusion, trouble, and anxiety it causes me."[83]

And Nasser responds to Abdel Kouddous in doubletalk, confessing his weakness before both Syria and Abdel Kouddous, written in a letter from Hashim to Rihab: "The secret of my misery isn't your insistence on putting tight limits on our relationship. It's my feeling of weakness. From our first day together, I was feeling weak. I tried to deny it. I was too conceited to admit that I was weak. I wasn't weak before you, but before myself."[84] With the split completed, Hashim experiences a nervous collapse and closes his clinic, paralleling Nasser's own physical and psychological decline at the dissolution of the United Arab Republic. As Saïd Aburish notes of Nasser during this time, "Nasser suffered something resembling a nervous breakdown. People who saw him soon after the breakup spoke of his health deteriorating considerably."[85] As Aburish explains, "It was in the 1963-65 period that Gamal Abdel Nasser became a shadow of his old self."[86]

The Third Eye ends suddenly and meekly, with Abdel Kouddous clearly wanting to put a quick end to the novel.[87] Rihab returns to Cairo a year later and calls Hashim. She discovers that he is engaged to the same woman to whom his mother had engaged him twenty years earlier. His fiancé is now a widow with three children. Hashim has overcome his weakness and discovered love by reconnecting with a woman from his past, seemingly returning to his roots, gesturing to Nasser's own retreat inwards by focusing on sober national development in the aftermath of his delusional chase after the exciting yet uncontrollable Syria. After their conversation, Rihab thinks, "Hashim had changed. He had changed into a stronger man, into another man, not the one in my memory. Maybe he was always this strong and only a moment of weakness made us intertwined."[88] In this, the novel ends with a sudden seemingly happy ending tacked onto the painful split between Rihab and Hashim, a likely indication that Abdel Kouddous, as he wrote in his letter to Tawfiq al-Hakim, simply wanted to resolve the novel quickly and without the controversies of the First or Second Eye. This neat, simplistic ending, however, belied the crisis of confidence that Abdel Kouddous was suffering when he wrote it.

The crisis surrounding the novel did not stop with the session of parliament on 8 June 1964. Sometime after this session, a complaint against Abdel Kouddous for harming public morality was presented to the district attorney, leading to Abdel Kouddous's interrogation. The case was then turned over to the public prosecutor, who also questioned him. When it was then transferred to the morals prosecutor, Abdel Kouddous had had enough. As he explained in a letter to Taha Hussein on 4 March 1966, "I couldn't bear that a novelist in our age could be held to account before the morals prosecutor like a prostitute or a pimp."[89] At the time, Abdel Kouddous called his close friend, fellow novelist, and army officer Youssef El Sebai to complain, refusing to go for another interrogation, arguing that all writers would be sent to the morals police after him if this case proceeded. El Sabai then called Nasser, who finally intervened to put an end to the scandal, serving as Abdel Kouddous's own deus ex machina. The case was immediately dropped, but it was far from the end of Abdel Kouddous's humiliation.

When Abdel Kouddous returned to Egypt in fall 1964 after his summer vacation, he was removed as president of the board of *Rose El Youssef*, replaced by Ahmed Fouad, whom Abdel Kouddous derisively described as a "tin-fish seller," according to Hanan al-Shaykh. He did not receive an official explanation, but he was convinced that it was because of his latest novel. During this crisis, as he explained to Taha Hussein, "I felt myself alone, alone, alone, far from all of life. I felt a horrible coldness flowing in my veins, a coldness as if it was a needle prick. I shook. I gripped myself as if I was searching for heat inside myself."[90] While he had experienced numerous campaigns against him and his fiction before, this time was different: "The world has changed. People now, I mean the people who talk in a loud voice, don't say their opinion but ask for the opinion of the government. . . . This is what has spread despair in me. This is what has made me feel loneliness, coldness, introversion, and even disgust."[91] While he continued to write editorials in late 1964, he had not published a single one of his usual obsequious editorials about Nasser for eighteen months, since the day that Anwar Sadat took him for that walk along the Nile. His silence was deafening.

### THE DEFEAT

**Every free noble writer—who maintains his honor—has to expect the worst at any moment because even his very existence as someone with a free pen represents, for the enemies of freedom, an unpardonable crime. The only option is to put an end to him by literary termination if terminating him physically is too difficult.**

—Ihsan Abdel Kouddous (1975)

In 1965, Abdel Kouddous continued to suffer from a mental breakdown. In his 1966 letter to Taha Hussein, he explained, "I found myself fighting a terrible psychological crisis that distanced me from everyone, all centers of movement, everyone whom I love. I discovered that I was weak. I bear my weakness inside and I try to hide it under a shade of false stubbornness and agitated delusion. . . . For the past two years, this suffering became more than I could bear, more than I could defeat so I submitted to my weakness. I haven't written much during this time except for a few short stories."[92] It was at this point that Hanan al-Shaykh began seeing Abdel Kouddous less and less. For her, his anxiety, depression, and sense of marginalization had turned him into a different person.

In what appears like a final attempt to save his position as editor in chief at *Rose El Youssef*, Abdel Kouddous wrote one more of his overly deferential editorials for Nasser on 15 March 1965, the only one that he published during a three-year period. It was not enough. When Ahmed Hamrush took over as editor in chief of *Rose El Youssef* on 10 May 1965, Abdel Kouddous felt that it was a much-anticipated "execution." As Abdel Kouddous explained in 1975 during his most direct interview about the scandal, "What they did to me was utter hypocrisy against everything that the revolution sought to achieve. They were able to isolate the revolution from all of its principles and values. Instead, they secretly erected a regime that guaranteed power for them and enabled them to achieve their personal goals.... All of my loyalty will remain tied to the 23 July Revolution as I dreamed of it in the forties. As for what I was seeing then... only the feeling of bitterness, defeat, and tyranny ties me to it. You can call this bitter feeling a shackle!"[93] His removal from *Rose El Youssef* was also the culmination of his regret over his central role in the nationalization of the press. Only later would Abdel Kouddous articulate this fully: "Governmental takeover of the press was more like entering a prison voluntarily and turning a journalist into a government employee because he only wrote what the government wants and that's what pays salary at the start of every month. If the government is angry with him, he'll starve and his kids will go homeless."[94]

Over the span of more than a year following his removal from *Rose El Youssef*, Abdel Kouddous published only two editorials, one of which was redacted without his permission.[95] Exiled from the revolution and the press, Abdel Kouddous left Egypt and embarked on a round-the-world trip that lasted for several months. As he explained in the 1980s, "The centers of power insisted on getting rid of everyone that defied them, to take possession of them and imprison their pen. They were determined to put an end to me.... I was convinced they considered what I was writing as lashes for all of the sins that they were committing in secret under the table of Egyptian politics."[96] During his trip around the world, Abdel Kouddous wrote a number of short stories, all set in foreign locales, an open admission of his distance from Egypt at the time.[97] While traveling, a distraught Abdel Kouddous harkened back to his old days as a journalist for *Rose El Youssef*, looking for revolution wherever he went. As he explained ten years later, hinting that he was still trying to grapple with his role in laying the groundwork for the 1952 revolution, "In each country I went to, I felt as if I was waiting for a popular revolution. A revolution in Thailand, Hong Kong, Japan, and even in Hawaii.... It might have been only a fantasy that my political imagination was pushing me to believe. I don't know why I look for and imagine revolution everywhere."[98] Abdel Kouddous had become even more alienated from and angry at Nasser's regime than he was at the monarchy in the 1940s, transferring his desire for revolution to foreign locales. Of course, he could not admit that he was once again hoping for revolution in Egypt.

Abdel Kouddous's alienation during this period was perhaps captured best by Gamal Kamel. Kamel was an artist who drew most of the illustrations and caricatures for *Rose El Youssef* and *Sabah al-Khayr* during the 1950s and 1960s as well as for most of the first editions of Abdel Kouddous's novels. When Kamel was arrested in the 1958 for suspected communist activities, Abdel Kouddous took the highly unusual step of writing a letter to Nasser directly pleading with him for Kamel's release, a move that was ultimately successful.[99] While almost all of Kamel's paintings—including one of Abdel Kouddous's wife, Lola—are traditional portraits, he painted a portrait of Abdel Kouddous in 1965 that was unique within his body of work. Entitled "The Son of Humanity," Abdel Kouddous appears in the center of the painting crucified, not with nails driven through his hands but with chains wrapping his wrists around the crucifix. The crucifix rises up above a patch of flowers, suggesting that the martyrdom of Abdel Kouddous originated with hopes and optimism. The background surrounding the crucifix is a deep, rich red, alluding to the hell that surrounds Abdel Kouddous during the experience of crucifixion, perhaps gesturing to what Egypt had become. To the left is a shadowy figure with a face blotched out by orange paint, looking at Abdel Kouddous, who is looking off in the other direction. Only by understanding the relationship that I have traced throughout this book—one that close friend and colleague Gamal Kamel no doubt understood himself—does it become clear that this shadowy figure must be Nasser.

In early 1966, against the crisis surrounding the novel, *A Nose and Three Eyes* was finally published as a book. Egyptian authorities refused

**Figure 25.** Ihsan Abdel Kouddous next to Gamal Kamel's 1965 painting "The Son Humanity." Courtesy of the Abdel Kouddous family.

to issue a publishing permit for the novel, so Abdel Kouddous had to publish it in Lebanon. Despite the charges stating that the novel should not be turned into a radio play, film, or television series, all three would eventually be produced. While the state would not issue a permit to publish the novel as a book in Egypt until 1980, it ironically bought the rights in 1968 in order to adapt it into a thirty-part radio series. Directed by Muhammad Elwan, the radio play starred Nadia Lutfi as Amina and Omar Sharif as Hashim. According to Elwan, Omar Sharif, who recorded his role when he was filming *Mayerling* in Austria, refused payment for the role because of his "love for Egypt." Recorded in summer 1968 and broadcast over two months in late 1968 and early 1969, the dramatic radio series is a sultry and largely faithful rendering of the novel, even if elements of the three parts are rearranged.[100] The film adaptation of the novel was announced in the press as early as 25 February 1967, but it would not be filmed and released until after Nasser's death in 1972. Directed by Hussein Kamal, the film starred Mahmoud Yassin as Hashim, Magda as Amina, Nagla Fathi as Nagwa, and an Egyptian Mervet Amine as Rihab. Although the film is unsurprisingly much less audacious than the novel, it ends with a broken Hashim horrified to discover that Amina has become a prostitute, perhaps suggesting metaphorically that Nasser, by the end of his life, had come face to face with the destruction that he had wrought on Egypt. Finally, the novel was adapted into a ten-part series for Egyptian television in 1978, directed by veteran Nour El-Demerdash and starring a young Yousra as Amina. Nearly fifteen years after the crisis had passed, El-Demardash clearly felt total freedom in altering the story, adding a number of carnivalesque plot twists, which Abdel Kouddous must have found truly bizarre.[101]

By 1966, Nasser's health was declining precipitously. Gone was the strong, confident, virile hero of the Arabs. He now had advanced diabetes and he suffered a heart attack that year. Abdel Kouddous's psychological crisis and shattering loss of confidence also escalated in early 1966, leading to his breakup with al-Shaykh. When he finally resumed writing short stories set in Egypt in spring 1966, he unsurprisingly focused on anxiety, depression, and psychological breakdown. "The Defeat," published in *Sabah al-Khayr* on 19 May 1966, continued the themes of prostitution and degradation in *A Nose and Three Eyes*, gesturing not only to Abdel Kouddous's own defeat and collapse but also, inauspiciously, to the coming national humiliation of June 1967. It would be Abdel Kouddous's final fictional work of resistance against Nasser. The story is the form of a letter from an unnamed woman to her former lover, Ahmed, yet another fictional double for Nasser. She has seen him on the street for the first time in fifteen years. He looks as if he has not aged with his strong personality and energetic eyes, "as if they are giving at each moment a military command."[102] As if picking up at the end of Nagwa's narrative in the Second Eye, she explains that she first met Ahmed when she was his student at the university, where he was a "philosophy" professor, a likely gesture to Nasser's *Philosophy of the Revolution*. Her father died years earlier and she lived alone with her mother. Her mother married her off to the first rich man who proposed. Pointing to Faiza's initial encounter with Munir in *The Barred Road*, the narrator describes trying to interact with her husband as an intellectual, but he only wants her as a sexual object. The husband turns their house into a gambling den and wants her "to get drunk, smoke hashish, and become friends with those kinds of women. Even more than that, he wanted me to be easy with his male friends."[103] Like Faiza in *The Barred Road*, the narrator of "The Defeat" clings to her principles and dignity, trying to convince her husband to end his debauchery and let her continue her university studies. Nonetheless, she writes, "I only felt the moments of defeat when he came to me and demanded his right from my body. I gave him a body colder than ice, feeling him degrade me."[104] A symbol of the corrupt and abusive monarchal era before the revolution, the husband exploits the narrator, once again serving as a double for the principled but abused Egyptian nation and Abdel Kouddous.

Laying the groundwork for revolt, she begins to call Ahmed, and they meet secretly, as Abdel Kouddous met with Nasser before the revolution. She resists him physically at first in order to maintain her dignity. She manages to leave her husband, but he refuses to divorce her, leaving her in limbo with no way to support herself. Now two years after she first met Ahmed—the same time gap between when Abdel Kouddous first met Nasser and 23 July 1952—she consummates her love with Ahmed, an act that serves as the symbol of the coup in the story. Echoing Hashim and Amina in the First Eye, Ahmed gives her money, because she has no other source of income: "Bit by bit, my mind drew a picture until it was finished. A picture of a prostitute. Yes, a prostitute. . . . I went to you as an intellectual and the wife of an important businessman. I left your house as a prostitute."[105] Through the female narrator's voice, Abdel Kouddous mourns his pre-revolutionary self, which Nasser has destroyed: "I cried for my intellectual self that I had lost. I cried for my pride and resistance. I cried for my defeat."[106] She refuses to take money like a prostitute and cuts off her relationship with Ahmed without explanation. She confesses in the letter, "I never loved you needing you to pay for me. I loved you needing your intellectualism, manliness, and tenderness. I'll never go to you needing your money.... You were wounding me, insulting me."

Released from the misery of the past but with no protector or support in the new era, she represents Abdel Kouddous abandoned by Nasser. She meets a man, sleeps with him as a betrayal to her absent husband, and then is appalled when he presses money into her palm when she leaves his apartment. When she uses the money for daily subsistence, she cannot escape the feeling that she has become a prostitute. As the same sequence keeps repeating itself, she feels the self-loathing and alienation that Abdel Kouddous wrote about in his letter to Taha Hussein: "I'm an orphan. No family, no money, no husband, no children, no love, no one respecting me and no one whom I respect, not even myself. I started letting out maniacal laughs. I've been defeated. I was defeated a long time ago."[107]

With her capitulation, her husband returns, along with his parties, gambling table, liquor, hashish, and prostitutes: "I participate in all of that.... I live in my defeat and my husband lives in his victory."[108] Metaphorically, the corruption of the old era had therefore returned but it is even worse now in Nasser's era. And the woman, the double for Abdel Kouddous, instead of resisting and clinging to self-respect and intellectualism, like Faiza in *The Barred Road*, has now fully submitted. Defeated, she lives in self-loathing. Nonetheless, she continues to cling to her love for Ahmed—maintaining her image of him and herself from fifteen years earlier—to sustain herself in her defeat: "I loved you as I was, victorious; not as I've become, defeated." The letter ends with her declaring that she is thankful that he did not see her now, pointing not only to her shame, disgrace, and disfigurement since she last saw him but also to the defeat of Egyptian society during the Nasser era, suggesting that it, like Abdel Kouddous, had already become degraded and rotted out well before the defeat of June 1967.

The stories from spring 1966 are not the only works of fiction from this period that point to Abdel Kouddous's despair, isolation, and depression from 1964 to 1966. Hanan al-Shaykh wrote her first novel,

*Suicide of a Dead Man*, in 1966, even though it was not published until 1970.[109] In this novel, al-Shaykh fictionalizes her experiences with Abdel Kouddous, turning the perspective of the Third Eye back on the famous writer. The unnamed male narrator is a famous forty-six-year-old journalist whose wife, whom he married twenty-one years earlier, knows about his affairs and monitors him. As the novel opens, the narrator has an illness that increases his irritation and anxiety. He is introduced to Daniya, al-Shaykh's double in the novel, who asks if she can publish her work in his newspaper. Once they start seeing each other every day, she can tell that he is sick with the look of someone dead in his eyes, pointing to the extent of Abdel Kouddous's anxiety and despair at the time. Like Hashim, the narrator soon becomes obsessed with Daniya. And like Rihab, Daniya is a flighty teenager whose youth undermines the narrator's confidence, making him feel weak and old. He desires her sexually but feels like her father. Sick and trying to suppress his pain, the narrator's experience with Dania leads to his breakdown: "She's the cause of all the confusion. Dania confuses me. The confusion causes me defeat and emptiness."[110] The two travel to Italy together, like Abdel Kouddous and al-Shaykh, and his wife mocks him for running after a child. As Hashim proposes to Rihab in the Third Eye, the narrator asks Daniya to marry him, but she too says no, leading him to sleep with other women and cut himself off from the world, like Hashim after his break from Rihab in the Third Eye. Fully unstable, the narrator now thinks, "Dania let me plunge into the sea and I'm afraid."[111] The novel ends as Daniya tells him that she is dating another man, leading the narrator to succumb to his illness and instability, just like Abdel Kouddous at the time of his split with Hanan al-Shaykh.

By late May 1966, Abdel Kouddous had spent two full years in isolation, anxiety, and crisis, losing his positions at *Rose El Youssef*, his lover Hanan al-Shaykh, and his sense of balance and stability, embodying the role of the crushed heroine of "The Defeat" or the distraught narrator of *Suicide of a Dead Man*. With *A Nose and Three Eyes*, he had launched a dramatic attack against Nasser, finally crossing the line and leading to the end of his years of protection. As punishment, he was not only removed from his professional home but also exiled from public life, cut adrift to face his abandonment, alienation, and breakdown alone. While he had been imprisoned for ninety-five days in 1954 for his editorials attacking Nasser, jail was not enough this time. Exile for two years was a far more severe punishment. Yet just as Nasser released Abdel Kouddous from jail and resuscitated his career in August 1954—presumably with the goal of the country's most popular fiction writer serving as his "translator" for the public—he did so once again in June 1966. With the dark clouds of June 1967 on the horizon, Nasser would suddenly resuscitate his former co-revolutionary Abdel Kouddous, summoning him to return as a major journalist and editor in chief. In this final opportunity to accommodate and please Nasser, Abdel Kouddous would be careful to serve as an unwavering pillar of support for the regime, abandoning fiction entirely as a means of defiance and using his editorials to perform his duties. By performing what was now a full-time role as apologist and "translator," Abdel Kouddous acted out his defeat in public before the nation. By fully repressing his instincts for dissent and resistance, he became, perhaps, the last major piece of Egyptian society to succumb to the decay of Nasser's regime as it approached its ultimate humiliation.

## CONCLUSION

## THE TIME OF DENIAL

> There should be no surprise then that we should cling to our leader after the defeat.... Without him there would be nothing, no men, no intelligence, and no power that could be relied on; the only thing ahead would be ruin.
>
> —*Tawfiq al-Hakim*,
> The Return of Consciousness (1974)

By early June 1966, after two years of alienation, despair, and instability, Ihsan Abdel Kouddous received another unexpected visit from Mohamed Hassanein Heikal. Instead of relaying Nasser's displeasure about something that he wrote—as he did in fall 1958—Heikal unexpectedly told him that Nasser was offering him the position of editor in chief of the well-known weekly *Akhbar al-Yawm* (News of the Day).[1] It was an offer that Abdel Kouddous could not refuse. After two years of intellectual and social exile, Abdel Kouddous had been punished enough. Just as Nasser had done nearly twelve years earlier when he released Abdel Kouddous from jail and gave him a radio program, Nasser decided it was time to resuscitate his former co-revolutionary again and put him in a high-profile position to serve as his "translator" for the public. Abdel Kouddous threw himself into his new post, raising the weekly circulation of *Akhbar al-Yawm* to a stunning 1.3 million, making it the first periodical to surpass the one million mark in the Arab world.[2]

With this new platform, Abdel Kouddous would never challenge Nasser again while the president was alive. Seemingly grateful for the opportunity to return to public life, Abdel Kouddous rushed to resume his bombastic praise of Nasser in his editorials, something he had abandoned since he left for his trip to Europe with Hanan al-Shaykh three years earlier. On 18 June 1966, in his very first issue in charge of *Akhbar al-Yawm*, only a month after he published his most desperate short story, "The Defeat," Abdel Kouddous celebrated the holiday marking the evacuation of the British from Egypt by declaring, "Our revolution is an incredible new reality that moves on Arab lands in depth and force. It will succeed in changing the formation of life."[3] To commemorate the fourteenth anniversary of the revolution on 23 July 1966, Abdel Kouddous focused on Nasser in particular: "The basic element that has guaranteed the continuity of our revolution is the character of Gamal Abdel Nasser, his revolutionary nature that formed his revolutionary feelings, his revolutionary thought, and his ability for revolutionary leadership, this constantly vigilant character, constantly conscious, inexhaustible, never bored or backtracking, this character that, with its ability for revolutionary dissemination, reaches the soul of every individual."[4] On 24 December 1966, Abdel Kouddous wrote to celebrate the "miracle" of the 1956 Suez War. The secret of the victory was, of course, Nasser himself: "Egypt was victorious by Gamal Abdel Nasser, this leadership in which our faith was concentrated, the unity of the nation was manifested. His leadership was a complete expression of the people. It had no personal interests. . . . From this strength—strength of the faith of the people and their unity—Gamal Abdel Nasser extended his genius in achieving victory."[5] Unlike in 1955, when Abdel Kouddous offered criticism of freedom in "Whisper" and depicted the "barred road" of democracy in his fiction, there was not a hint of dissent in these obsequious pieces.

In the days leading up to the June 1967 War, Abdel Kouddous, like other prominent journalist at the time, echoed Nasser's blind confidence and delusions about the coming conflict. As Nasser declared publicly that "we're ready for a total war with Israel" and threatened that "we'll destroy Israel if it begins the aggression," Abdel Kouddous wrote, "We're on the path of victory, not only the victory of armies, but also the victory of the Arab people everywhere."[6] On 3 June 1967, only two days before the start of the war, Abdel Kouddous boasted, "Gamal Abdel Nasser has grabbed Israel by the neck and shaken it violently, confirming his political and military brilliance."[7] Abdel Kouddous then declared, full of belligerence, "We're waiting for the first shot so we can fire the second, third, tenth and the last, which will write victory for us."

Even the total catastrophe of the *naksa*—the "setback," or shattering Arab defeat in only six days of war in June 1967—did not break through his performance of allegiance to the Nasser in his editorials. On 10 June 1967, the first issue of *Akhbar al-Yawm* after the defeat, Abdel Kouddous echoed Nasser's initial excuse that Egypt faced an international plot that caused its loss but still gestured to his earlier image of Nasser as the sun that would never set: "Always, before the darkest days of history, we haven't ever lost the light of hope."[8] In his initial writings after the defeat, Abdel Kouddous suggested, seemingly in delusion, that the fundamental situation in the Middle East had not changed, despite the loss. Palestine simply remained occupied, and all that Israel won from Egypt was land that it could not occupy forever. Moreover, Israel did not win because of Egyptian weakness. Instead, Israel was victorious because it was a base for Western imperialism.

By 8 July 1967, Abdel Kouddous had dug in so deeply that he was denying that Egypt had even suffered a defeat. He argued that Israel and the United States had not achieved their imperial goal of Arab submission and the destruction of the revolution: "And if Israel wasn't victorious, we weren't defeated."[9] Echoing his articles during the 1956 Suez crisis—as well as Nasser's own resignation speech on 9 June 1967—Abdel Kouddous argued that Egypt would have lost the war if and only if Nasser had been removed from power. As Abdel Kouddous explained on 22 July 1967, in his editorial celebrating the anniversary of the ill-fated revolution that he had helped spark, "During these fifteen years, every enemy has failed because the revolution continues and its principles remain. And this latest enemy will fail too because our weapon that we've been victorious with hasn't changed and won't change. Our weapon is our revolution, our principles, our pact: Gamal Abdel Nasser."[10] While Abdel Kouddous had contested Nasser in both his editorials and fiction from fall 1952 through spring 1966, he was now operating in public with the blind embrace that Tawfiq al-Hakim would later claim was the hallmark of the response of Egyptian intellectuals to the *naksa*: "Not one of us in Egypt retreated a bit or even suspected the truth of what [Nasser] set forth before us."[11]

By fall 1967, Abdel Kouddous appeared even more delusional and bellicose. He shifted his framework for grappling with the *naksa*, arguing that the war was simply ongoing. Israel may have won a particular battle in June, but the war was not over. As Abdel Kouddous would argue until 1973, the military solution was the political solution. This meant that Egypt had become a "society of ceasefire" and that Nasser was simply biding his time for the next battle while decisively rebuilding the Egyptian army and society. As Egypt had achieved "miracles" in rapid periods of building in the past, Abdel Kouddous was confident that it would do so again. In this context, Abdel Kouddous framed Nasser as the one who projected strength and confidence, a sharp contrast for a people who had internalized the *naksa* as "a kind of general psychological anxiety."[12] As far as Abdel Kouddous was concerned, the necessary condition for Egyptian victory was that the people needed to return to their past psychological fortitude and stability. If there was a weakness in Egypt, it was the people, not their cherished leader.

His public performances of allegiance to Nasser in the aftermath of the *naksa*—even as his own sons participated in the street protests against the regime in February and March 1968—must have pained Abdel Kouddous tremendously; it surely required him to bury his feelings of horror about the implications of the defeat. While the warning signs of the crumbling of the regime seem to have been clear to him as early as when he was writing *A Nose and Three Eyes*, it must have still been traumatic to see the impotence of the Egyptian army in the war and the shocking failure of the leader whom he felt he had inadvertently brought to power. Years later, Abdel Kouddous claimed in interviews that he wrote only days before 5 June 1967 that people would have had to have been naïve to believe the leaders' rhetoric about victory and that, soon after the *naksa*, he wrote that it was necessary to find those responsible for the catastrophe and hold them accountable.[13] Instead, the record shows that it would take nearly five years, well after Nasser's death, before Abdel Kouddous would feel able to express in writing his first criticism of what happened. On 1 April 1972, with old friend Anwar Sadat firmly in place as president, Abdel Kouddous published an editorial in which he claimed that Egypt was now an occupied country as a result of the defeat. Nonetheless, he argued the *naksa* was not simply a loss of land: "It's a defeat of the 1952 Revolution and the system that Gamal Abdel Nasser erected. It's a defeat for the socialist society. More serious than that, it's a defeat for the Egyptian generation that assumed power after the 1952 Revolution."[14] This article would inaugurate for Abdel Kouddous a hesitant process of opening up to the public through interviews and articles about his past with Nasser and his traumatic feelings about the pivotal role that he felt that he had played in sparking revolution and embedding dictatorship Egypt. It was only in 1975 that he finally admitted openly how he felt when he first heard the news of the 1967 defeat: "I was stunned.... I was struck that day by complete stupor that paralyzed my ability even to cry.... I was fleeing from a reality whose failure the terrible truth had proven.... I was one of the writers who had been deceived just as the entire Egyptian people had been deceived."[15] Despite confessions like this, Abdel Kouddous never acknowledged his own denial of the implications of the *naksa* in the press at the time.

In the months and years immediately following the shattering June 1967 loss, Abdel Kouddous expressed his horror in what he had not been writing—fiction. He began planning a new novel in early 1967, but he abandoned it as soon as the *naksa* happened.[16] He wrote three short stories in fall 1967, all published in *Akhbar al-Yawm*, but then stopped writing fiction entirely for over five years, his longest hiatus by far. As he suggested in his 1966 letter to Taha Hussein, he could not write fiction if he felt that he had no freedom. That he stopped writing fiction almost entirely—and for such a long time—spoke volumes. With no freedom of expression, he simply stopped writing fiction. As usual, Nasser, his longtime devoted reader, understood the message. In the final year of Nasser's life, Sadat came to Abdel Kouddous with yet another message of displeasure from the president. This time, Nasser wanted to know why he had stopped writing fiction and asked him to write a new novel.[17] Abdel Kouddous was shocked at the request, perhaps reading it as yet another attempt to micromanage and humiliate him. He responded that Nasser would read his next novel whenever he was able to write it.

Nasser never did. On 27 September 1970, Nasser convened an emergency Arab League summit to ease tensions in the aftermath of Black September. When King Hussein and Yasser Arafat continued bickering despite mediation, Nasser ironically yelled at them to "call a psychiatrist."[18] Clearly, Nasser understood that he was unable to serve as an effective analyst for them. After the summit ended the following day,

Nasser suffered a heart attack and died at only fifty-two years old. In his article to mark Nasser's death, Abdel Kouddous could not grasp what had happened. Like Nawal after Ibrahim's death in *There's a Man in Our House*, Abdel Kouddous remained unable to face and accept Nasser's demise. He wrote in denial, "Nasser hasn't left. He's not simply a human being, or a leader of a revolution, or a leader of the people, or a president of a republic. He's something else. He's a message, a creed, principles, faith, life.... All that lives on inside us, in our minds, hearts, and actions. He forged all of the components of the Egyptian character."[19] Abdel Kouddous was even more emotional and direct in an undated note that I found in his personal papers and was published posthumously in 2001. It reads, "Even though I knew the details of Nasser's illness and how serious it was, I never expected him to die. His passing was a violent shock for me that I could never comprehend maybe because Nasser had become a continuing reality that couldn't change no matter what.... I could never comprehend the incredible emptiness that his death would leave behind. It never occurred to me that I'd be forced to bear the responsibility of this emptiness."[20]

It should come as no surprise that Abdel Kouddous faced Nasser's death with a mixture of grief and denial. Nasser had indeed become an omnipresent reality for Abdel Kouddous, someone who intervened in seemingly all aspects of his existence, leading Abdel Kouddous to internalize Nasser in his political writing, fiction, and personal life. Just as Abdel Kouddous had blurred the lines between himself and Nasser in his fiction, it was as if part of him, his double, had died. Unsurprisingly, Nasser's death was no liberation but a burden that he would have to bear. Abdel Kouddous did begin to speak in detail about his relationship with Nasser in interviews in 1974, but he was clearly uncomfortable doing so, in stark contrast to the vitriol of someone like Tawfiq al-Hakim at the time. In these initial interviews, Abdel Kouddous commonly did not identify Nasser by name but instead referred to him as "my friend" or "the very important official." And many of the details of these first interviews—his mother's visit to his jail cell in 1954 or Nasser pushing him to be his translator—he never repeated again, despite discussing the episodes in many subsequent interviews.

Abdel Kouddous did air criticisms of the Nasser era in the late 1970s, but even nearly ten years after Nasser's death, he still could not bring himself to do so openly. Instead, he wrote a series of dialogues between a pessimistic and world-weary "old man," a thinly veiled double for himself, and an ill-informed but enthusiastic young man. The series was titled "On the Political Street" and was later published in three volumes. In this series, the old man levels a few stinging rebukes of the revolution, arguing that it did not achieve any of its goals. Moreover, he argues, the only thing that the revolution achieved was its continuity, thanks to the postponement of democracy and the embrace of military dictatorship: "It has even been said that Egyptian society is built on a military class ruling a civilian class."[21] This kind of criticism, however, was never aired openly and directly in any of his interviews.

After Nasser's death, Abdel Kouddous continued writing editorials and Sadat subsequently appointed him as chairman of *al-Ahram*, Egypt's daily newspaper of record. He finally resumed writing fiction in the mid-1970s, much of which grappled with the *infitah*—or economic opening—of the Sadat era. He remained close personal friends with Sadat after he became president of Egypt, with Sadat attending the wedding of each of his sons. Abdel Kouddous claimed on several occasions that Sadat offered him the opportunity to become minister of culture, but he refused. Nonetheless, they spoke weekly, with Sadat asking his opinion on political matters. Abdel Kouddous later claimed that he turned down Sadat's request to write his memoirs and speeches. Their friendship faded once when Sadat began the peace process with Israel, a move that Abdel Kouddous strongly opposed. It seems that Abdel Kouddous was once again unable to guide a president, leading to his distance once again from the inner circle of power.

### HISTORY REPEATS HISTORY

**Our bodies are never safe from the people who rule this place. Not in life, not even in death.**
—*Sharif Abdel Kouddous*,
**City Limits of the Dead (2020)**

Ihsan Abdel Kouddous died on 11 January 1990. His striking tombstone, made of white granite with black etched letters, gestures to rectifying his erasure by Nasser. It reads in part, "Ihsan Abdel Kouddous faced assassination and jail numerous times because of his political writings, especially about the case of the Rotten Weapons that were used in the Palestine War. These writings had a big influence on preparing public opinion for the 23 July 1952 Revolution." Despite his continued prominence during the Sadat era as well as his many interviews during the 1970s and 1980s, Abdel Kouddous never received public recognition for what he saw as his critical role in sparking the revolution. His repeated hints during his post-Nasser interviews and articles that his fiction served as political allegory and metaphor during the 1950s and 1960s also never spurred researchers to explore his archive and look beyond the veneer of romantic melodrama in his fiction. In this, his tombstone continues to point to the validation that he clearly desired for his political role in making modern Egypt.

Shockingly, on 18 July 2020, Ihsan Abdel Kouddous faced one more humiliation, this time by the current military president of Egypt, Abdel Fattah El-Sisi. On that day, under the watchful eye of the police, the Abdel Kouddous family mausoleum was callously bulldozed to make way for a new overpass in Cairo. The state informed the family only days before, giving them little time to move the remains of not only Ihsan Abdel Kouddous but also his wife, Lola, and father, Mohammed. Sharif Abdel Kouddous, Ihsan's grandson and an award-winning journalist and documentary filmmaker, described with horror and outrage as he watched the remains of his grandparents and great grandfather exhumed and exposed to the sun.[22] He asked, "How can all this be happening around us without our consent?" In the face of this callous humiliation, Ihsan Abdel Kouddous would have been immensely proud of how his grandson continued his tradition of defying the military ruler, despite the very real threat of harm for doing so. At the end of his courageous article, Sharif Abdel Kouddous even acknowledges, "I am afraid to tell [my father] my worst fears. That eventually I may have to leave, by choice or by force."

This tragic scene provides yet another marker for the complexity of the entrenchment of military dictatorship in Egypt. Ihsan Abdel Kouddous, to his horror, believed that he was an unwitting partner in bringing a dictator to power and embedding him in rule. It was this military regime that pushed him into the seemingly endless pendulum swing between appeasement and defiance, fueling the production of his massive oeuvre of novels, short stories, editorials, and commentaries written on a weekly basis for decades. It is this oeuvre that was not only so beloved by the broad Arab public but also recorded in real time the complexities of the evolving relationship between one of the most important intellectuals of the Nasser era and the state. It was his oscillating relationship with the military ruler, with all of its complexity and nuance, hopes, and despair, that tragically helped produce the current Egyptian political regime that could do something as callous as bulldoze his grave with impunity. Yet thanks to the tireless efforts of the family, the Abdel Kouddous mausoleum was quickly rebuilt, a burial site even more beautiful than the first, a monument for both the present—continuing the family tradition of courageously defying the ruler in the face of intolerable humiliation—and the future, which many hope will finally bring the democratic rule of law that Ihsan Abdel Kouddous dreamed of for so long.

# NOTES

**Introduction**

1. Ihsan 'Abd al-Quddus, "95 Yawman fi al-Sijn," *Ruz al-Yusuf*, 6 September 1954.

2. Muhammad al-Shinnawi, *Ihsan 'Abd al-Quddus bayna al-Adab wa-l-Siyasa* (Cairo: Manshurat Battana, 2019), 552.

3. Ibid., 554.

4. Ibid.

5. Ibid., 555.

6. On Nasser's messianism, see Yoav Di-Capua, "Revolutionary Decolonization and the Formation of the Sacred: The Case of Egypt," *Past and Present* 256, no. 1 (2022).

7. Nasser has been the subject of a massive secondary literature. On his rise to power, see Joel Gordon, *Nasser's Blessed Movement: Egypt's Free Officers and the July Revolution*, new paperback edition (Cairo and New York: The American University in Cairo Press, 2016). Recent important books include Laura Bier, *Revolutionary Womanhood: Feminisms, Modernity, and the State in Nasser's Egypt* (Stanford: Stanford University Press, 2011); Sharif Yunis, *Nida' al-Sha'ab: Tarikh Naqdi li-l-Idiyulujiyya al-Nasiriyya* (Cairo: Dar al-Shuruq, 2012); Omar Khalifah, *Nasser in the Egyptian Imaginary* (Edinburgh: Edinburgh University Press, 2017); Fawaz A. Gerges, *Making the Arab World: Nasser, Qutb, and the Clash That Shaped the Middle East* (Princeton and Oxford: Princeton University Press, 2018); Alex Rowell, *We Are Your Soldiers: How Gamal Abdel Nasser Remade the Arab World* (New York: W.W. Norton & Company, 2024).

8. Saïd K. Aburish, *Nasser: The Last Arab* (New York: St. Martin's Press, 2004), 28.

9. Ahmed Abul-Fath, *L'Affaire Nasser* (Paris: Plon, 1962), 92.

10. Gerges, *Making the Arab World*, 89ff.

11. Israel Gershoni, "An Intellectual Source for the Revolution: Tawfiq al-Hakim's Influence on Nasser and His Generation," in *Egypt from Monarchy to Republic: A Reassment of Revolution and Change*, ed. Shimon Shamir (Boulder, CO: Westview Press, 1995).

12. Tawfiq al-Hakim, *The Return of Consciousness*, trans. Bayly Winder (New York and London: New York University Press, 1985), 61.

13. Ibid., 19.

14. Ibid.

15. Miles Copeland, *The Game of Nations: The Amorality of Power Politics* (New York: Simon and Schuster, 1969), 62.

16. Laura M. James, *Nasser at War: Arab Images of the Enemy* (New York: Palgrave Macmillan, 2006), 3.

17. Khaled Mohi El Din, *Memories of a Revolution: Egypt 1952*, trans. TRIACC Translation Services (Cairo: American University in Cairo Press, 1995), 127.

18. Joel Gordon, *Revolutionary Melodrama: Popular Film and Civic Identity in Nasser's Egypt*, Chicago Studies on the Middle East (Chicago: Middle East Documentation Center, 2002), 137.

19. Abdel Kouddous's magnum opus, *The Sun Never Sets*, was adapted into a thirty-part television series for Ramadan in 2017. His classic 1963–64 novel *A Nose and Three Eyes* was also adapted into a new film in 2023.

20. Ihsan Abdel Kouddous, *I Do Not Sleep*, trans. Jonathan Smolin (Cairo and New York: Hoopoe, 2021). An English translation of Abdel Kouddous's *I'm Free* appeared in Egypt in 1978 and has been long out of print. See Ihsan 'Abd al-Quddus, *I Am Free, and Other Stories*, trans. Trevor Le Gassick (Cairo: General Egyptian Book Organization, 1978).

21. Ihsan Abd al-Quddus and Mahmud Murad, *I'tirafat Ihsan 'Abd al-Quddus: al-Hurriya, al-Jins* (Cairo: al-'Arabi li-l-Nashr wa-l-Tawzi', 1980), 91.

22. Ihsan 'Abd al-Quddus, *Ayyam Shababi* (Cairo: al-Maktab al-Misri al-Hadith, 1980), 10.

23. Amira Abu al-Futuh, "Mishwar Ihsan 'Abd al-Quddus: 1," *al-Siyasa*, 19 July 1980.

24. Ihsan 'Abd al-Quddus, "Lughat Bini Hamir," *Akhir Sa'a*, 26 September 1943.

25. On the *nahda*, see Tarek El-Ariss, ed., *The Arab Renaissance: A Bilingual Anthology of the Nahda* (New York: Modern Language Association of America, 2018).

26. Ahmad 'Abd al-Mu'ti Hijazi, "Ba'd Sab'at Shuhur min al-Samt Ihsan Yatakallam (1)," *Ruz al-Yusuf*, 28 October 1968. This is one of the few interviews that take Abdel Kouddous's fiction seriously as works of literature.

27. Amira Abu al-Futuh, *Ihsan 'Abd al-Quddus Yatadhakkar* (Cairo: al-Hay'a al-Misriyya al-'Amma li-l-Kitab, 1982).

28. Ihsan ʿAbd al-Quddus, "Katib al-Qissa," *Ruz al-Yusuf*, 20 December 1954. This was confirmed by Abdel Kouddous's wife and son as well. See Muhammad ʿAbd al-Quddus, *Hikayat Ihsan ʿAbd al-Quddus* (Cairo: al-Hay'a al-ʿAmma li-l-Kitab, 2011), 44–49; Niʿam al-Baz, "Awraq Khassa wa-Hamma min Sanawat Ihsan ʿAbd al-Quddus: al-Majmuʿ al-Thalith," *Akhir Saʿa*, 2 March 1983.

29. Jonathan Smolin, *Moroccan Noir: Police, Crime, and Politics in Popular Culture* (Bloomington: Indiana University Press, 2013).

30. This should not come as a surprise. According to P. J. Vatikiotis, "Nasser conducted his state business face to face and largely by word of mouth." See Vatikiotis, *Nasser and His Generation* (New York: St. Martin's Press, 1978), 315.

31. Al-Hakim, *Return of Consciousness*, 27.

32. Anwar El-Sadat, *In Search of Identity: An Autobiography* (New York: Harper Colophon Books, 1977), 210.

33. Abdel Kouddous, *I Do Not Sleep*.

34. Ihsan Abdel Kouddous, "'Girl Three,' Translated by Raphael Cohen," *Banipal*, no. 71 (2021).

35. Ihsan Abdel Kouddous, *A Nose and Three Eyes*, trans. Jonathan Smolin, foreword by Hanan al-Shaykh (Cairo and New York: Hoopoe, 2024).

36. The model of *iltizam* has also come under reconsideration recently in the work of Benjamin Koerber. See Koerber, *Conspiracy in Modern Egyptian Literature* (Edinburgh: Edinburgh University Press, 2018).

37. Huda Jamal ʿAbd al-Nasir, ed. *Jamal ʿAbd al-Nasir Taliban wa-Zabitan*, vol. 1, Jamal ʿAbd al-Nasir: al-Awraq al-Khassa (Cairo: al-Hay'a al-ʿMisriyya al-ʿAmma li-l-Kitab, 2015), 53ff.

38. Margaret Litvin, *Hamlet's Arab Journey* (Princeton and Oxford: Princeton University Press, 2011), 40.

39. Omnia El Shakry, *The Arabic Freud: Psychoanalysis and Islam in Modern Egypt* (Princeton and Oxford: Princeton University Press, 2017).

40. Abdel Kouddous discussed this many times in interviews. See, for example, al-Shinnawi, *Ihsan ʿAbd al-Quddus bayna al-Adab wa-l-Siyasa*, 602.

41. Rami Ghinat, *Egypt's Incomplete Revolution: Lutfi al-Khuli and Nasser's Socialism in the 1960s* (Portland, OR: Frank Cass, 1997).

42. For other examples, see Mark Lilla, *The Reckless Mind: Intellectuals in Politics* (New York: New York Review of Books, 2001).

43. Lynn Hunt, *The Family Romance of the French Revolution* (Berkeley: University of California Press, 1992).

44. See Bier, *Revolutionary Womanhood*.

45. Vatikiotis, *Nasser and His Generation*, 306.

46. Abul-Fath, *L'Affaire Nasser*, 222ff.

47. John Waterbury, *Egypt: Burdens of the Past/Options for the Future* (Bloomington: Indiana University Press in Association with the American Universities Field Staff, 1978), 235ff.

48. Gershoni, "Intellectual Source for the Revolution," 233.

49. Fredric Jameson, *The Political Unconscious: Narrative as a Socially Symbolic Act* (Ithaca, NY: Cornell University Press, 1981).

## Chapter 1

1. Abdel Kouddous did not discuss the attack publicly until two years later. See Ihsan 'Abd al-Quddus, "Man Alladhi I'tada 'ala Ra'is al-Tahrir?," *Ruz al-Yusuf*, 9 November 1953.

2. Ibrahim 'Abd al-'Aziz, *Ihsan 'Abd al-Quddus: Sira Ukhra* (Cairo: Manshurat Battana, 2019), 171.

3. Raphael Cormack, *Midnight in Cairo: The Divas of Egypt's Roaring '20s* (New York: W.W. Norton and Company, 2021), 127ff.

4. Ibid., 28. Abdel Kouddous himself would later mention that the one time he saw his mother perform on the stage, he felt so ashamed that he lowered his head to avoid watching her. See 'Abd al-'Aziz, *Ihsan 'Abd al-Quddus: Sira Ukhra*, 147.

5. "Autograph," Egyptian state television program, audio recording, 1976. I would like to thank the Abdel Kouddous family for access to this recording.

6. On the magazine, see Fatima al-Yusuf, *Dhikriyat* (Cairo: Mu'assasat Ruz al-Yusuf, 2010).

7. Magda al-Jindi, "al-Hurriyya Khuliqat min Ruz al-Yusuf," *Sabah al-Khayr*, 5 January 1989, 20; Ni'am al-Baz, "Awraq Khassa wa-Hamma min Mudhakkirat Ihsan 'Abd al-Quddus," *Akhir Sa'a*, 9 March 1983, 22.

8. Nadiya Khalifa, "Ihsan 'Abd al-Quddus: al-Tha'ir, al-Sahafi, wa-l-Rawa'i," *Sabah al-Khayr*, 10 September 1987, 21.

9. al-Baz, "Awraq Khassa wa-Hamma min Mudhakkirat Ihsan 'Abd al-Quddus," 22.

10. Suna [Ihsan Abdel Kouddous], "al-Khulasa al-Wafiyya fi al-Tabaqa al-Raqiyya wa-Ghayr al-Raqiyya," *Ruz al-Yusuf*, 19 August 1936.

11. Ihsan 'Abd al-Quddus, "al-I'tiraf al-Akhir," *Ruz al-Yusuf*, 18 April 1938.

12. "Khatwa Muwaffaqa wa-Lakinnaha nahwa al-Mawt al-Zu'am," *Ruz al-Yusuf*, 2 September 1936.

13. Suna [Ihsan Abdel Kouddous], "Thalathat Ayyam ma'a al-Wafd," *Ruz al-Yusuf*, 1 October 1939, 39.

14. Ihsan 'Abd al-Quddus, "Haddathani Wazir Sabiq," *Ruz al-Yusuf*, 15 August 1941. Presumably, this was Ali Maher, who was prime minister in 1936 and would return twice to the office in 1952, with Abdel Kouddous's strong support.

15. 'Abd al-'Aziz, *Ihsan 'Abd al-Quddus: Sira Ukhra*, 147.

16. Ibid., 148.

17. El-Tabii was more than just a professional mentor to Abdel Kouddous. When Abdel Kouddous and Lola eloped, the marriage ceremony took place at El-Tabii's house.

18. Ihsan 'Abd al-Quddus, "Hawaltu an Akun Jarsun," *Akhir Sa'a*, 13 December 1942.

19. Hilmi al-Namnam, "Rasa'il Ihsan 'Abd al-Quddus al-Majhula: 8," *al-Musawwir*, 20 April 2001, 51.

20. Ihsan 'Abd al-Quddus, "Nahnu," *Ruz al-Yusuf*, 23 March 1944.

21. Ihsan 'Abd al-Quddus, "Man fikum al-Za'im?," *Ruz al-Yusuf*, 10 August 1944.

22. Ihsan 'Abd al-Quddus, "al-Za'im al-Muntazar," *Ruz al-Yusuf*, 18 January 1945.

23. Ihsan 'Abd al-Quddus, "Zu'ama' " *Ruz al-Yusuf*, 29 March 1945.

24. Muhammad al-Shinnawi, *Ihsan 'Abd al-Quddus bayna al-Adab wa-l-Siyasa* (Cairo: Manshurat Battana, 2019), 154.

25. Ihsan 'Abd al-Quddus, "al-'Ummal," *Ruz al-Yusuf*, 11 January 1945.

26. Jamil al-Bajuri, "Nazra Ba'ida: Ihsan 'Abd al-Quddus," *al-Kawakib*, 8 August 1961, 36.

27. Ihsan 'Abd al-Quddus, "al-Rajul Alladhi Yajib an Yadhhab!," *Ruz al-Yusuf*, 9 August 1945.

28. Ihsan 'Abd al-Quddus, "96 Sa'a ma'a al-Hurriyyat al-Arba'a," *Ruz al-Yusuf*, 23 August 1945.

29. Fatima al-Yusuf, "Ila Waladi al-Sajin," *Ruz al-Yusuf*, 16 August 1945.

30. al-Baz, "Awraq Khassa wa-Hamma min Mudhakkirat Ihsan 'Abd al-Quddus," 22.

31. Fatima al-Yusuf, "'Ishrun 'Amman fi al-Intizar," *Ruz al-Yusuf*, 24 October 1945.

32. Amira Abu al-Futuh, *Ihsan 'Abd al-Quddus Yatadhakkar* (Cairo: al-Hay'a al-Misriyya al-'Amma li-l-Kitab, 1982), 79.

33. Amira Abu al-Futuh, "Mishwar Ihsan 'Abd al-Quddus: 4," *al-Siyasa*, 22 July 1980.

34. Abu al-Futuh, *Ihsan 'Abd al-Quddus Yatadhakkar*: 85.

35. Ihsan 'Abd al-Quddus, "al-Rajul Alladhi Yatba'uhu Nisf Milyun," *Ruz al-Yusuf*, 5 September 1945.

36. Ihsan 'Abd al-Quddus, "Hatta La Takun Farda Hadha'!," *al-Ahram*, 23 August 1974, 4.

37. Ihsan 'Abd al-Quddus, "Laysa fina Damm!," *Ruz al-Yusuf*, 2 October 1946.

38. Frantz Fanon, *The Wretched of the Earth*, trans. Constance Farrington (New York: Grove Press, 1968), 86.

39. Ihsan 'Abd al-Quddus, "Harb al-'Isabat," *Ruz al-Yusuf*, 23 July 1947.

40. Ihsan 'Abd al-Quddus, "al-Jihad Fann!," *Ruz al-Yusuf*, 28 August 1947.

41. "Masra' Amin 'Uthman Basha," *al-Ahram*, 6 January 1946; "Hadith Amin 'Uthman," *Ruz al-Yusuf*, 10 January 1946.

42. Al-Shinnawi, *Ihsan 'Abd al-Quddus bayna al-Adab wa-l-Siyasa*, 162.

43. Anwar El-Sadat, *In Search of Identity: An Autobiography* (New York: Harper Colophon Books, 1977), 59.

44. "Li-madha Uhibb al-Ingliz?," *Akhir Sa'a*, 30 May 1943.

45. Ihsan 'Abd al-Quddus, "Lughat Bini Hamir," *Akhir Sa'a*, 26 September 1943.

46. "Baqiyat Hadith ma'a Su'adat Amin 'Uthman Basha," *Ruz al-Yusuf*, 16 November 1944.

47. "Hal Kana Amin 'Uthman Kha'inan?," *Ruz al-Yusuf*, 24 January 1946.

48. "Al-Muttaham bi-Qatl Amin 'Uthman Yatahaddath," *Ruz al-Yusuf*, 5 November 1947.

49. "Al-Muttaham bi-Qatl Amin 'Uthman . . . Hal Huwwa Majnun?," *Ruz al-Yusuf*, 4 February 1948, 33.

50. Ihsan 'Abd al-Quddus, "Muhakamat al-Hay'a al-Tanfidhiyya," *Ruz al-Yusuf*, 10 December 1947, 3.

51. Ibid., 5.

52. "Hadith Harab Husayn Tawfiq," *al-Ahram*, 11 June 1948.

53. "Hariba Husayn Tawfiq min al-Dabit al-Haris," *al-Ahram*, 10 June 1948. Incredibly, Tawfik boasted months earlier that he "will escape from jail when he wants to." See "Al-Muttaham bi-Qatl Amin 'Uthman . . . Hal Huwwa Majnun?," 33.

54. Husayn Tawfiq, "Khitab min Husayn Tawfiq ila Ra'is al-Tahrir," *Ruz al-Yusuf*, 16 June 1948, 5.

55. "Hal al-Gharad min Kitaba al-Tadlil?," *al-Ahram*, 15 June 1948.

56. "Walidat al-Dabit al-Mu'taqal Tunashiduhu al-Zuhur," *al-Ahram*, 18 June 1948.

57. Ihsan 'Abd al-Quddus, "Da'uhu Yadhhab," *Ruz al-Yusuf*, 16 June 1948.

58. Isma'il al-Habruk, "Rasa'il min Husayn Tawfiq," *Ruz al-Yusuf*, 30 June 1948; Ihsan 'Abd al-Quddus, "Li-madha?," *Ruz al-Yusuf*, 21 June 1948.

59. 'Abd al-Quddus, "Li-madha?"

60. "al-Qissa al-Haqiqiyya li-Harb Husayn Tawfiq," *al-Misri*, 8 February 1953.

61. Ihsan 'Abd al-Quddus, "Min Sujun Suriya," *Ruz al-Yusuf*, 9 July 1956.

62. al-Shinnawi, *Ihsan 'Abd al-Quddus bayna al-Adab wa-l-Siyasa*, 117–18.

63. Abu al-Futuh, *Ihsan 'Abd al-Quddus Yatadhakkar*, 92.

64. Ihsan 'Abd al-Quddus, "al-Jil al-Jadid," *Ruz al-Yusuf*, 20 October 1948.

65. Ihsan 'Abd al-Quddus, "Muhakamat Mujrimi Harb Filistin!," *Ruz al-Yusuf*, 20 July 1949.

66. Ihsan 'Abd al-Quddus, "Mar'at Misr," *Ruz al-Yusuf*, 17 November 1948.

67. Ihsan 'Abd al-Quddus, "al-Jaysh wa-l-Siyasa," *Ruz al-Yusuf*, 6 April 1949.

68. Ihsan 'Abd al-Quddus, "Man Huwwa al-Dabit Alladhi Yamlik Qasran fi Jazirat Kabri?," *Ruz al-Yusuf*, 6 June 1950.

69. Fawaz A. Gerges, *Making the Arab World: Nasser, Qutb, and the Clash That Shaped the Middle East* (Princeton and Oxford: Princeton University Press, 2018), 170.

70. Gamal Abdel Nasser and David Wynne-Morgan, "My Revolutinary Life: President Nasser's Own Story: 1: How We Overthrew Farouk," *The Sunday Times*, 17 June 1962, 26.

71. Khaled Mohi El Din, *Memories of a Revolution: Egypt 1952*, trans. TRIACC Translation Services (Cairo: American University in Cairo Press, 1995), 41.

72. Mohammed Neguib, *Egypt's Destiny* (London: Victor Gollancz, 1955), 17.

73. P. J. Vatikiotis, *Nasser and His Generation* (New York: St. Martin's Press, 1978), 42.

74. Ihsan 'Abd al-Quddus, "Muhakamat Mujrimi Harb Filistin," *Ruz al-Yusuf*, 13 June 1950.

75. It was Halim who was so furious at being named that he hired someone to kill Abdel Kouddous as he was leaving the Immobilia. The man confessed to the attack only after the revolution, and no charges were brought. Abu al-Futuh, *Ihsan 'Abd al-Quddus Yatadhakkar*, 110-11.

76. 'Abd al-'Aziz, *Ihsan 'Abd al-Quddus: Sira Ukhra*, 41.

77. al-Shinnawi, *Ihsan 'Abd al-Quddus bayna al-Adab wa-l-Siyasa*, 202-3.

78. Ihsan 'Abd al-Quddus, "3: Muhakamat Mujrimi Harb Filistin," *Ruz al-Yusuf*, 20 June 1950.

79. Ihsan 'Abd al-Quddus, "4: Muhakamat Mujrimi Harb Filistin," *Ruz al-Yusuf*, 27 June 1950.

80. Ihsan 'Abd al-Quddus, "1—Inni Utalib bi-l-Tahqiq ma'a al-Fariq Muhammad Haydar Basha," *Ruz al-Yusuf*, 24 October 1950.

81. Amal al-Umdah, "Kunuz Amal al-Umdah," *Ruz al-Yusuf*, 15 January 2022, 82.

82. Din, *Memories of a Revolution*, 48.

83. Huda Jamal 'Abd al-Nasir, ed. *Jamal 'Abd al-Nasir Taliban wa-Zabitan*, vol. 1, Jamal 'Abd al-Nasir: al-Awraq al-Khassa (Cairo: al-Hay'a al-'Misriyya al-'Amma li-l-Kitab, 2015), 410.

84. Ihsan 'Abd al-Quddus, "1—Kayfa Ushrif Tahqiqat al-Jaysh amam al-Niyaba?," *Ruz al-Yusuf*, 9 January 1951, 4.

85. Premier Gamal Abdul Nasser, *Egypt's Liberation: The Philosophy of the Revolution*, trans. Dorothy Thompson (Washington, DC: Public Affairs Press, 1955), 52.

86. Muhammad Fawzi, *Ihsan 'Abd al-Quddus bayna al-Ightiyal al-Siyasi wa-l-Shaghb al-Jinsi* (Cairo: Maktabat Madbuli, 1988), 60.

87. 'Abd al-'Aziz, *Ihsan 'Abd al-Quddus*, 41.

88. For example, see 'Abd al-Mun'im al-Dusuqqi al-Jami'i, *al-Asliha al-Fasida wa-Dawruha fi Harb Filistin 1948*, Tarikh al-Misriyin (Cairo: al-Hay'a al-'Amma li-l-Kitab, 1990).

89. Abu al-Futuh, *Ihsan 'Abd al-Quddus Yatadhakkar*, 97.

90. Courtesy of the family of Ihsan Abdel Kouddous.

91. Tawfiq al-Hakim, *Return of the Spirit*, trans. William Maynard Hutchins and Russel Harris (New York: Penguin Classics, 2019), 187.

92. Israel Gershoni, "An Intellectual Source for the Revolution: Tawfiq al-Hakim's Influence on Nasser and His Generation," in *Egypt from Monarchy to Republic: A Reassment of Revolution and Change*, ed. Shimon Shamir (Boulder, CO: Westview Press, 1995), 230.

93. al-Nasir, *Jamal 'Abd al-Nasir Taliban wa-Zabitan*, 64.

94. Gershoni, "Intellectual Source for the Revolution," 220–21.

95. Ihsan 'Abd al-Quddus, "Man Huwwa al-Za'im al-Muntazir?," *Ruz al-Yusuf*, 5 September 1950.

96. Ihsan 'Abd al-Quddus, "Man Huwwa "Rabb al-Qanun" fi Misr?," *Ruz al-Yusuf*, 19 September 1950.

97. Al-Shinnawi, *Ihsan 'Abd al-Quddus bayna al-Adab wa-l-Siyasa*, 158.

98. Ihsan 'Abd al-Quddus, "Dawlat al-Fashal," *Ruz al-Yusuf*, 8 July 1951.

99. Ahmad Husayn, *Qadiyat al-Tahrid 'ala Harq Madinat al-Qahira wa-Muqaddimat Thawrat 23 Yuliyu 1952: Maqalat, Taqarir, Ittiham, Ahkam* (Cairo: al-Matba'at al-'Alimiyah, 1957).

100. Ihsan 'Abd al-Quddus, "Riyad wa-'Abd Allah . . . Hal Yakuna Akhir al-Dahaya?," *Ruz al-Yusuf*, 24 July 1951.

101. Al-Shinnawi, *Ihsan 'Abd al-Quddus bayna al-Adab wa-l-Siyasa*, 307–8.

102. Ihsan 'Abd al-Quddus, "Ayna al-Qumsan al-Zurq, ya Shabab al-Wafd?," *Ruz al-Yusuf*, 6 November 1951.

103. Ihsan 'Abd al-Quddus, "Qatarat al-Damm fi Finjin al-Shay," *Ruz al-Yusuf*, 25 December 1951.

104. Ihsan 'Abd al-Quddus, "al-Rajul al-Wahid Alladhi Yajib an Yu'min bi-Bara'at al-Sha'b!," *Ruz al-Yusuf*, 4 February 1952.

105. Ihsan 'Abd al-Quddus, "Inna Misr fi Haja ila Diktatur. Fa-hal Huwwa 'Ali Mahir?," *Ruz al-Yusuf*, 11 February 1952.

## Chapter 2

1. The audio is on YouTube: https://www.youtube.com/watch?v=ELtS2TLYIJM. Accessed 15 January 2024.

2. Ihsan 'Abd al-Quddus, "Li-madha Rafada Muhammad Najib Ta'lif Wizara 'Askariyya?," *Ruz al-Yusuf*, 2 September 1952. Abdel Kouddous named Nasser as the one who called him only much later. See 'Abd al-Rahman Abu 'Awf, *Ihsan 'Abd al-Quddus bayna al-Sihafa wa-l-Riwaya* (Cairo: al-Majlis al-A'la li-l-Thaqafa, 2006), 16.

3. 'Abd al-Quddus, "Li-madha Rafada Muhammad Najib Ta'lif Wizara 'Askariyya?"

4. Ahmed Abdel Kouddous, Ihsan's son, explained to me that his cousin was in the room when Ihsan made the call and overheard the conversation. Personal communication, 27 March 2019. In Nasser's first publication in the press printed under his name, he cryptically wrote that a "well-known nationalist

journalist" warned the Officers of the impending arrest. See Jamal 'Abd al-Nasir, "Kayfa Dabbarna Hadha al-Inqilab?," *al-Tahrir*, 15 October 1952.

5. Ahmed Abul-Fath, *L'Affaire Nasser* (Paris: Plon, 1962), 19; Tharwat 'Ukasha, "Hakadha Qumna bi-l-Thawra," *al-Tahrir*, 29 July 1953.

6. Amira Abu al-Futuh, *Ihsan 'Abd al-Quddus Yatadhakkar* (Cairo: al-Hay'a al-Misriyya al-'Amma li-l-Kitab, 1982), 143.

7. 'Abd al-Quddus, "Li-madha Rafada Muhammad Najib Ta'lif Wizara 'Askariyya?"

8. Ihsan 'Abd al-Quddus, "al-Nasr li-l-Rijal," *Ruz al-Yusuf*, 28 July 1952.

9. Ihsan 'Abd al-Quddus, "al-Mawqif al-Hadir," *al-Idha'a al-Misriyya*, 2 August 1952.

10. Abu al-Futuh, *Ihsan 'Abd al-Quddus Yatadhakkar*, 141.

11. 'Abd al-Quddus, "al-Mawqif al-Hadir."

12. 'Abd al-Quddus, "al-Nasr li-l-Rijal."

13. Abu 'Awf, *Ihsan 'Abd al-Quddus bayna al-Sihafa wa-l-Riwaya*, 17.

14. Ibid.

15. 'Abd al-Quddus, "Li-madha Rafada Muhammad Najib Ta'lif Wizara 'Askariyya?"

16. Muhammad al-Shinnawi, *Ihsan 'Abd al-Quddus bayna al-Adab wa-l-Siyasa* (Cairo: Manshurat Battana, 2019), 369.

17. Ibid., 370.

18. Ibid., 374.

19. Ibrahim 'Abd al-'Aziz, *Ihsan 'Abd al-Quddus: Sira Ukhra* (Cairo: Manshurat Battana, 2019), 41.

20. al-Shinnawi, *Ihsan 'Abd al-Quddus bayna al-Adab wa-l-Siyasa*, 401-2.

21. Muhammad Fawzi, *Ihsan 'Abd al-Quddus bayna al-Ightiyal al-Siyasi wa-l-Shaghb al-Jinsi* (Cairo: Maktabat Madbuli, 1988), 98.

22. Ihsan 'Abd al-Quddus, "Li-madha Rafada Muhammad Najib Ta'lif Wizara 'Askariyya?," *Ruz al-Yusuf*, 2 September 1952.

23. Abul-Fath, *L'Affaire Nasser*, 32.

24. Sayyid Qutb, "Idha Lam Takun Thawra fa-Hakimu Muhammad Najib!," *Ruz al-Yusuf*, 18 August 1952.

25. Abul-Fath, *L'Affaire Nasser*, 209-10.

26. Joel Gordon, *Nasser's Blessed Movement: Egypt's Free Officers and the July Revolution*, new paperback edition (Cairo and New York: The American University in Cairo Press, 2016), 10.

27. 'Abd al-Quddus, "al-Nasr li-l-Rijal."

28. Ihsan 'Abd al-Quddus, "al-Dustur Lam Yu'zil al-Malik wa-Lakin Yutahhir al-Ahzab," *Ruz al-Yusuf*, 4 August 1952.

29. Ihsan 'Abd al-Quddus, "Faruq Lam Yakun al-Wahid Alladhi Taqarrar an Natakhallas Min-hu," *Ruz al-Yusuf*, 11 August 1952.

30. Ihsan 'Abd al-Quddus, "Li-madha Istaqala 'Ali Mahir wa-Li-madha Allafa al-Wizara Muhammad Najib," *Ruz al-Yusuf*, 8 September 1952.

31. Ibid.

32. Anwar El-Sadat, *In Search of Identity: An Autobiography* (New York: Harper Colophon Books, 1977), 121.

33. Ihsan 'Abd al-Quddus, "Mata Ya'ud al-Dustur wa-Mata Tajri al-Intikhabat?," *Ruz al-Yusuf*, 15 September 1952.

34. Ihsan 'Abd al-Quddus, "Ghaddan Lan Yataqarrar Idha Taharrarna min 'Aqaliyyat al-'Abid!," *Ruz al-Yusuf*, 22 September 1952.

35. Ihsan 'Abd al-Quddus, "Man La Yazal Yakhaf fa-Huwwa Kharij 'ala Mabadi' al-Harika," *al-Idha'a al-Misriyya*, 1 November 1952.

36. Ihsan 'Abd al-Quddus, "al-Afwah al-Samita wa-l-Malayin al-Samita!," *Ruz al-Yusuf*, 24 November 1952.

37. Ihsan 'Abd al-Quddus, "4: Kayfa Nurid an Tahkum Misr?," *Ruz al-Yusuf*, 3 November 1952.

38. Ihsan Abd al-Quddus and Mahmud Murad, *I'tirafat Ihsan 'Abd al-Quddus: al-Hurriya, al-Jins* (Cairo: al-'Arabi li-l-Nashr wa-l-Tawzi', 1980), 58.

39. Ibid., 48.

40. 'Abd al-Quddus, "al-Mawqif al-Hadir."

41. Clifton Daniel, "Position of Farouk Is Clouded by Coup," *New York Times*, 24 July 1954.

42. Muhammad Najib, "Indhar Qa'id 'Amm al-Quwwat al-Musallaha ila al-Malik al-Sabiq," *al-Idha'a al-Misriyya*, 2 August 1952.

43. *Al-Misri*, 25 August 1952.

44. Jamal 'Abd al-Nasir, "Kayfa Dabbarna Hadha al-Inqilab?," *al-Tahrir*, 1 October 1952.

45. Ihsan 'Abd al-Quddus, *Dami wa-Dumu'i wa-Ibtisamati* (Cairo: Dar al-Shuruq, 1974), 14.

46. On the film, see Joel Gordon, "Nasser's Free Officer Mutiny," in *Rebellion, Repression, Reinvention: Mutiny in Comparative Perspective*, ed. Jane Hathaway (Westport, CT: Praeger Publishers, 2001).

47. The full-page advertisement appeared in the 14 March 1955 issue of *Rose El-Youssef*. I thank the Abdel Kouddous family for access to the film program.

48. Ihsan 'Abd al-Quddus, "Man Kan Aqwa min al-Hakim?," *al-Ahram*, 20 September 1974.

49. In a 1948 letter, Nasser wrote, "Our country is a second Faluga." See Saïd K. Aburish, *Nasser: The Last Arab* (New York: St. Martin's Press, 2004), 26.

50. Talimat married Fatima Youssef in 1924; they divorced in 1938.

51. While no footage of Talimat as Mohammed Neguib survives, Joel Gordon was able to locate a still of a scene with Talimat and Hamama. See Gordon, "Nasser's Free Officer Mutiny."

52. This article is cited in 'Abd al-'Aziz, *Ihsan 'Abd al-Quddus*, 317–21.

53. Ibid., 187-93.

54. Ihsan 'Abd al-Quddus, "Man Alladhi Yahkum: al-Jaysh 'am 'Ali Mahir?," *Ruz al-Yusuf*, 18 August 1952.

55. Al-Shinnawi, *Ihsan 'Abd al-Quddus bayna al-Adab wa-l-Siyasa*, 415ff.

56. Amira Abu al-Futuh, "Mishwar Ihsan 'Abd al-Quddus: 11," *al-Siyasa*, 29 July 1980.

57. Abu al-Futuh, *Ihsan 'Abd al-Quddus Yatadhakkar*, 157.

58. Nasser rejected articles by Ahmed Abul-Fath in order to intimidate him as well. See Abul-Fath, *L'Affaire Nasser*, 159.

59. Al-Shinnawi, *Ihsan 'Abd al-Quddus bayna al-Adab wa-l-Siyasa*, 420-21.

60. Ni'am al-Baz, "Awraq Khassa wa-Hamma min Sanawat Ihsan 'Abd al-Quddus: al-Majmu' al-Thani," *Akhir Sa'a*, 23 February 1983, 22.

61. Al-Shinnawi, *Ihsan 'Abd al-Quddus bayna al-Adab wa-l-Siyasa*, 423.

62. Fawaz A. Gerges, *Making the Arab World: Nasser, Qutb, and the Clash That Shaped the Middle East* (Princeton and Oxford: Princeton University Press, 2018), 89.

63. Ibid., 92.

64. Ibid., 97.

65. Ihsan 'Abd al-Quddus, "Dustur Mu'aqqat li-Fatrat Intiqal Mu'aqqat!," *Ruz al-Yusuf*, 15 December 1952.

66. Abul-Fath, *L'Affaire Nasser*, 158.

67. Ihsan 'Abd al-Quddus, "Innana Nu'min bi-l-Mabadi' wa-bi-l-Mukhlisin li-Hadhihi al-Mabadi'," *Ruz al-Yusuf*, 12 January 1953.

68. Ni'am al-Baz, "Awraq Khassa wa-Hamma min Sanawat Ihsan 'Abd al-Quddus: al-Majmu' al-Thalith," *Akhir Sa'a*, 2 March 1983, 33.

69. Ihsan 'Abd al-Quddus, "La Mustabid Adil wa-La Adil Mustabid," *Ruz al-Yusuf*, 9 February 1953.

70. Fatima Yusuf, "Min Haqqi an Ashhad fi Yawm Qarib Khatimat al-Mufawadat," *Ruz al-Yusuf*, 4 May 1953.

71. Abd al-Quddus and Murad, *I'tirafat Ihsan 'Abd al-Quddus: al-Hurriya, al-Jins*, 62.

72. Khaled Mohi El Din, *Memories of a Revolution: Egypt 1952*, trans. TRIACC Translation Services (Cairo: American University in Cairo Press, 1995), 121.

73. El-Sadat, *In Search of Identity*, 165.

74. 'Ukasha, "Hakadha Qumna bi-l-Thawra;" Khalid Muhi al-Din, "Khalid Muhi al-Din Yarwi Qissat Manshurat al-Dubbat al-Ahrar," *al-Tahrir*, 29 July 1953.

75. Mohammed Neguib, *Egypt's Destiny* (London: Victor Gollancz, 1955), 122.

76. Anwar El Sadat, *Revolt on the Nile* (New York: John Day, 1957), 145; Abd al-Latif Baghdadi, *Mudhakkirat 'Abd al-Latif Baghdadi* (Cairo: al-Maktab al-Misri al-Hadith, 1977), 57.

77. Tharwat 'Ukasha, *Mudhakkirati fi al-Siyasa wa-l-Thaqafa* (Cairo: Maktabat Madbuli, 1987-88), vol. 1, 54.

78. Gamal Abdul Nasser, *Egypt's Liberation: The Philosophy of the Revolution*, trans. Dorothy Thompson (Washington, DC: Public Affairs Press, 1955), 19-20.

79. Ibid., 21.

80. Ibid., 34.

81. Ibid., 76.

82. Ibid., 118.

83. Ihsan 'Abd al-Quddus, "Ha'ula'i al-Wuzara' Aqwiya' wa-Hadha al-Sha'b Qawi!," *Ruz al-Yusuf*, 22 June 1953.

84. Ihsan 'Abd al-Quddus, "Li-l-Asif," *Ruz al-Yusuf*, 7 November 1950.

85. Ihsan 'Abd al-Quddus, "Raqisa fi Ijaza," *Ruz al-Yusuf*, 21 August 1951.

86. Ihsan 'Abd al-Quddus, "al-Nazzara al-Sawda'," *Ruz al-Yusuf*, 28 January 1952. This novella would later be adapted into the classic 1963 film *Sunglasses*, starring Nadia Lotfi, Ahmed Mazhar, and Ahmed Ramzy.

87. Fathi Ghanim, "Masir Alladhina Yajlisun fawq al-Hirab," *Akhir Sa'a*, 19 September 1956.

88. Ihsan 'Abd al-Quddus, "al-Islam La Yakfi!," *Ruz al-Yusuf*, 24 September 1956.

89. Interview with Lobna Abdel Aziz in Cairo, 1 April 2019.

90. Fawzi, *Ihsan 'Abd al-Quddus bayna al-Ightiyal al-Siyasi wa-l-Shaghb al-Jinsi*, 23.

91. Ihsan 'Abd al-Quddus, "Ana Hurra," *Ruz al-Yusuf*, 29 June 1953, 36.

92. Ibid., 37.

93. Ihsan 'Abd al-Quddus, "Ana Hurra," *Ruz al-Yusuf*, 3 August 1953, 21.

94. Ibid., 36.

95. Ibid., 37.

96. *I'm Free* was adapted into the classic 1959 film with a screenplay by Naguib Mahfouz and starring Lobna Abdel Aziz as Amina and Shoukry Sirhan as Abbas. In the film, Sirhan, who played Muhsin Abdel Mawgoud in *God Is with Us*, once again takes on the role of a revolutionary journalist double of Ihsan Abdel Kouddous.

97. Ihsan 'Abd al-Quddus, "Ana Hurra," *Ruz al-Yusuf*, 10 August 1953, 21.

98. Ibid., 35.

99. Ibid.

100. Ibid.

101. Ibid., 36.

102. Ibid.

103. Ibid., 37.

104. Tarek El-Ariss, "Ottomania: Boy Love, Incest, and the Arab Spring," in *Essays on Heritage, Tourism, and Society in the MENA Region: Proceedings of the International Heritage Conference 2013 at Tangier, Morocco*, ed. Dieter Haller, Achime Lichtenberger, and Meike Meerpohl (Paderborn, Germany: Wilhelm Fink, 2015), 33-34.

105. 'Abd al-Quddus, "Ana Hurra," 37.

106. Ihsan 'Abd al-Quddus, "Ana Hurra," *Ruz al-Yusuf,* 17 August 1953, 35.

107. Ibid., 36.

108. Ibid., 37.

109. Ihsan 'Abd al-Quddus, *al-Hazima Kana Ismuha Fatima* (Misr: Dar al-Ma'arif, 1975), 30.

110. Ahmad Hashim al-Sharif, "Hiwar ma'a Ihsan 'Abd al-Quddus," *Sabah al-Khayr,* 17 August 1974.

111. Salwa al-'Anani, "Hiwar Lam Tunshar ma'a Ihsan 'Abd al-Quddus," *al-Ahram,* 14 January 1990.

## Chapter 3

1. Ihsan 'Abd al-Quddus, "Ard al-Din wa-l-Duniya!," *Ruz al-Yusuf,* 22 March 1954.

2. Ihsan 'Abd al-Quddus, "al-Bahth 'an Allah," *Ruz al-Yusuf,* 15 March 1954.

3. Ihsan 'Abd al-Quddus, "Ard al-Din wa-l-Duniya!," *Ruz al-Yusuf,* 22 March 1954.

4. Ihsan 'Abd al-Quddus, "Innana Nasir fi al-Tariq al-Tabi'i al-Muhattam 'ala al-Thawra," *Ruz al-Yusuf,* 15 March 1954.

5. Ihsan 'Abd al-Quddus, "al-Jam'iyyya al-Sirriyya Alladhi Tahkum Misr!," *Ruz al-Yusuf,* 22 March 1954.

6. Ihsan 'Abd al-Quddus, "Masir al-Thawra wa-Masir Rijal al-Thawra!," *Ruz al-Yusuf,* 29 March 1954.

7. "*Ruz al-Yusuf* Tastafta al-Sha'b: Jumhuriyya am Malikiyya?," *Ruz al-Yusuf,* 27 October 1952.

8. Joel Gordon, *Nasser's Blessed Movement: Egypt's Free Officers and the July Revolution,* new paperback edition (Cairo and New York: The American University in Cairo Press, 2016), 139.

9. Mohammed Neguib, *Egypt's Destiny* (London: Victor Gollancz, 1955), 204.

10. Ahmad Abu al-Fath, "Siyadat al-Sha'ab," *al-Misri,* 15 March 1954.

11. Ahmed Abul-Fath, *L'Affaire Nasser* (Paris: Plon, 1962), 71.

12. Ibrahim 'Abd al-'Aziz, *Ihsan 'Abd al-Quddus: Sira Ukhra* (Cairo: Manshurat Battana, 2019), 50.

13. According to Mohammed Abdel Kouddous, Ihsan's oldest son, this was an intentional strategy to express her outrage. Muhammad 'Abd al-Quddus, *Hikayat Ihsan 'Abd al-Quddus* (Cairo: al-Hay'a al-'Amma li-l-Kitab, 2011), 114.

14. Muhammad al-Shinnawi, *Ihsan 'Abd al-Quddus bayna al-Adab wa-l-Siyasa* (Cairo: Manshurat Battana, 2019), 517.

15. Ibid., 520.

16. Ihsan 'Abd al-Quddus, "Dhikriyat," *Ruz al-Yusuf,* 24 October 1955.

17. Amal al-Umdah, "Kunuz Amal al-Umdah," *Ruz al-Yusuf,* 15 January 2022.

18. Ni'am al-Baz, "Awraq Khassa wa-Hamma min Mudhakkirat Ihsan 'Abd al-Quddus," *Akhir Sa'a,* 9 March 1983.

19. Al-Shinnawi, *Ihsan 'Abd al-Quddus bayna al-Adab wa-l-Siyasa*, 531.

20. Lynn Hunt, *The Family Romance of the French Revolution* (Berkeley: University of California Press, 1992). xiv.

21. Al-Shinnawi, *Ihsan 'Abd al-Quddus bayna al-Adab wa-l-Siyasa*, 532.

22. Ibid., 548-50.

23. Muhammad Fawzi, *Ihsan 'Abd al-Quddus bayna al-Ightiyal al-Siyasi wa-l-Shaghb al-Jinsi* (Cairo: Maktabat Madbuli, 1988), 73-74.

24. Omnia El Shakry, *The Arabic Freud: Psychoanalysis and Islam in Modern Egypt* (Princeton and Oxford: Princeton University Press, 2017), 4.

25. Ibid., 39.

26. Premier Gamal Abdul Nasser, *Egypt's Liberation: The Philosophy of the Revolution*, trans. Dorothy Thompson (Washington, DC: Public Affairs Press, 1955), 39.

27. Anwar El-Sadat, *In Search of Identity: An Autobiography* (New York: Harper Colophon Books, 1977), 77.

28. Neguib, *Egypt's Destiny*, 215.

29. Ihsan 'Abd al-Quddus, "Ayna 'Umri?," *Ruz al-Yusuf*, 23 November 1953, 35.

30. Ihsan 'Abd al-Quddus, "Ayna 'Umri?," *Ruz al-Yusuf*, 30 November 1953, 34.

31. Abul-Fath, *L'Affaire Nasser*, 73.

32. Ibid., 224.

33. See al-Shinnawi, *Ihsan 'Abd al-Quddus bayna al-Adab wa-l-Siyasa*, 557ff.

34. Ibid., 562.

35. Ibid., 561-62.

36. Ibid., 575.

37. Abul-Fath, *L'Affaire Nasser*, 158.

38. Khaled Mohi El Din, *Memories of a Revolution: Egypt 1952*, trans. TRIACC Translation Services (Cairo: American University in Cairo Press, 1995), 159.

39. Abul-Fath, *L'Affaire Nasser*, 226.

40. Tawfiq al-Hakim, *The Return of Consciousness*, trans. Bayly Winder (New York and London: New York University Press, 1985), 28.

41. Ibid., 29.

42. Laura Bier, *Revolutionary Womanhood: Feminisms, Modernity, and the State in Nasser's Egypt* (Stanford: Stanford University Press, 2011).

43. Ibid., 17.

44. Shakry, *Arabic Freud*, 72.

45. al-Shinnawi, *Ihsan 'Abd al-Quddus bayna al-Adab wa-l-Siyasa*, 563.

46. Ibid., 562.

47. Ibid., 561.

48. Ihsan 'Abd al-Quddus, "Man Huwwa al-Katib al-Hurr?," *Ruz al-Yusuf*, 30 August 1954.

49. 'Abd al-'Aziz, *Ihsan 'Abd al-Quddus*, 50.

50. Ihsan 'Abd al-Quddus, "95 Yawman fi al-Sijn," *Ruz al-Yusuf*, 6 September 1954.

51. 'Abd al-Rahman Abu 'Awf, "Ihsan 'Abd al-Quddus: Arfud al-Madi wa-Afrud al-Hadir Li-anni Udin bi-l-Mustaqbal," *Ruz al-Yusuf*, 28 October 1974.

52. Amira Abu al-Futuh, "Mishwar Ihsan 'Abd al-Quddus: 14," *al-Siyasa*, 2 August 1980.

53. al-Shinnawi, *Ihsan 'Abd al-Quddus bayna al-Adab wa-l-Siyasa*, 504–5.

54. In a single interview, Abdel Kouddous was pressed if he had been tortured physically in jail or not, but he refused to speak about it. See ibid., 491.

55. Amira Abu al-Futuh, "Mishwar Ihsan 'Abd al-Quddus: 13," *al-Siyasa*, 31 July 1980.

56. Ihsan 'Abd al-Quddus, "al-Wisada al-Khaliyya," *Ruz al-Yusuf*, 6 September 1954, 40.

57. Ibid., 41.

58. Ibid.

59. Ihsan 'Abd al-Quddus, "al-Wisada al-Khaliyya," *Ruz al-Yusuf*, 13 September 1954, 22.

60. I thank Joel Gordon for suggesting this.

61. Ibid., 41.

62. Ihsan 'Abd al-Quddus, "al-Wisada al-Khaliyya," *Ruz al-Yusuf*, 27 September 1954, 22.

63. Ibid.

64. Ibid.

65. Ibid., 40.

66. Ibid.

67. Ihsan 'Abd al-Quddus, "al-Wisada al-Khaliyya," *Ruz al-Yusuf*, 4 October 1954, 40.

68. Ihsan 'Abd al-Quddus, "al-Wisada al-Khaliyya," *Ruz al-Yusuf*, 11 October 1954, 41.

69. Ibid.

70. Mustafa 'Abd al-Ghani, *al-Muthaqqafun wa-Thawrat Yuliyu: al-Shahadat al-Akhira* (Cairo: Markaz al-Ahram, 2010), 100.

71. Ahmad 'Abd al-Mu'ti Hijazi, "Ba'd Sab'at Shuhur min al-Samt Ihsan Yatakallam (3)," *Ruz al-Yusuf*, 16 November 1968.

72. 'Abd al-'Aziz, *Ihsan 'Abd al-Quddus: Sira Ukhra*, 57.

73. Ahmed Abul-Fath discusses how Nasser repeatedly punished and then resuscitated "friends of the past." See Abul-Fath, *L'Affaire Nasser*, 224.

74. Saïd K. Aburish, *Nasser: The Last Arab* (New York: St. Martin's Press, 2004), 56.

75. Din, *Memories of a Revolution*, 159.

76. Ihsan 'Abd al-Quddus, "Hamsa," *al-Idha'a al-Misriyya*, 16 October 1954.

77. Shakry, *Arabic Freud*, 107.

78. Al-Shinnawi, *Ihsan 'Abd al-Quddus bayna al-Adab wa-l-Siyasa*, 29.

79. Ihsan 'Abd al-Quddus, "Hamsa," *al-Idha'a al-Misriyya*, 23 October 1954.
80. Ihsan 'Abd al-Quddus, "Hamsa," *al-Idha'a al-Misriyya*, 30 October 1954.
81. Al-Muwatin al-Misri, "al-Sha'ab wa-l-Hurriyya wa-l-Sihafa fi al-'Alim al-Jadid," *Ruz al-Yusuf*, 25 October 1954.
82. Ihsan 'Abd al-Quddus, "Hamsa," *al-Idha'a al-Misriyya*, 6 November 1954.
83. Ihsan 'Abd al-Quddus, "Imani," *Ruz al-Yusuf*, 1 November 1954.
84. Al-Shinnawi, *Ihsan 'Abd al-Quddus bayna al-Adab wa-l-Siyasa*, 581ff. I have been unable to determine the exact date of this arrest.
85. Amira Abu al-Futuh, *Ihsan 'Abd al-Quddus Yatadhakkar* (Cairo: al-Hay'a al-Misriyya al-'Amma li-l-Kitab, 1982), 210.
86. Ibid., 212.
87. Ibid., 213.
88. Ibid., 214.
89. Al-Shinnawi, *Ihsan 'Abd al-Quddus bayna al-Adab wa-l-Siyasa*, 596.
90. Abu al-Futuh, *Ihsan 'Abd al-Quddus Yatadhakkar*, 216.
91. Ibid., 217.
92. Ihsan 'Abd al-Quddus, *'Ala Maqha fi al-Shari' al-Siyasi* (Cairo: Maktabat Misr, 1979), 4.
93. 'Abd al-Quddus, *Hikayat Ihsan 'Abd al-Quddus*, 197.
94. Ihsan 'Abd al-Quddus, "al-Tariq al-Masdud," *Ruz al-Yusuf*, 10 January 1955, 26.
95. Ibid., 36.
96. Ibid.
97. Ibid., 37.
98. Ibid.
99. Ibid.
100. Ibid., 48.
101. Ibid.
102. Ibid.
103. Ihsan 'Abd al-Quddus, "al-Tariq al-Masdud," *Ruz al-Yusuf*, 17 January 1955, 37.
104. Ihsan 'Abd al-Quddus, "al-Tariq al-Masdud," *Ruz al-Yusuf*, 4 April 1955, 37.
105. Ibid.
106. Ibid.
107. Ibid., 37, 48.
108. Ihsan 'Abd al-Quddus, "al-Tariq al-Masdud," *Ruz al-Yusuf*, 11 April 1955, 36.
109. Ibid.
110. Ibid., 37.
111. Ibid.
112. Ibid.

113. Ihsan 'Abd al-Quddus, "al-Tariq al-Masdud," *Ruz al-Yusuf*, 23 May 1955.

114. The ending of the film *The Barred Road* was indeed changed. Directed by Salah Abou Seif with a screenplay by Naguib Mahfouz, the 1958 film starred Faten Hamama as Faiza and Ahmed Mazhar as Munir. In the film, Faiza clings to her faith and idealism to the end, eventually convincing Munir to give up his life of sin and corruption. In the final moments of then film, Munir declares to Faiza, "We'll break through the barred road!"

115. Ihsan 'Abd al-Quddus, "Hamsa," *al-Idha'a al-Misriyya*, 19 March 1955.

116. Ihsan 'Abd al-Quddus, "Sa'uhawil . . . Sa'uhawil!," *Ruz al-Yusuf*, 31 December 1956.

117. Abu al-Futuh, *Ihsan 'Abd al-Quddus Yatadhakkar*, 207-8.

118. Ihsan 'Abd al-Quddus, *Finjan Shay'*, ed. Samiya Sadiq (1959). I thank the Abdel Kouddous family for providing me with the full recording of this interview.

119. Amani Farid, "al-Udaba' lahum Mashakil ma'a al-Iza'a," *al-Kawakib*, 26 May 1981.

## Chapter 4

1. Ihsan 'Abd al-Quddus, "al-Nawm wa-l-Mawt," *Ruz al-Yusuf*, 28 February 1955.

2. Ihsan 'Abd al-Quddus, "Hawadith wa-Khawatir," *Ruz al-Yusuf*, 29 August 1955.

3. Khaled Mohi El Din, *Memories of a Revolution: Egypt 1952*, trans. TRIACC Translation Services (Cairo: American University in Cairo Press, 1995), 238.

4. The link between *Bonjour Tristesse* and *I Do Not Sleep* was suggested by a reader letter published in *Rose El Youssef* on 11 June 1956. While Abdel Kouddous denied that he even read Sagan's novel, a cursory reading of both shows that Abdel Kouddous was almost certainly inspired by it.

5. Ihsan 'Abd al-Quddus, *Ba'i al-Hubb*, Kutub li-l-Jami' (Cairo: Dar al-Jumhuriyya, 1949).

6. Ihsan Abdel Kouddous, *I Do Not Sleep*, trans. Jonathan Smolin (Cairo and New York: Hoopoe, 2021), 11.

7. Ihsan 'Abd al-Quddus, "Hawadith wa-Khawatir," *Ruz al-Yusuf*, 9 January 1956.

8. In this Abdel Kouddous reverses the typical gender of the symbol of Egypt from female to male. See Beth Baron, *Egypt as a Woman: Nationalism, Gender, and Politics* (Berkeley: University of California Press, 2005).

9. Ihsan Abdel Kouddous, *I Do Not Sleep*, trans. Jonathan Smolin (Cairo and New York: Hoopoe, 2021), 45.

10. Ibid., 47.

11. Ibid., 49.

12. Ibid., 51.

13. Ibid., 49.

14. Ibid., 53.
15. Ibid., 62.
16. Ibid., 63.
17. Ibid., 65. As in *God Is with Us*, Abdel Kouddous is careful to include some details about Mustafa to avoid making the identification with Nasser too obvious. For example, Mustafa is wealthy, has studied at Cambridge, and loves whiskey, all stark contrasts with Nasser's modest background and conservative lifestyle.
18. Ibid., 67-68.
19. Ibid., 78.
20. Ibid., 84.
21. Ibid., 129.
22. Ibid., 134.
23. Ibid., 136.
24. Ibid., 142.
25. Ibid., 181.
26. Ibid., 60.
27. Ibid., 152-53.
28. Ibid., 153.
29. Ibid., 155.
30. Ibid., 156.
31. Ibid., 166.
32. Ibid., 172-73.
33. Ibid., 194.
34. Ibid.
35. Ibid., 196.
36. Ibid.
37. Ibid., 198.
38. Peter Brooks, *The Melodramatic Imagination: Balzac, Henry James, Melodrama, and the Mode of Excess* (New York: Columbia University Press, 1985), ix.
39. Ibid., 42.
40. Ibid., 56.
41. al-Muwatin al-Misri, "Innana Nurid al-Dustur li-anna Nu'min bi-l-Dimuqratiyya," *Ruz al-Yusuf*, 19 December 1955.
42. Abdel Kouddous, *I Do Not Sleep*, 201.
43. Ibid., 208.
44. Ibid., 222.
45. Ibid., 211.
46. Ibid., 211-12.
47. Ibid., 212.
48. Ibid., 216.
49. Ibid., 235.
50. Ibid., 240.

51. Ibid., 241.
52. Ibid., 219.
53. Ibid., 249.
54. Ibid., 255.
55. Ibid., 257.
56. Ibid., 279.
57. Ibid., 280.
58. Ibid., 282.
59. Ibid., 287.
60. Ibid.
61. Ibid., 296.
62. Ihsan 'Abd al-Quddus, *Finjan Shay'*, ed. Samiya Sadiq (1959).
63. Abdel Kouddous, *I Do Not Sleep*, 309.
64. Saïd K. Aburish, *Nasser: The Last Arab* (New York: St. Martin's Press, 2004), 136.
65. Abdel Kouddous, *I Do Not Sleep*, 310.
66. Ibid.
67. Ibid., 351.
68. Ibid., 353.
69. Ibid., 354.
70. Ihsan 'Abd al-Quddus, "La Anam," *Ruz al-Yusuf*, 12 March 1956.
71. Ihsan 'Abd al-Quddus, "Hawadith wa-Khawatir," *Ruz al-Yusuf*, 19 March 1956.
72. On the cultural implications of existentialism in the Arab world during this time, see Yoav Di-Capua, *No Exit: Arab Existentialism, Jean-Paul Sartre, and Decolonization* (Chicago: University of Chicago Press, 2018).
73. 'Abd al-Hamid Ibrahim, ed., *Watha'iq Taha Hussayn al-Sirriyya* (Cairo: Dar al-Shuruq, 2006), 95ff.
74. Ihsan 'Abd al-Quddus, "al-'Uyun al-Maghmuda," *Ruz al-Yusuf*, 28 November 1955.
75. It was an ending that disturbed people familiar with the novel, including the well-known writer Fathi Ghanim, who argued in *Rose El Youssef*, no doubt with Abdel Kouddou's support, that the ending was changed to suit the censor. Fathi Ghanim, "La Anam fi al-Sinima," *Ruz al-Yusuf*, 11 November 1957.
76. Ihsan 'Abd al-Quddus, "al-Rajul Alladhi Nu'min bihi," *Ruz al-Yusuf*, 21 May 1956.
77. Ihsan 'Abd al-Quddus, "Hadha al-Rajul Huwwa al-Sha'ab," *Ruz al-Yusuf*, 30 July 1956.
78. Israel Gershoni, "An Intellectual Source for the Revolution: Tawfiq al-Hakim's Influence on Nasser and His Generation," in *Egypt from Monarchy to Republic: A Reassment of Revolution and Change*, ed. Shimon Shamir (Boulder, CO: Westview Press, 1995), 237.

79. Ihsan 'Abd al-Quddus, "Tahiyya ila Rusiya," *Ruz al-Yusuf*, 13 August 1956.

80. Ihsan 'Abd al-Quddus, "Fi al-Mu'tamar al-Sahafi," *Sabah al-Khayr*, 16 August 1956.

81. Ihsan 'Abd al-Quddus, "al-'Alim Alladhi Iktashafnahu," *Ruz al-Yusuf*, 20 August 1956.

82. Ihsan 'Abd al-Quddus, "Fadiha Amrikiyya fi Mu'tamar Landan," *Ruz al-Yusuf*, 27 August 1956.

83. Ihsan 'Abd al-Quddus, "al-Ni'am fi Bayrut," *Ruz al-Yusuf*, 7 May 1956.

84. Ihsan 'Abd al-Quddus, "Min Sujun Suriya," *Ruz al-Yusuf*, 9 July 1956.

85. Ihsan 'Abd al-Quddus, "al-Malika wa-Qissa," *Ruz al-Yusuf*, 15 October 1956.

86. Ibrahim 'Abd al-'Aziz, *Ihsan 'Abd al-Quddus: Sira Ukhra* (Cairo: Manshurat Battana, 2019), 69.

87. See, for example, Ihsan 'Abd al-Quddus, "Da'uhu Yadhhab," *Ruz al-Yusuf*, 16 June 1948.

88. Ihsan 'Abd al-Quddus, "Fi Baytina Rajul," *Ruz al-Yusuf*, 7 January 1957, 22.

89. Ibid.

90. Ibid., 24.

91. Ibid., 25.

92. Ihsan 'Abd al-Quddus, "Fi Baytina Rajul," *Ruz al-Yusuf*, 28 January 1957, 22.

93. Ihsan 'Abd al-Quddus, "Fi Baytina Rajul," *Ruz al-Yusuf*, 14 January 1957, 25.

94. Ihsan 'Abd al-Quddus, "Fi Baytina Rajul," *Ruz al-Yusuf*, 10 June 1957, 35.

95. Ihsan 'Abd al-Quddus, "Fi Baytina Rajul," *Ruz al-Yusuf*, 27 May 1957, 34.

96. Tawfiq al-Hakim, *Return of the Spirit*, trans. William Maynard Hutchins and Russel Harris (New York: Penguin Classics, 2019), 325.

97. Ihsan 'Abd al-Quddus, "Fi Baytina Rajul," *Ruz al-Yusuf*, 21 January 1957, 21.

98. Ihsan 'Abd al-Quddus, "Fi Baytina Rajul," *Ruz al-Yusuf*, 11 March 1957, 35.

99. Ibid., 37.

100. Ibid.

101. Ihsan 'Abd al-Quddus, "Hawadith wa-Khawatir," *Ruz al-Yusuf*, 3 June 1957.

102. Muhammad al-Shinnawi, *Ihsan 'Abd al-Quddus bayna al-Adab wa-l-Siyasa* (Cairo: Manshurat Battana, 2019), 670.

103. Perhaps not coincidentally, Abdel Kouddous wrote almost no political editorials in *Rose El Youssef* as he was serializing the novel.

104. Amira Abu al-Futuh, *Ihsan 'Abd al-Quddus Yatadhakkar* (Cairo: al-Hay'a al-Misriyya al-'Amma li-l-Kitab, 1982), 43.

105. Ihsan 'Abd al-Quddus, "Hawadith wa-Khawatir," *Ruz al-Yusuf*, 17 June 1957, 7.

106. The classic 1961 film adaptation of the novel, which was directed by Henry Barakat and starred Omar Sharif and Zubaida Tharwat, reinforces this point to avoid any misinterpretation that the story suggests the killing of Nasser.

107. Ihsan 'Abd al-Quddus, "Fi Baytina Rajul," *Ruz al-Yusuf*, 27 May 1957, 34.

108. Ibid.

109. Ibid., 35.

110. Ihsan 'Abd al-Quddus, "Fi Baytina Rajul," *Ruz al-Yusuf*, 10 June 1957, 34.

111. Ibid.

112. Omnia El Shakry, *The Arabic Freud: Psychoanalysis and Islam in Modern Egypt* (Princeton and Oxford: Princeton University Press, 2017), 75.

113. Ihsan 'Abd al-Quddus, "Fi Baytina Rajul," *Ruz al-Yusuf*, 10 June 1957, 34.

## Chapter 5

1. Ibrahim 'Abd al-'Aziz, *Ihsan 'Abd al-Quddus: Sira Ukhra* (Cairo: Manshurat Battana, 2019), 109.

2. Ihsan 'Abd al-Quddus, "al-Za'im wa-l-Mabda'," *Ruz al-Yusuf*, 24 February 1958.

3. Ihsan 'Abd al-Quddus, "Jamal . . . wa-Kull Shu'ub al-'Alam," *Sabah al-Khayr*, 26 December 1957.

4. Ihsan 'Abd al-Quddus, "Innahu fi Kull Makan," *Sabah al-Khayr*, 20 March 1958.

5. Tawfiq al-Hakim, *The Return of Consciousness*, trans. Bayly Winder (New York and London: New York University Press, 1985), 24-25.

6. Muhammad Fawzi, *Ihsan 'Abd al-Quddus bayna al-Ightiyal al-Siyasi wa-l-Shaghb al-Jinsi* (Cairo: Maktabat Madbuli, 1988), 91-92.

7. Hilmi al-Namnam, "Rasa'il Ihsan 'Abd al-Quddus al-Majhula (2)," *al-Musawwir*, 9 March 2001.

8. Ihsan 'Abd al-Quddus, "Hawadith wa-Khawatir," *Ruz al-Yusuf*, 9 September 1957.

9. Fatima al-Yusuf, "Sabah al-Khayr," *Sabah al-Khayr*, 12 January 1956.

10. Ihsan 'Abd al-Quddus, "al-Bayt al-Jadid," *Sabah al-Khayr*, 12 January 1956.

11. Al-Yusuf, "Sabah al-Khayr."

12. Ihsan 'Abd al-Quddus, "Mujtama' Jadid . . . wa-Akhlaq Jadida," *Sabah al-Khayr*, 9 January 1958.

13. The novel was initially advertised in both *Rose El Youssef* and *Sabah al-Khayr* in June 1958 as *Three Girls in Summer*, suggesting that Abdel Kouddous originally conceived of the work as an expanded version of the first three stories.

14. Ihsan Abdel Kouddous, "'Girl Three,' Translated by Raphael Cohen," *Banipal*, no. 71 (2021), 139. I have used the title Third Girl throughout.

15. Ibid.
16. Ibid.
17. Ibid.
18. Ibid., 140.
19. Ibid.
20. Ibid.
21. Ibid., 144-45.
22. Ibid., 145.
23. Ibid., 147.
24. Ibid., 148. I have modified the translation slightly.
25. Ibid., 149.
26. Ibid.
27. Ibid.
28. Ibid.
29. Ibid.
30. Ibid., 150.
31. Ibid., 152. I have modified the translation.
32. Ibid., 156.
33. Ibid., 160.
34. Ibid.
35. Ibid.
36. Ibid., 161.
37. Ibid.
38. Ibid., 164.
39. Ibid., 165.
40. Ibid.

41. Ihsan 'Abd al-Quddus, *Asif Lam A'ud Astati'* (Cairo: al-Dar al-Misriyya al-Lubnaniyya, 1980; repr., 2015), 6. Abdel Kouddous mistakenly writes in the introduction that he wrote the letter in 1955 and that *Girls in Summer* was published in *Rose El Youssef*.

42. Ibid.

43. Ibid., 7.

44. This also foreshadows the 1969 classic film adaptation of an Abdel Kouddous short story, *My Father's Up a Tree*, which returns to sexual scandal on the beaches of Alexandria. See Ihsan 'Abd al-Quddus, *Dami wa-Dumu'i wa-Ibtisamati* (Cairo: Dar al-Shuruq, 1974), 143-209. On the political dimensions of the film, see Joel Gordon, "The Slaps Felt around the Arab World: Family and National Melodrama in Two Nasser-Era Musicals," *International Journal for Middle Eastern Studies* 39 (2007).

45. 'Abd al-'Aziz, *Ihsan 'Abd al-Quddus: Sira Ukhra*, 58.

46. 'Abd al-Quddus, *Asif Lam A'ud Astati'*, 8.

47. Ihsan 'Abd al-Quddus, "al-Sud wa-l-Bayd," *Ruz al-Yusuf*, 4 April 1960.

48. 'Abd al-Quddus, *Asif Lam A'ud Astati'*, 13.

49. Ihsan 'Abd al-Quddus, *Finjan Shay'*, ed. Samiya Sadiq (1959).

50. Amira Abu al-Futuh, "Mishwar Ihsan 'Abd al-Quddus: 1," *al-Siyasa*, 19 July 1980.

51. Fawzi, *Ihsan 'Abd al-Quddus bayna al-Ightiyal al-Siyasi wa-l-Shaghb al-Jinsi*, 171.

52. Abdel Kouddous wrote in *Rose El Youssef* on 2 February 1959 that he had been looking for a title for his new novel for two months. In mid-May 1959, Abdel Kouddous wrote in *Rose El Youssef* that he had been living with the characters of *The Sun Never Sets* for six months. See Ihsan 'Abd al-Quddus, "Hawadith wa-Khawatir," *Ruz al-Yusuf*, 18 May 1959.

53. Ihsan 'Abd al-Quddus, "'Awdat al-Shakhsiyya," *Sabah al-Khayr*, 23 August 1956.

54. See Friedrich Nietzsche, *The Birth of Tragedy: Out of the Spirit of Music*, ed. Michael Tanner, trans. Shaun Whiteside (New York: Penguin Books, 1993).

55. Abdel Kouddous only discovered this when he flipped through the magazine at the printer. Ihsan 'Abd al-Quddus, "Ams wa-Yawm wa-Ghaddan," *Ruz al-Yusuf*, 2 February 1959.

56. 'Abd al-Quddus, "Hawadith wa-Khawatir."

57. Ihsan 'Abd al-Quddus, "La Tutfi' al-Shams," *Ruz al-Yusuf*, 2 March 1959, 34.

58. Ihsan 'Abd al-Quddus, "La Tutfi' al-Shams," *Ruz al-Yusuf*, 9 March 1959, 42.

59. 'Abd al-Quddus, "La Tutfi' al-Shams," *Ruz al-Yusuf*, 2 March 1959, 36.

60. Ihsan 'Abd al-Quddus, "La Tutfi' al-Shams," *Ruz al-Yusuf*, 24 June 1959, 40.

61. Ihsan 'Abd al-Quddus, *La Tutfi' al-Shams*, 1st ed. (Cairo: al-Sharika al-Qawmiyya, 1960), vol. 1, 50.

62. Ihsan 'Abd al-Quddus, "La Tutfi' al-Shams," *Ruz al-Yusuf*, 16 March 1959, 23.

63. 'Abd al-Quddus, *La Tutfi' al-Shams*, vol. 1, 348.

64. Ihsan 'Abd al-Quddus, "La Tutfi' al-Shams," *Ruz al-Yusuf*, 7 December 1959, 28.

65. Ihsan 'Abd al-Quddus, "La Tutfi' al-Shams," *Ruz al-Yusuf*, 11 January 1960, 22.

66. Ihsan 'Abd al-Quddus, "Ana wa-l-Majanin," *Ruz al-Yusuf*, 14 December 1959.

67. Ihsan 'Abd al-Quddus, "Sana'at al-Insan," *Ruz al-Yusuf*, 18 January 1960.

68. Ihsan 'Abd al-Quddus, "La Tutfi' al-Shams," *Ruz al-Yusuf*, 1 February 1960, 22.

69. Ibid., 23.

70. Ibid.

71. Ibid.

72. Ibid., 35.

73. Ihsan 'Abd al-Quddus, "La Tutfi' al-Shams," *Ruz al-Yusuf*, 15 February 1960, 23.

74. Ihsan 'Abd al-Quddus, "La Tutfi' al-Shams," *Ruz al-Yusuf*, 22 February 1960, 26–27.

75. Ibid., 40.

76. For a digital archive of Nasser's speeches and papers, see http://nasser.bibalex.org/Home/Home.aspx?lang=ar.

77. Ihsan 'Abd al-Quddus, "La Tutfi' al-Shams," *Ruz al-Yusuf*, 14 March 1960, 23.

78. Ihsan 'Abd al-Quddus, "Mujtama' al-Thawra," *Ruz al-Yusuf*, 20 July 1959.

79. Ihsan 'Abd al-Quddus, "La Tutfi' al-Shams," *Ruz al-Yusuf*, 14 March 1960, 23.

80. Ibid., 42.

81. Ibid.

82. Ihsan 'Abd al-Quddus, "La Tutfi' al-Shams," *Ruz al-Yusuf*, 14 March 1960, 43.

83. Ibid., 29.

84. Ibid., 48.

85. The series is on YouTube: https://www.youtube.com/watch?v=NeZF7_OUX2A&t. Accessed 20 January 2024.

86. See Joel Gordon, *Revolutionary Melodrama: Popular Film and Civic Identity in Nasser's Egypt*, Chicago Studies on the Middle East (Chicago: Middle East Documentation Center, 2002), 205ff.

87. Ihsan 'Abd al-Quddus, "al-Ittihad al-Qawmi wa-l-Sihafa," *Ruz al-Yusuf*, 1 February 1960.

88. 'Abd al-'Aziz, *Ihsan 'Abd al-Quddus: Sira Ukhra*, 104.

89. 'A'isha Abu al-Nur, "Rihla ila 'Aql Ihsan 'Abd al-Quddus," *Akhir Sa'a*, 14 February 1979.

90. Ni'am al-Baz, "Awraq Khassa wa-Hamma min Mudhakkirat Ihsan 'Abd al-Quddus," *Akhir Sa'a*, 9 March 1983, 22.

91. Ibid.

92. Ihsan 'Abd al-Quddus, "al-Qawmiya," *Ruz al-Yusuf*, 28 March 1960.

93. Ihsan 'Abd al-Quddus, "al-Sihafa wa-l-Ishtirakiyya," *Ruz al-Yusuf*, 30 May 1960.

94. As seen in the photo of Abdel Kouddous's office, published in *al-Kawakib* on 13 September 1960.

95. Ihsan 'Abd al-Quddus, "Muddat 4000 Sana," *Ruz al-Yusuf*, 25 July 1960.

96. Ihsan 'Abd al-Quddus, "Innana La Nakrah al-Aghniya' wa-Lakinnana Nuhibb al-Fuqara'," *Ruz al-Yusuf*, 24 July 1961.

97. Ihsan 'Abd al-Quddus, "Kayfa Hadatha Kull Dhalik?," *Ruz al-Yusuf*, 23 July 1962.

98. Ihsan 'Abd al-Quddus, *Bi'r al-Hirman* (Beirut: Dar al-Nashr al-Hadith, 1962).

## Chapter 6

1. Ihsan 'Abd al-Quddus, "al-Iktishaf al-Dakhm," *Ruz al-Yusuf*, 22 July 1963.
2. Hanan al-Shaykh, "La Takhunani," *Ruz al-Yusuf*, 21 January 1963.
3. Al-Shaykh writes for the first time about her relationship with Abdel Kouddous in the foreword of my translation of *A Nose and Three Eyes*. See Ihsan Abdel Kouddous, *A Nose and Three Eyes*, trans. Jonathan Smolin; foreword by Hanan al-Shaykh (Cairo and New York: Hoopoe, 2024).
4. Personal correspondence, 27 June 2019.
5. The Arabic is "sharin ha'ir." Interview with Hanan al-Shaykh, 8 May 2019, London.
6. Only years later did Abdel Kouddous ever mention in an interview that he suffered from panic attacks. See Muhammad al-Shinnawi, *Ihsan 'Abd al-Quddus bayna al-Adab wa-l-Siyasa* (Cairo: Manshurat Battana, 2019), 61. Abdel Kouddous's wife also spoke once about her husband's anxiety: "Ihsan was always anxious. When he wrote an article or a novel, he stayed anxious until it saw the light of day. I always gave him calm and I soaked up his anxiety.... Nonetheless, anxiety constantly followed him." Ibrahim 'Abd al-'Aziz, *Ihsan 'Abd al-Quddus: Sira Ukhra* (Cairo: Manshurat Battana, 2019), 262.
7. Interview with Hanan al-Shaykh, 8 May 2019.
8. Ahmed Abul-Fath, *L'Affaire Nasser* (Paris: Plon, 1962), 215.
9. Ibid., 216–20.
10. Ibid., 215.
11. See Joel Gordon, *Revolutionary Melodrama: Popular Film and Civic Identity in Nasser's Egypt*, Chicago Studies on the Middle East (Chicago: Middle East Documentation Center, 2002), 217–20.
12. This was not the first scandal sparked by fiction in Egypt. See, for example, Mohamed Shoair, *The Story of the Banned Book: Naguib Mahfouz's Children of the Alley* (Cairo: American University in Cairo, 2022).
13. Abdel Kouddous, *A Nose and Three Eyes*, 13.
14. Ibid., 13–15.
15. Al-Shaykh explained to me that Abdel Kouddous modeled the lovers in the novel after his own affairs with particular women. I have chosen throughout this book not to delve into aspects of his personal life that are not germane to my argument.
16. Abdel Kouddous, *A Nose and Three Eyes*, 28.
17. Ibid.
18. Ibid., 46.
19. Ibid., 59–60.
20. Ibid., 76.
21. Ibid., 89.
22. Ibid., 96–97.
23. Ibid., 108.
24. Ibid., 131.

25. Ibid., 128.
26. Ibid., 132.
27. Ibid., 112.
28. Ibid., 150.
29. Muhammad Fawzi, *Ihsan 'Abd al-Quddus bayna al-Ightiyal al-Siyasi wa-l-Shaghb al-Jinsi* (Cairo: Maktabat Madbuli, 1988), 148.
30. Abdel Kouddous, *A Nose and Three Eyes*, 157.
31. Ihsan 'Abd al-Quddus, "Anf wa-Thalath 'Uyun," *Ruz al-Yusuf*, 23 December 1963, 39. I cite the original serialization for lines that have been cut from the published translation.
32. Abdel Kouddous, *A Nose and Three Eyes*, 176. Translation slightly modified.
33. Ihsan 'Abd al-Quddus, "Anf wa-Thalath 'Uyun," *Ruz al-Yusuf*, 6 January 1964, 33.
34. Ibid., 35.
35. Ibid.
36. Abdel Kouddous, *A Nose and Three Eyes*, 215.
37. Ihsan 'Abd al-Quddus, "Anf wa-Thalath 'Uyun," *Ruz al-Yusuf*, 10 February 1964, 32.
38. Abdel Kouddous, *A Nose and Three Eyes*, 219.
39. Ihsan 'Abd al-Quddus, "Anf wa-Thalath 'Uyun," *Ruz al-Yusuf*, 10 February 1964, 33.
40. Abdel Kouddous, *A Nose and Three Eyes*, 217.
41. Ibid., 225.
42. Ibid., 230.
43. Ibid., 231. Translation modified.
44. Ihsan 'Abd al-Quddus, "Anf wa-Thalath 'Uyun," *Ruz al-Yusuf*, 17 February 1964, 42.
45. Abdel Kouddous, *A Nose and Three Eyes*, 271.
46. Ibid., 272.
47. Ihsan 'Abd al-Quddus, "Anf wa-Thalath 'Uyun," *Ruz al-Yusuf*, 16 March 1964, 34-35.
48. Abdel Kouddous, *A Nose and Three Eyes*, 313-14.
49. Ihsan 'Abd al-Quddus, "Anf wa-Thalath 'Uyun," *Ruz al-Yusuf*, 16 March 1964, 34-35.
50. Abdel Kouddous, *A Nose and Three Eyes*, 337.
51. Ibid., 342.
52. Ibid., 345.
53. Ibid., 358.
54. Ibid., 361.
55. Ibid., 362.
56. Ibid., 368.
57. Ibid., 371.

58. Ibid., 378.
59. Ibid., 379.
60. Ibid., 380.
61. Ibid., 389.
62. Ihsan 'Abd al-Quddus, "Ba'd Mi'at 'Amm," *Ruz al-Yusuf*, 27 February 1956.
63. For the legal text of the complaint, see Ihsan Abd al-Quddus and Mahmud Murad, *I'tirafat Ihsan 'Abd al-Quddus: al-Hurriya, al-Jins* (Cairo: al-'Arabi li-l-Nashr wa-l-Tawzi', 1980), 66–68.
64. 'Abd al-Rahman Abu 'Awf, "Ihsan 'Abd al-Quddus: Arfud al-Madi wa-Afrud al-Hadir Li-anni Udin bi-l-Mustaqbal," *Ruz al-Yusuf*, 28 October 1974.
65. Fawzi, *Ihsan 'Abd al-Quddus bayna al-Ightiyal al-Siyasi wa-l-Shaghb al-Jinsi*, 11.
66. Ahmad Hashim al-Sharif, "Hiwar ma'a Ihsan 'Abd al-Quddus," *Sabah al-Khayr*, 17 August 1974, 22.
67. 'Abd al-'Aziz, *Ihsan 'Abd al-Quddus: Sira Ukhra*, 85.
68. Ibid.
69. Ibid., 86.
70. Ibid., 86–88.
71. Abdel Kouddous, *A Nose and Three Eyes*, xii.
72. 'Abd al-'Aziz, *Ihsan 'Abd al-Quddus*, 89.
73. Abdel Kouddous, *A Nose and Three Eyes*, 396.
74. Ibid., 433.
75. Ibid., 451.
76. Ibid., 460.
77. Abdel Kouddous based this on a story that al-Shaykh told to her father and brother. See ibid., x.
78. Ibid., 468.
79. 'Abd al-'Aziz, *Ihsan 'Abd al-Quddus: Sira Ukhra*, 53.
80. Abdel Kouddous, *A Nose and Three Eyes*, 480.
81. Ibid., 499.
82. Ibid., 509.
83. Ibid.
84. Ibid., 511.
85. Saïd K. Aburish, *Nasser: The Last Arab* (New York: St. Martin's Press, 2004), 205.
86. Ibid., 219.
87. No doubt, Abdel Kouddous had originally planned for the Third Eye to last longer than it did since it was much shorter than the First or Second Eye.
88. Abdel Kouddous, *A Nose and Three Eyes*, 518.
89. 'Abd al-Hamid Ibrahim, ed. *Watha'iq Taha Hussayn al-Sirriyya* (Cairo: Dar al-Shuruq, 2006), 99.
90. Ibid., 100.
91. Ibid.

92. Ibid.

93. Al-Shinnawi, *Ihsan 'Abd al-Quddus bayna al-Adab wa-l-Siyasa*, 635-36.

94. 'Abd al-'Aziz, *Ihsan 'Abd al-Quddus*, 108.

95. Ihsan 'Abd al-Quddus, "Afkar Hurra fi Dawla Shuyu'iyya," *Ruz al-Yusuf*, 2 August 1965.

96. Amira Abu al-Futuh, *Ihsan 'Abd al-Quddus Yatadhakkar* (Cairo: al-Hay'a al-Misriyya al-'Amma li-l-Kitab, 1982), 222.

97. Ihsan 'Abd al-Quddus, *Sayyida fi Khidmatik* (Cairo: Dar al-Ma'arif, 1967).

98. Ihsan 'Abd al-Quddus, "Dimuqratiyya bila Za'ama wa-Za'ama bila Dimuqratiyya," *al-Ahram*, 14 February 1975.

99. Hilmi al-Namnam, "Rasa'il Ihsan 'Abd al-Quddus al-Majhula (2)," *al-Musawwir*, 9 March 2001.

100. The series without the first seven episodes is available on YouTube: https://www.youtube.com/watch?v=RT7XvKjGYr0&t. Accessed 21 January 2024.

101. These include Nagwa's father revealing that he faked his paralysis as he shoots her mother to death; Nagwa dying of heart rheumatism; Hashim becoming a morphine addict out of grief over Nagwa's death; Amina placed in a psychiatric hospital for treatment; and, perhaps most bizarre, Rihab is not a Lebanese teenager but, instead, Amina's Egyptian psychiatrist who undertakes a personal investigation to try to save both Amina and Hashim. The series is available on YouTube: https://www.youtube.com/watch?v=kS10Mquom_ 0&list=PLUOtJ4Uut5ULKhW8JEeeKLfozbKA23vyU. Accessed 1 February 2024.

102. Ihsan 'Abd al-Quddus, "al-Hazima," *Sabah al-Khayr*, 19 May 1966, 3.

103. Ibid., 5.

104. Ibid.

105. Ibid., 20.

106. Ibid.

107. Ibid., 21.

108. Ibid.

109. Hanan al-Shaykh, *Intihar Rajul Mayyit* (Beirut: Dar al-Nahar, 1970).

110. Ibid., 57.

111. Ibid., 78.

## Conclusion

1. Ni'am al-Baz, "Awraq Khassa wa-Hamma min Sanawat Ihsan 'Abd al-Quddus: al-Majmu' al-Thalith," *Akhir Sa'a*, 2 March 1983, 34.

2. Muhammad Fawzi, *Ihsan 'Abd al-Quddus bayna al-Ightiyal al-Siyasi wa-l-Shaghb al-Jinsi* (Cairo: Maktabat Madbuli, 1988), 159.

3. Ihsan 'Abd al-Quddus, "al-Mawqif al-Siyasi," *Akhbar al-Yawm*, 18 June 1966.

4. Ihsan 'Abd al-Quddus, "Istimrar al-Thawra. Limadha? wa-Kayfa?," *Akhbar al-Yawm*, 23 July 1966.

5. Ihsan 'Abd al-Quddus, "Li-madha Intasarna?," *Akhbar al-Yawm*, 24 December 1966.

6. Ihsan 'Abd al-Quddus, "al-Mas'uliyya al-Kabira," *Akhbar al-Yawm*, 27 May 1967.

7. Ihsan 'Abd al-Quddus, "al-Mabadi' al-Jamida," *Akhbar al-Yawm*, 3 June 1967.

8. Ihsan 'Abd al-Quddus, "al-Mawqif al-Siyasi," *Akhbar al-Yawm*, 10 June 1967.

9. Ihsan 'Abd al-Quddus, "Khawatir wasta al-Dukhkhan: 4," *Akhbar al-Yawm*, 8 July 1967.

10. Ihsan 'Abd al-Quddus, "Silahuna," *Akhbar al-Yawm*, 22 July 1967.

11. Tawfiq al-Hakim, *The Return of Consciousness*, trans. Bayly Winder (New York and London: New York University Press, 1985), 41.

12. Ihsan 'Abd al-Quddus, "Marakiz al-Quwwa," *Akhbar al-Yawm*, 25 November 1967.

13. Amira Abu al-Futuh, *Ihsan 'Abd al-Quddus Yatadhakkar* (Cairo: al-Hay'a al-Misriyya al-'Amma li-l-Kitab, 1982), 229.

14. Ihsan 'Abd al-Quddus, "al-Jil al-Mas'ul wa-l-Jil Ghayr al-Mas'ul," *Akhbar al-Yawm*, 1 April 1972.

15. Muhammad al-Shinnawi, *Ihsan 'Abd al-Quddus bayna al-Adab wa-l-Siyasa* (al-Qahira: Manshurat Battana, 2019), 647.

16. Ihsan 'Abd al-Quddus, *Dami wa-Dumu'i wa-Ibtisamati* (Cairo: Dar al-Shuruq, 1974), 18.

17. Amira Abu al-Futuh, "Mishwar Ihsan 'Abd al-Quddus: 1," *al-Siyasa*, 19 July 1980.

18. Saïd K. Aburish, *Nasser: The Last Arab* (New York: St. Martin's Press, 2004), 310.

19. Ihsan 'abd al-Quddus, "al-'Ayb Kabir. Hal Nastati' an Natahammaluha?," *al-Akhbar*, 30 September 1970.

20. Hilmi al-Namnam, "Ihsan wa-l-Sadat: Halqa Jadida fi Rasa'il Ihsan al-Majhula: 4," *al-Musawwar*, 23 March 2001.

21. Ihsan 'Abd al-Quddus, *'Ala Maqha fi al-Shari' al-Siyasi 3: al-Bahth 'an al-Thawra* (Cairo: Maktabat Misr, 1980), 33.

22. Sharif Abdel Kouddous, "City Limits of the Dead," *Mada Masr*, 21 July 2020, https://madamasr.com/en/2020/07/21/opinion/u/city-limits-of-the-dead/.

# BIBLIOGRAPHY

'Abd al-'Aziz, Ibrahim. *Ihsan 'Abd al-Quddus: Sira Ukhra*. Cairo: Manshurat Battana, 2019.

'Abd al-Ghani, Mustafa. *Al-Muthaqqafun wa-Thawrat Yuliyu: Al-Shahadat al-Akhira*. Cairo: Markaz al-Ahram, 2010.

'Abd al-Nasir, Jamal. "Kayfa Dabbarna Hadha al-Inqilab?" *Al-Tahrir*, 15 October 1952, 10-12.

'Abd al-Quddus, Ihsan. *Finjan Shay'*. Edited by Samiya Sadiq, 1959.

———. "1—Inni Utalib bi-l-Tahqiq ma'a al-Fariq Muhammad Haydar Basha." *Ruz al-Yusuf*, 24 October 1950, 3-4.

———. "1—Kayfa Ushrif Tahqiqat al-Jaysh amam al-Niyaba?" *Ruz al-Yusuf*, 9 January 1951, 3-4.

———. "3: Muhakamat Mujrimi Harb Filistin." *Ruz al-Yusuf*, 20 June 1950, 3-5, 31.

———. "4: Kayfa Nurid an Tahkum Misr?" *Ruz al-Yusuf*, 3 November 1952, 3.

———. "4: Muhakamat Mujrimi Harb Filistin." *Ruz al-Yusuf*, 27 June 1950, 3-5.

———. "95 Yawman fi al-Sijn." *Ruz al-Yusuf*, 6 September 1954, 6-7.

———. "96 Sa'a ma'a al-Hurriyyat al-Arba'a." *Ruz al-Yusuf*, 23 August 1945, 12-14.

———. "Afkar Hurra fi Dawla Shuyu'iyya." *Ruz al-Yusuf*, 2 August 1965, 3-6, 61.

———. "al-Afwah al-Samita wa-l-Malayin al-Samita!" *Ruz al-Yusuf*, 24 November 1952, 3.

———. *'Ala Maqha fi al-Shari' al-Siyasi*. Cairo: Maktabat Misr, 1979.

———. *'Ala Maqha fi al-Shari' al-Siyasi 3: Al-Bahth 'an al-Thawra*. Cairo: Maktabat Misr, 1980.

———. "al-'Alam Alladhi Iktashafnahu." *Ruz al-Yusuf*, 20 August 1956, 3.

———. "Ams wa-Yawm wa-Ghaddan." *Ruz al-Yusuf*, 2 February 1959, 6-7.

———. "Ana Hurra." *Ruz al-Yusuf*, 29 June 1953, 20-21, 24-25, 36-37.
———. "Ana Hurra." *Ruz al-Yusuf*, 3 August 1953, 21-22, 35-37.
———. "Ana Hurra." *Ruz al-Yusuf*, 10 August 1953, 21-22, 35-37.
———. "Ana Hurra." *Ruz al-Yusuf*, 17 August 1953, 21-22, 35-37.
———. "Ana wa-l-Majanin." *Ruz al-Yusuf*, 14 December 1959, 6-7.
———. "Anf wa-Thalath 'Uyun." *Ruz al-Yusuf*, 23 December 1963, 34-41.
———. "Anf wa-Thalath 'Uyun." *Ruz al-Yusuf*, 6 January 1964, 32-36.
———. "Anf wa-Thalath 'Uyun." *Ruz al-Yusuf*, 10 February 1964, 30-36.
———. "Anf wa-Thalath 'Uyun." *Ruz al-Yusuf*, 17 February 1964, 40-45.
———. "Anf wa-Thalath 'Uyun." *Ruz al-Yusuf*, 16 March 1964, 30-37.
———. "Ard al-Din wa-l-Duniya!" *Ruz al-Yusuf*, 22 March 1954, 18-19, 40-41.
———. *Asif Lam A'ud Astati'*. Cairo: Al-Dar al-Misriyya al-Lubnaniyya, 1980.
———. "'Awdat al-Shakhsiyya." *Sabah al-Khayr*, 23 August 1956, 3.
———. "al-'Ayb Kabir. Hal Nastati' an Natahammaluha?" *Al-Akhbar*, 30 September 1970, 2.
———. "Ayna al-Qumsan al-Zurq, ya Shabab al-Wafd?" *Ruz al-Yusuf*, 6 November 1951, 3.
———. "Ayna 'Umri?" *Ruz al-Yusuf*, 23 November 1953, 22-23, 34-35.
———. "Ayna 'Umri?" *Ruz al-Yusuf*, 30 November 1953, 22-23, 34-35, 40.
———. *Ayyam Shababi*. Cairo: Al-Maktab al-Misri al-Hadith, 1980.
———. "al-Bahth 'an Allah." *Ruz al-Yusuf*, 15 March 1954, 18-19, 39.
———. "Ba'd Mi'at 'Amm," *Ruz al-Yusuf*. 27 February 1956. 7.
———. *Bi'r al-Hubb*. Kutub li-l-Jami'. Cairo: Dar al-Jumhuriyya, 1949.
———. "al-Bayt al-Jadid." *Sabah al-Khayr*, 12 January 1956, 6.
———. *Bi'r al-Hirman*. Beirut: Dar al-Nashr al-Hadith, 1962.
———. "Da'uhu Yadhhab." *Ruz al-Yusuf*, 16 June 1948, 11-12.
———. *Dami wa-Dumu'i wa-Ibtisamati*. Cairo: Dar al-Shuruq, 1974.
———. "Dawlat al-Fashal." *Ruz al-Yusuf*, 8 July 1951, 3.
———. "Dhikriyat." *Ruz al-Yusuf*, 24 October 1955, 4-5.
———. "Dimuqratiyya bila Za'ama wa-Za'ama bila Dimuqratiyya." *Al-Ahram*, 14 February 1975, 8-9.
———. "al-Dustur Lam Yu'zil al-Malik wa-Lakin Yutahhir al-Ahzab." *Ruz al-Yusuf*, 4 August 1952, 3.
———. "Dustur Mu'aqqat li-Fatrat Intiqal Mu'aqqat!" *Ruz al-Yusuf*, 15 December 1952, 3.
———. "Fadiha Amrikiyya fi Mu'tamar Landan." *Ruz al-Yusuf*, 27 August 1956, 3-4.
———. "Faruq Lam Yakun al-Wahid Alladhi Taqarrar an Natakhallas Min-hu." *Ruz al-Yusuf*, 11 August 1952, 3.
———. "Fi al-Mu'tamar al-Sahafi." *Sabah al-Khayr*, 16 August 1956, 8-9.
———. "Fi Baytina Rajul." *Ruz al-Yusuf*, 7 January 1957, 22-25, 32-33, 42.
———. "Fi Baytina Rajul." *Ruz al-Yusuf*, 14 January 1957, 22-25, 32-33.
———. "Fi Baytina Rajul." *Ruz al-Yusuf*, 21 January 1957, 21-25, 42.
———. "Fi Baytina Rajul." *Ruz al-Yusuf*, 28 January 1957, 22-25, 42.

———. "Fi Baytina Rajul." *Ruz al-Yusuf*, 11 March 1957, 20-21, 34-38.

———. "Fi Baytina Rajul." *Ruz al-Yusuf*, 27 May 1957, 20-21, 34-35, 38.

———. "Fi Baytina Rajul." *Ruz al-Yusuf*, 10 June 1957, 20-21, 34-35.

———. "Ghaddan Lan Yataqarrar Idha Taharrarna min 'Aqaliyyat al-'Abid!" *Ruz al-Yusuf*, 22 September 1952, 3.

———. "Ha'ula'i al-Wuzara' Aqwiya' wa-Hadha al-Sha'b Qawi!" *Ruz al-Yusuf*, 22 June 1953, 3.

———. "Haddathani Wazir Sabiq." *Ruz al-Yusuf*, 15 August 1941, 10-11.

———. "Hadha al-Rajul Huwwa al-Sha'ab." *Ruz al-Yusuf*, 30 July 1956, 3.

———. "Hal al-Dimuqratiyya fi Haja ila Silah?" *Ruz al-Yusuf*, 20 September 1954, 6.

———. "Hamsa." *Al-Idha'a al-Misriyya*, 16 October 1954, 13.

———. "Hamsa." *Al-Idha'a al-Misriyya*, 23 October 1954, 19.

———. "Hamsa." *Al-Idha'a al-Misriyya*, 30 October 1954, 19.

———. "Hamsa." *Al-Idha'a al-Misriyya*, 6 November 1954, 11.

———. "Hamsa." *Al-Idha'a al-Misriyya*, 19 March 1955, 15.

———. "Harb al-'Isabat." *Ruz al-Yusuf*, 23 July 1947, 3.

———. "Hatta La Takun Farda Hadha'!" *Al-Ahram*, 23 August 1974, 4-5.

———. "Hawadith wa-Khawatir." *Ruz al-Yusuf*, 29 August 1955, 6.

———. "Hawadith wa-Khawatir." *Ruz al-Yusuf*, 9 January 1956, 6.

———. "Hawadith wa-Khawatir." *Ruz al-Yusuf*, 19 March 1956, 7.

———. "Hawadith wa-Khawatir." *Ruz al-Yusuf*, 3 June 1957, 7.

———. "Hawadith wa-Khawatir." *Ruz al-Yusuf*, 17 June 1957, 7.

———. "Hawadith wa-Khawatir." *Ruz al-Yusuf*, 9 September 1957, 7.

———. "Hawadith wa-Khawatir." *Ruz al-Yusuf*, 2 March 1959, 6-7.

———. "Hawadith wa-Khawatir." *Ruz al-Yusuf*, 18 May 1959, 6-7.

———. "Hawaltu an Akun Jarsun." *Akhir Sa'a*, 13 December 1942, 16-17.

———. "Al-Hazima." *Sabah al-Khayr*, 19 May 1966, 3-5, 20-21.

———. *Al-Hazima Kana Ismuha Fatima*. Cairo: Dar al-Ma'arif, 1975.

———. "Al-Iktishaf al-Dakhm." *Ruz al-Yusuf*, 22 July 1963, 3.

———. "Imani." *Ruz al-Yusuf*, 1 November 1954, 6-7.

———. "Inna Misr fi Haja ila Diktatur. Fa-hal Huwwa 'Ali Mahir?" *Ruz al-Yusuf*, 11 February 1952, 3.

———. "Innahu fi Kull Makan." *Sabah al-Khayr*, 20 March 1958, 10.

———. "Innana La Nakrah al-Aghniya' wa-Lakinnana Nuhibb al-Fuqara'." *Ruz al-Yusuf*, 24 July 1961, 3-4.

———. "Innana Nasir fi al-Tariq al-Tabi'i al-Muhattam 'ala al-Thawra." *Ruz al-Yusuf*, 15 March 1954, 3-5.

———. "Innana Nu'min bi-l-Mabadi' wa-bi-l-Mukhlisin li-Hadhihi al-Mabadi'." *Ruz al-Yusuf*, 12 January 1953, 3.

———. "Al-Islam La Yakfi!" *Ruz al-Yusuf*, 24 September 1956, 6-7.

———. "Istimrar al-Thawra. Limadha? Wa-Kayfa?" *Akhbar al-Yawm*, 23 July 1966, 8.

———. "Al-I'tiraf al-Akhir." *Ruz al-Yusuf*, 18 April 1938, 47–49.
———. "Al-Ittihad al-Qawmi wa-l-Sihafa." *Ruz al-Yusuf*, 1 February 1960, 3.
———. "Jamal . . . wa-Kull Shu'ub al-'Alam." *Sabah al-Khayr*, 26 December 1957, 12.
———. "Al-Jam'iyya al-Sirriyya Alladhi Tahkum Misr!" *Ruz al-Yusuf*, 22 March 1954, 3–5.
———. "Al-Jaysh wa-l-Siyasa." *Ruz al-Yusuf*, 6 April 1949, 3.
———. "Al-Jihad Fann!" *Ruz al-Yusuf*, 28 August 1947, 3.
———. "Al-Jil al-Jadid." *Ruz al-Yusuf*, 20 October 1948, 14–15.
———. "Al-Jil al-Mas'ul wa-l-Jil Ghayr al-Mas'ul." *Akhbar al-Yawm*, 1 April 1972, 8.
———. "Katib al-Qissa." *Ruz al-Yusuf*, 20 December 1954, 6–7.
———. "Kayfa Hadatha Kull Dhalik?" *Ruz al-Yusuf*, 23 July 1962, 11.
———. "Khawatir wasta al-Dukhkhan: 4." *Akhbar al-Yawm*, 8 July 1967, 4.
———. "La Anam." *Ruz al-Yusuf*, 12 March 1956, 23–24, 43–43, 48–49.
———. "La Mustabid Adil wa-La Adil Mustabid." *Ruz al-Yusuf*, 9 February 1953, 3.
———. *La Tutfi' al-Shams*. Cairo: Al-Sharika al-Qawmiyya, 1960.
———. "La Tutfi' al-Shams." *Ruz al-Yusuf*, 2 March 1959, 22–25, 34–36, 42.
———. "La Tutfi' al-Shams." *Ruz al-Yusuf*, 9 March 1959, 22–24, 35, 40–42.
———. "La Tutfi' al-Shams." *Ruz al-Yusuf*, 16 March 1959, 22–24, 35–36, 40–42.
———. "La Tutfi' al-Shams." *Ruz al-Yusuf*, 24 June 1959, 22–25, 34–35, 40–42.
———. "La Tutfi' al-Shams." *Ruz al-Yusuf*, 7 December 1959, 26–29, 34–35, 42.
———. "La Tutfi' al-Shams." *Ruz al-Yusuf*, 11 January 1960, 22–25, 34–35, 40–42.
———. "La Tutfi' al-Shams." *Ruz al-Yusuf*, 1 February 1960, 22–25, 34–35, 40–41.
———. "La Tutfi' al-Shams." *Ruz al-Yusuf*, 15 February 1960, 22–25, 34–35, 40–41.
———. "La Tutfi' al-Shams." *Ruz al-Yusuf*, 22 February 1960, 26–29, 40, 42–44.
———. "La Tutfi' al-Shams." *Ruz al-Yusuf*, 14 March 1960, 22–25, 40–42.
———. "La Tutfi' al-Shams." *Ruz al-Yusuf*, 14 March 1960, 26–29, 42–43, 48.
———. "Laysa fina Damm!" *Ruz al-Yusuf*, 2 October 1946, 3.
———. "Li-l-Asif." *Ruz al-Yusuf*, 7 November 1950, 19.
———. "Li-madha Intasarna?" *Akhbar al-Yawm*, 24 December 1966, 8.
———. "Li-madha Istaqala 'Ali Mahir wa-Li-madha Allafa al-Wizara Muhammad Najib." *Ruz al-Yusuf*, 8 September 1952, insert.
———. "Li-madha Rafada Muhammad Najib Ta'lif Wizara 'Askariyya?" *Ruz al-Yusuf*, 2 September 1952, 5, 30–31.
———. "Li-madha?" *Ruz al-Yusuf*, 21 June 1948, 14.
———. "Lughat Bini Hamir." *Akhir Sa'a*, 26 September 1943, 9.
———. "Al-Mabadi' al-Jamida." *Akhbar al-Yawm*, 3 June 1967, 4.
———. "Al-Malika wa-Qissa." *Ruz al-Yusuf*, 15 October 1956, 6.
———. "Man Alladhi I'tada 'ala Ra'is al-Tahrir?" *Ruz al-Yusuf*, 9 November 1953, 12–13, 40.

———. "Man Alladhi Yahkum: Al-Jaysh am 'Ali Mahir?" *Ruz al-Yusuf*, 18 August 1952, 3.

———. "Man fikum al-Za'im?" *Ruz al-Yusuf*, 10 August 1944, 9.

———. "Man Huwwa "Rabb al-Qanun" fi Misr?" *Ruz al-Yusuf*, 19 September 1950, 3-5.

———. "Man Huwwa al-Dabit Alladhi Yamlik Qasran fi Jazirat Kabri?" *Ruz al-Yusuf*, 6 June 1950, 5-7.

———. "Man Huwwa al-Katib al-Hurr?" *Ruz al-Yusuf*, 30 August 1954, 6-7.

———. "Man Huwwa al-Za'im al-Muntazir?" *Ruz al-Yusuf*, 5 September 1950, 4.

———. "Man Kan Aqwa min al-Hakim?" *Al-Ahram*, 20 September 1974, 5.

———. "Man La Yazal Yakhaf fa-Huwwa Kharij 'ala Mabadi' al-Harika." *Al-Idha'a al-Misriyya*, 1 November 1952, 8.

———. "Mar'at Misr." *Ruz al-Yusuf*, 17 November 1948, 3.

———. "Marakiz al-Quwwa." *Akhbar al-Yawm*, 25 November 1967, 6.

———. "Masir al-Thawra wa-Masir Rijal al-Thawra!" *Ruz al-Yusuf*, 29 March 1954, 3-5.

———. "Al-Mas'uliyya al-Kabira." *Akhbar al-Yawm*, 27 May 1967, 8.

———. "Mata Ya'ud al-Dustur wa-Mata Tajri al-Intikhabat?" *Ruz al-Yusuf*, 15 September 1952, 3.

———. "Al-Mawqif al-Hadir." *Al-Idha'a al-Misriyya*, 2 August 1952.

———. "Al-Mawqif al-Siyasi." *Akhbar al-Yawm*, 10 June 1967, 4.

———. "Al-Mawqif al-Siyasi." *Akhbar al-Yawm*, 18 June 1966, 8.

———. "Min Sujun Suriya." *Ruz al-Yusuf*, 9 July 1956, 7.

———. "Muddat 4000 Sana." *Ruz al-Yusuf*, 25 July 1960, 3.

———. "Muhakamat al-Hay'a al-Tanfidhiyya." *Ruz al-Yusuf*, 10 December 1947, 3-5.

———. "Muhakamat Mujrimi Harb Filistin." *Ruz al-Yusuf*, 13 June 1950, 3-5.

———. "Muhakamat Mujrimi Harb Filistin!" *Ruz al-Yusuf*, 20 July 1949, 3.

———. "Mujtama' al-Thawra." *Ruz al-Yusuf*, 20 July 1959, 3.

———. "Mujtama' Jadid . . . wa-Akhlaq Jadida." *Sabah al-Khayr*, 9 January 1958, 10-12.

———. "Nahnu." *Ruz al-Yusuf*, 23 March 1944, 9.

———. "Al-Nasr li-l-Rijal." *Ruz al-Yusuf*, 28 July 1952, 5.

———. "Al-Nawm wa-l-Mawt." *Ruz al-Yusuf*, 28 February 1955, 6-7.

———. "Al-Nazzara al-Sawda'." *Ruz al-Yusuf*, 28 January 1952, 26-27, 32-33.

———. "Al-Ni'am fi Bayrut." *Ruz al-Yusuf*, 7 May 1956, 6-7.

———. "Qatarat al-Damm fi Finjin al-Shay." *Ruz al-Yusuf*, 25 December 1951, 3.

———. "Al-Qawmiya." *Ruz al-Yusuf*, 28 March 1960, 6-7.

———. "Al-Rajul al-Wahid Alladhi Yajib an Yu'min bi-Bara'at al-Sha'b!" *Ruz al-Yusuf*, 4 February 1952, 3.

———. "Al-Rajul Alladhi Nu'min bihi." *Ruz al-Yusuf*, 21 May 1956, 8.

———. "Al-Rajul Alladhi Yajib an Yadhhab!" *Ruz al-Yusuf*, 9 August 1945, 3.

―――. "Al-Rajul Alladhi Yatba'uhu Nisf Milyun." *Ruz al-Yusuf*, 5 September 1945, 6-7.

―――. "Raqisa fi Ijaza." *Ruz al-Yusuf*, 21 August 1951, 26-27, 33-34.

―――. "Riyad wa-'Abd Allah . . . Hal Yakuna Akhir al-Dahaya?" *Ruz al-Yusuf*, 24 July 1951, 3.

―――. "Sa'uhawil . . . Sa'uhawil!" *Ruz al-Yusuf*, 31 December 1956, 6.

―――. "Sana'at al-Insan." *Ruz al-Yusuf*, 18 January 1960, 4-5.

―――. *Sayyida fi Khidmatik*. Cairo: Dar al-Ma'arif, 1967.

―――. "Al-Sihafa wa-l-Ishtirakiyya." *Ruz al-Yusuf*, 30 May 1960, 3-5, 40-41.

―――. "Silahuna." *Akhbar al-Yawm*, 22 July 1967, 4.

―――. "Al-Sud wa-l-Bayd." *Ruz al-Yusuf*, 4 April 1960, 6-7.

―――. "Tahiyya ila Rusiya." *Ruz al-Yusuf*, 13 August 1956, 3.

―――. "Al-Tariq al-Masdud." *Ruz al-Yusuf*, 10 January 1955, 26-27, 36-37, 48-49.

―――. "Al-Tariq al-Masdud." *Ruz al-Yusuf*, 17 January 1955, 26-27, 36-37, 49.

―――. "Al-Tariq al-Masdud." *Ruz al-Yusuf*, 4 April 1955, 26-27, 36-37, 48-49.

―――. "Al-Tariq al-Masdud." *Ruz al-Yusuf*, 11 April 1955, 26-27, 36-37.

―――. "Al-Tariq al-Masdud." *Ruz al-Yusuf*, 23 May 1955, 7.

―――. "Al-'Ummal." *Ruz al-Yusuf*, 11 January 1945, 13.

―――. "Al-'Uyun al-Maghmuda." *Ruz al-Yusuf*, 28 November 1955, 6-7.

―――. "Al-Wisada al-Khaliyya." *Ruz al-Yusuf*, 6 September 1954, 22-23, 40-41.

―――. "Al-Wisada al-Khaliyya." *Ruz al-Yusuf*, 13 September 1954, 22-23, 40-41.

―――. "Al-Wisada al-Khaliyya." *Ruz al-Yusuf*, 20 September 1954, 22-23, 40-41.

―――. "Al-Wisada al-Khaliyya." *Ruz al-Yusuf*, 27 September 1954, 22-23, 40-41.

―――. "Al-Wisada al-Khaliyya." *Ruz al-Yusuf*, 4 October 1954, 22-23, 40-41.

―――. "Al-Wisada al-Khaliyya." *Ruz al-Yusuf*, 11 October 1954, 22-23, 40-41.

―――. "Al-Za'im al-Muntazar." *Ruz al-Yusuf*, 18 January 1945, 10.

―――. "Al-Za'im wa-l-Mabda'." *Ruz al-Yusuf*, 24 February 1958, 3.

―――. "Zu'ama'" *Ruz al-Yusuf*, 29 March 1945, 14.

'Abd al-Quddus, Ihsan, and Mahmud Murad. *I'tirafat Ihsan 'Abd al-Quddus: Al-Hurriya, al-Jins*. Cairo: Al-'Arabi li-l-Nashr wa-l-Tawzi', 1980.

'Abd al-Quddus, Muhammad. *Hikayat Ihsan 'Abd al-Quddus*. Cairo: Al-Hay'a al-'Amma li-l-Kitab, 2011.

Abdel Kouddous, Ihsan. "'Girl Three,' Translated by Raphael Cohen." *Banipal*, no. 71 (Summer 2021): 136-65.

―――. *I Do Not Sleep*. Translated by Jonathan Smolin. Cairo and New York: Hoopoe, 2021.

―――. *A Nose and Three Eyes*. Translated by Jonathan Smolin. Foreword by Hanan al-Shaykh. Cairo and New York: Hoopoe, 2024.

Abdel Kouddous, Sharif. "City Limits of the Dead." *Mada Masr*, 21 July 2020. https://madamasr.com/en/2020/07/21/opinion/u/city-limits-of-the-dead/.

Abu 'Awf, 'Abd al-Rahman. "Ihsan 'Abd al-Quddus: Arfud al-Madi wa-Afrud al-Hadir Li-anni Udin bi-l-Mustaqbal." *Ruz al-Yusuf*, 28 October 1974, 8-10.

———. *Ihsan 'Abd al-Quddus bayna al-Sihafa wa-l-Riwaya*. Cairo: Al-Majlis al-A'la li-l-Thaqafa, 2006.
Abu al-Fath, Ahmad. "Siyadat al-Sha'ab." *Al-Misri*, 15 March 1954, 1, 9.
Abu al-Futuh, Amira. *Ihsan 'Abd al-Quddus Yatadhakkar*. Cairo: Al-Hay'a al-Misriyya al-'Amma li-l-Kitab, 1982.
———. "Mishwar Ihsan 'Abd al-Quddus: 1." *Al-Siyasa*, 19 July 1980, 17.
———. "Mishwar Ihsan 'Abd al-Quddus: 4." *Al-Siyasa*, 22 July 1980, 15.
———. "Mishwar Ihsan 'Abd al-Quddus: 11." *Al-Siyasa*, 29 July 1980, 22.
———. "Mishwar Ihsan 'Abd al-Quddus: 13." *Al-Siyasa*, 31 July 1980, 15.
———. "Mishwar Ihsan 'Abd al-Quddus: 14." *Al-Siyasa*, 2 August 1980, 15.
Abul-Fath, Ahmed. *L'Affaire Nasser*. Paris: Plon, 1962.
Aburish, Saïd K. *Nasser: The Last Arab*. New York: St. Martin's Press, 2004.
al-'Anani, Salwa. "Hiwar Lam Tunshar ma'a Ihsan 'Abd al-Quddus." *Al-Ahram*, 14 January 1990.
El-Ariss, Tarek, ed. *The Arab Renaissance: A Bilingual Anthology of the Nahda*. New York: Modern Language Association of America, 2018.
———. "Ottomania: Boy Love, Incest, and the Arab Spring." In *Essays on Heritage, Tourism, and Society in the MENA Region: Proceedings of the International Heritage Conference 2013 at Tangier, Morocco*, edited by Dieter Haller, Achime Lichtenberger, and Meike Meerpohl, 17-40. Paderborn, Germany: Wilhelm Fink, 2015.
"Autograph." Egyptian state television program. Audio recording, 1976.
Baghdadi, Abd al-Latif. *Mudhakkirat 'Abd al-Latif Baghdadi*. Cairo: Al-Maktab al-Misri al-Hadith, 1977.
Al-Bajuri, Jamil. "Nazra Ba'ida: Ihsan 'Abd al-Quddus." *Al-Kawakib*, 8 August 1961, 35-36, 43.
"Baqiyat Hadith ma'a Su'adat Amin 'Uthman Basha." *Ruz al-Yusuf*, 16 November 1944, 7.
Baron, Beth. *Egypt as a Woman: Nationalism, Gender, and Politics*. Berkeley: University of California Press, 2005.
Al-Baz, Ni'am. "Awraq Khassa wa-Hamma min Mudhakkirat Ihsan 'Abd al-Quddus." *Akhir Sa'a*, 9 March 1983, 21-24.
———. "Awraq Khassa wa-Hamma min Sanawat Ihsan 'Abd al-Quddus: Al-Majmu' al-Thalith." *Akhir Sa'a*, 2 March 1983, 32-24, 42.
———. "Awraq Khassa wa-Hamma min Sanawat Ihsan 'Abd al-Quddus: Al-Majmu' al-Thani." *Akhir Sa'a*, 23 February 1983, 21-23.
Bier, Laura. *Revolutionary Womanhood: Feminisms, Modernity, and the State in Nasser's Egypt*. Stanford: Stanford University Press, 2011.
Brooks, Peter. *The Melodramatic Imagination: Balzac, Henry James, Melodrama, and the Mode of Excess*. New York: Columbia University Press, 1985.
Copeland, Miles. *The Game of Nations: The Amorality of Power Politics*. New York: Simon and Schuster, 1969.
Cormack, Raphael. *Midnight in Cairo: The Divas of Egypt's Roaring '20s*. New York: W.W. Norton and Company, 2021.

Daniel, Clifton. "Position of Farouk Is Clouded by Coup." *New York Times*, 24 July 1954, 3.

Di-Capua, Yoav. *No Exit: Arab Existentialism, Jean-Paul Sartre, and Decolonization.* Chicago: University of Chicago Press, 2018.

———. "Revolutionary Decolonization and the Formation of the Sacred: The Case of Egypt." *Past and Present* 256, no. 1 (August 2022): 239-81.

Din, Khaled Mohi El. *Memories of a Revolution: Egypt 1952.* Translated by TRIACC Translation Services. Cairo: American University in Cairo Press, 1995.

Fanon, Frantz. *The Wretched of the Earth.* Translated by Constance Farrington. New York: Grove Press, 1968.

Farid, Amani. "Al-Udaba' lahum Mashakil ma'a al-Iza'a." *Al-Kawakib*, 26 May 1981, 10-11.

Fawzi, Muhammad. *Ihsan 'Abd al-Quddus bayna al-Ightiyal al-Siyasi wa-l-Shaghb al-Jinsi.* Cairo: Maktabat Madbuli, 1988.

Gerges, Fawaz A. *Making the Arab World: Nasser, Qutb, and the Clash That Shaped the Middle East.* Princeton and Oxford: Princeton University Press, 2018.

Gershoni, Israel. "An Intellectual Source for the Revolution: Tawfiq al-Hakim's Influence on Nasser and His Generation." In *Egypt from Monarchy to Republic: A Reassment of Revolution and Change*, edited by Shimon Shamir. 213-49. Boulder, CO: Westview Press, 1995.

Ghanim, Fathi. "La Anam fi al-Sinima." *Ruz al-Yusuf*, 11 November 1957, 30.

———. "Masir Alladhina Yajlisun fawq al-Hirab." *Akhir Sa'a*, 19 September 1956, 27.

Ghinat, Rami. *Egypt's Incomplete Revolution: Lutfi al-Khuli and Nasser's Socialism in the 1960s.* Portland, OR: Frank Cass, 1997.

Gordon, Joel. *Nasser's Blessed Movement: Egypt's Free Officers and the July Revolution.* New paperback edition. Cairo and New York: The American University in Cairo Press, 2016.

———. "Nasser's Free Officer Mutiny." In *Rebellion, Repression, Reinvention: Mutiny in Comparative Perspective*, edited by Jane Hathaway. 253-71. Westport, CT: Praeger Publishers, 2001.

———. *Revolutionary Melodrama: Popular Film and Civic Identity in Nasser's Egypt.* Chicago Studies on the Middle East. Chicago: Middle East Documentation Center, 2002.

———. "The Slaps Felt around the Arab World: Family and National Melodrama in Two Nasser-Era Musicals." *International Journal for Middle Eastern Studies* 39 (2007): 209-28.

Al-Habruk, Isma'il. "Rasa'il min Husayn Tawfiq." *Ruz al-Yusuf*, 30 June 1948, 16-17.

"Hadith Amin 'Uthman." *Ruz al-Yusuf*, 10 January 1946.

"Hadith Harab Husayn Tawfiq." *Al-Ahram*, 11 June 1948, 2.

Al-Hakim, Tawfiq. *The Return of Consciousness*. Translated by Bayly Winder. New York and London: New York University Press, 1985.

———. *Return of the Spirit*. Translated by William Maynard Hutchins and Russell Harris. New York: Penguin Classics, 2019.

"Hal al-Gharad min Kitaba al-Tadlil?" *Al-Ahram*, 15 June 1948, 2.

"Hal Kana Amin 'Uthman Kha'inan?" *Ruz al-Yusuf*, 24 January 1946, 15.

"Hariba Husayn Tawfiq min al-Dabit al-Haris." *Al-Ahram*, 10 June 1948, 4.

Hijazi, Ahmad 'Abd al-Mu'ti. "Ba'd Sab'at Shuhur min al-Samt Ihsan Yatakallam (1)." *Ruz al-Yusuf*, 28 October 1968, 51-53.

———. "Ba'd Sab'at Shuhur min al-Samt Ihsan Yatakallam (3)." *Ruz al-Yusuf*, 16 November 1968, 34-36.

Hunt, Lynn. *The Family Romance of the French Revolution*. Berkeley: University of California Press, 1992.

Husayn, Ahmad. *Qadiyat al-Tahrid 'ala Harq Madinat al-Qahira wa-Muqaddimat Thawrat 23 Yuliyu 1952: Maqalat, Taqarir, Ittiham, Ahkam*. Cairo: Al-Matba'at al-'Alimiyah, 1957.

Ibrahim, 'Abd al-Hamid, ed. *Watha'iq Taha Hussayn al-Sirriyya*. Vol. 1. Cairo: Dar al-Shuruq, 2006.

al-Jami'i, 'Abd al-Mun'im al-Dusuqqi. *Al-Asliha al-Fasida wa-Dawruha fi Harb Filistin 1948*. Tarikh al-Misriyin. Cairo: Al-Hay'a al-'Amma li-l-Kitab, 1990.

James, Laura M. *Nasser at War: Arab Images of the Enemy*. New York: Palgrave Macmillan, 2006.

Jameson, Fredric. *The Political Unconscious: Narrative as a Socially Symbolic Act*. Ithaca, NY: Cornell University Press, 1981.

al-Jindi, Magda. "Al-Hurriyya Khuliqat min Ruz al-Yusuf." *Sabah al-Khayr*, 5 January 1989, 18-23.

Khalifa, Nadiya. "Ihsan 'Abd al-Quddus: Al-Tha'ir, al-Sahafi, wa-l-Rawa'i." *Sabah al-Khayr*, 10 September 1987, 20-22.

Khalifah, Omar. *Nasser in the Egyptian Imaginary*. Edinburgh: Edinburgh University Press, 2017.

"Khatwa Muwaffaqa wa-Lakinnaha nahwa al-Mawt al-Zu'am." *Ruz al-Yusuf*, 2 September 1936, 3.

Koerber, Benjamin. *Conspiracy in Modern Egyptian Literature*. Edinburgh: Edinburgh University Press, 2018.

Lilla, Mark. *The Reckless Mind: Intellectuals in Politics*. New York: New York Review of Books, 2001.

"Li-madha Uhibb al-Ingliz?" *Akhir Sa'a*, 30 May 1943, 3-4.

Litvin, Margaret. *Hamlet's Arab Journey*. Princeton and Oxford: Princeton University Press, 2011.

"Masra' Amin 'Uthman Basha." *Al-Ahram*, 6 January 1946, 2.

Muhi al-Din, Khalid. "Khalid Muhi al-Din Yarwi Qassat Manshurat al-Dubbat al-Ahrar." *Al-Tahrir*, 29 July 1953, 12, 44.

"Al-Muttaham bi-Qatl Amin 'Uthman Yatahaddath." *Ruz al-Yusuf*, 5 November 1947, 8.

"Al-Muttaham bi-Qatl Amin 'Uthman . . . Hal Huwwa Majnun?" *Ruz al-Yusuf*, 4 February 1948, 9.

Al-Muwatin al-Misri. "Innana Nurid al-Dustur li-anna Nu'min bi-l-Dimuqratiyya." *Ruz al-Yusuf*, 19 December 1955, 3.

———. "Al-Sha'ab wa-l-Hurriyya wa-l-Sihafa fi al-'Alim al-Jadid." *Ruz al-Yusuf*, 25 October 1954, 3.

Najib, Muhammad. "Indhar Qa'id 'Amm al-Quwwat al-Musallaha ila al-Malik al-Sabiq." *Al-Idha'a al-Misriyya*, 2 August 1952, 5.

Al-Nasir, Jamal 'Abd. "Kayfa Dabbarna Hadha al-Inqilab?" *Al-Tahrir*, 1 October 1952, 8–9.

Al-Nasir, Huda Jamal 'Abd, ed. *Jamal 'Abd al-Nasir Taliban wa-Zabitan*. Vol. 1, Jamal 'Abd al-Nasir: Al-Awraq al-Khassa. Cairo: Al-Hay'a al-'Misriyya al-'Amma li-l-Kitab, 2015.

Nasser, Gamal Abdul. *Egypt's Liberation: The Philosophy of the Revolution*. Translated by Dorothy Thompson. Washington, DC: Public Affairs Press, 1955.

Nasser, Gamal Abdel, and David Wynne-Morgan. "My Revolutionary Life: President Nasser's Own Story: 1: How We Overthrew Farouk." *The Sunday Times*, 17 June 1962, 25–26.

Neguib, Mohammed. *Egypt's Destiny*. London: Victor Gollancz, 1955.

Nietzsche, Friedrich. *The Birth of Tragedy: Out of the Spirit of Music*. Translated by Shaun Whiteside. Edited by Michael Tanner. New York: Penguin Books, 1993.

Al-Namnam, Hilmi. "Ihsan wa-l-Sadat: Halqa Jadida fi Rasa'il Ihsan al-Majhula: 4." *Al-Musawwar*, 23 March 2001, 58–60.

———. "Rasa'il Ihsan 'Abd al-Quddus al-Majhula (2)." *Al-Musawwir*, 9 March 2001, 56–58.

———. "Rasa'il Ihsan 'Abd al-Quddus al-Majhula: 8." *Al-Musawwir*, 20 April 2001, 50–52.

Al-Nur, 'A'isha Abu. "Rihla ila 'Aql Ihsan 'Abd al-Quddus." *Akhir Sa'a*, 14 February 1979, 32–34.

"Al-Qissa al-Haqiqiyya li-Harb Husayn Tawfiq." *Al-Misri*, 8 February 1953, 3.

Al-Quddus, Ihsan 'Abd. *I Am Free, and Other Stories*. Translated by Trevor Le Gassick. Cairo: General Egyptian Book Organization, 1978.

Qutb, Sayyid. "Idha Lam Takun Thawra fa-Hakimu Muhammad Najib!" *Ruz al-Yusuf*, 18 August 1952, 10.

Rowell, Alex. *We Are Your Soldiers: How Gamal Abdel Nasser Remade the Arab World*. New York: W.W. Norton & Company, 2024.

"*Ruz al-Yusuf* Tastafta al-Sha'b: Jumhuriyya am Malikiyya?" *Ruz al-Yusuf*, 27 October 1952, 8.

El-Sadat, Anwar. *In Search of Identity: An Autobiography*. New York: Harper Colophon Books, 1977.

———. *Revolt on the Nile*. New York: John Day, 1957.
Shakry, Omnia El. *The Arabic Freud: Psychoanalysis and Islam in Modern Egypt*. Princeton and Oxford: Princeton University Press, 2017.
Al-Sharif, Ahmad Hashim. "Hiwar ma'a Ihsan 'Abd al-Quddus." *Sabah al-Khayr*, 17 August 1974, 20-22.
Al-Shaykh, Hanan. *Intihar Rajul Mayyit*. Beirut: Dar al-Nahar, 1970.
———. "La Takhunani." *Ruz al-Yusuf*, 21 January 1963, 40.
Al-Shinnawi, Muhammad. *Ihsan 'Abd al-Quddus bayna al-Adab wa-l-Siyasa*. Cairo: Manshurat Battana, 2019.
Shoair, Mohamed. *The Story of the Banned Book: Naguib Mahfouz's Children of the Alley*. Cairo: American University in Cairo, 2022.
Smolin, Jonathan. *Moroccan Noir: Police, Crime, and Politics in Popular Culture*. Bloomington: Indiana University Press, 2013.
Suna [Ihsan Abdel Kouddous]. "Al-Khulasa al-Wafiyya fi al-Tabaqa al-Raqiyya wa-Ghayr al-Raqiyya." *Ruz al-Yusuf*, 19 August 1936, 32-33.
———. "Thalathat Ayyam ma'a al-Wafd." *Ruz al-Yusuf*, 1 October 1939, 39-41.
Tawfiq, Husayn. "Khitab min Husayn Tawfiq ila Ra'is al-Tahrir." *Ruz al-Yusuf*, 16 June 1948, 4-5.
'Ukasha, Tharwat. "Hakadha Qumna bi-l-Thawra." *Al-Tahrir*, 29 July 1953, 4ff.
———. *Mudhakkirati fi al-Siyasa wa-l-Thaqafa*. 2 vols. Cairo: Maktabat Madbuli, 1987-88.
Al-Umdah, Amal. "Kunuz Amal al-Umdah." *Ruz al-Yusuf*, 15 January 2022, 81-83.
Vatikiotis, P. J. *Nasser and His Generation*. New York: St. Martin's Press, 1978.
"Walidat al-Dabit al-Mu'taqal Tunashiduhu al-Zuhur." *Al-Ahram*, 18 June 1948, 2.
Waterbury, John. *Egypt: Burdens of the Past/Options for the Future*. Bloomington: Indiana University Press in Association with the American Universities Field Staff, 1978.
Yunis, Sharif. *Nida' al-Sha'ab: Tarikh Naqdi li-l-Idiyulujiyya al-Nasiriyya*. Cairo: Dar al-Shuruq, 2012.
Al-Yusuf, Fatima. *Dhikriyat*. Cairo: Mu'assasat Ruz al-Yusuf, 2010. 1959.
———. "Ila Waladi al-Sajin." *Ruz al-Yusuf*, 16 August 1945, 7.
———. "'Ishrun 'Amman fi al-Intizar." *Ruz al-Yusuf*, 24 October 1945, 3.
———. "Min Haqqi an Ashhad fi Yawm Qarib Khatimat al-Mufawadat." *Ruz al-Yusuf*, 4 May 1953, 3.
———. "Sabah al-Khayr." *Sabah al-Khayr*, 12 January 1956, 2.
———. "Sabah al-Khayr." *Sabah al-Khayr*, 9 February 1956, 2.

# INDEX

23 July 1952 Revolution, 1-3, 7-8, 15, 18, 23, 26, 28-30, 46-47, 71, 97-98, 113, 115, 138, 181, 184, 243, 291, 295, 300, 305-6; Black Saturday, 69. *See also* Free Officers

Abdallah, Emir, 170
Abdeen Palace incident, 4, 43, 45
Abdel Aziz, Lobna, 107-8, 145, 320n96
Abdel Halim Hafez, 231
Abdel Kouddous, Ahmed, 316-17n4
Abdel Kouddous, Ihsan, 49, 51-52, 58, 72, 105, 168, 312n4, 312n14, 325n4, 325n8; address to nation, 74-75, 86-88; *Akhbar al-Yawm*, editor in chief of, 299-300; alienation from Egypt, 291-92; al-Shaykh, affair with, 252-58, 287-88; anxiety of, 213, 237, 290-91, 297; as apprentice lawyer, 37; archive of, 15, 22-23; arrest of, 43-44, 119, 124, 136-37, 149-52, 202; assassination attempts against, 27-28, 315n75; background of, 30-31; balancing act of, 135; Bandung Conference, covering of, 163; Black Saturday, appalled by, 69; call for revolution, 12, 38-42, 44-47, 50, 53, 60-61, 63, 66-67, 70-71, 74; censorship of, 207, 211-13, 215, 223-25, 235-37, 245-46; confession and self-purification, connection between, 167; as coopted intellectual, 249; corruption, attacks against, 36-37, 40, 42, 80; corruption, disgust with, 5, 60, 64; death of, 305-6; depression of, 164, 187, 257-58, 296; as duped, 80; Egyptian army, as mirror of new generation, 56; Egyptian army, support for, 57; as Egypt's most popular author, 133; elopement of, 37, 312n17; erasure of, 73, 75, 93, 103-5, 118, 135-36, 170-71, 180-81, 205, 260, 305-6; family mausoleum, bulldozing of, 306-7; firing from *Rose El Youssef* and *Sabah al-Khayr*, 257; Free Officers, challenging/criticism of, 120-23, 138; Free Officers, disavowing of, 100; Free Officers, influence on, belief in, 98; Free Officers coup, role in, 28-30, 56, 59, 61-63, 75-84, 86-88, 94; Free Officers, support of, 84-86, 88, 90; *God Is with Us* (film), 88-94, 102, 106, 118-19; humiliation of, 128, 138, 186, 250, 256, 260, 272, 289, 298, 306; idealized nation, vision of, 36-37, 39; imprisonment of, 1-2, 119, 124-25, 128, 134, 137-38, 160-61, 200-201, 257, 297-98, 323n54; as inflammatory journalist, 105; insomnia of, 165-66; July revolution, laying groundwork for, 23; letters from young women, seeking advice, 169; Kaaba, circumambulation of, 116-18; marginalization of, 93, 290-91; mental breakdown of, 290; military dictatorship, anxieties

Abdel Kouddous, Ihsan (*continued*) and guilt about, 94-95, 98-99, 166-67, 260; military dictatorship, blame for laying groundwork for, 23, 100-101, 104, 112; military dictatorship, disavowing of, 106; misunderstanding of, 13-14; mother, complex relationship with, 32-34, 37-38, 44, 125-26; mother, rejection of, 20; nationalization of press, call for, 213, 245-46, 272; on *naksa*, 302-3; new Egypt, fantasies about, 6-7, 50; Order of First Merit, rewarding of, 249; panic attacks, 19, 253, 333n6; as paradoxical figure, 26; parliamentary democracy, support of, 120; permanent split from revolution, 119; private life, as hands-off, 256; as prolific writer, 8; as political journalist, 12; as public intellectual, 93; public morality, charge of harming, 257, 283-84, 289; public soul searching of, 137; RCC, 120-22; as rebel, 252; rebellion and appeasement, oscillating between, 22; regret toward role played in revolution, 24-25; removal as president of *Rose El Youssef*, 290-91; Rotten Weapons scandal, 28, 62-64; secret police, monitoring of, 254; "Son of Humanity" painting of (Kamel), 292; as state employee, 251, 255; Suez fighting, support of, 67; "Suna," nickname of, 34; threat to kill, 237; "Whisper" radio program, 147-52, 160, 162-63, 212, 229-30, 255, 300. *See also* Abdel Kouddous editorials, Abdel Kouddous fiction, Abdel Kouddous and Nasser

Abdel Kouddous, Ihsan editorials, 10, 13, 27, 29, 53, 57; censorship of, 15; "Does Egypt Need a Dictator? Is It Ali Maher?" 69; "Leader and the Principle," 208; "Let Him Go," 51; "Man We Believe In, The," 191; "Man Who Has to Go, The," 42-43; "On the Political Street," 305; "Prosecute the Palestine War Criminals!" 56; "Secret Gang That Rules Egypt, The," 120-21; "Sleep and Death," 165, 187; "State of Failure," 65-66; "This Man Is the People," 192; "We Want the Constitution Because We Believe in Democracy," 180; "Who Is the Awaited Leader?" 65

Abdel Kouddous, Ihsan fiction, 206, 210-11, 303; accommodation, rejection of, 152; acts of resistance in, 15; as apolitical, 13; appeal for women, 21; *Barred Road, The*, 101, 151-60, 162-63, 165-66, 171, 182, 188, 191, 203, 218, 260, 262, 271, 276, 280, 295-96, 325n114; breaking taboos, 8, 15, 17; censoring of, by Nasser, 136; critical dismissal of, 11; critics and academics, ignored by, 9; as criticism of Nasser, 135; "Dancer on Vacation," 105; "Defeat, The," 294-97, 300; defying Nasser in, 106-7, 110; dissemination of, 8; *Empty Pillow, The*, 139-46, 148, 150-55, 163, 179, 188, 212, 238, 262, 268; film adaptations of, 9, 17, 25, 53-55, 88-94, 102, 106, 108, 118-19, 189-90, 225, 227-29, 243, 294, 310n19, 320n96, 325n114; *Girls in Summer*, 17, 209, 211-20, 222-25, 227-29, 231-32, 244, 255-56, 260, 265-66, 268-70, 278, 330n41; guilt and remorse, expression of through, 20, 119-20, 164; *Holes in Black Cloth*, 249-50; *I Do Not Sleep*, 114-15, 133, 166-67, 169-73, 175-89, 191, 195, 201, 203, 205, 207-8, 215, 217-23, 228, 234, 242, 244, 260-62, 264-65, 267, 282, 325n4; "I Found Her," 33; *I'm Free*, 106-15, 119, 129-30, 135, 153-54, 156, 167, 171, 188, 218, 260, 262-63, 265, 269, 271, 274-75, 279; immorality in, 10; lives of wealthy, focus on, 10-11; as medium for confession and therapy, 106; melodrama, appeal to, 179-80; metaphors of revelation and confession, 19; "My Friend's in Love," 169; *nahda*, employing of, 18; Nasser, criticism of in, 135-36, 139, 164; Nasserism, 21; neglect of, 26; "New Generation," 53-54, 56, 107, 198-99, 203; *Nose and Three Eyes, The*, 17, 256-60, 262-67, 268-73, 279, 283-89, 292-95, 297, 302, 310n19, 335n86; political aspects of, 12, 16, 21-22, 105; political regret, expression in, 53; as political vehicle, 114-15; politics in, as inseparable, 13-14; popular appeal of, 11; as prolific writer, 28; reckless with, 55; "Return of the Character, The," 230-32, 238-37; revenge in, 204; romantic melodramas of, 8, 13, 15, 17-18; romantic melodrama, use of to condemn 1952 revolution, 18; *Sorry, I Can't Anymore*, 224; state censorship of, 15; "Sunglasses," 105-6; *Sun Never Sets, The*, 212, 231-49, 271, 273, 284, 310n19, 331n52; therapy, as form of, 19-20, 212, 228,-29, 256; *There's a Man in Our House*, 9, 53-55, 194-205,

207-8, 213, 219, 223, 225, 234, 248, 262, 304; using allegory and metaphor to express despair over revolution, 24; *Well of Deprivation*, 250; *Where's My Life?*, 129-31, 133, 141-42, 203, 262, 273-82; as widely remembered, 1, 8, 15; "Woman of the Salon," 105; as "writer of the bed," 9; writing, as internal performance, 185
Abdel Kouddous, Lola, 128, 292, 306, 312n17
Abdel Kouddous, Mohammed, 30, 306, 321n13
Abdel Kouddous, and Nasser: abandoned by, 296; accommodation of, 127, 133-35, 145, 148, 150, 191, 208-9, 260; as apologist for, 298; attacking of, 24, 297-98; capitulating to, 218; conflict between, 96-97, 101-2; criticism of, 119, 122, 135-36, 139, 162, 164; deference to, 291; defying of, 106-7, 110; deluded by, 138-40, 144, 146; denial of death, 304; disillusionment with, 285; dissent toward, 22; family heritage and assets, seizing of Nasser, 247; fictional appearances of, 135-36, 139, 164, 167-70, 199-205, 207, 219-20; forced invitations from, 2; humiliation of by, 186, 250, 256, 260, 272, 298; internalizing conflict with, 134-35; as Nasser's "echo," 247; as Nasser's "translator," 251, 298; parallels between, 3-4; plot to assassinate, learning of, 210; praising of, 191-92, 209-10, 229-30, 248-49, 251, 300; prostitution to, 272; protection by, need for, 228, 270; pushed aside by, 5-6; rebellion against, 6, 274-75; resuscitation of by, 298; as secret collaborator with, 29; submissive to, 207-8; as his "therapist," 23, 26, 128-29, 131-32, 138, 141-42, 146, 182, 238-39, 250, 262; waning influence over Nasser, 12
Abdel Kouddous, Sharif, 305-6
Abdel Mawgoud, Muhsin, 90-91, 96
Abdel Samad, Muhammad Abdel, 283
Abdel Wahab, Mohamed, 32, 147, 261
Abdul-Fath, Ahmed, 6, 8, 12, 19, 23-24, 29, 73-74, 79-80, 86, 94, 99, 101, 118, 123, 131, 133, 147, 255-56, 323n73
Abou Seif, Salah, 189
Aburish, Saïd, 147, 186
*al-Ahram* (The Pyramids) (publication), 12, 51, 305
*al-Akhbar* (The News) (newspaper), 79

*Akhbar al-Yawm* (News of the Day) (publication), 12, 299-301, 303
*Akhir Sa'a (Latest Hour)* (magazine), 38
Ali, Mohammed, 58
Amer, Abdel Hakim, 150
American University in Cairo, 8, 108, 133
Anglo-Egyptian Treaty, 4, 45, 66; cancellation of, by Egypt, 67
Amine, Mervet, 294
Anwar, Ahmed, 149-50
al-Aqqad, Abbas Mahmoud, 9, 32
Arab dictatorship, 16-18, 26, 99, 112
Arabism, 57
Arab-Israeli War, 258
Arab League, 303
Arab nationalism, 3, 206-7, 235
Arafat, Yasser, 303
El-Ariss, Tarek, 112
authoritarianism, 7
Automobile Club, 60

Badrakhan, Ahmed, 88, 92
Baghdadi, Abdellatif, 120
Bandung Conference, 160, 163-64, 166, 235-36
al-Banna, Hassan, 45
*Barred Road, The* (Abdel Kouddous), 153-57, 162, 165, 171, 188, 191, 203, 218, 260, 262, 271, 276, 280, 295-96; accommodation, rejection of, 152; dictatorship, as theme, 101; ending of, 158, 163, 166, 182; ending of, readers objection to, 159-60; film adaptation of, 325n114; serialization of, 151
Bier, Laura, 21, 133
Black Saturday riots, 69-70
Black September, 303
*Bonjour Tristesse* (Sagan), 167-68, 174, 325n4
Britain, 3, 4, 34, 35, 43, 45-46, 48, 148, 176, 192, 194, 206-7, 224
British colonialism, 4, 17, 52, 54, 74, 109
Brooks, Peter, 179-80

Caffery, Jefferson, 7, 8
Cairo (Egypt), 1-2, 27, 30, 47, 51, 72-73, 87, 168, 306; Black Saturday riots in, 69, 92
Capri (Italy), 57
censorship, 38-39, 42, 101-2, 114, 163, 166, 207, 211-13, 215, 223-25, 229, 235-37, 245-46; ending of, 104, 120; restoration of, 123

Communist Party, 45
colonialism, 6, 10, 51, 64, 167; British, 4, 17, 52, 54, 74, 109
Cormack, Raphael, 20, 30
corruption, 51-52, 58, 60, 87, 124, 147-48, 157, 160, 163, 272, 280, 325n114; in Egypt, 3, 5, 36, 40, 58, 62, 64, 69-70, 72, 75, 80-81, 128; in Nasser era, 29, 153, 296
Council for the Union of the Press: dissolving of, 123

"Dancer on Vacation" (Abdel Kouddous), 105
"Defeat, The" (Abdel Kouddous), 294-97, 300
El-Demerdash, Nour, 243-44, 294
dictatorship, 5-6, 17, 20, 23, 30, 94-95, 98-101, 104, 106, 112, 114, 120, 122, 144-45, 166-67, 181, 184-85, 191, 193, 214, 225, 227, 228, 260, 306. *See also* Arab dictatorship
Dina, Queen (Jordan), 195, 202
"Does Egypt Need a Dictator? Is It Ali Maher?" (Abdel Kouddous), 69
"Don't Betray Me" (al-Shaykh), 252

Eddine, Ahmed Bahaa, 231
Effendi, Misri, 36, 66-68, 90
Egypt, 1-3, 8-10, 20, 23, 26, 32, 34-35, 37, 42, 45, 48-49, 51, 63, 65-67, 74, 83, 89, 92, 98, 105, 113-14, 118, 124, 126, 136, 143, 152-54, 156, 163-64, 172-73, 176, 180, 183, 191, 193-95, 198-99, 204, 208, 221-23, 227, 236, 246, 248-49, 260, 262, 272, 285-88, 291-93, 300-303, 305-6, 325n8; betrayal of, by Nasser, 18, 58, 184-85, 205, 220, 296; censorship in, 151; corruption in, 3, 5, 36, 40, 58, 62, 64, 69-70, 72, 75, 80-81, 128; democratic Egypt, fantasy of, 144-45; "Holiday of Victory," 229; love and nationalism, link between, 147-49; as military dictatorship, 17, 30, 95, 99, 120, 122, 144-45, 167, 181, 214, 306; Nasser, romance with, 110, 184, 186; nationalism, 43; new Egypt, vision of, 7, 11, 50, 86, 111, 133-34, 214; Period of Great Victories, 166; psychoanalysis, discussions of, 129; revolution in, 4; totalitarian regime, necessity for, 99; virile leader, need for, 21, 41, 46, 109, 112, 129-31, 174, 215, 217, 263, 273, 294

*Egyptian Radio Magazine*, 147
Elwan, Muhammad, 294
*Empty Pillow, The* (Abdel Kouddous), 141-44, 146, 148, 150-55, 163, 179, 188, 212, 238, 262, 268; as accommodating and apologetic, 145; as AK's first attempt to explore deluded by fantasy, 140; serialization of, 139-40
Euripides, 232

Fahim, Amin, 77-78
Fakhreddine, Maryam, 225
Faisal al-Saud, Abdullah bin, 117
Fanon, Frantz, 45-46
Farouk, King, 4, 42-43, 48, 58-59, 73, 77-78, 80, 103, 175-76, 263
Fathi, Nagla, 294
feminism, 133-34
First Indochina War, 124
*For Freedom* (Nasser), 18, 64, 90
Fouad, Ahmed, 290
Fouad, King, 134
Fouad Serageddin, 86
France, 3, 194, 206, 207, 224
Free Officers, 1-2, 4, 10, 12-13, 16, 22, 23, 30, 41, 48, 56, 58, 59, 61-65, 70, 84-85, 90, 96, 98, 111-14, 116, 119-20, 127, 139-40, 144, 147-48, 161-62, 174, 247, 255-56, 260-61, 264, 268; coup, 12, 18, 20-21, 29, 34, 36, 46, 52, 72-80, 86-88, 91-95, 102-3, 121-23, 126, 130, 138, 175, 177, 179-80, 183, 194; corruption of, 5; disavowing of, 100; founding of, 3, 58; lack of planning, 82, 83; military government, 83-84, 86; passivity of, 81-82. *See also* Revolutionary Command Council (RCC)
French Revolution, 127, 180
Freud, Sigmund, 127, 129, 174
Fuad I, 30

Gamal Abdel Nasser Museum, 202
Gaza, 58
Geneva Conference, 124
Gerges, Fawaz, 58, 97-98
Gershoni, Israel, 24, 64-65
Ghanim, Fathi, 327n75
*Girls in Summer* (Abdel Kouddous), 211, 213, 216-18, 222, 231-32, 244, 255-56, 260, 265-66, 268-69, 278, 330n41; allegory of dictatorship, 225, 227-28; betrayal by fictional Nasser, 219-20; as crossing the line, 212, 223;

fantasy of killing Nasser, 219; Fifth Girl, 225; Fourth Girl, 225; Nasser's anger toward, 209, 212, 215, 224-25, 227, 270; serialization of, 214; Third Girl, 215, 223-25, 227, 229
*Girls in Summer* (film), 17, 225, 227-29
*God Is with Us* (film), 88-91, 96, 102-3, 106, 111, 118-19, 153-54, 163, 167, 243, 265, 320n96, 326n17; as hagiography of coup, 94; Neguib, cut from, 92-94
Gordon, Joel, 9, 80, 92, 318n51
*al-Gumhuriyya* (The Republic) (newspaper), 21, 132

Hafez, Abdel Halim, 9, 145
al-Hakim, Tawfiq, 7-8, 16, 18, 24, 27, 29, 64, 90, 209, 257, 283-84, 288-89, 299, 301, 304
Halim, Abbas, 59, 315n75
Hamama, Faten, 9, 89, 151, 189, 243, 325n114
Hamdy, Emad, 89, 189, 243
Hamrush, Ahmed, 291
Haydar Pasha, Mohammed, 61-62
Heikal Hassanein, Mohamed, 4, 16, 124, 126, 134, 206-7, 209, 211-12, 223-24, 228-29, 299
*Holes in Black Cloth* (Abdel Kouddous), 249-50
Hudaybi, Hassan, 6-8, 97-98
Hunt, Lynn, 21, 127, 217
Hussein, Ahmed, 29, 66-67
Hussein, Kamel el-Din, 76-77
Hussein, King, 303
Hussein, Taha, 8, 11, 189, 257, 289-90, 296, 303

*I Do Not Sleep* (Abdel Kouddous), 171, 176-82, 184-85, 191, 195, 201, 203, 205, 207-8, 215, 217-19, 221-23, 228, 234, 242, 244, 260, 262, 264, 265, 267, 282, 325n4; blurring of fiction and reality, 169-70; denouncing of, as immoral, 188-89; ending of, 186-87, 189; first edition of, 187; letters about, 169, 188; killing of Nasser double in, 167-70, 220; plot of, 172-73; rewriting of coup, 167, 175, 188; as sensational, 188; serializing of, 166-67, 169, 180, 186-89; as self-therapy, 167; as work of sexual deviancy, 188
*I Do Not Sleep* (film), 9, 17; ending, change in, 189-90

"I Found Her" (Abel Kouddous), 33
*iltizam*, 18
*I'm Free* (Abdel Kouddous), 106-7, 109-13, 119, 129-30, 135, 153-54, 156, 167, 171, 188, 218, 260, 262-63, 265, 269, 271, 274-75, 279; film adaptation of, 108, 320n96; as political critique, 115; as political novel, 114; revolutionary womanhood, 133; rewriting of, 261
Immobilia Building, 27-28
Iron Guard, 48
Israel, 3, 194-96, 206-7, 224, 300-302, 305

Jameson, Fredric, 25
June 1967 war, 3, 300-301

Kader Hatem, Abdel, 74
Kamal, Hussein, 294
Kamel, Gamal, 292
Kamel, Ihsan, 54
Kamil, Mustafa Pasha, 49
Khayri, Adil, 225, 227
Khoury, Georges, 252, 285
al-Khuli, Lutfi, 19
Korean War, 124
Kulthum, Umm, 147

Lampson, Sir Miles, 42-43, 48, 136
"Leader and the Principle, The" (Abdel Kouddous), 208
Lebanon, 292-93
"Let Him Go" (Abdel Kouddous), 51
Litvin, Margaret, 18
Louis XIV, 232
Luna 1, 235
Lutfi, Nadia, 294

Magda (actress), 294
Maher, Ali, 69, 76-77, 94, 96, 103, 312n14; resignation of, 70, 78, 81-82, 97-98, 255
Mahfouz, Naguib, 8, 11, 14, 30, 107, 251, 257, 283, 320n96, 325n114
Mahmoud, Fathi, 136
"Man We Believe In, The" (Abdel Kouddous), 191
"Man Who Has to Go, The" (Abdel Kouddous), 42-43
March Crisis (1954), 93, 118-19, 123-24, 129, 137-38, 151-52, 206, 210
Mar'i, Mustafa, 57
Mazhar, Ahmed, 325n114
al-Mehelmy, Lawahez (Lola), 37
Middle East, 3, 26, 56, 166, 301

*Midnight in Cairo* (Cormack), 20
*al-Misri* (The Egyptian) (newspaper), 6, 29, 52, 79, 87, 94, 99, 101, 132, 255; shutting down of, 123
Mohi El Din, Khaled, 58-59, 62, 72, 102, 120, 131-32, 166
Motawea, Karam, 243-44
Murad, Yusuf, 129, 133, 204
Murray, James, 95-96, 181, 267
Muslim Brotherhood, 4-7, 45, 79, 149
*My Father's Up a Tree* (film), 9, 330n44
"My Friend's in Love" (Abdel Kouddous), 169

*nahda*, 11, 18
*naksa* (setback), 301-2
Nasser, Gamal Abdel, 1, 8-9, 12-14, 25, 36, 41-43, 50, 53, 55, 59-60, 62, 66, 71-76, 79-80, 86, 89, 91-93, 111, 113-16, 118-20, 122-24, 127-28, 134-42, 144-45, 148, 150-52, 154-59, 163-65, 175-76, 180-81, 183, 188-89, 194-96, 199-203, 215-19, 221, 227-28, 238-40, 242, 246, 249-51, 257, 260-62, 264, 268, 272, 275, 281, 283-84, 286, 290, 292, 297-98, 300-301, 306-7, 311n30, 316-17n4, 326n17, 329n106; and Abdel Kouddous, 2-4, 15-16, 22-23, 26, 96-97, 101-3, 106-7, 110, 146-47, 182, 191-92; ascendency of, 166-67; assassination attempts on, 7, 149, 160-61, 192, 210; betrayal of Egypt, 18, 58, 184-85, 205, 220, 296; blackmail, use of, 255-56; condemning of, 24, 287; controlling media, 21; corruption of, 29, 153, 296; criticism, prickly attitude toward, 22; cult of personality, 7; death of, 302-5; as degrading Egypt, 287; democracy, betrayal of, 18; as deus ex machina, 231-32, 237, 241, 243-45, 263, 271, 273; dissent toward, 16-17, 162; Egyptian romance with, 110, 184, 186; Egypt and Syria, orchestrating unity between, 3; as embodiment of Egypt, 208, 285; *For Freedom*, 18, 64, 90; Free Officers, founding of, 3, 58; *Girls in Summer* (Abdel Kouddous), anger toward, 209, 212, 269-70; health of, 294; as hero, image of, 7, 18-19, 28, 29, 64-65, 70, 174; humiliating of dissenters, savoring of, 23, 255; as icon, 3; as idolized, 209; intimidation of journalists, 131; media, micromanaging of, 132-33; messianic status of, 19, 166; meteoric rise, 3; micromanagement of former co-revolutionaries, 23; military dictatorship of, 6, 20, 30, 184-85; mission of press, to build respectable society, 247; Muslim Brotherhood, assault on, 149; nationalization of press, 247-48; as new masculinity of, 112; as personification of Egypt, 192-93; *Philosophy of the Revolution*, 63, 90, 103, 104, 129, 182, 197, 295; as pliable, mistaken perception of, 18-19, 29, 94, 97-98, 174, 204; popularity of, 206, 208-9, 223, 235-36; protests, crushing of, 102; punishing and resuscitating friends, 323n73; romance with Egypt, 110, 184, 186; Rotten Weapons scandal, 87-88, 103; sensitive to rivals, 102; as shadow of former self, 288-89; Suez Canal, nationalizing of, 3, 167, 206-7, 224, 229-31; totalitarian regime, necessity for, 99

Nasserism, 18, 21-22, 234, 258; de-Nasserization, 24, 224
Nationalist Party, 45
National Union, 245
Neguib, Mohammed, 58-59, 73, 76-77, 83, 86, 92, 94-95, 98, 100, 102-3, 120, 123, 129, 147, 318n51; cleaning of army, 87; under house arrest, 93; resignation of, 118
"New Generation, The" (Abdel Kouddous), 53-54, 56, 107, 198-99, 203
1919 Revolution, 198
El Nokrashi Pasha, Mahmoud, 43, 136
*Nose and Three Eyes, A* (Abdel Kouddous), 17, 259, 264-67, 269-70, 279, 292, 302; as angry revolt against Nasser, 256-57; film adaptation of, 294, 310n19; First Eye, 260, 262-63, 268, 271-73, 289, 295, 335n86; as modernist, 258; public morality, as harmful to, 283; as radio series, 293-94; Second Eye, 260, 272, 284, 289, 295, 335n86; serializing of, 258, 284; television adaptation, 294; Third Eye, 260, 263, 284-89, 297, 335n86

Okasha, Sarwat, 73, 102
"On the Political Street" (Abdel Kouddous), 305

Othman Pasha, Amin, 47-49, 51-52, 194, 196

Palestine, 56, 57, 60, 61, 63, 72, 74, 89-90, 301
Palestine War (1948), 3-5, 28-29, 51, 56-57, 58, 87, 89, 103, 305-6
*Philosophy of the Revolution* (Nasser), 63, 90, 103-4, 129, 182, 197, 295
psychoanalysis, 129

Qutb, Sayyid, 6-8, 79

regressivism, 10
"Return of Character, The" (Abdel Kouddous), 230-32, 238-39
*Return of Consciousness, The* (al-Hakim), 283
*Return of the Spirit* (al-Hakim Tawfiq), 7, 18, 64-65, 90, 198, 200
Revolutionary Command Council (RCC), 120-22; end of press censorship, 118; restoration of censorship, 123. *See also* Free Officers
Ridwan, Ahmed, 30, 31
romantic melodrama, 8, 12-13, 15, 17, 20, 26, 107, 112, 119, 133-34, 167, 170-71, 179, 188-90, 262, 306; as apolitical, 140; cinematic, 9; as democratic, 180; as metaphorical vehicle, 18
*Rose El Youssef* (magazine), 4-5, 10, 12, 18, 20, 28-29, 34-36, 38, 41, 43-45, 47-52, 55-56, 59-61, 69-70, 72-74, 77-80, 83-84, 86, 90-91, 95, 99, 101, 105, 107-9, 111, 118, 122-24, 127, 136, 139-40, 144, 148-50, 156, 159-62, 165-66, 168, 174, 177, 180, 184, 187-89, 195-96, 198, 200, 205, 209, 211-12, 214-15, 218, 224, 228, 230-32, 235, 237-38, 241, 244-49, 251-52, 254, 256-58, 268, 282-83, 290-92, 297; boycott of articles about Nasser, 206; caricatures of British figures, 66; censorship of, 32, 224; *I Do Not Sleep*, letters about, 169-70;importance and popularity of, 32; military dictatorship, disavowing of, 106; push for revolution, 67-68; storehouse of weapons, 66; *There's a Man in Our House*, angry letters about, 201-2
Rotten Weapons scandal, 4-5, 12-13, 28-29, 57, 61-64, 70, 74-75, 81-82, 86-88, 90-94, 102-5, 111, 113, 175-78, 260, 305-6

al-Sa'adani, Mahmoud, 211
*Sabah al-Khayr* (Good Morning) (magazine), 12, 213, 215, 231, 242, 246, 249, 256-57, 268, 292, 294; *Girls in Summer*, serialization of, 214
Sabry, Hasan, 224-25
Sadat, Anwar, 16, 23-24, 48-50, 56, 72, 74, 76-77, 82-83, 91-92, 103, 116, 129, 131, 170, 254-56, 283, 290, 302-3, 305; de-Nasserization, 224
Sagan, Françoise, 167-68, 325n4
Salem, Gamal, 97
Salem, Madiha, 243-44
Saud, King, 116
Saudi Arabia, 116, 118, 210
El Sebai, Youssef, 289
"Secret Gang That Rules Egypt, The" (Abdel Kouddous), 120-21
Seif, Salah Abou, 325n114
Serageddin, Fouad Pasha, 65, 263
Shafei, Hussein, 102
El Shakry, Omnia, 19, 129, 133, 147, 204
Shahin, Yahya, 189
Sharif, Omar, 9, 189, 294, 329n106
Shawqi, Ahmed, 32
al-Shaykh, Hanan, 15, 252-58, 283-85, 287-88, 290, 294, 296-97, 300
El-Shennawi, Kamal, 225
Shishakli, Adib, 117-18, 194
Sirhan, Shoukry, 90, 243, 320n96
El-Sisi, Abdel Fattah, 306
"Sleep and Death" (Abdel Kouddous), 165, 187
"Son of Humanity, The" (Kamel), 292
*Sorry, I Can't Anymore* (Abdel Kouddous), 224
"State of Failure" (Abdel Kouddous), 65-66
*Story of Zahra, The* (al-Shaykh), 15, 252
Studio Misr, 92
Sudan, 34-35
Suez, 101-2, 195; British occupation of, 116; fighting in, 67, 69
Suez Canal, 4, 34-35, 70; nationalization of, 3, 167, 192, 194, 206-7, 224, 229-31
Suez War, 167, 229, 239, 241, 243-44, 300
*Suicide of a Dead Man* (al-Shaykh), 296-97
"Sunglasses" (Abdel Kouddous), 105-6
*Sun Never Sets, The* (Abdel Kouddous), 212, 233, 235-36, 238-40, 242, 246, 248-49, 271, 273, 284, 331n52; ending of, 242-43; film adaptation of, 243; Nasser, as deus ex machina, 231-32,

*Sun Never Sets, The* (Abdel Kouddous) (*continued*)
  237, 241, 243-45; Nasserism, critique of, 234; television series adaptation, 243-44, 310n19
Syria, 3, 194-95, 199, 208, 223, 285-88

El-Tabii, Mohamed, 38, 79, 312n17
*al-Tahrir* (Liberation) (magazine), 21, 92, 101-2, 132
Talimat, Zaki, 92, 318n50, 318n51
Tawfik, Hussein, 48-56, 60-61, 78, 81, 195, 198; escape from prison, 50-52, 199, 314n53; imprisonment of, 194; Iron Guard, 196
El-Tawil, Kamal, 231
Tawila, Abdel Sattar, 201
Tharwat, Zubaida, 329n106
*There's a Man in Our House* (Abdel Kouddous), 9, 53-55, 194, 208, 213, 219, 223, 234, 248, 262, 304; blurring of fiction and reality, 196; censorship, 225; fictional killing of Nasser, 199-205, 207; nationalism in, 198; rewriting history of coup, 199-200, 205; serializing of, 195-96, 202; Tawfik and Nasser, blurring between, 195, 197
"This Man Is the People" (Abdel Kouddous), 192

United Arab Republic, 3, 206-9, 223-35, 245, 260, 285, 287-88
United Nations (UN), 46
United States, 301
*Until the Moon Returns* (al-Sa'adani), 211

Vatikiotis, P. J., 22
Victoria Club, 47

Wafd Party, 32
Waterbury, John, 24
*Well of Deprivation, The* (Abdel Kouddous), 250
Western imperialism, 301
"We Want the Constitution Because We Believe in Democracy" (Abdel Kouddous), 180
*Where's My Life?* (Abdel Kouddous), 130-31, 141-42, 203, 262, 273, 276-82; revolutionary womanhood, 133; rewriting of, 274-75; serialization of, 129
"Whisper" (radio program), 147-52, 156, 160, 212, 300; cancelling of, 162-63, 229-30, 255; dissent toward Nasser regime, 162
"Who Is the Awaited Leader?" (Abdel Kouddous), 65
"Woman of the Salon" (Abdel Kouddous), 105
*Women of Sand and Myrrh* (al-Shaykh), 252
World War II, 39, 41-42
Wynnne-Morgan, David, 58

Yassin, Mahmoud, 294
Young Egypt Society, 29, 66
Yousra (actress), 294
Youssef, Fatima (mother of Abdel Kouddous), 20-21, 32, 37-38, 43-44, 54, 90, 124-28, 145, 161-62, 171, 191, 206, 213-14, 217, 246-47, 265, 272, 312n4, 318n50; as diva, 30; fame of, 33-34. *See also* El Youssef, Rose
El Youssef, Rose, 20, 30. *See also* Youssef, Fatima

Zagloul, Saad, 32, 49
Zulficar, Ezzedine, 225

The authorized representative in the EU for product safety and compliance is:
Mare Nostrum Group B.V.
Mauritskade 21D
1091 GC Amsterdam
The Netherlands
Email address: gpsr@mare-nostrum.co.uk

KVK chamber of commerce number: 96249943

The authorized representative in the EU for product safety and compliance is:
Mare Nostrum Group
B.V Doelen 72
4831 GR Breda
The Netherlands

www.ingramcontent.com/pod-product-compliance
Lightning Source LLC
Chambersburg PA
CBHW030603230426
43661CB00053B/1825